E J[...]
R[...]AMA[...]N OF
JESU[...]

THE JEWISH RECLAMATION OF JESUS

An Analysis and Critique
of Modern Jewish
Study of Jesus

DONALD A. HAGNER

With a foreword by
Gösta Lindeskog

Academie
Books Grand Rapids,
Michigan
Zondervan Publishing House

THE JEWISH RECLAMATION OF JESUS
Copyright © 1984 by The Zondervan Corporation
Grand Rapids, Michigan

ACADEMIE BOOKS is an imprint of Zondervan Publishing House,
1415 Lake Drive, S.E., Grand Rapids, Michigan 49506.

Library of Congress Cataloging in Publication Data

Hagner, Donald Alfred.
    The Jewish reclamation of Jesus.

    Bibliography: p.
    Includes indexes.
    1. Jesus Christ—Jewish interpretations—History—
20th century. I. Title.
BM620.H33   1983   232   83-23570
ISBN 0-310-33431-4

Edited by Gerard Terpstra
Designed by Louise Bauer

Printed in the United States of America

Unless otherwise indicated, Scripture quotations are taken from the Revised
Standard Version. Copyright © 1946, 1952 by The Division of Christian
Education, National Council of the Churches of Christ in the United States
of America.

86 87 88 89 90/10 9 8 7 6 5 4 3 2

Contents

Foreword

Professor Donald A. Hagner has asked me to write a foreword to his work *The Jewish Reclamation of Jesus: An Analysis and Critique of Modern Jewish Study of Jesus.*

I have studied the manuscript carefully and with growing interest, and I am able to state that the author is particularly well oriented regarding the relevant literature and problems.

As the title indicates, the author's starting point is the phenomenon that in German literature is called "die Heimholung Jesu" (the bringing home of Jesus). The heretic, whose name the Jews refused to utter because of everything they had suffered on his account, is now welcomed home to his own, to a people who themselves have again received a homeland. It is, however, not as "the heretic" that he is welcomed home, but rather as one of the great persons in the history of the Jewish faith.

This welcoming has been made possible through a process that is now more than a hundred years old. Hagner recapitulates important data in this history, but he constantly focuses on what has happened and is happening: the Jewish reclamation of Jesus. He asks, What has happened that has led to this reclamation? Further on he asks the question, To what degree is this reclamation possible? Jesus was a Jew. This Jew nevertheless was responsible for the rise of a world-wide religion. He was called the Son of God and became the object of divine worship. Indeed, it was said that he was God become man. The church's christology, having finally deified him, has radically de-Judaized Jesus of Nazareth.

A question that is constantly before the reader in Hagner's presentation is this: Is it possible to "bring home" this Jew to his origin, that rigorously monotheistic religion, and give him a place in the history of its faith? This is a central question. Jewish theologians of significance maintain that it is possible, and I share their optimism. Hagner, on the other hand, is very doubtful about the validity of this process. The issue concerns "the Jewishness of Jesus": Jesus is turned into an ordinary Jewish teacher. But thereby—in the opinion of Hagner—"the uniqueness of Jesus" has been violated.

This does not mean, however, that Hagner minimizes the value of the process within Judaism that has culminated in this reclamation. This process has been made possible through Jewish research that has great significance for the relationship between Judaism and Christianity. By way of example, Jewish scholars have taught Christians that the Pharisees, who in Christian preaching and teaching have been rudely caricatured, represented the best in contemporary Judaism.

We live in an era of dialogue, and this means direct conversation between the church and the synagogue at the scientific level. The purpose of this conversation is that both religions may come to know each other better and even cooperate in common goals and tasks. This matter is also considered in Hagner's book, which contains many important observations on this phenomenon.

From what has been said, as well as from the title of the book, it is clear that Hagner is not content simply to analyze and describe without also entering into debate with the Jewish authors discussed in the book. He does not guard himself against giving his opponents the occasion and possibility for critical objections. Obviously the work involves sensitive and controversial subjects, as well as assertions whose correctness can be questioned.

For my own part—in order to take up the key question again—I am of the opinion that the Jewish "reclamation" is not only justified but also reasonable, and that it is not impossible to combine the Jewishness with the uniqueness. I will clarify my point by saying that there are today two Jesus-images: the Jewish and the Christian—both the result of historical research—and that these two views are indeed more related to one another than "the

Jesus of history and the Christ of faith'' of which scholars earlier spoke.

The Jewish research on Jesus—of very great significance for the Christian—has given rise to a Christian literature concerning that research. The genre is still of very small compass, but with Donald A. Hagner's solid investigation, in which he provides an extensive review of controversial questions, it has received an important addition, which will certainly stimulate new contributions from both the Jewish and Christian side. This work contains many valuable and thought-provoking observations. One can say confidently that it cannot fail to arouse debate.

Gösta Lindeskog
Uppsala

Preface

In 1925 Harry A. Wolfson, the great Philo scholar of Harvard University, wrote an introductory essay to Joseph Jacobs's book *Jesus as Others Saw Him,* entitled "How the Jews Will Reclaim Jesus." According to Wolfson, the Jews will reclaim Jesus as one of their own rabbis whose parables and sermons have a rightful place in Jewish literature alongside those of other ancient sages. The Jewish reclamation of their own will be complete when readers will be able to "pass on from Talmudic and Midrashic selections to those of the Gospels without being conscious of any difference."

Although the Jewish reclamation of Jesus was already well under way when Wolfson wrote his essay, his words have proved to be an accurate description of the Jewish study of Jesus over the nearly sixty years since they were written. Today the Jewish reclamation of Jesus appears to be a healthy enterprise. But how successful is it in dealing with the data of the Gospels? And how convincing? These are the questions I have attempted to answer in this book.

It is only fair at the outset to indicate my own orientation to this subject in order to help readers understand what is before them. I write avowedly as a Christian and not as a "neutral" observer. I write furthermore as an evangelical Christian, viz., as one who holds to the basic doctrines of the Christian faith and the inspiration of the biblical writings and who attempts to employ historical-critical methodologies in a way that is fair to what is being studied. I do *not* claim that I am more "objective" than the Jewish writers examined here. Nor is it my intent to argue that because Jewish scholars have not accepted Jesus as Messiah their scholarship is necessarily unsuccessful.

Simply put, my claim in the present book is this: the Jewish reclamation of Jesus has been possible only by being unfair to the Gospels. In order to arrive at their modern portraits of Jesus, Jewish scholars are forced to select from the Gospels what seems to agree with their views and to reject everything that does not. It seems to me, therefore, that Jewish scholars bring expectations (not to say a priori conclusions) to the Gospels that are far from congenial to these writings. The Gospels after all are documents of faith and present a kerygmatic Christ, and not simply a human Jesus. The Gospels reflect the faith of the postresurrection community.

But this last statement is two-edged and has been used by radical critical Christian scholarship to argue against the historical reliability of the Gospels—something that Jewish scholars have quickly picked up as support for their own perspective. Thus in this book I have been forced to take a stand against radical gospel criticism from the Christian side. This I have had to do very briefly and inadequately, of course, since I cannot here present arguments for the reliability of each saying or passage to which I refer. A main point I want to make in this connection is simply that the radical critical scholars to whom Jewish scholars can appeal are a minority at the extreme left of the spectrum and that many, if not most, New Testament scholars who use critical methodologies in the study of the Gospels would not agree with their consistently negative assessment of the historical worth of what we may call the christologically significant passages in the Gospels. It seems to me that critical scholars are increasingly recognizing that because history is written with theological interests (and commitment), it does not follow that the history has no worth. History and theology need not be mutually exclusive.

I write furthermore from the standpoint of a New Testament specialist. This accounts for the fact that this study focuses on the teaching of Jesus. I am not addressing here the theological differences between Judaism and Christianity, nor do I here intend to make a statement concerning the Jewish-Christian dialogue. My sole concern is to ask whether the Jewish reclamation of

Jesus does justice to the data of the synoptic Gospels. Even if we restrict ourselves to these documents to the exclusion of the rest of the New Testament writings—as does Jewish scholarship— can we fairly arrive at a picture of Jesus that falls within the limits of Jewish acceptability? In my view, the Jewish reclamation of Jesus, done with such apparent confidence and skill, is manifestly unsuccessful because the data of the Gospels cannot be separated from or understood apart from the christological perspective of their authors. Only when the personal claims of Jesus (the key to the Gospel narratives) are recognized does his teaching fall into place. No Jewish rabbi, prophet, or even messianic-pretender spoke as did this Jew, just as none had the effect that he had.

It may be asked whether I do Jewish scholars an injustice by often discussing them in the singular phrase "Jewish scholarship" and in terms of a common, or relatively common, perspective. Are there not varieties of Jewish perspectives and differing portraits of Jesus? The answer is, of course, yes. But there is at the same time a sufficiently recognizable pattern in the Jewish approach to Jesus to justify the generalizing statements in this book. These statements do not overlook or nullify the differences between scholars that are noted frequently in my presentation. I have tried carefully not to misrepresent any author, and this accounts for my preference of direct quotation in the following pages. I have tried to use these quotations not as proof texts, but with an awareness of the contexts from which they are derived and with the goal of presenting a true picture of what Jewish scholars are saying.

Finally, I want to say that I am very much aware that this book is out of step with the current trend of Jewish-Christian dialogue with its mood of mutual acceptance and affirmation. For some it may indeed seem to be in particularly bad taste to write critically of Jewish scholarship. These are difficult and controversial questions, after all, and Jewish sensitivities, not without justification, run high in these matters. I have nevertheless taken up my courage and have attempted to write candidly. Although what I have written is by nature polemical as well as descriptive, I hope I have written in an irenic spirit.

I do not, furthermore, see this book as presenting a hindrance to Jewish-Christian dialogue. To my mind genuine dialogue occurs only when the parties involved speak honestly, share their differences, and explore these differences together, with the result that they understand each other better and become friends despite their disagreements. More than once I have witnessed Jewish-Christian "dialogue" in which the Christian representative presented such a radically liberal view of Jesus that it hardly differed from the liberal Jewish statements about him. To try to ignore or explain away the differences that separate Jews and Christians does not promote dialogue; it obstructs it. I believe therefore that it is advantageous for both sides to write honestly; this is what I have tried to do in the present book. I sincerely hope that my critique of the Jewish reclamation of Jesus will not be taken to mean that I am not grateful for the good that has come from the Jewish study of Jesus or that I wish to see the latter come to an end.

Although I have tried to be fair and honest, I realize that this book will probably frustrate some Jewish readers in the same way that many Jewish books on Jesus frustrate me. There is perhaps no way around this. But it does remain important for us to keep listening to each other despite our differences. As an example of the attitude needed, I would like, if I may be permitted, to refer to that great Jewish scholar the late Samuel Sandmel, who, when I told him of this project a few years ago, although he knew my perspective as an evangelical Christian and that his own writing on Jesus would be criticized, nevertheless graciously encouraged me to complete the work and to publish it.

I am glad here to offer thanks to all who have helped me to produce this book. I am especially grateful to Professor Gösta Lindeskog for consenting to write the foreword and to Professor Ludwig Dewitz of Columbia Theological Seminary, himself a Hebrew Christian, for reading an early draft of the book. Thanks are also due my graduate assistants Tom Schreiner and especially John Simpson for their help at various stages, and Dolores Loeding and Lynn Losie for help in typing. Finally, I would like to thank Stan Gundry and Zondervan Publishing House who have enabled this book to become available to the reading public.

Abbreviations

ANT	*The Authentic New Testament,* H. J. Schonfield, 1955; reprinted, New York: Mentor, 1958.
BJ	*Bruder Jesus. Der Nazarener in jüdischer Sicht,* S. Ben-Chorin, Munich, 1967.
BT	Babylonian Talmud
DCG	*A Dictionary of Christ and the Gospels,* ed. J. Hastings, 2 vols., Edinburgh, 1906–1908.
EJ	*Encyclopedia Judaica,* ed. C. Roth, 16 vols., Jerusalem, 1971.
ET	English translation
EvTheol	*Evangelische Theologie*
ExpT	*Expository Times*
FCS	*For Christ's Sake: A Discussion of the Jesus Enigma,* H. J. Schonfield, London: MacDonald and Jane's, 1975.
GJJ	*The Gospel of Jesus the Jew,* G. Vermes, University of Newcastle upon Tyne, 1981.
HJ	*Hibbert Journal*
HTR	*Harvard Theological Review*
HUCA	*Hebrew Union College Annual*
JAAR	*Journal of the American Academy of Religion*
JBL	*Journal of Biblical Literature*
JBLMS	*Journal of Biblical Literature Monograph Series*
JE	*The Jewish Encyclopedia,* ed. I. Singer, 12 vols., New York, 1901–1906.
JES	*Journal of Ecumenical Studies*
JETS	*Journal of the Evangelical Theological Society*
JJ	*Jesus the Jew. A Historian's Reading of the Gospels.* G. Vermes, 1973; reprinted, New York: Collins, 1977.
JJS	*Journal of Jewish Studies*

JN	*Jesus of Nazareth. His Life, Times and Teaching,* J. Klausner, 1922; ET by H. Danby, 1925; reprinted, Boston: Beacon, 1964.
JPJC	*The Jewish People and Jesus Christ,* J. Jocz, 1949; third edition, Grand Rapids: Baker, 1979.
JPJCA	*The Jewish People and Jesus Christ after Auschwitz,* J. Jocz, Grand Rapids: Baker, 1981.
JQR	*Jewish Quarterly Review*
JR	*Journal of Religion*
JSSM	*The Jewish Sources of the Sermon on the Mount,* G. Friedlander, 1911; reprinted, New York: Ktav, 1969.
JSNT	*Journal for the Study of the New Testament*
JT	Jerusalem Talmud
JTS	*Journal of Theological Studies*
M	*Mishna*
NTS	*New Testament Studies*
ÖCJ	*Ökumene aus Christen und Juden,* P. Lapide, Neukirchen-Vluyn, 1972.
PP	*The Passover Plot. A New Interpretation of the Life and Death of Jesus,* H. J. Schonfield, New York: Bernard Geis, 1966; many reprints.
PT	*Palestinian Talmud*
RJ	*Revolution in Judaea,* H. Maccoby, 1973; reprinted, New York: Taplinger, 1981.
RLGT	*Rabbinic Literature and Gospel Teachings,* C. G. Montefiore, 1930; reprinted, New York: Ktav, 1970.
RN	*Der Rabbi von Nazareth. Wandlungen des jüdischen Jesusbildes,* P. Lapide, Trier, 1974.
RT	*Some Elements of the Religious Teaching of Jesus According to the Synoptic Gospels,* C. G. Montefiore, 1910; reprinted, New York: Arno, 1973.
SBT	*Studies in Biblical Theology* (SCM)
SG	*The Synoptic Gospels,* C. G. Montefiore, 2 vols., 1927[2]; reprinted, New York: Ktav, 1968.
SNTSMS	*Society of New Testament Studies Monograph Series*
SP	*Studies in Pharisaism and the Gospels,* I. Abrahams, 2 vols., 1917–1924; reprinted, New York: Ktav, 1967.
USR	*Union Seminary Review*
WJJ	*We Jews and Jesus,* S. Sandmel, 1965; reprinted, New York: Oxford University Press, 1973.

THE JEWISH
RECLAMATION OF
JESUS

CHAPTER ONE

Introduction:
Jews and the Study of Jesus

THE FACT THAT Jesus of Nazareth, the Christ of Christianity, was fully a Jew is increasingly recognized in our day. Biblical scholarship has continued to demonstrate that the roots of the New Testament are deepest in the soil of Judaism and that a thorough knowledge of the Jewish background is indispensable to any adequate interpretation of the New Testament. While this is true even of such a Hellenistically influenced writer as Paul,[1] it is especially true of the Gospels and preeminently of the central figure of the Gospels, Jesus.

THE JEWISHNESS OF JESUS

We are particularly indebted to Jewish scholars, though by no means has this emphasis been limited to them, for the widespread realization of the full Jewishness of Jesus. It is rightly insisted on nowadays that in every regard the upbringing of Jesus was typically Jewish. He was born of Jewish parents in the homeland of the Jews, circumcised according to Jewish custom, and dedicated in the temple; he received the education of the Jewish child in Torah, became *bar mitzvah* at the age of thirteen, and—as we have every reason to believe—passed into manhood faithfully practicing his religion in both deed and word, as well as in regular attendance at synagogue. When he received the call to preach at the beginning of his ministry, he continually presupposed the synagogue framework and the final authority of the

---

[1]See especially W. D. Davies, *Paul and Rabbinic Judaism,* 4th ed. (Philadelphia: Fortress, 1980).

Jewish Scriptures. His teaching indeed is very Jewish in tone, and it is quite possible as one reads his words to imagine that one is listening to a member of the great prophetic tradition of Israel, an Amos or an Isaiah.

THE JEWS AND JESUS

From the beginning many Jews accepted Jesus, his teaching, and his personal claims. The earliest Christian church consisted exclusively of Jews, and the very idea that Gentiles could be admitted to this fellowship without initially converting to Judaism caused no small controversy at first (see Acts 15). Even after the church became predominantly Gentile, there continued to be a remnant of believing Jews who welcomed Jesus as Messiah and Lord. When the apostle Paul wrestles with the theological problem of Israel's unbelief he finds the notion that God has rejected his people quite unacceptable. "God has not rejected his people whom he foreknew," he writes, but as it was in the past history of Israel, "so too, at the present time there is a remnant chosen by grace" (Rom. 11:1–5). While this is not Paul's final answer to his problem—that he finds in a yet future response of Israel, after "the full number of the Gentiles come in" (11:25)—it is quite clear that the concept of a remnant of believing Jews was very important to him.

On the other hand, it is a sad and remarkable fact that Jesus also experienced a singular alienation from his fellow countrymen almost from the beginning of his ministry. Despite all the continuity between Jesus and his Jewish heritage, it is clear that what Jesus brings to his nation becomes the source of a discontinuity that grows ever more painful in the narrative of the Gospels and increases to catastrophic proportions in the history of the early church. This indeed is the central tragedy of the New Testament story: the Jews, the elect and covenant people of God, reject Jesus and his message and in so doing reject their rightful hope, their Messiah. The paradox of this rejection is poignantly expressed in the words of the prologue of the fourth Gospel: "He was in the world, and the world was made through him, yet the world knew him not. He came to his own home, and his own people received him not" (John 1:10–11). The pattern of this rejection is seen throughout Luke's history of the early church, and it serves as the climactic note that brings that narrative to a close. According to Acts, Paul, a prisoner in chains "because of the hope of Israel," calls together the leading Jews of Rome to hear the exposition of his gospel. When the majority of Jews reject his message, he quotes a passage from the prophet Isaiah (6:9–10) concerning the dullness of hearing, the blindness, and the hardness of heart that characterized their fathers (and now characterizes them), adding the somber dictum, "Let it be known to you then that this salvation of God has been sent to the Gentiles; they will listen" (Acts 28:28). These words not only predict the increasing response of Gentiles to the apostolic message but also implicitly anticipate the great chasm that would come to separate Jews and Gentile Christians.

THE MODERN ERA

Nineteen hundred years later we find that this situation has changed little. The church has remained overwhelmingly Gentile, but with a continuing remnant of Jewish believers. In the past few years the evangelization of Jews seems to have gained somewhat of a new impetus, and we have seen a new movement calling itself "Jews for Jesus" receive extensive publicity.[2] Yet it remains true that most Jews have been unable to accept the Christ of Christianity. In this respect we have not moved much beyond the state of affairs that existed toward the end of the first century.

---

[2]Cf. *Time,* June 13, 1972. For a full and interesting study of this phenomenon, see B. Z. Sobel, *Hebrew Christianity: The Thirteenth Tribe* (New York: Wiley, 1974). See too Arnold G. Fruchtenbaum, *Hebrew Christianity: Its Theology, History and Philosophy* (Washington, D.C.: Canon, 1974). The modern Jewish-Christian movement rightfully attempts to preserve its Jewish identity. Some within the movement prefer the designation "Messianic Judaism." See P. E. Goble, *Everything You Need to Grow a Messianic Synagogue* (South Pasadena: William Carey, 1974). For a Jewish response to the movement, see D. Berger and M. Wyschograd, *Jews and "Jewish Christianity"* (New York: Ktav, 1980). For further pertinent material, see *Christianity Today* 26.7 (April 24, 1981); and Jocz, *JPJCA,* 140–51. (For *JPJCA* and other abbreviations in footnotes, see list of abbreviations, pp. 17–18.)

Nevertheless, there have been some extraordinarily important developments in the past two hundred years, particularly in our own century. The emancipation of the Jew from the oppression of the ghetto and the gradual lessening of social prejudice that began in the second half of the eighteenth century have continued to the present, despite some unspeakable setbacks. This general trend has brought about an entirely new climate of Jewish-Christian relationships, especially in recent years. In place of the traditional animosity and blind prejudice that formerly characterized both sides has come a climate of acceptance and dialogue. On each side an increasing attitude of liberalism is evident, and, in keeping with the ecumenical spirit of our times, emphasis is now on matters held in common rather than on matters that divide. Most noteworthy, perhaps, among recent signs of this trend from the Christian side are the long overdue statements of Vatican II that exculpate the Jews as a race from the death of Jesus and deny the vicious doctrine that the Jews are a people cursed and repudiated by God.[3] While there is still much work to be done, we can only be grateful for the warming trend that has come on both sides.[4]

This new climate of our modern era has brought about something that hitherto was virtually impossible: the constructive study of Jesus by Jewish scholars. In contrast to the centuries preceding the Emancipation, characterized mainly by an alternation between purposeful silence and biting criticism, modern Jews have increasingly been able to approach the New Testament with new open-mindedness and a genuine willingness to evaluate Jesus positively from within their Jewish perspective. The number of Jewish writers on Christianity began to increase in the past

---

[3]Declaration on the Relationship of the Church to Non-Christian Religions (*Nostra Aetate*), section 4.

[4]The number of writings in this area continues to grow rapidly. I mention here three recent symposia that themselves contain useful bibliographical information: J. E. Wood, Jr., ed., *Jewish-Christian Relations in Today's World* (Waco: Baylor University Press, 1971); F. E. Talmage, ed., *Disputation and Dialogue: Readings in the Jewish-Christian Encounter* (New York: Ktav and Anti-Defamation League of B'nai B'rith, 1975); M. H. Tanenbaum, M. R. Wilson, and A. J. Rudin, eds., *Evangelicals and Jews in Conversation on Scripture, Theology and History* (Grand Rapids: Baker, 1978). See also *Christianity Today* 26.7 (April 24, 1981).

century and has mushroomed in our own century.[5] Thirty years ago the Hebrew Christian Jacob Jocz stated that the Jewish study of Jesus had only reached its initial stages.[6] The truth of this statement is underlined by Israeli scholar Pinchas Lapide, who wrote the following in 1975:

> The 187 Hebrew books, research articles, poems, plays, monographs, dissertations, and essays that have been written about Jesus in the last twenty-seven years since the foundation of the state of Israel, justify press reports of a "Jesus wave" in the present-day literature of the Jewish state. The fact is that much more has been written about Jesus in Hebrew in the last quarter century than in the eighteen previous centuries.[7]

As further indication of the current vitality of Jewish interest in Jesus, we may note with gratitude the recent republication of important Jewish works on Jesus and the Gospels. The Jewish publishing house Ktav has reprinted Claude Goldsmid Montefiore's two-volume commentary, *The Synoptic Gospels,*[8] a classic first published in 1909, and also the closely related and highly esteemed work of Montefiore's friend, Israel Abrahams, *Studies in Pharisaism and the Gospels,*[9] originally published in two parts (1917 and 1924). Also from Ktav is a reprinting of Montefiore's *Rabbinic Literature and Gospel Teachings* (1930)[10] and G. Friedlander's *The Jewish Sources of the Sermon on the Mount* (1911).[11] Arno Press, publisher of a large number of older

---

[5]See, for example, the expansive Jewish bibliographies in G. Lindeskog, *Die Jesusfrage im neuzeitlichen Judentum* (Uppsala, 1938; reprinted with new postscript, Darmstadt, 1973), 328–62; and J. A. Vorster, "Jewish Views on Jesus. An Assessment of the Jewish Answer to the Gospel of Jesus Christ," unpublished doctoral dissertation (University of Pretoria, 1975), 405–56.

[6]*The Jewish People and Jesus Christ* (London, 1949), 145.

[7]*Israelis, Jews and Jesus*, trans. P. Heinegg (Garden City, N.Y.: Doubleday, 1979), 31–32. Cf. the similar, earlier statement by Lapide in "Jesus in Israeli Literature," *Christian Century* 87 (1970): 1248. See also Schalom Ben-Chorin, "The Image of Jesus in Modern Judaism," *JES* 11 (1974):401–30.

[8]New York: Ktav, 1968, with a prolegomenon by Lou H. Silberman (1–18). Silberman, whose prolegomenon seems querulous, is apparently unenthusiastic about the reprinting of the commentary.

[9]New York, 1967, with a prolegomenon by the Christian scholar Morton S. Enslin (v-xxvii).

[10]New York, 1970 (rev. ed.) with a prolegomenon by Eugene Mihaly (vii-xxv).

[11]New York, 1969, with a prolegomenon by Solomon Zeitlin (ix-xxxv).

Jewish books in the series "The Jewish People, History, Religion, Literature," has reprinted Montefiore's *Some Elements of the Religious Teaching of Jesus According to the Synoptic Gospels* (1910),[12] as well as Joseph Jacobs's *Jesus As Others Saw Him* (1925).[13] Also available from Arno is a reprint of the brief survey *Jewish Views of Jesus* (1931) by the Christian author Thomas Walker.[14] As further evidence of the continuing interest in Jewish discussions of Jesus, we may also mention the reprintings of the writings of contemporary scholars such as Sandmel[15] and Vermes.[16]

THE JEWISH APPROACH

Despite certain differences among individual scholars, it is now possible to speak of a distinctly Jewish approach to the life of Jesus and Christian origins. This approach, of course, has its own traits. Limiting themselves almost exclusively to the synoptic Gospels, Jewish scholars seek only the so-called Jesus of history, which to them as Jews cannot be the Christ of Christian faith. This Christ—indeed, Christianity itself—is regarded as largely the creation of the apostle Paul, who, by importing Hellenistic ideas, subverted the message of Jesus and so brought a new religion into existence. Jewish scholars are not interested in the Christ of Paul's Christianity. They are interested instead in Jesus the Jew and the extent to which he may be reclaimed for Judaism. As a result of this overriding interest, there is a clear avoidance of the claims of Christianity about the personal identity of Jesus.[17] Jewish scholars prefer to focus their attention on the teaching of Jesus, for here the promise of reclamation is great-

---

[12]New York, 1973.

[13]New York, 1973.

[14]New York, 1973, with a new introduction by Seymour Siegel.

[15]Sandmel's important book *We Jews and Jesus* (original 1965) has been reprinted by Oxford University Press (1973). Ktav has joined with the Anti-Defamation League of B'nai B'rith in reprinting Sandmel's *A Jewish Understanding of the New Testament* (original 1956; reprint 1974).

[16]G. Vermes, *Jesus the Jew* (1973; reprint ed., London: SCM, 1983).

[17]Jocz rightly sets forth as one of the striking characteristics of modern Jewish scholarship "the preoccupation with the *teaching* of Jesus to the neglect of a closer study of his personality, its innermost motives and self-consciousness." *JPJC*, 145.

est—although even this material, as we will see, is not without problems for such an undertaking. Since it is the teaching of Jesus that dominates the interest of recent Jewish scholarship, it is here that one can best begin to understand the modern Jewish approach to Jesus.

It will be obvious that Jewish scholars are in a particularly advantageous position to understand the teaching of Jesus. Familiar with the Bible (Old Testament), the development of early Judaism, the Jewish background of the Gospels, and often learned in the difficult world of rabbinic literature, they are often able not only to place Jesus in historical context but also to enter the mental world of Jesus and to capture every Jewish nuance in his words. Indeed, as has already been said, we are indebted in large measure to Jewish scholars for the realization of the necessity of seeing Jesus as a first-century Jew. In repeatedly drawing attention to the Jewishness of Jesus, these scholars have shed considerable light on him and his teaching as well as on contemporary Jewish religion itself. For this, Christian scholars, though sensing an incompleteness in the Jewish approach, continue to be grateful.

As we have noted, the amount of Jewish writing devoted to the study of Jesus and his teaching has continued to grow in volume to the present day. It is interesting to note that despite this proliferation of literature, the substantial shape of the Jewish approach to Jesus *has not altered significantly*. While the more recent writers may often differ in the details of their presentation, the basic contours are rather easily recognizable. There are, to be sure, differences between Reform Jews, Conservative Jews, and Orthodox Jews on the reclamation of Jesus and the positive evaluation of him that goes with it. Nevertheless, this is of little consequence to our study as almost all current Jewish writing on Jesus is positive in approach and stems from a liberalized Judaism.

OUTSTANDING JEWISH SCHOLARS

For my purposes I have selected from this voluminous literature certain important and influential Jewish scholars who have written specifically on Jesus and Christian origins and who are the outstanding representatives of the Jewish perspective on Jesus. This study, of course, will not be limited to them, but they must serve as important guideposts in any portrayal of the modern Jewish viewpoint.[18] Taken more or less chronologically, they are Claude Goldsmid Montefiore, Israel Abrahams, Joseph Klausner, Samuel Sandmel, Schalom Ben-Chorin, David Flusser, Pinchas E. Lapide, and Geza Vermes. Each of these men has devoted considerable time and energy to the study of the New Testament and Christian origins—until recent times a very unusual preoccupation for Jewish scholars.

It is especially appropriate to head this list with the distinguished British scholars C. G. Montefiore (1858–1938) and Israel Abrahams (1858–1925). While earlier Jewish scholars had written on Jesus and the Gospels, none gave himself to the subject as completely as Montefiore, who was one of the first Jews to write a full-scale commentary (two volumes) on the synoptic Gospels.[19] Educated at Balliol College, Oxford, Montefiore was deeply influenced by his mentor and friend, Benjamin Jowett—a man known for his constant emphasis on the spirit over the letter and the major issues over the trifling.[20] Thus prepared, Montefiore became the foremost proponent of Liberal Judaism in his day (in 1926 he became president of the World Union for Progressive Judaism), and it is no coincidence that he also became the outstanding Jewish writer on Jesus.

Montefiore was an eclectic scholar who devoted himself to the task of mediation[21] rather than originality; yet he was an avid

---

[18]For a survey of previous studies of Jewish scholarship on Jesus, see the bibliographical note, pp. 305ff.

[19]Probably the first Jew to write a commentary on the Gospels was Elie Soloweyczyk, who wrote in Hebrew and published his work in Paris in 1875. It was later translated into French and German. See Vorster, "Jewish Views on Jesus," 89–90.

[20]L. H. Silberman attributes what he regards as Montefiore's "condescending attitude" toward the rabbis to the fact that the rabbis "had not been at Balliol when Jowett was Master." When Silberman points out that Montefiore was "purely English," he implies he was less Jewish for that reason. Prolegomenon to the Ktav edition of C. G. Montefiore's *Synoptic Gospels* (New York: Ktav, 1968), 4–5.

[21]H. A. Fisher has well described Montefiore's accomplishments in these words: "His own task was to break down the barriers which separated Jew from Christian, to show the Jews what they might learn from the New Testament, and to teach the Christians what depths of religious truth and beauty might be found not only in the Old Testament,

seeker of truth, and his scholarship was and continues to be held in high regard by Jew and non-Jew alike. As a Liberal Jew he regarded himself as being somewhere between an Orthodox Jew and a Christian.[22] Having the advantages of being a Jew, he was also free from the restricted perspective of orthodoxy and thus capable of a higher degree of objectivity in his study of Christianity. He frankly admitted that his views would probably satisfy neither Jew nor Christian, but added that for this very reason they were the more likely to be true.[23] Liberal Judaism, fully open to the conclusions of scientific criticism, enabled one to accept the good freely and to reject the bad. So far as Judaism and Christianity are concerned, Montefiore wrote, "The Daughter learnt much from the Mother; why should not the Mother learn also from the Daughter?"[24]

Montefiore's most significant works for our purpose are the two-volume commentary *The Synoptic Gospels* (first edition, 1909; second edition, 1927), a volume that grew out of the commentary *Some Elements of the Religious Teaching of Jesus* (1910) and a later supplementary volume containing rabbinic parallels entitled *Rabbinic Literature and Gospel Teachings* (1930). Although the last volume was published after the exhaustive work of Paul Billerbeck in the five-volume *Kommentar Zum Neuen Testament aus Talmud und Midrasch* (München 1922–28)—and indeed made extensive use of that work—it nonetheless was and remains useful because of its brief compass, being limited to specifically religious and ethical teachings. Montefiore, as we will see, also meant this volume to be a corrective to Billerbeck at certain crucial points.[25] Also to be added to this is the

---

but also in the Rabbinic literature of the Middle Ages." Foreword to Lucy Cohen, *Some Recollections of Claude Goldsmid Montefiore* (London, 1940), 12.

[22] "Though I myself stand in different ways outside both sanctuaries, I have lived as much among those who are within both that I can appreciate their feelings." *RT*, 116.

[23] *RT*, 64.

[24] "Has Judaism a Future?" *HJ* 19 (1920–21):35.

[25] The Strack-Billerbeck *Kommentar* has received an increasing amount of criticism from both Jewish and Christian scholars for being unreliable in its presentation of Rabbinic Judaism. Billerbeck's rabbinic quotations are often taken out of context and little attention is given to the problem of their dates. Most grievous is the selectivity employed in favor of Christian apologetics. See most recently E. P. Sanders, *Paul and Palestinian Judaism* (Philadelphia: Fortress, 1977), 42–44.

large number of articles relevant to our interests that appeared in the *Jewish Quarterly Review,* of which journal Montefiore was cofounder, and in the *Hibbert Journal,* the last of which, "What a Jew Thinks of Jesus" (vol. 33, 1934–35), also appeared as a small book.

When Montefiore wrote his famous commentary, he sought the assistance of his friend Israel Abrahams, who had been appointed Reader in Talmudic and Rabbinic Literature at Cambridge University in 1902. The plan was for Abrahams to use his expertise in the rabbinic literature by elucidating certain points in Montefiore's commentary. Some sixty notes—each of which really called for a lengthy excursus—were to have been supplied by Abrahams and together to have formed a third volume of the commentary. Unfortunately, as Montefiore sadly notes in his second edition, this turned out to be impossible primarily because of the failing health of Abrahams. A note on the ʿam hā-āretz (the people of the land) did appear in Montefiore's second edition at the end of volume 2, but the original plan had to be abandoned. Some of the studies were written, but they took a shape of their own and eventually reached the public in a separate work by Abrahams, *Studies in Pharisaism and the Gospels,* printed in two "series," i.e., two volumes (1917 and 1929). These studies were written as a general vindication of Pharisaism but at the same time as an attempt to evaluate Jesus fairly and appreciatively.[26] Abrahams, like Montefiore, was a leading proponent of liberal Judaism and, with his friend, was cofounder and co-editor (1889–1907) of the *Jewish Quarterly Review.* Together Montefiore and Abrahams epitomize Liberal Judaism and today they stand as truly representative of the finest Jewish scholarship.

One of the best known Jewish books on Jesus, and almost certainly the most influential, is Joseph Klausner's *Jesus of Nazareth: His Life, Times, and Teaching.* Klausner (1874–1960)

---

[26]M. S. Enslin has correctly described the approach of Abrahams in these words: "Against the double temptation, on the one hand for Christians to darken the colors in which they draw the picture of the contemporaries and opponents of Jesus, and on the other, for Jews to minimize the originality of the one destined to be, if not the founder, certainly the foundation stone of Christianity—against this double temptation Abrahams was unalterably opposed." Prolegomenon to the Ktav edition of Israel Abrahams' *Studies in Pharisaism and the Gospels* (New York: Ktav, 1967), xv.

was a Lithuanian Jew who received his doctorate from the University of Heidelberg for a thesis on the subject of Jewish messianic ideas in the tannaitic period (i.e., the first two centuries of the Christian era).[27] In 1905 he succeeded Ahad ha' Am (literally "one of the people," a pen name for Asher Ginsberg) as editor of the important Hebrew literary periodical *Ha-Shiloach.* Having been greatly influenced by Ginsberg's Zionism, Klausner emigrated to Palestine in 1920, where he taught Modern Hebrew (he made significant contributions to the modernization of the language) and literature at Hebrew University. His two books most important for our purpose were written in Hebrew and published in Jerusalem: *Jesus of Nazareth* in 1922 (English translation by Herbert Danby, published in 1925) and *From Jesus to Paul* in 1939 (English translation by William F. Stinespring, published in 1943). In the introduction to *Jesus of Nazareth* Klausner describes his purpose as objective and scientific history and suggests that his book will be the first Hebrew book on Jesus that avoids both the propagandist aim of converting Jews to Christianity and the religious aim of making Christianity obnoxious to Jews.[28] For that reason, he—like Montefiore before him—expects the book to be objectionable to many Christians and Jews. Klausner, who was much more conservative in his Judaism than Montefiore, believed that Montefiore had too high a view of the Gospels (often at the expense of the Talmud).[29]

Turning to contemporary Jewish writers on Jesus, we may begin with the late Samuel Sandmel (1911–1979), the distinguished American scholar who established himself as the leading Jewish authority on the New Testament and early Christianity in this country. An ordained rabbi, Sandmel had decided to pursue a doctorate in Old Testament studies at Duke University but was persuaded by Harvie Branscomb, chairman of Duke University's New Testament department, to devote himself to New Tes-

---

[27]This was published in German in 1904 and is now available in English translation and revised form as volume iii of a three-volume work *The Messianic Idea in Israel* (volume 1 deals with the period of the Prophets; volume 2 with the apocalyptic and pseudepigraphic literature), New York: Beacon, 1955.

[28]*JN,* 11.

[29]Ibid., 114.

tament studies.[30] After the war, Sandmel completed his Ph.D. at
Yale, where he subsequently took a professorial chair in Jewish
Studies. He spent most of his academic career, however, as a
professor at the Hebrew Union College–Jewish Institute of Religion in Cincinnati of which he was Provost (1957–66) and
where he held the title of Distinguished Service Professor. The
prolific Sandmel was the author of, among other books, a full
introduction to the New Testament for Jewish readers entitled *A
Jewish Understanding of the New Testament* (Cincinnati, 1956;
new augmented edition, New York, 1974), *The Genius of Paul*
(New York, 1958; reprint, 1970), *We Jews and You Christians:
An Inquiry Into Attitudes* (New York, 1967), and *The First Christian Century in Judaism and Christianity* (New York, 1969), the
last a most interesting blend of scholarship and personal comment. A collection of essays, some of which bear on our subject,
is found in *Two Living Traditions: Essays on Religion and the
Bible* (Detroit: Wayne State University, 1972). His most important book for our purposes, however, is *We Jews and Jesus* (New
York, 1965). In this helpful volume Sandmel briefly reviews the
history of the Jewish study of Jesus and presents his view of a
"reasoned and reasonable" Jewish approach to Jesus. He writes
from the standpoint of a liberal Jew in the lineage of Montefiore
and Abrahams but, much more than they, Sandmel assumes and
builds on the substructure of modern critical scholarship. Sandmel was a classical liberal in the very best sense of that word.

Another very important contemporary Jewish author is
Schalom Ben-Chorin. Ben-Chorin, a student and friend of Martin
Buber, was born in Germany (1913) and studied at the University
of Munich before he moved to Israel in 1935 (he changed his
original name, Fritz Rosenthal, in 1937). In 1958 Ben-Chorin
founded the first congregation of Reform Jews in Jerusalem. He
has won several medals for his ecumenism and his leadership in
Jewish-Christian dialogue. Ben-Chorin pursued a career in jour-
nalism in Jerusalem while at the same time authoring several
books in the area of Judaism and Christianity, including books on

---

[30]S. Sandmel, *The First Christian Century in Judaism and Christianity* (New York:
Oxford, 1969), x.

Paul and Mary: *Paulus* (Munich, 1970) and *Mutter Mirjam* (Munich, 1971).[31] Most important for our purpose, however, are his *Bruder Jesus: Der Nazarener in jüdischer Sicht* (Munich, 1967) and *Jesus im Jüdentum* (Wuppertal, 1970), both presently available only in German. In these books Ben-Chorin records his own Jewish encounter with Jesus. In *Bruder Jesus* he carefully roots his study in the texts of the Gospels as well as in the Jewish background of the first century. The conclusion that emerges is that Jesus was neither Messiah nor a prophet but "a revolutionary of the heart." Ben-Chorin's writings are both perceptive and sensitive, and when he speaks of his own struggles with, and even his closeness to, Jesus, his eloquence is moving.

A third contemporary Jewish scholar is David Flusser, a specialist in early Christianity and currently a professor of comparative religion at Hebrew University in Jerusalem. Flusser, who was born in Vienna (1917), studied and taught classical philology at the University of Prague before taking his doctorate at Hebrew University. Among the areas of Flusser's expertise are the Dead Sea Scrolls, Judaism of the New Testament period, and Essene Christianity. While most of his writing has been in the form of articles (some quite lengthy) rather than books, in 1968 Flusser published in German a book on Jesus that in 1969 became available in English translation under the simple title *Jesus*.[32] Going against the stream of modern critical scholarship, Flusser contends that "it is possible to write the story of Jesus' life" and that the Gospels are more trustworthy as historical sources than is commonly thought.[33] Jesus, however, he argues, is truly understood only against the Jewish background of the Gospels and not against the backdrop of the later church's faith in him. Flusser's

---

[31]See too "Jesus und Paulus in jüdischer Sicht," *Annual of the Swedish Theological Institute*, X, ed. B. Knutsson (Leiden: Brill, 1976), 17–29.

[32]The German original was entitled *Jesus in Selbstzeugnissen und Bilddokumenten* (Hamburg, 1968). The English translation is by Ronald Walls (New York: Herder and Herder, 1969) and has been sharply criticized by Robert Lisle Lindsey in his pamphlet *A Review of David Flusser's "Jesus"* (Jerusalem: Dugith Publishers, Baptist House, 1973). Much of the material of this book is also available in Flusser's article "The Son of Man: Jesus in the Context of History" in Arnold Toynbee, ed., *The Crucible of Christianity*, (London: Thames & Hudson, 1969), 215–34.

[33]D. Flusser, *Jesus*, 7–8.

book is notable in that it is the first book on Jesus by a Jew in which little is made of the Jewishness of the author,[34] indicating the extent to which the Jewish perception is becoming widely understood as the truly historical view of Jesus.

Pinchas Lapide (b. 1922) moved from his native Canada to Israel in 1938 and was involved in the establishment of the first American kibbutz in Israel. For many years a diplomat in service of the State of Israel, Lapide has in the past decade turned to university lecturing in the field of religion, first in Israel, but most recently in Germany in the University of Göttingen.[35] Lapide is the author of several books having to do with Jews and Christians, such as *Juden und Christen* (1976), and a dialogue with Hans Küng, *Signposts for the Future* (Garden City, N.Y., 1978). More central to our purpose are *Ökumene aus Christen und Juden* (Neukirchen-Vluyn, 1972), *Der Rabbi von Nazareth: Wandlungen des jüdischen Jesusbildes* (Trier, 1974) and *Israelis, Jews and Jesus* (New York, 1976).[36] Lapide's approach is solidly within the modern trend to reclaim Jesus by affirming his genuine Jewishness and finds its primary motivation in the desire to bring Jews and Christians closer together.[37]

The last of the contemporary scholars with whom we are concerned is Geza Vermes, the author of the most recently pub-

---

[34]S. Ben-Chorin calls attention to this fact in his book, *Jesus im Judentum* (Wuppertal, 1970), 20.

[35]It was there in 1979 that Lapide caused considerable stir when he announced that he was willing to accept the resurrection of Jesus as a historical event. See "Resurrection: A Jew Looks at Jesus," *Time* (May 7, 1979). What was *not* pointed out, however, was that since Lapide puts the resurrection of Jesus alongside other resurrections from the dead recorded in the Bible and the Talmud, it is no longer the appearance of a new order as the New Testament claims; Jesus presumably was raised from the dead only to die again. In a recent book, Lapide has used this theme of resurrection in the Jewish and Christian traditions as a further aid to ecumenical discussion. See his *Auferstehung: Ein jüdisches Glaubenserlebnis* (Munich, 1977). Cf. J. P. Galvin, "A Recent Jewish View of the Resurrection," *ExpT* 91 (1980):277–79.

[36]A translation of *Ist das nicht Josephs Sohn?: Jesus im heutigen Judentum* (Munich, 1976). See too Lapide's article "Two Famous Rabbis" in B. Knutsson, ed., *Annual of the Swedish Theological Institute,* X (Leiden: Brill, 1976), 97–109, in which he compares Jesus and Rabbi Israel Mezibezh (=Besht).

[37]For a summary and brief assessment of Lapide's contribution, see U. Laepple, "Die Sache Jesu—die Sache Israels. P. Lapides Beiträge zum jüdisch-christlichen Dialog," *Theologische Beiträge* 10 (1979): 178–83. See now also P. Lapide, *Er predigte in ihren Synagogen: Jüdische Evangelienauslegung* (Gütersloh: Mohn, 1981).

lished Jewish book on Jesus, *Jesus the Jew* (London: Collins, 1973; first American edition, New York: Macmillan, 1974). Vermes was born in Hungary (1924); attended the University of Budapest and studied Oriental history, philology, and theology at Louvain, Belgium; and is now Reader in Jewish Studies at Oxford University. One of the first to study the finds at Qumran, he is well known for his book *The Dead Sea Scrolls in English*, which has enjoyed a large paperback circulation. In addition to authoring several other books, Vermes has been the editor of the *Journal of Jewish Studies* since 1971. His book on Jesus is a significant work; it has been described by one reviewer as "likely to replace Klausner's *Jesus of Nazareth* as the most authoritative Jewish study of our time."[38] Vermes, however, resists the suggestion that his book is Jewish in any sense other than in its attempt to understand Jesus in his total Jewish context.[39] He wants his approach to be understood as nonpartisan, as a serious search for historical fact, as the book's subtitle, "A Historian's Reading of the Gospels," indicates. Nonetheless, Vermes's book does bear the distinctive traits of the Jewish approach and is worth considering as such despite the author's disclaimer. Also to be noted are Vermes's lectures entitled *The Gospel of Jesus the Jew* (The Riddell Memorial Lectures, Newcastle upon Tyne: University of Newcastle upon Tyne, 1981), the precursors of a full volume by the same title promised by Vermes.[40]

Our examination of the modern Jewish approach to Jesus and his teaching will be enriched by reference to additional Jewish writers, among whom are the following (listed chronologically according to year of birth): Isaac M. Wise (1819–1900; born in Bohemia, moved to New York in 1846; rabbi, pioneer of Reform Judaism, first president of Hebrew Union College); Kaufmann Kohler (1843–1926; born in Bavaria, moved to the United States in 1869; rabbi, advocate for Reform Judaism, pres-

---

[38]Edward Quinn in the *Yorkshire Post,* as cited on the dust cover of the American edition.

[39]*Jesus the Jew,* 9. We may compare the way in which Flusser's book made little of the fact that the author was a Jew (see above, note 36).

[40]A further article by Vermes that anticipates this volume and overlaps considerably the content of the lectures is "The Gospels without Christology," in A. E. Harvey, ed., *God Incarnate: Story and Belief* (London: SPCK, 1981), 55–68.

ident of Hebrew Union College); Joseph Jacobs (1854–1916; born in Australia, moved to England; Jewish historian and scholar); Gerald Friedlander (1871–1923; British rabbi); Leo Baeck (1873–1956; German rabbi, leader of Progressive Judaism; imprisoned in Theresienstadt, moved to London in 1945); Paul Goodman (1875–1949; born in Estonia, moved to England in 1891; Zionist, served Zionist Organization); Hyman G. Enelow (1877–1934; born in Lithuania, moved to the United States as a youth; Reform rabbi); Jules M. Isaac (1877–1963; French historian); Ernest M. Trattner (1898—; American rabbi); Hugh J. Schonfield[41] (1901—; British writer); David Daube (1909—; born in Germany; jurist and biblical scholar; professor in England and the United States); Hans Joachim Schoeps (1909—; German professor); and Hyam Maccoby (1924—; British historian).[42]

There are, of course, many other Jewish writers who have given some attention to Jesus, the Gospels, and early Christianity. The present work is representative and not exhaustive in its survey of Jewish views of Jesus. Moreover, in the present work novelists, playwrights, and lyricists,[43] as well as those writers whose interest centers on the trial and execution of Jesus, have been excluded from consideration. The latter, which understandably has held a great fascination for Jewish scholars, is really a subject unto itself, and I have intentionally omitted it from this study. The Jewish literature is extensive and has been carefully studied by David R. Catchpole in his excellent book *The Trial of Jesus,* subtitled "A Study in the Gospels and Jewish

---

[41]Some may object to the inclusion of Schonfield in this list because he is a popularizer whose views are somewhat eccentric and whose work is respected neither by Jewish nor by Christian scholars. Although Schonfield's perspective is not typical or representative of Jewish scholarship, nevertheless at many points his views are in line with those of other Jewish scholars. Nor can Schonfield be ignored. He is without question the most widely known among the Jewish scholars discussed in the present work, primarily because of several paperbacks that have been best sellers, including, of course, *The Passover Plot* (New York: Geis, 1966), which has even been made into a movie.

[42]For the works of these men, see part one of the bibliography at the end of the present work.

[43]This material is surveyed by Ben-Chorin in "The Image of Jesus in Modern Judaism," *JES* 11 (1974):417–24; cf. also P. Lapide, *Israelis, Jews and Jesus,* ET by P. Heinegg (Garden City, N.Y.: Doubleday, 1979), 3–34.

Historiography from 1770 to the Present Day'' (Leiden: Brill, 1971).[44]

Other well-known persons in the Jewish-Christian dialogue, such as Martin Buber and Franz Rozensweig, have not addressed the specific questions concerning the interpretation of the teaching of Jesus, which is our interest here. For this reason they are not important for this book.

It should be noticed that the Jewish scholars that are the focus of our attention span nearly a century, are from different countries, and represent different varieties of Judaism. They often differ in their viewpoints—sometimes markedly—and each has his own analysis and reconstruction of the historical Jesus worthy of discussion in itself. In this book I do not pretend to do justice to the totality of any single author's work. I attempt instead to examine what each of the Jewish authors has to say on a variety of topics concerning the teaching of Jesus. And although I am therefore forced to select statements pertinent to this study, in no case has this been done in violation of context, and nowhere have I willfully distorted the meaning of an author.

It is my contention that all of these writers share to some extent in the enterprise known as the Jewish reclamation of Jesus and furthermore that there is a recognizable pattern in what they say concerning the topics before us. Despite the differences among these writers, there is general agreement on many fundamental points. The similarity of outlook is so evident that it becomes possible to speak of a composite Jewish perspective to which each of these writers has contributed in his own way. It is of course always a simplification to speak of "the Jewish view." Given the similarities that confront us in the present study, however, such a simplification seems justifiable.

The eight scholars who assume special importance for this study do so because of their significant writing on Jesus and his

---

[44]See also W. Horbury, "The Trial of Jesus in Jewish Tradition," in E. Bammel, ed., *The Trial of Jesus*, Cambridge Studies in Honour of C.F.D. Moule (London: SCM, 1970), 103–21, and G. Lindeskog, "Der Prozess Jesu im jüdisch-christlichen Religionsgespräch," in *Abraham Unser Vater*, Festschrift for O. Michel (Leiden: Brill, 1963), 325–36.

teaching. Each is to some degree typical of the Jewish viewpoint. Montefiore holds the important place he does, not simply because of the volume of his writing on the subject but also because of the remarkable extent to which he anticipates what later Jewish scholars have written about Jesus. When one is familiar with his writings, one finds little that is really new in the burgeoning Jewish literature of our day. At the same time, as we will see, there is a discernible trend in more recent Jewish scholarship toward what we may call a more ambitious reclamation of Jesus. That is, more and more of the teaching of Jesus is by one means or another designated as "Jewish," and a portrait of Jesus is set forth that increasingly contradicts the Christian view.

It should be noted, finally, that the views of these Jewish scholars set forth here are not widely held among the Jewish populace. Most of the latter would probably deny the feasibility and perhaps even the desirability of the Jewish reclamation of Jesus.

THE JEWISH INTEREST

Almost all the Jewish scholars mentioned in this book have as a primary interest the Jewish reclamation of Jesus. This, as we have already noted, involves them in a consistent attempt to elucidate fully the Jewishness of Jesus. It is always Jesus the Jew they are interested in and not the Jesus of Christianity. While this in itself raises interesting problems, which we will be concerned with later, it must be pointed out here that this Jewish approach inevitably requires the discussion of Judaism generally, and of the character of Judaism in the first century.

This is immediately evident from the fact that in the Gospel narratives, among the foremost enemies of Jesus are the Pharisees, and Jesus speaks to no one more harshly than to the Pharisees (cf. Matt. 23). But Pharisaic Judaism represents the finest expression of Judaism: it alone survived the destruction of the Jewish nation and its capital in A.D. 70; it inspired the compilation of the Mishna and the production of the Talmudic commentaries and has continued as "normative" Judaism down to the present.

How then can Jesus be reclaimed for Judaism when he seems to have stood against the Pharisees? How can Jesus the Jew be appreciated when in the fourth Gospel it is repeatedly "the Jews" who are the enemies of Jesus?

Jewish scholars have long felt that the portrayal of the Pharisees in the Gospel narratives is unjust. They have, accordingly, labored to bring about a positive appreciation of Pharisaic Judaism and to show that rather than being contrary to the spirit of Jesus' teachings, Pharisaic Judaism is consistent with, and often runs parallel to, the teaching of Jesus. In this deserving effort, Jews have received considerable aid from such non-Jewish scholars as Travers Herford, George Foot Moore, James Parkes, and A. Lukyn Williams.[45] In their positive understanding of Judaism and the Jewish spirit, these writers essentially reflect what can be called the Jewish viewpoint, and their work has frequently called forth praise from Jewish scholars for its impartiality.

In demonstrating the Jewishness of Jesus, Jewish scholars thus have an unavoidable interest in vindicating the Judaism of his day. While the methods may vary, the interest is a common one. For these scholars it is impossible that Jesus the Jew could truly have spoken against the Judaism in the name of which he is being reclaimed in their writings.

Before we pursue these matters further, however, it is important for us to understand the evolution of the Jewish approach to Jesus. Only then will we have the background necessary for our task.[46]

---

[45]For the books of these men, see part two of the bibliography.

[46]A recent Jewish book on Jesus, which appeared too late to be included in the present study, deserves to be mentioned here: G. Cornfeld, ed., *The Historical Jesus: A Scholarly View of the Man and His World* (Macmillan: New York/London, 1982). In this book Cornfeld leans heavily on the views of Flusser and Vermes and, like Schonfield, propounds the view that Jesus did not die on the cross. Cornfeld's book fits solidly into the emerging Jewish perspective on Jesus and adds little that is new. According to Cornfeld, Jesus was not a Zealot and did not claim to be the Messiah. He was instead a charismatic holy man who was probably influenced by the Essenes. Much of the criticism of the representative authors used in the present study is also applicable to this newest Jewish volume.

CHAPTER TWO

The History of
the Jewish Study of Jesus

A TRUE UNDERSTANDING and appreciation of the attitude of modern Jewish scholarship toward Jesus is quite impossible apart from seeing the Jewish position in historical perspective. Understandably there is a direct—indeed, causal—relationship between the Jewish perception of Jesus and the treatment accorded Jews by Christendom. Tracing the Jewish experience is a painful undertaking, but the Christian must not shut his eyes to his past, however repugnant it may be. It is not possible here to give a full history of the Jewish attitude toward Jesus,[1] but it is necessary at least to outline that history and characterize the different periods by conspicuous examples drawn from each.

THE PREMODERN JEWISH ATTITUDE

The premodern period is that grim span of some seventeen hundred years in which Jews suffered at the hands of Christian society prior to the European emancipation. As the Christian church grew in power, so grew her oppression of the Jews and, in turn, the Jewish response of hostility toward the church. The disheartening story of the treatment of the Jews by Christians through these long, dark centuries constitutes one of the saddest chapters in the history of the church. Castigated as "enemies of God" and "murderers of Christ," the Jews became the victims of a particularly vile persecution that not only contradicted the ethical teaching of the Lord of the church but also burned hatred of Christianity into the hearts of the Jews.

---

[1]For previous surveys available, see the bibliographical note at the end of the present work, pp. 305ff.

In the earliest Christian church, which was of course entirely Jewish, Jewish believers in Jesus apparently encountered little significant hostility from their Jewish brethren. The rift between the two groups had not yet occurred. The earliest description of the church shows Christian Jews persevering in their Jewish way of life, having added to it the dimension of Christian worship: "And day by day, attending the temple together and breaking bread in their homes, they partook of food with glad and generous hearts, praising God and having favor with all the people" (Acts 2:46–47). To be sure, the Jewish authorities were upset with the teaching of the apostles from the beginning, but their primary concern appears to have been the meeting of their Roman-delegated responsibility of keeping the peace and averting rebellions, actual or potential.

The rift appears to begin in earnest with Stephen, a Hellenistic Jew and the first Christian martyr, who apparently had been drawing out the implications of the work of Jesus Christ and the nature of Christian salvation with an increasing emphasis on discontinuity with Judaism (cf. Acts 6:13–14; 7). There is an ever-growing mood of hostility in the succeeding narrative of Acts, which culminates in Paul's denunciation of unbelieving Jews through the quotation of Isaiah 6:9–10 (Acts 28:25ff.). In this final interview with Paul the Jews in Rome had reported "with regard to this sect [i.e., Christian Jews] we know that everywhere it is spoken against" (Acts 28:22).

The actual "parting of the ways," however, did not take place until the generation following the destruction of Jerusalem in A.D. 70.[2] Until this period, Jewish Christians were apparently able to continue attending synagogue and thus to engage in proselytizing activities. As Judaism reconstituted itself at Yavneh (Jamnia) following the national catastrophe, the rabbis decided that measures had to be taken against the threat of a continued presence of Hebrew Christians in the synagogue services. Judaism was facing a new situation, a time when her very existence

---

[2] "The Parting of the Ways" is the chapter title of an outstanding history of the entire subject: James Parkes, *The Conflict of the Church and the Synagogue* (London: Soncino, 1934; reprinted, New York: Atheneum, 1969). Cf. F. J. Foakes-Jackson, ed., *The Parting of the Roads: Studies in the Development of Judaism and Early Christianity* (London: Arnold, 1912).

was endangered, and it was thus natural that her primary concern should be with the Jews who had turned from Judaism to Christianity rather than with Gentile Christians.[3] Gentile Christianity was largely ignored in the early period and the references to the *minim* (heretics) in the Talmudic literature refer in the main probably to Jewish Christians.[4] Klausner calls attention to the animosity against these *minim* in the following words: "In the earlier period they [the Tannaim] were more averse to the *Minim* than to Jesus himself, since in them they saw a danger to the national existence."[5]

It was probably in the decade of the eighties, but at least by the end of the first century, that a change in the liturgy was initiated with the specific purpose of driving Jewish Christians out of the synagogue. This was accomplished by the insertion of an added "benediction" to the recitation of the so-called Eighteen Benedictions (*Shemoneh Esreh*).[6] This benediction is numbered as the twelfth and brings the total to nineteen, although the collection continued to bear its original name.[7] In reality it is a curse and not a blessing, and in its present form reads as follows:

> And for slanderers let there be no hope, and let all wickedness perish as in a moment; let all thine enemies be speedily cut off, and the dominion of arrogance do thou uproot and crush, cast down and humble speedily in our days. Blessed art thou, O Lord, who breakest the enemies and humblest the arrogant.[8]

---

[3]Israel Abrahams calls attention to the "extraordinary fact that it is scarcely possible to cite a single clear attack against Gentile Christianity in the early Rabbinic literature." *SP* 11:56.

[4]This is argued by Abrahams, ibid., 56, and J. Jocz, *JPJC*, 45 and 180; cf. also R. Travers Herford, *Christianity in Talmud and Midrash* (London: Williams and Norgate, 1903; reprinted, Clifton, N. J.: Reference Book Publishers, 1966).

[5]*JN*, 47.

[6]According to BT (Berakoth 28b), Rabban Gamaliel (2) requested such an addition, and it was actually composed by Samuel the Lesser.

[7]May there originally have been seventeen benedictions, the addition of the benediction of the *minim* bringing the number to eighteen? See JT (Berakoth 4.3) and S. Zeitlin, "The Tefillah, the Shemoneh Esreh: An Historical Study of the First Canonization of the Hebrew Liturgy," originally published in *JQR*, n.s. 54 (1964): 208–49 and reprinted in Zeitlin's Studies in the *Studies in Early History of Judaism*, vol. 1 (New York: Ktav, 1973): 92–133. Hanoch Avenary concurs in his article "Amidah" in *EJ*, 2:841.

[8]As found in *The Authorised Daily Prayer Book*, revised edition by Joseph H. Hertz (New York, 1948), 143–45.

There is some question as to what the original wording of this twelfth benediction may have been. Among the variations, for example, that are in the version found in the Cairo Genizah,[9] representing probably the oldest form of the text, is the explicit reference to *ha-nozrim,* the Nazarenes, alongside the mention of *ha-minim* (the heretics), neither of which occurs in the present form of the benediction.[10] It cannot be established with certainty that the original form of the benediction did refer specifically to the Nazarenes, i.e., the Christians, those who followed the Nazarene.[11] But there can be little doubt that whatever the original wording of the benediction, and whether or not the original itself was a modification of a previously existing, more general benediction, as Flusser argues,[12] there were added to the larger liturgical prayer elements that aimed at ridding the synagogue of Jews who had become Christians.[13] A person who was unable to recite this twelfth benediction, and recite it correctly, was removed from the synagogue under suspicion of being a *min* (heretic).[14]

Although there were certainly other *minim,* none posed so

---

[9]The Cairo Genizah (=storeroom) was the repository of the Old Cairo Synagogue (established in A.D. 882), where old, unused manuscripts were kept. In the last half of the nineteenth century, a great quantity of highly significant manuscripts from the storeroom came to light. See Paul E. Kahle, *The Cairo Genizah* (London, 1947).

[10]For the text translated see ibid., 26. For the Hebrew text, S. Schechter in *JQR* 10 (1898): 657. The reference to "Nazarene" in the benediction is also noted by Jerome, *On Isaiah,* 5:18.

[11]See the cautious discussion in the appendix "The Shema^c and the Shemoneh 'Esreh" in the new edition of Schürer, *The History of the Jewish People in the Age of Jesus Christ (175 B.C.–A.D. 135)* rev. and ed. G. Vermes, F. Millar, and Matthew Black (Edinburgh: T. & T. Clark, 1979), 11:454–63.

[12]"Das Schisma zwischen Judentum und Christentum," *EvTheol* 40 (1980): 229ff. Flusser's conclusion is that the benediction "was apparently not so decisive a step in the separation of Christianity from Judaism as is generally thought." Ibid., 233.

[13]For skepticism on this point, see R. Kimelman, "*Birkat Ha-Minim* and the Lack of Evidence for an Anti-Christian Jewish Prayer in Late Antiquity," in E. P. Sanders, A. I. Baumgarten, and Alan Mendelson, eds., *Jewish and Christian Self-Definition,* vol. 2 (London: SCM, 1981), 226–44. But see now the thorough and convincing article by William Horbury, "The Benediction of the *Minim* and Early Jewish-Christian Controversy," *JTS* 33 (1982):19–61.

[14]In BT (Berakoth 28b, 29a) the amusing anecdote is told concerning Samuel the Lesser, who, although he himself had composed the new benediction, could not recall its exact wording and thus came into no small danger of being ostracized.

great a threat to the synagogue as did the Jewish Christians. For that reason they were treated with utter contempt and were ostracized from the Jewish community. The benediction concerning the heretics, other liturgical alterations,[15] and the prohibition of the Greek language and the use of the Septuagint—all came about in stern answer to this challenge. The gap was increasingly widened between Jews and Jewish Christians. Gentile Christians, on the other hand, were not of immediate concern to the synagogue. Yet the actions taken specifically against Jewish Christians inevitably had an impact on the church as a whole. The hostility between church and synagogue continued to heighten. To curse Jewish Christians is to curse all Christians, and thus Justin Martyr (c. 150) writes, "In your synagogues ye curse all who have become Christians,"[16] quite probably alluding to the added benediction concerning the heretics.

There are not a few references to Jewish Christians under the name *minim* within the rabbinic literature.[17] Possible references to Jesus in the Talmud are not frequent and most of them are denied by Jewish scholars.[18] Christian censorship, actual or threatened, may be responsible for some of the silence of the rabbinic writings as they have come down to us, even as it appears to account for the modifications in the form of the twelfth benediction mentioned above. There are other reasons, however, for the sparseness of references to Jesus. As Klausner points out, the period of the second temple is in fact seldom referred to in the Talmud, and initially, at least, the appearance of Jesus and the rise of Christianity were inconspicuous events.[19] The rabbis,

---

[15]See J. Jocz, *JPJC*, 47–50.

[16]*Dialogue with Trypho*, ch. 96; cf. ch. 16.

[17]The evidence is collected and evaluated by R. Travers Herford in *Christianity in Talmud and Midrash* (1903; reprint ed., Clifton, N.J.: Reference Book Publishers, 1966).

[18]Klausner is a notable exception. Though not uncritical of the Talmudic references, he does accept a number of tannaitic references as authentic references to Jesus. See *JN*, 24–47.

[19]*JN*, 19; cf. H. J. Schoeps, "The growing church was not taken seriously during the first centuries of this era. For this reason, remarkably few passages can be found in the Talmud referring indisputably to the historical Jesus." *The Jewish-Christian Argument*, trans. David E. Green from 3rd German ed. (New York: Holt, Rinehart & Winston, 1963), 19.

moreover, are not likely to have gone out of their way to refer to
Jesus and probably preferred to ignore Jesus and Christianity in
writings they produced for study.

Whether there are any actual references to Jesus in the Talmud and Midrash (the rabbinic commentaries on Scripture) is
debatable. In the most recent thorough study of the subject,[20]
Johann Maier concludes that no tannaitic passages (first century
B.C. to A.D. 200) refer to Jesus and that references to him in
amoraic passages (200 to the fifth century) are the result of post-
Talmudic influence. The rabbis themselves, therefore, reveal little or no interest in Jesus. It was apparently only later (beginning
in the fifth century) that certain rabbinic passages were interpreted to refer to Jesus. The references are nonetheless valuable, not for ascertaining the rabbinic perspective, but for understanding the polemics of post-Talmudic Judaism. In that connection, it is worth giving a sample of the data.

In the Talmud and Midrash Jesus is seldom referred to explicitly. We do encounter the name Yeshu (an abbreviation of the
more popular Yeshua), occasionally with ben Pandera (in a variety of spellings) or ben Stada, and even Yeshu ha-nozri (a later
addition, according to Maier). Elsewhere a name such as Balaam, or the anonymous expression "such a one" or "that man,"
came to be understood as referring to Jesus. It became easy for
Jews to identify this or that despicable person in the Talmud with
Jesus on the basis of some superficial similarity between the two.

Aspects of the Christian story about Jesus therefore find
their parody in this material. Thus Jesus had no father, not because of a virgin birth, we read, but because of an illegitimate
birth (Mishnah, Jebamoth iv 13). His mother, although a descendant of royal families, is said to have played the harlot with
carpenters (BT Sanhedrin 106a). In the latter passage she is referred to as the mother of Balaam, about whom R. Johanan said,

[20]*Jesus von Nazareth in der Talmudischen Überlieferung* (Darmstadt, 1978). See
also the much earlier investigation of the evidence in "Jesus Christ in the Talmud" by
Heinrich Laible (ET by A. W. Streane) in G. Dalman, *Jesus Christ in the Talmud,
Midrash, Zohar, and the Liturgy of the Synagogue* (Cambridge, 1893; reprint, Arno,
New York, 1973), 1–98; J. Klausner, *JN*, 18–47; R. Travers Herford, *Christianity in
Talmud and Midrash*. A summary of the last mentioned work may be found in *DCG*
2:877.

"In the beginning a prophet, in the end a deceiver"—words that apparently seemed particularly suitable as referring to Jesus. Elsewhere she is identified with Miriam, a dresser of women's hair (by virtue of a play on the name Magdalene), who had been false to her husband (BT Shabbath 104b). Jesus had indeed been to Egypt and there had learned the sorcery by which he subsequently led astray and deceived Israel, causing Israel to sin (ibid.; BT Sanhedrin 107b). He was a heretic who claimed to be God, but was a liar; to be the son of man, but was mocked; and to go up to heaven, but did not do so (JT Taanith 65b). He scoffed at the wisdom of the wise, was excommunicated, and has no part in the world to come (BT Sanhedrin 107b; Mishnah, Sanhedrin x 2). Yeshu had five disciples, each deserving of death. He himself was put to death on the eve of Passover for the practicing of magic and his deception of Israel, but only after a plea had gone out in vain for anything that might be found in his favor (BT Sanhedrin 43a). The punishment of this prophet of a false religion is "by boiling filth" (BT Gittin 56b, 57a).

It is admitted by all that these Talmudic references possess no historical value.[21] This material is important only insofar as it reflects the Jewish attitude of the late Talmudic and post-Talmudic periods. Given their plight, it is understandable that Jews should react with such strong distaste. Jesus is perceived as a Jew, but a Jew who had defected from Israel and led many astray with him. He was a mere man and cannot have been what he claimed himself to be. Nothing in him calls for appreciation or admiration; he is only to be ridiculed and rejected. Certainly this distaste did not come about suddenly. The rabbis must have shared this negative attitude even if it does not find expression in their writings. But the aversion to Jesus undoubtedly increased with the passing of the centuries, and some scholars (e.g., Klausner) have called attention to the fact that the later Talmudic passages are the more acerbic ones. This increasing aversion eventually finds its climax in the medieval compilation known as *Toledot Yeshu,* our next major illustration of the premodern Jewish attitude.

---

[21]Klausner says the "single historical value" of these references is that they make impossible the claim that Jesus never existed. *JN,* 20. Cf. Sandmel, *WJJ,* 28.

The *Toledot Yeshu* (literally "generations [life]" of Yeshu) makes use of much of the Talmudic and Midrashic material referred to above, but differs from the latter in that an extended, more or less coherent, story of the life of Jesus is presented. The complete narrative appears not to have been written earlier than the tenth century, although the oral sources must go back as early as the fifth century, and perhaps earlier. As with most folklore material of this kind, many different versions came into existence, and today nearly a dozen are extant.[22] The story is a kind of farce, a mocking distortion and elaboration of the gospel story that well reflects the animosity and hatred of the Jews for Christianity and its Christ. No attempt is made to refute or deny items of the gospel narrative, but as in the Talmudic references, certain of its aspects are altered and presented in keeping with the special interests of the Jewish community. Although scholars admit that there is no historical worth to the narrative,[23] this story provided many generations of Jews through the Middle Ages with virtually their only knowledge about the founder of Christianity.

The tale begins with an account of the seduction of Miriam, the mother of Yeshu, by one Joseph Pandira and her eventual desertion by both the latter and her betrothed, Yochanan by name. The child Yeshu, by his irreverent and intolerable conduct toward the rabbis entrusted with his education, soon reveals his illegitimate birth and is expelled from the community. Yeshu is eventually successful in attempting to steal the "Ineffable Name" from the temple in Jerusalem. This he accomplished by writing it on a scrap of leather and sewing it into an incision on his thigh. It is by the power of this Name that Yeshu was able to do his miracles of healing and even of raising the dead. He added to his miracle-working the proclamation of himself as the virgin-born Son of God and the Messiah of Israel. Gathering a considerable following in Upper Galilee, Yeshu attracted the attention of

---

[22]See the article "Toledot Yeshu" by Joseph Dan in *EJ* 16:1208.

[23]E. Bammel argues, however, that certain traditions incorporated in *Toledot Yeshu* are very old and may be of some indirect historical value. See "Christian Origins in Jewish Tradition," *NTS* 13 (1966–67), 317–35; cf. also "Ex illa itaque die consilium fecerunt . . ." in E. Bammel, ed., *The Trial of Jesus*. Studies in honor of C. F. D. Moule (London: SCM, 1970), 30ff.; 36–37.

the leading Jews in Jerusalem. These leaders arranged for Yehuda (=Judas Iscariot) to receive the Name with its power and to challenge the power of Yeshu in a contest. After Yeshu lost the contest, he escaped only to be followed by Yehuda, who managed to steal from him the leather fragment containing the Name. It was after this that Yeshu was apprehended by the authorities in the temple precincts, where he once again tried to abscond with the Ineffable Name. He was stoned and hung on a cabbage stalk, since no other tree consented to bear his body (or alternately, because Yeshu had in advance, by the power of the Name, prohibited every tree from bearing his body). After his burial, the gardener took the body from the tomb and threw it into a ditch, causing the disciples to encounter an empty tomb and to conclude that Yeshu had risen from the dead. When Queen Helena (a historical confusion), who had believed in Yeshu, was about to bring persecution on the Jews for the execution of Yeshu, the body was found, tied to the tail of a horse and dragged before her. The story continues with information about Shimeon Kepha (Simon Peter), who, though he was at first on the side of the Jews, learned the Ineffable Name, worked miracles, and essentially brought a new religion into existence. This new religion, however, was eventually corrupted by his successor in Rome.[24]

A brief summary such as the preceding cannot convey satisfactorily the cruel, mocking spirit and the low comedy of the full-length narrative. But one need not look far for the motive underlying such a scandalous view of Jesus. R. Travers Herford, who calls the story "an unseemly relic of evil days," is quite correct in pointing out that "if it bears witness against those who wrote it, it does so no less against those whose cruelty drove them to write it."[25]

And indeed they were driven to such an attitude. The total-

---

[24]For longer summaries (of different versions) see Klausner, *JN,* 48–51 and Herford, *DCG* 2:879. Cf. also H. J. Schonfield, *According to the Hebrews* (London, 1937), for an English translation and discussion of sources. The definitive scholarly treatment remains S. Krauss, *Das Leben Jesu nach jüdischen Quellen* (Berlin, 1902), but see now also the thorough study of a version of the *Toledot* hitherto unknown: G. Schlichting, *Ein jüdisches Leben Jesu: Die verschollene Toledot-Jeschu-Fassung Tam ū-mūʿād* (Tübingen: Mohr, 1982).

[25]*DCG* 2:879.

itarian church exerted the full force of its power against the
Jewish brood of Christ-killers, as they were commonly called.
They were imprisoned within crowded ghettos and thus increasingly isolated from society and culture; they were victimized
by a welter of legal restrictions; they were expelled from country
after country; and they were discriminated against in every possible dimension. They were sometimes forcibly subjected to Christian baptism and at other times offered the alternative of conversion or execution. There can be little question but that the
church's treatment of the Jews is responsible for the Jewish perception of Christ in this period. Jocz rightly calls the church of
history "the first and foremost stumbling-block in the Jewish
appreciation of Jesus."[26] It is not surprising that apart from such
a travesty as the *Toledot,* the Jew closed his mind to the Jesus
Christ of Christianity.

A remarkable exception to the perspective of Orthodox Judaism is found in the sect known as the Karaites which, beginning in the eighth century, rejected the authority of the Talmud.
The Karaites exhibit a surprisingly positive view of Jesus. For
them, Jesus was a great Jewish martyr, who in fact belonged to
Judaism and not to Christianity. In this conclusion and in the
insistence that the evangelists and the apostles are guilty of mis-
representing Jesus, the Karaites constitute a remarkable anticipation of the modern Jewish perspective.[27]

There is not much Orthodox Jewish mention of Jesus prior to
the Enlightenment beyond what we have already looked at in the
Talmudic and Midrashic sources and in the *Toledot.* Most of the
references that exist stem not from any interest in Jesus, but from
the polemics that various Jewish-Christian disputations brought
forth in the era preceding the Emancipation.[28] Needless to say, in
such a context any comments about Jesus would be characterized

---

[26]*JPJC,* 92. Sandmel's paraphrase of the early Luther is appropriate: "When I see
how Christians have treated the Jews, if I were a Jew, I would rather be a hog than a
Christian." *WJJ,* 62.

[27]See Bammel, "Christian Origins in Jewish Tradition," 333–34.

[28]For surveys of this material, see I. Broydé, "Polemics and Polemical Literature,"
JE 10:102-9 and Haim Hillel Ben-Sasson, "Disputation and Polemics," *EJ* 6:79–103.
Cf. also R. T. Herford, *DCG* 2:879–80.

by a decided restraint lest the Christians be offended and intensify their persecution of the Jews. Insofar as discussion bears on Jesus, two kinds of material tend to surface with some regularity. First, there is the repeated denial that the Talmud speaks blasphemously of Jesus. It is insisted by the disputants that the chronological setting of several passages must point to a different time and thus to a different Jesus (the name, after all, being a common one). Second, there is a philosophical protestation against the possibility of a trinity that does not violate the unity of God.

There are in this tradition of disputation and polemics some outstanding examples of courteous and dispassionate discussions of sensitive subjects. Lapide mentions some of the significant Jewish representatives of this era and those of the succeeding centuries—and also provides lengthy quotations—in his useful survey "Rabbis Speak of Jesus."[29] In the famed Maimonides (1135–1204), who does not mention Jesus specifically, there is the suggestion that Christianity can be perceived favorably by the Jews as ordained by God for the spread of true religion among the Gentiles. Such Jews as the Spaniard Hasdai Crescas (15th century), the Pole Isaac Troki (16th century), and the philosopher Baruch Spinoza (17th century), without compromising their own position, spoke directly, forcefully, and yet peaceably to the most difficult of questions. Troki in particular anticipates certain tendencies that later were to be exhibited in the modern Jewish attitude toward Jesus. He was able to separate, or at least to distinguish, Jesus from his professed followers, sensing a Jewishness on the part of Jesus that had been ignored by most Christians.[30] Abraham Farissol, who lived in Italy at the end of the fifteenth and the beginning of the sixteenth century, was able to take a position similar to Maimonides' and allow that Jesus, though not the Jewish messiah, could be regarded as a Christian messiah. On the other side, there was an occasional Christian who spoke out for the human rights of the Jews. Mention may be made of the outstanding example of Johannes Reuchlin

---

[29]*Israelis, Jews and Jesus,* 70–156.

[30]Troki, however, is a clear exception in the era in which he wrote. Jocz attributes this to the liberty of speech in the Poland of Troki's day. *JPJC,* 99.

(1455–1522), a learned Hebraist, who argued that the Jew is to be regarded as one's neighbor, and whose endeavors helped preserve the Talmud from destruction at the hands of Christians.

These exceptions, however, serve only to underline the tragedy of the hostility that characterized both sides. The Jewish embitterment was deep and was inevitably reflected in the Jewish attitude toward Jesus. The remnants of the Jewish bitterness that persevered into the twentieth century were inflamed by the Holocaust, and that bitterness remains a factor today, certainly in the Jewish perception of Christians,[31] and to a lesser extent in the Jewish perception of Jesus. It must frankly be admitted that the premodern Jewish attitude toward Jesus was to a large degree determined by the church. The natural antipathy caused by the juxtaposition of two very similar and yet very different religions was aggravated by the grievous stance taken by the church toward the Jews. Herbert Danby's observation is that the "Jewish attitude has varied with almost mathematical certainty according to the precise degree in which Christians have shown themselves real followers, in spirit and deed, of their Savior."[32]

To summarize, the rise of Christianity, together with the dissolution of national Israel, meant far-reaching changes for Judaism. In reality, so drastic were these changes that we may speak of the necessity of a rebirth of the Jewish religion.[33] The Jewish reaction during the premodern period expressed itself not only in the establishment and consolidation of rabbinic piety as normative Judaism, but more particularly in the careful definition of Jewish doctrine, especially in those areas relevant to the claims of Christianity. The boundaries of Judaism were thus carefully and rigidly marked. Among other things, there was in this reactionary crystallization of doctrine a strong reaffirmation of the unity of God, a limitation of the concept *Messiah*, and a corresponding glorification of the Torah.[34]

---

[31]Cf. Sandmel, *WJJ*, 61; Montefiore, "What a Jew Thinks About Jesus," *HJ* 33 (1934–35): 512.

[32]*The Jew and Christianity* (London, 1927), 3.

[33]G. Lindeskog thus refers to the first century of our era as the beginning, not of one, but of two new religions. "Jesus als religionsgeschichtliches und religiöses Problem in der modernen jüdischen Theologie," *Judaica* 6 (1950):194.

[34]Cf. Jocz, *JPJC*, 189–90, and H. J. Schoeps, *The Jewish-Christian Argument*, ET by D. E. Green, 3rd ed. (London: Faber & Faber, 1965), 53–54.

The most striking fact of premodern Judaism is its consistently defensive posture. We encounter here, by way both of reaction and self-protection, at worst a wholly negative, destructive attitude toward Jesus, and at best a cold neutrality. The first demand on the human being is self-preservation. It can cause no wonder then that under the threatened destruction, first of the Jewish religion, and second, of the Jewish people, the Jewish view of Jesus during this vexatious era was what it was.

ENLIGHTENMENT AND EMANCIPATION

It is above all the Emancipation of the Jews that marks the turning point in the Jewish attitude toward Jesus. The acquisition of personal rights and liberties by the ordinary Jew was symbolized most dramatically in the tearing down of ghetto gates. The new freedom of the Jew brought with it the dawn of a new day in Jewish-Christian relationships and made possible the beginnings of a new assessment of Jesus and, indeed, of Christianity itself.[35]

The Emancipation was the fruit neither of the Renaissance nor of the Reformation, but of the Enlightenment of the eighteenth century. Here emerged the concepts of the equality of man, his "natural rights," and truly humanitarian principles. For the first time in history Jews were enabled to participate in the social, political, economic, and cultural life of their respective countries. The full rights of citizenship, which were previously denied to Jews, now became theirs. Indeed, it may be said that for the first time the Jews became Europeans in the full sense of the word.[36]

However, the Emancipation did not take place overnight. It was a process that lasted nearly two hundred years, and one that can be divided into three stages.[37] The first stage was the fifty-

---

[35]Schoeps calls the emancipation "the decisive caesura" in the debate between Judaism and Christianity. *The Jewish-Christian Argument,* 95.

[36]So G. Lindeskog, *Die Jesusfrage im neuzeitlichen Judentum* (Uppsala: Almquist & Wiksells, 1938), 29; cf. Montefiore's pride in being an *English* Jew: "Anti-Semitism in England," *HJ* 19 (1920–21):337–46.

[37]Thus Benzion Dinur in the article "Emancipation" in *EJ* 6:696–718, on which this and the succeeding paragraph are dependent.

year period preceding the French Revolution of 1789, a period
when the philosophical impetus of the movement began. It is
obvious that the same kind of thinking that spawned the French
Revolution and other liberating movements lay behind the Jewish
Emancipation. It was freely admitted by many of those who
defended the latter that the Jews had serious defects at that moment in history. But it was further and aptly argued that these
defects were a result of the kind of treatment the Jews had received for generations in European society. If they were back-
ward, peculiar, and closed-minded, it was because they had had
no opportunity to be otherwise. The ghetto Jew was, after all, the
creation of "civilized" society.

The second stage in the process of emancipation lasted for
nearly a century (1789–1878) and included the actual implementing of emancipation in Western and Central Europe by means of
political and social legislation. The third stage (1878–1933) completed the process with the emancipation of the Jews of Eastern
Europe. These countries were the slowest to be influenced by the
new thinking, and the emancipation of the Jews here was not able
to proceed very far.

It must be admitted that the Emancipation—as grateful as
we must remain for it—was not an immediate success, but involved a long and often painful process of adjustment. Indeed,
emancipation was never a complete success. A main reason for
this is that Jews were as little prepared for it as were non-Jews.
Educationally and culturally Jews had become pitifully im-
poverished. They were ill-equipped to take advantage of the new
opportunities that were now becoming theirs, and it was not easy
for them to cope with the social demands they encountered outside the ghetto. In response to this need, the *Haskalah* ("Enlightenment") movement was born in the last half of the eighteenth century. A child of the Enlightenment, the *Haskalah*
movement served to mediate the spirit of the new age to the
Jewish people. It purposed to educate Jews and help them to
adapt to their new social environment. Emancipation made possible, but did not guarantee, the transition to a new status. If the
latter was to be achieved by the Jews, they needed to be educated
in subjects other than the Talmud; they needed to speak lan-

guages other than Yiddish; they needed to adopt the dress and manners of society—in short, they needed to acquire those traits that mark the complete and honorable citizens of any particular country. They had to prepare to enter a variety of occupations, avoiding those positions that were responsible for the popular image of Jews as unscrupulous profiteers.[38] Even their religion had to be shown to be nonsuperstitious and compatible with the rationalism of the day. It was to these things that the *Haskalah* movement dedicated itself. In the fullest sense, the Jews needed to become Europeans whose religion could be shown to be an enlightened one and whose bad name could be shown to have been unwarranted.[39]

But as Jews broke into European society after centuries of isolation, non-Jews too were forced to make an adjustment. The "natural rights of man" was an admirable motto, but the actual implementing of those rights for the Jews was another matter. Prejudice dies hard. The traditional hostility and aversion did not cease. The common reaction of non-Jews to the realities of emancipation was unfavorable, and thus paradoxically the Emancipation had the effect of fostering a new anti-Semitism more vicious than the earlier one. This new anti-Semitism, which became widely prevalent in the third stage of the Emancipation, was for the first time based primarily on racial rather than religious grounds. Hatred of Jews was now motivated by ethnic differences. While these differences included religion as a social phenomenon, the doctrinal disparity between Christianity and Judaism became relatively unimportant. The result was that anti-Semitism became independent of Christianity; the two could no longer be equated. When the glory and power of the church began to fade, albeit without any lessening of anti-Semitism in European society, it became possible for Jews to look at Jesus somewhat more objectively. This was one of the important fac-

---

[38]It is worth remembering that the church had forced the role of money-lender on the Jew, regarding this profession as incompatible with the teaching of Scripture, and thus as unsuitable for the Christian. The Jew, in turn, suffered hatred and hostility for prospering in what had been forced on him.

[39]For further information see the article "Haskalah" by Azriel Shochat in *EJ*, 7:1433–45.

tors that contributed to the possibility of a new, more open approach toward Jesus.[40] It was the failure of the Emancipation, seen in this newest blot of anti-Semitism, that turned the hearts of the Jews to longing for a Jewish national sovereignty and produced the Zionist movement in the late nineteenth century.

Any attempt to understand the Emancipation and its effects on the Jews must depend on a knowledge of the intellectual climate of the Enlightenment and its broader impact on religion. We have already seen that the roots of the Emancipation itself are to be found in the liberal thinking of the Enlightenment. However, the significance of the Enlightenment, for our purpose, is broader than the subject of human rights. For the Enlightenment spoke loudly to established religion, both Jewish and Christian.

The Enlightenment was before all things the triumph of rationalism. The glory of man was discovered—human reason became the measure of all things. And man reveled in the power of his newly found critical faculties. He exposed every area of his existence to the penetrating scrutiny of the critical method. With an apparent vengeance he applied this method to things that hitherto had been regarded as sacred. It was inevitable that scientific criticism should turn to the writings of the sacred canon. Given the anti-authoritarian mood and rationalistic presuppositions of the times, the Scriptures and revealed religion did not fare well. The claims of orthodoxy notwithstanding, the plain humanity of these writings became evident, and the religion in them was made to appear as nothing more than the product of human creativity.[41]

This was the intellectual climate of the world the Jews had been thrust into. "Free inquiry" was the slogan of the times, and there was abundant evidence all around of its practice. It can readily be seen how conducive this new climate was for a more objective and positive attitude toward Jesus on the part of the

---

[40]Cf. Jocz, *JPJC,* 102.

[41]For the early history of biblical criticism see Herbert F. Hahn, *The Old Testament in Modern Research* (Philadelphia, 1970[2]). For the same background as it affected the study of the New Testament, see W. G. Kümmel, *The New Testament: The History of the Investigation of Its Problems,* trans. MacLean Gilmour and Howard Clark Kee (Nashville: Abingdon, 1972).

Jews. Jewish scholar Hans Joachim Schoeps rightly stresses the importance of a climate of freedom, when he writes:

> Real encounter can become possible only within the realm of freedom, in which all participants in the conversation are allowed openly to declare the truth to which they bear witness, without the constant fear that thereby they may suffer harm, or encounter invisible prejudices on the part of the other side from the outset.[42]

Many Christians, drinking deeply of the spirit of this era, themselves denied or expressed doubtfulness concerning the key doctrines of Christianity. Jews had the strange experience of hearing some of their own objections to Christianity in the mouths of Christian scholars. Ironically, when the Jewish attitude toward Jesus finally became vocal, it was the pronouncement of similar views by Christians themselves that made the expression of that attitude possible.[43]

Of course, in this new climate the doctrines of traditional Judaism were also subject to reexamination. The rise of historical criticism had as much an impact on Judaism itself as it did on Christianity. The new climate was thus responsible for the spawning of the Reform movement within Judaism. This movement picked up the challenge offered by the *Haskalah* movement but focused on the religion of the Jews and was designed to redefine Judaism in keeping with the spirit of the age. The reformers minimized the traditional aspects of Judaism, so central to the Orthodox Jews. They were instead interested only in the essence of Judaism, which they found exclusively in its ethical teachings. The Reform movement, rooted as it was in rationalism and free thought, conceived Judaism to be something quite different from what it had been through the centuries.

Since not all Jews could bring themselves to accept the new movement, it became the cause of a schism that had profound effects on Jewish life—effects that remain evident in our own

---

[42]*The Jewish-Christian Argument*, 125.

[43]"Circles that were previously Christian now created their own skepticism and disparagement. A Western Jew could find support for his negativism about Christianity from the philosophical atmosphere of that age." Sandmel, *WJJ*, 14.

day. Within Judaism two groups became clearly distinguishable: (1) the Orthodox Jews and (2) the Reform or (as they were also called) Liberal Jews. In recent times a third group, "Conservative Judaism," has come into existence, especially in America. This group mediates between the Orthodox and the Reform Jews, attempting to combine the best of both worlds.[44]

The Orthodox Jews regarded the ancient traditions as sacred. To them, Judaism was an all-encompassing way of life. It claimed sovereignty over every aspect of a person's life, whether in the realm of the religious or of the secular. Orthodox Judaism was thus especially insistent on the preservation of the Jewish national identity.[45] Somehow, in spite of the newly acquired status of the Jews, the Orthodox Jews desired to retain the purity and socio-religious exclusivism of the ghetto. In contrast to this attitude, the Reform Jews, following the stimulus of *Haskalah* ideology, viewed Judaism specifically as the religion of the Jew, and nothing more. Reform Judaism was thus initially characterized by a nonnational outlook. To the reformers, the Jew was a European who practiced the Jewish religion.

Reform Jews, moreover, regarded the accumulation of tradition over the centuries as an obstacle to the religious belief of the enlightened man of the modern era. Judaism, according to them, was meant to be in the process of continual development, leaving behind the old and outdated, ever adapting itself to the present.[46] There was, however, something within Judaism that was timeless in its value and that the reformers consequently emphasized. This was the rich tradition of ethical teaching, exemplified preeminently in the prophets of Israel. For the reformers, Judaism was succinctly defined as an ethical world view.[47] It was only natural

---

[44]See M. Sklare, *Conservative Judaism. An American Religious Movement* (1955; new augmented edition, New York: Schocken, 1972).

[45]Jocz calls attention to the national renaissance that took place in reaction to the stress caused by the triumph of rationalism. He differentiates between the older nationalism rooted in the religious consciousness and the modern nationalism (e.g., as exemplified in political Zionism), which is self-contained and gives rise to the religious consciousness. *JPJC*, 109.

[46]See Lindeskog, *Die Jesusfrage*, 66; cf. Jocz, *JPJC*, 106.

[47]Thus Lindeskog, *Die Jesusfrage*, 65.

that this view of Judaism would eventually turn the attention of Reform Jews particularly to the ethical teaching of Jesus.

The endeavor of the Reform movement to preserve and defend Judaism in the age of the Enlightenment led also to the vigorous study of the history of Israel by means of the use of critico-historical methodology, thus giving rise to "the science of Judaism" (*die Wissenschaft des Judentums*). The *Haskalah* movement was again an important stimulus here, and many of the scholarly conclusions of the new science promoted the advance of Reform Judaism. The attempt was made by the new scientific criticism to grasp the development of Judaism through the biblical period. Special attention was directed to the study of Pharisaism and the nature of Jewish religion in the New Testament period, especially with an eye to its exoneration. But, more than this, Jewish scholars took on themselves the task of presenting their explanation of the origin of Christianity—an explanation arrived at by means of scientific principles of historical research, but nonetheless with plain apologetic motives. In the process of these studies the Jewishness of Jesus emerged with striking clarity. This rediscovery brought forth a new appreciation of Jesus as a Jew—to such an extent that it became possible to speak of a Jewish reclamation of Jesus.[48] G. Lindeskog thus regards this rise of the science of Judaism as the most important factor in making possible a new Jewish attitude toward Jesus.[49]

The importance of the Emancipation for the change in the Jewish attitude toward Jesus is now plainly evident. The modern Jewish attitude is essentially the result of the assimilation[50] of Jews into European life and culture at a unique era in the history of man. Assimilation necessitated the *Haskalah* movement with its attempt to adapt Judaism to its new environment and ultimately was responsible for the birth of the Reform movement. The spirit and mood of the Western world that made emancipation, and thus assimilation, possible is itself of equal significance. The new era brought with itself a new climate of freedom, a new spirit

---

[48]S. Sandmel, *WJJ*, 51; cf. 14.

[49]*Die Jesusfrage*, 70.

[50]Lindeskog calls the new Jewish attitude "ein Assimilationsphänomen." Ibid., 63.

of critical enquiry. Jews were for the first time free to speak what they thought about Jesus without fear of the consequences. The rationalistic tendencies that dominated the period made possible the questioning of both Christian and Jewish dogma and concomitantly produced an emphasis on ethics as the heart of religion. The rise of the science of Judaism meant extensive research into biblical Judaism and the origin of Christianity. All of these factors contributed to, and indeed necessitated, a new and distinctively Jewish position regarding the question of Jesus.[51] As never before, Jews were thus able to—and thus had to— discuss Jesus objectively. We turn now to look at the beginnings of the new study of Jesus and to mark some of the traits that become noticeable in the Jewish approach to the subject.

THE MODERN JEWISH APPROACH

Samuel Sandmel begins his book on Jesus with these words: "In the past one hundred and fifty years there has taken place what amounts to a reversal of eighteen centuries of Jewish and Christian attitudes toward each other."[52] These words are also true of the Jewish attitude toward Jesus. The Emancipation, the emergence of the Jews out of the darkness of the ghetto, brought a complete turnabout in the Jewish evaluation of Jesus. And given the climate just a few years earlier, the results can only be described as astonishing.

The first fruits of the Emancipation, so far as the study of Jesus is concerned, began to appear in the nineteenth century as Jewish scholars turned their attention to Jesus in the new climate of scholarly objectivity. Jewish historiography began with Isaac Markus Jost's nine-volume work, *Geschichte der Israeliten seit der Zeit Maccabäer bis auf unsere Tage* (1820–29) (History of the Israelites From the Time of the Maccabees to Our Age), which included information on Jesus and Christian origins. Al-

---

[51]Jocz sums up the matter in these words: "The entry into European civilization demanded an attitude towards Christianity and thus brought to the forefront the problem of the Jewish attitude to Jesus." *JPJC*, 110; cf. Sandmel, *WJJ*, 13.

[52]*WJJ*, 3.

though not important in itself, Jost's treatment of the subject indicated its propriety and the need for Jewish scholarship to address the question. It thus in some degree prepared the path for later Jewish authors.[53] The first really notable break, however, in the centuries of calumniation of the person of Jesus on the one hand and deliberate silence on the other came with Joseph Salvador's two-volume work, *Jésus-Christ et sa doctrine,* which was published in Paris in 1838.[54] Salvador was a descendant of Spanish Jews, but his mother was a Roman Catholic. He was later to argue for a universal religion, a kind of amalgamation of Judaism and Christianity. In his pioneering work on Jesus, he anticipated some later historico-critical methodology in the study of the origins of Christianity and set forth arguments that were to become stock-in-trade for Jewish writers in the modern era: e.g., the ethical teaching of Jesus is wholly Jewish, and includes nothing new; Jesus was concerned with the individual and the future life, not with society or the present world; Christianity arose as a compromise between Judaism and paganism. Thus in Salvador and those who followed him we see the Jewish reclamation of Jesus clearly at work.[55]

In the last half of the nineteenth century two Jewish writers whose work was vastly more influential than Salvador's deserve mention: Abraham Geiger and Heinrich Graetz. Like Salvador, both of these writers emphasize the Jewishness of Jesus, Geiger calling him a Pharisee, Graetz an Essene. According to both, Jesus was in no way original in what he taught. Although far from extolling him, both writers are able to speak sympathetically concerning Jesus, occasionally even finding him worthy of commendation. Like Jost before him, Graetz was the author of a comprehensive history of the Jews from its beginnings

---

[53]Ibid., 54.

[54]Klausner is indignant at Schweitzer's brief note on Salvador—in which he is referred to as "one of the most ingenious of the followers of Venturini"—in Albert Schweitzer, *The Quest of the Historical Jesus,* trans. W. Montgomery (London, 1954[3]), 162, n.2. Not only is Salvador misrepresented, says Klausner, but his name is misspelled (Salvator). *JN,* 106–7.

[55]It is worth noting that Salvador's view of the trial of Jesus caused a great public outcry and ultimately "brought him to the criminal dock." Klausner, *JN,* 109. The Emancipation had hardly come to full fruition.

to the present (*Geschichte der Juden von den ältesten Zeiten bis zur Gegenwart*, 1853–1876).[56] In volume three of this history, he includes a section on the subject of Jesus and the origin of Christianity, which later appeared in the format of a separate monograph in French translation under the title *Sinai et Golgotha* (Paris, 1867).[57] Graetz was very impressed with the similarities between the doctrines of the Essenes and the teaching of Jesus on such matters as the virtue of poverty and the sharing of property, the undesirability of marriage, and the rejection of oath-taking. On the basis of these similarities, he proceeded to understand Jesus' renunciation of life in the present world as an indication that he was a member of the Jewish sect of the Essenes. The purpose of Jesus, he argues, was not to create a new religion, but rather to reform Judaism. Accordingly, Graetz denies that there was anything new in the teaching of Jesus. Apart from his ministry of healing, which Graetz does not deny, Jesus may be likened to a contemporary rabbi such as Hillel. He himself never abolished the ceremonial law as did his disciples some time later. Although Graetz shows some sympathy for Jesus, his antagonism toward Christianity remains unabated. It is very interesting to note that Graetz was able to take this positive stance despite the fact that he was not in agreement with Reform Judaism and became known as a champion of Orthodoxy.

Geiger, whom some have called the father of modern theology, was by contrast an ardent advocate of Reform Judaism and a leader in the promotion of the "science of Judaism."[58] His lectures on the history of Judaism were collected and began to be published in Breslau in 1864 (*Das Judenthum und seine Geschichte*). Three of these lectures were devoted to Jesus and his disciples. Like Graetz, Geiger became interested in Jesus'

---

[56]This monumental work appeared in many editions and translations. In English the translation by Bella Löwy, Israel Abrahams, et al., is available in a six-volume edition, *History of the Jews*, printed by the Jewish Publication Society of America (Philadelphia, 1891–98).

[57]The translator and editor was Moses Hess. The German original was apparently never published except as it appeared in the *History*.

[58]In 1835 he founded the periodical *Wissenschäftliche Zeitschrift für Jüdische Theologie*.

pessimism concerning the present world and sought to explain it. Rather than finding it central to his message, however, Geiger argued that this attitude was a historical accident arising from the severe Roman oppression of the Jews at that time. In the last analysis Jesus belongs fully and completely to Judaism and is to be understood as a Pharisaic Jew who mistakenly believed that he was central to the realization of the commonly longed-for messianic hope. Although he was not always consistent, basically Jesus affirmed the eternal validity of the Law. He himself brought nothing new and had nothing to do with the rise of Christianity.

With the pioneers Geiger and Graetz we again find conclusions that are to recur many times in the Jewish study of Jesus: Jesus came to bring nothing that was essentially new, but to reform Judaism; he was a Jewish rabbi who taught Jewish ethics and who was tragically misinterpreted by his later followers. In all of this Jesus is understood separately from Christianity. He is appreciated, and even admired, with no lessening of the Jewish hatred of Christianity. Other important Jewish writers of the nineteenth and early twentieth centuries wrote for the most part only what amounts to variations on the same theme. Among these may be mentioned, in addition to those with whom we are directly concerned in the present work, S. Formstecher, S. Hirsch, and Moriz Friedländer.[59]

All of this new Jewish literature about Jesus displayed the new attitude of the emancipated Jew—indeed, as we have seen, the very existence of such a literature was the result of the changed climate. The fullest and richest expression of the new Jewish attitude came from the exponents of the Reform or Liberal wing of Judaism. Some Jews were willing to go further in their appreciation of Jesus than others. Those who did speak appreciatively of him were often looked on with disfavor by their brethren. In particular, the more orthodox Jews were reluctant to concede too much to the Christian view of Jesus. Thus Rabbi H. G. Enelow notes that in certain Jewish circles ''consideration of Jesus on the part of a Jew is regarded as a sign of weakness, if not

---

[59]See part one of the bibliography for the titles by these authors.

disloyalty, as a leaning in the wrong direction, particularly if it shows symptoms of admiration for Jesus."[60]

It can be regarded as no surprise, then, that the outstanding contribution of Jewish scholarship comes from Liberal Judaism with its less defensive stance. It was those who strove for a fresh understanding and revitalizing of Judaism who were most able to take a new look at Jesus. Thus very few of the writers we are concerned with in this book are of the Orthodox persuasion. Among the eight major writers[61] an exception is found in Joseph Klausner; among the secondary writers, we may mention Paul Goodman and Gerald Friedlander. Klausner's views concerning Jesus, despite his own brand of Judaism, are quite clearly more in keeping with Liberal Judaism than they are with Orthodox Judaism.

Reform Judaism, especially in its more liberal manifestations, was understandably hated and opposed by those who held to Orthodoxy. When strong advocacy of Liberal Judaism was combined with a positive and genuine appreciation for Jesus—as it was supremely in Montefiore—there poured forth a spontaneously hostile reaction from the Orthodox Jews. Montefiore in particular, as a leading figure in both enterprises, became the focal point of sharp criticism. Thus M. Friedländer is representative of Orthodox Judaism when he declares he saw in Montefiore's writings "an anti-Jewish tendency."[62] Gerald Friedlander, writing from a similar perspective in his volume *The Jewish Sources of the Sermon on the Mount* (London, 1911), strongly opposed Montefiore's ascription of originality to Jesus: "The Jews [i.e., the Orthodox] have refused steadfastly to see in the hero of the Gospels either a God, or an inspired prophet, or a qualified law giver, or a teacher in Israel with a new message for his people" (xxii–xxiii). Montefiore was also hotly attacked by Ahad ha'Am, as Zionist Asher Ginsberg preferred to call him-

[60]*A Jewish View of Jesus* (New York: Macmillan, 1920), 1; cf. Montefiore, "Liberal Judaism in England: Its Difficulties and Its Duties," *JQR* 12 (1900):628.

[61]See above, p. 28.

[62]"Notes in Reply to My Critic," *JQR* 3 (1892):437; cf. Montefiore "Jewish Conceptions of Christianity," *HJ* 28 (1929–30):248.

self. He maintained the superiority of Jewish ethics with its rule of absolute justice and accused Montefiore of verging on conversion to Christianity.[63]

The hostility not only was directed against representatives of Liberal Judaism, such as Montefiore, but it could even be turned against the avowed Zionist and disciple of Ahad ha'Am, Joseph Klausner, when he cautiously expressed appreciation of Jesus as a Pharisaic rabbi. A. Kaminka thus characterized Klausner's book on Jesus as "a truckling and kow-towing to the Christian religion, and an assertion of great affection for the foggy figure of its founder, a denial of the healthy sense of our saintly forefathers."[64] Some specific objections of Orthodox Jews to the Liberal Jewish understanding of the teaching of Jesus will be mentioned in the chapters that follow.

Jewish scholars who embody a positive attitude toward Jesus are often criticized by other Jews on purely scholarly grounds, as well as for their supposedly anti-Jewish tendencies. This raises the whole question of the Jewish stance toward modern biblical criticism. During the early decades of the Emancipation the field of biblical studies was undergoing a revolution at the hands of such men as D. F. Strauss and F. C. Baur. This was not without its effect on the study of Judaism itself, and we have seen in turn how the atmosphere thus created facilitated the development and expression of the new Jewish attitude toward Jesus. To what extent, however, did Jewish scholars accept the results of non-Jewish critical scholarship applied to the Gospels?

Sandmel expresses amazement at Geiger's and Graetz's uncritical acceptance of the historical reliability of the Gospels, writing as they did after Strauss.[65] Sandmel is particularly critical of Klausner, who, writing in 1922, ought to have indicated an

---

[63]See the essay "Judaism and the Gospels" (1910) in the collection of Ginsberg's writings entitled *Nationalism and the Jewish Ethic,* ed. H. Kohn (New York, 1962), 289–319.

[64]Quoted from the periodical *Ha-Toren* (August 1922) by H. Danby, *The Jew and Christianity* (London: Sheldon, 1927), 103; cf. G. F. Moore, "A Jewish Life of Jesus," *HTR* 16 (1923):100–101.

[65]*WJJ,* 63–64.

awareness of the work of form criticism.[66] He also calls Klausner an amateur Talmudist, accuses him of "applying dilettantism rather whimsically to the Gospel passages," and concludes that Klausner would have done well to draw on Montefiore's far better scholarship.[67] Sandmel, indeed, is unhappy with the general Jewish neglect of modern gospel criticism: "As to the scholarship by Jews on the matter, I must comment that all too often Jewish scholars have by-passed the Christian scholarship on the Gospels and have trespassed directly into the Gospels themselves, with the result that very often Jews have attributed to the Gospels a historical reliability which Christian scholars do not."[68]

Sandmel regards Montefiore's commentary on the synoptic Gospels as exemplifying the best of Gospel scholarship in the early part of the century.[69] G. Friedlander, however, accuses Montefiore, on the one hand, of ignoring "the present crisis in the Christian Church, due to the failure of the theologians to discover the historic Jesus" and, on the other hand, of an inordinate reliance on Christian scholars at points.[70] Montefiore himself admits a certain reliance on Christian scholars, but reserves for himself the right to disagree with them and to correct them.[71]

It may be said that almost without exception modern Jewish scholars are cognizant of and capitalize on the contention that the Gospels are in large measure reflections of the theology of the early church. They are also aware of the difficulty of arriving at

---

[66]Cf. ibid., 116, n. 31. Klausner, however, did come to grips with form criticism in the fourth Hebrew edition of *Jesus of Nazareth: His Life, Times, and Teaching* (1925; reprint ed., New York: Beacon, 1964). Cf. his depreciation of radical form criticism as "sophistical skepticism" in *From Jesus to Paul*, trans. W. F. Stinespring (1943; reprint ed., New York: Beacon, 1961), 256ff.

[67]*WJJ*, 92–93.

[68]"The Jewish Scholar and Early Christianity" in A. A. Neuman and S. Zeitlin, eds., *The Seventy-Fifth Anniversary Volume of the Jewish Quarterly Review, JQR* (1967):477. Sandmel continues: "One sometimes suspects that the New Testament has, as it were, become a *kosher* field, but Christian scholarship seems to remain *traif*. How otherwise can one account for the almost fundamentalism of some Jewish scholars when they approach the Gospels and New Testament literature?"

[69]*WJJ*, 89.

[70]*JSSM*, 52.

[71]*SG* l:xxii.

the *ipsissima verba* of Jesus,[72] and thus they approach the Gospel material with a certain amount of caution. Yet, on the whole, it is true that they surprisingly tend to ascribe more reliability to these materials than do many of the more radical non-Jewish critics. We will explore this subject more fully in the excursus that follows.

Jewish scholars have limited themselves to the synoptic Gospels in their attempt to understand Jesus and his teaching, arguing that as Jews they are interested in history, not theology. Indeed, as Montefiore has noted, both the fourth Gospel and Paul are too antithetical to Judaism to receive a very fair treatment at the hands of Jews.[73] Jewish authors can, on occasion, however, speak of the reliability of the fourth Gospel as well as of its religious value.[74]

In their zeal to keep Jesus within Judaism, either as the one who presented the culmination of its religious teaching or simply as a misled Israelite, Jewish scholars insist on a cleavage between Jesus and Paul and regard the latter as the true originator of Christianity,[75] thus adopting F. C. Baur's dichotomy between Paul and primitive Christianity. Many Jewish scholars completely dissociate Paul from rabbinic Judaism and conceive Hellenism to be the sole source of his ideas.[76] The Hellenistic Judaism of the Diaspora that Paul knew was far different from the rabbinic Judaism of Palestine, it is claimed.[77] While Klausner somewhat modifies these characteristically Jewish views by al-

---

[72]See, e.g., Enelow, *A Jewish View of Jesus*, 64; Sandmel, *WJJ*, 27.

[73]*RT*, 8.

[74]E.g., I. Abrahams, who writes, "My own general impression, without asserting an early date for the Fourth Gospel, is that that Gospel enshrines a genuine tradition of an aspect of Jesus' teaching which has not found a place in the Synoptics." *SP* 1:12. Cf. Montefiore, "Notes on the Religious Value of the Fourth Gospel," *JQR* 7 (1895):24–74.

[75]E.g., K. Kohler, *The Origins of the Synagogue and the Church* (New York: Macmillan, 1929), 260; Enelow, *A Jewish View of Jesus*, 1959.

[76]Kohler, *Origins of the Synagogue and the Church*, 261ff.; cf. Sandmel, *WJJ*, 79.

[77]C. G. Montefiore, "Rabbinic Judaism and the Epistles of St. Paul," *JQR* 13 (1901); J. Parkes, *Jesus, Paul and the Jews* (London: SCM, 1936); cf. the reply to this argument in W. D. Davies, *Paul and the Rabbinic Judaism* (1955; reprint ed., Philadelphia, Fortress, 1980), ch. 1; cf. also, however, Abrahams's remarkable anticipation of Davies's view. "The supposition that Hellenistic and Pharisaic Judaism were opposed forces will, I am convinced, not survive fuller research." "Rabbinic Aids to Exegesis," *Cambridge Biblical Essays*, ed. H. B. Swete (London: 1909), 183.

lowing a definite dependency of Paul on Jesus, for him Jesus nevertheless remains only a reformer of Judaism, and Paul is the creator of a new religion.[78] Sandmel too cautions that "it does not seem reasonable to detach Jesus from the historical origins of Christianity," though he does argue that in Paul Christianity experienced a "*second* beginning."[79] Vermes writes, "I would suggest that once Paul was acknowledged 'apostle to the Gentiles' and a specifically Gentile mission sanctioned by the church leadership came into being, the original bias of Jesus' ministry suffered a radical transformation."[80] Thus Christianity has been regarded by many scholars, Jewish and non-Jewish, as a compromise between paganism and Judaism, brought about by contact with the Gentiles in the propagation of the Gospel.[81]

One further dimension of considerable importance in the modern Jewish approach to Jesus concerns the newly discovered importance of the rabbinic literature to understanding the New Testament. Montefiore produced a most interesting volume entitled *Rabbinic Literature and Gospel Teachings* in which he demonstrated the help that the rabbinic materials can be in understanding the Gospels (he focuses on Matthew and Luke). The significance of the rabbinic literature for the study of the New Testament had of course been clearly recognized at least as early as Geiger, who had insisted that this literature was fully as important as, if not more important than, the Apocrypha, Pseudepigrapha, and various Hellenistic writings in understanding the background of the New Testament. However, since the rabbinic literature for the most part remained untranslated,[82] it was ac-

[78]Klausner, *From Jesus to Paul*, 580–81.

[79]S. Sandmel, *Anti-Semitism in the New Testament?* (Philadelphia: Fortress, 1978), 161.

[80]*GJJ*, 45.

[81]For a survey of Jewish views of Paul see D. A. Hagner, "Paul in Modern Jewish Thought," in D. A. Hagner and M. J. Harris, eds. *Pauline Studies. Essays Presented to Professor F. F. Bruce on His 70th Birthday* (Grand Rapids: Eerdmans, 1980), 143–65.

[82]The first complete translation of the Babylonian Talmud was the translation into English by I. Epstein, 35 vols. (London, 1935–52). Prior to this, there was only the German translation of selected portions by L. Goldschmidt, 9 vols. (Berlin, 1897–1935). The Jerusalem Talmud was first translated, into French, by M. Schwab, 11 vols. (Paris, 1878–89). Other rabbinic writings, e.g., *Tosephta* and midrashic commentaries, began to be translated as well. See M. Waxman, *A History of Jewish Literature*, 5 vols. (New York and London, 1960²), IV, part two, 710ff.

cessible only to a handful of Christian scholars.[83] Jewish scholars capitalized on their knowledge of rabbinics in understanding Jesus, the Gospels, and Christian origins. The amount of light shed was considerable. As Israel Abrahams wrote in an essay entitled "Rabbinic Aids to Exegesis," reflecting the new Jewish contribution: "Rabbinic explains the idioms. The real Jesus emerges then to the clearer light of day."[84]

Jewish scholars, however, were highly sensitive to what they considered to be the distortion and misuse of the rabbinic literature by Christians. The latter—often with only an imperfect knowledge of the literature,[85] a concern to retain a sharp demarcation between Christianity and Judaism, and an eye on the Gospel portrayal of the Pharisees—generally characterized rabbinic religion as unspiritual and wholly legalistic, containing nothing good or admirable. In the first of his many articles written for the *Hibbert Journal*,[86] Montefiore bemoans the fact that Christians were ignoring the work of Jewish scholars in rabbinic religion— indeed, to such an extent, he says, that it might almost as well have remained unprinted. Christians seem adamant in insisting that all light is on their side and that on the rabbinic side all is darkness.[87] Thus, for example, Montefiore speaks of the outstanding work of Schechter in this field, and then remarks:

> In spite of all Schechter has to say, the Rabbinic God is still "remote," the Rabbis do not know what spiritual prayer means, the law is a burden, Rabbinic holiness is "outward" and hypo-

---

[83]The contribution of these scholars, however, has not been insignificant. One need only recall such early works as Christopher Cartwright's *Mellificium Hebraicum* (1649) and John Lightfoot's *Horae Hebraicae et Talmudicae* (1658–78; ed., Grand Rapids: Baker, reprint, 1979) as well as the work of Buxtorf, Schoettgen, and others. Cf. G. F. Moore, "Christian Writers on Judaism," *HTR* 14 (1921):187–254. Nor are modern writers lacking: e.g., Delitzsch, Wünsche, Strack, Dalman, R. T. Herford, P. Billerbeck, and G. F. Moore himself—all of whom have employed the rabbinic literature in the elucidation of the New Testament.

[84]In *Cambridge Biblical Essays,* 192.

[85]Cf. S. Schechter's indignant amazement at those who interpret the rabbinic literature "by mere intuition." He wryly remarks that "it is impossible to argue with transcendental ignorance." "Some Rabbinic Parallels to the New Testament," *JQR* 12 (1900):418.

[86]"Jewish Scholarship and Christian Silence," *HJ* 1 (1902–03):335–46.

[87]"All that is best and that you like best, is new and Christian; all that you dislike is Jewish." Ibid., 340.

critical, the only religious motive is the "lust" for reward, and all the rest of the familiar jargon.[88]

Schechter himself said that the problem was due to the failure to gain acquaintance with the "inner life" of the rabbis and their religion.[89]

In this whole matter we see the interrelationship between the Jewish perception of Jesus and the nature of rabbinic Judaism. If Jesus is to be understood in his own context, what was that context so far as the Jewish religion is concerned? If Jesus is to be reclaimed for Judaism, it needed to be shown that the highest aspects of his religious and ethical teachings are akin to, or at least not incompatible with, rabbinic Judaism. Thus Jewish scholars were called to a defense of rabbinic religion. Montefiore in his *Rabbinic Literature and Gospel Teachings* (1930; reprint ed., New York: Ktav, 1970) purposed to correct some of the distortion contained in the extensive and influential *Kommentar zum Neuen Testament aus Talmud und Midrasch* (München, 1922–28) by P. Billerbeck. Later he collaborated with H. Loewe to produce *A Rabbinic Anthology* (London, 1938) containing a selection of rabbinic passages with comments on them designed to make possible a fairer assessment of the piety of rabbinic Judaism. The rabbinic literature was of the greatest importance in understanding the New Testament, but that literature itself had to be understood properly—from within rather than without. On this subject, too, more will be said in the following pages.

In summary, we have seen the pivotal significance of the Emancipation in determining the attitude of Jews toward Jesus. It meant in the first instance the entry of Jews into European life, and it resulted most importantly in the bifurcation of Judaism into orthodox and liberal wings and the rise of the "science of Judaism" with its study of the first-century Jewish milieu from which Christianity sprang. The Emancipation came to full fruition in the modern Jewish approach to Jesus, which from Salvador onward can be summed up as the emphatic affirmation of the Jewishness

---

[88]Ibid., 338.

[89]"Some Rabbinic Parallels to the New Testament," *JQR* 12 (1900):429. Cf. S. Sandmel, *WJJ*, 129.

of Jesus. In conjunction with this affirmation, Jewish scholars increasingly stressed the importance of the rabbinic literature in understanding the Gospels. To the extent that the conclusions of nineteenth-century critical scholarship supported Jewish claims concerning Jesus, they were gladly accepted. Jesus became the reformer of Judaism; Paul, the creator of Christianity. In short, for Jewish scholarship the modern period is best characterized by the phrase "the Jewish reclamation of Jesus." The primary purpose of the present work is to look specifically at the most important area of this Jewish reclamation—Jewish study of the teaching of Jesus.

The Use of Gospel Criticism

THE CONCLUSIONS OF radical critical scholarship have been welcomed warmly by Jewish scholars. Negative assessments of the historical reliability of the Gospels from Christian scholars themselves have reinforced the general Jewish opinion about the Gospels and have facilitated the Jewish reclamation of Jesus. Indeed, this development has been seen by many as the way forward to a true meeting of minds. Lapide comments that only when Christian faith "gets the courage to expose itself to the challenge of scientific biblical criticism" will we have "a reasonable prospect of discovering together that historical Jew named Yeshua."[1]

Critical scholarship has shown in particular that the Gospels are products of the community of faith. That is, we do not have in the Gospels historical writing that is objective and impartial, but rather accounts designed to bring the reader to believe in Jesus as the early church believed in him. Moreover, it is clear that the portrayal of Jesus in the Gospels is such that it reflects a postresurrection understanding of him. Indeed, among the more radical critical scholars this has led to the peculiar criterion of "dissimilarity," which disallows confidence in the historicity of any of Jesus' words where they can be paralleled in the theology of the early church.[2] Jesus as he actually was is all but lost to

---

[1]P. Lapide, *Israelis, Jews and Jesus* (Garden City, N.Y.: Doubleday, 1979), 130–31. Schonfield writes in a similar vein: "The wrestling of modern theologians with texts and terms, their struggle to make it appear that things do not mean what we have thought they meant, their anxiety to save something from the wreck, eloquently betrays the discomfort they feel in being confronted with evidence which integrity refuses to allow them to reject outright." *FCS,* 111.

[2]E.g., N. Perrin, *Rediscovering the Teaching of Jesus* (London: SCM, 1967), 39; *What Is Redaction Criticism?* (London: SPCK, 1970), 71. What is often not noted by Jewish scholars, however, is that "dissimilarity" is also applied to the Jewish aspects of the tradition: "Material may be ascribed to Jesus only if it can be shown to be distinctive of him, which usually will mean dissimilar to known tendencies in Judaism before him or the church after him." 71. C. F. D. Moule's response is the only sensible one: "No historian in his right mind would try to construct a portrait of a figure of the past solely from views, sayings or characteristics which he shared neither with his predecessors nor with his successors." *The Origin of Christology* (Cambridge: Cambridge University Press, 1977), 156.

Maccoby has a peculiar twist on the criterion of dissimilarity, which is related to his

us. What we encounter in the Gospels is *Gemeindetheologie*, the theologizing of the early Christian community, which is understood as obscuring the real Jesus. Anything, therefore, that is consonant with what the early church believed about Jesus is thus attributable to the church's faith. For many, however, the impact of this new perspective transforms the Gospel tradition to such a great extent that the end result is a skepticism about the historicity of what is recorded in the Gospels, ranging from a relative to an absolute uncertainty.

Jewish scholars are well aware of this tendency in Gospel criticism to understand considerable portions of the Gospel materials as embodying the theology of the church and indeed they regularly utilize it themselves in handling the more awkward materials that do not readily fit their theories.[3] Probably the most forceful Jewish writing on this point is Leo Baeck's essay "The Gospel as a Document of the History of the Jewish Faith."[4] Baeck argues at length that the theology of Paul had an inevitable impact on the Gospel tradition, with the odd result that Jesus appears un-Jewish. Concerning the Gospel of John he writes, "It is no longer a question of the place of Jesus within the Jewish people or of something new in Judaism, as it had been in the old tradition of the congregation; one is concerned exclusively with something new that is opposed to Judaism, with the position of Jesus in opposition to the Jewish people."[5] But the fault is not simply that of the fourth Gospel.

> Certainly none of them was written down in the form in which these four Gospels confront us today. . . . Old traditions are clearly and recognizably preserved in them; but what each of them exhibits primarily in its overall contents is nevertheless not what Jesus had said, hoped, and experienced. What each of the Gospels, taken as a whole, presents to us is rather what was believed, thought, wished, and desired by Christian communities under the guidance of authoritative teachers at the turn from the first to the second century.[6]

---

controlling thesis about Jesus as a political revolutionary. Thus he writes that if "an incident *contradicts* the prevailing pro-Roman tenor of the narratives one can assume it is authentic, since such an incident would not have been added at a late stage in the development of the Gospels and must be a survival from the earliest versions." *RJ*, 104.

[3]"And when Jewish scholars started to develop an interest in Jesus they based their interpretation on the concepts of liberal German scholarship." E. Bammel, "Christian Origins in Jewish Tradition." *NTS* 13 (1966–67):317.

[4]ET of German original (*Das Evangelium als Urkunde der jüdischen Glaubensgeschichte* [1938]) in L. Baeck, *Judaism and Christianity*, trans. W. Kaufmann (New York: Leo Baeck Institute, 1958), 39–136.

[5]Ibid., 81.

[6]Ibid., 86–87.

Other Jewish scholars indicate the importance of understanding the impact of the church's theology on the Gospels. Ben-Chorin refers to the necessity of freeing the picture of Jesus in the Gospels "from their Christian overpainting."[7] According to Sandmel, "the stamp of the church was put on virtually every pericope about Jesus," with the result that a Gospel is like "an impressionistic painting."[8] Trattner notes that the evangelists make Jesus say what they wanted to say rather than recording what he actually said.[9] Schonfield writes the following: "Modern study of the Gospels and of Christian origins has unveiled a process of development which establishes that new thinking about Jesus, and statements attributed to him, were imposed upon the earliest recollections of his life and teaching." Pauline christology thus came to be reflected in the Gospels.[10] For Baeck the task of historical research is "to recognize and penetrate all these layers. What has to be accomplished is comparable to an excavation."[11]

Jewish skepticism about attaining any real knowledge of the Jesus of history seldom approaches the absolute point. A few, of course, but only a few, have been led to deny the existence of Jesus.[12] Some Jewish scholars, to be sure, are very doubtful about the possibility of reconstructing the historical Jesus. In this conclusion they generally reflect the influence of radical Protestant criticism. According to Kohler, "the chief difficulty in ascertaining the real character of Jesus is that neither he nor any of his disciples wrote a word of the contents of the New Testament."[13] "Because the Gospels, while containing valuable material, are all written in a polemical spirit and for the purpose of substantiating the claim of the messianic and superhuman character of Jesus, it is difficult to present an impartial story of his life."[14] Vermes notes that the evangelists' life of Jesus "was intended principally as a vehicle for the preaching of the early Church" and concludes, "In consequence,

---

[7]*BJ*, 13.

[8]S. Sandmel, *A Jewish Understanding of the New Testament* (1956; reprint ed., New York: Ktav, 1974), 110, 114.

[9]E. R. Trattner, *As a Jew Sees Jesus* (New York: Scribner, 1931), 108.

[10]*FCS*, 2, 54. Schonfield attributes to this influence, among other things, the notion of a mission to the nations, the atonement, and "a medley of inconsistencies." 56, 68, 93. Cf. *PP*, 6.

[11]L. Baeck, "The Gospel as a Document of the History of the Jewish Faith," in *Judaism and Christianity*, ET by W. Kaufmann (New York: Leo Baeck Institute, 1958), 92.

[12]E.g., Israel Sach, B. Kellerman, S. Lublinski, G. Brandes. See Vorster, "Jewish Views on Jesus," 99–103.

[13]K. Kohler, *The Origins of the Synagogue and the Church* (New York: Macmillan, 1929), 211.

[14]K. Kohler, *JE*, 7:166.

however brilliantly analysed, the Gospels cannot be expected to provide more than a skeletal outline of Jesus of Nazareth as he really was.''[15] Yet he can also write, "My guarded optimism concerning a possible recovery of the genuine features of Jesus is in sharp contrast with Rudolf Bultmann's historical agnosticism.''[16] Friedlander writes, ''I cannot ignore the fact, confirmed by recent historical criticism, that it is impossible to extract from the Gospels sufficient incontestable evidence necessary for a biography of the Gospel hero.''[17] In the same vein, Schoeps comments that the Gospels do not in the main communicate historical information but rather the tradition of the community. The sources are "unsatisfactory" for exact history, mixing legend and fact, and therefore the reconstruction of Jesus as he actually was "is altogether impossible.''[18]

By far the most pessimistic of Jewish scholars on this question is Sandmel who, by no coincidence, is also the Jewish scholar most influenced by radical Protestant Gospel criticism. He writes:

> It is a hopeless task to disentangle history from non-history in the narratives of Tanak, or of the extra-biblical literature, or of the New Testament. We cannot be precise about Jesus. We can know what the Gospels say, but we cannot know Jesus. If our objective is an accurate history of Jesus, then we are more apt to find that the Gospels obscure than reveal him.[19]

He says elsewhere, ''I have an uneasy feeling . . . that there is no real sense in which one can move from the Gospels back to Jesus. . . . And I have no unchallengeable way of objectively distinguishing between the history and the non-history. If I know anything, it is the Gospels, not Jesus.''[20] S. Zeitlin is nearly as skeptical as Sandmel. Following the Christian scholar M. S. Enslin, Zeitlin stresses the inadequacy of the Gospels—even to the absurd extreme of concluding that "there are no

---

[15]*JJ*, 42.

[16]Ibid., 235, n.l. Vermes quotes the famous words of Bultmann that "we can now know almost nothing concerning the life and personality of Jesus" (*Jesus and the Word* [London: Fontana, 1962], 14). Cf. *GJJ*, 3–4.

[17]*JSSM*, XLVI.

[18]"Jesus," 47–48, in *Gottheit und Menschheit* (Stuttgart, 1950). Maccoby speaks of the "considerable distortion" of the gospel tradition. *RJ*, 95.

[19]*WJJ*, 124; and cf. 108. Cf. *Judaism and Christian Beginnings*, 340–41.

[20]S. Sandmel, *The First Christian Century in Judaism and Christianity* (New York: Oxford University Press, 1978), 191. Sandmel refers to the whole subject as one of "impenetrable uncertainty." 193. "It is my opinion that the reliable data about Jesus are too small to justify any sound opinion about him." "The Jewish Scholar and Early Christianity," in A. A. Newman and S. Zeitlin, eds., *The Seventy-Fifth Anniversary Volume of the Jewish Quarterly Review* (Philadelphia: Jewish Quarterly Review, 1967), 479. Cf. above, p. 66.

sources that can be called historical."[21] Despite the fact that Zeitlin writes a fair amount about Jesus, the net result for him is that "the historical Jesus is still an enigma."[22]

Yet in this extreme degree of skepticism, Sandmel and Zeitlin are exceptions among Jewish scholars. Some of them, indeed, seem actually to ridicule the critical enterprise of Protestant scholarship for its excessive negativism. Klausner notes that

> nearly all the many Christian scholars, and even the best of them, who have studied the subject deeply, have tried their hardest to find in the historic Jesus something which is not Judaism; but in his actual history they have found nothing of this whatever, since this history is reduced almost to zero.[23]

Referring in the same way to the refusal of Christian scholarship to accept the Jewish interpretation of the Gospel data, Vermes points out that the Gospels remain subject to a criticism that results in "an agnostic tendency in regard to the historical authenticity of most of these words" even to the point of rejecting "the possibility of knowing anything historical about Jesus himself."[24] In response to Perrin's placing of the burden of proof on the claim of authenticity, and the resultant principle of radical gospel criticism "when in doubt discard," Vermes writes, "Bearing in mind the basic Jewish respect for tradition in general, and attachment to the words of a venerated master in particular, I myself would advocate *a priori* an open mind, and would not tip the balance in favour of inauthenticity."[25] Lapide indeed wonders why Christian scholars in their study of the Gospels "have in such a great hurry and unconditionally declared their task as hopeless" (i.e., reconstructing the historical Jesus).[26]

---

[21]*The Rise and Fall of the Judaean State* (Philadelphia: Jewish Publication Society of America, 1967), 2:152.

[22]Ibid., 1959. Kaminka, in his reply to Klausner, is also very pessimistic about the historical value of the Gospels. He says that the attempt to extract from the Gospels either the events of Jesus' life or the substance of his teaching is futile. Quoted in Moore, "A Jewish Life of Jesus," *HTR* 16 (1923):101.

[23]*JN*, 105.

[24]*JJ*, 225. This excessive skepticism, according to Vermes, results from the absence among NT interpreters of "any *real* familiarity with the literature, culture, religion and above all spirit, of the post-biblical Judaism from which Jesus and his first disciples sprang." *GJJ*, 3–4.

[25]*GJJ*, 17, n. 60.

[26]*RN*, 131. Lapide, however, had himself earlier written, "No known means of science will reveal the historical Jesus from beneath the mountainous layers of subsequent fable and fiction." *The Last Three Popes and the Jews* (London, 1967), 33.

In the face of this radical Christian skepticism, most Jewish scholars seem relatively conservative. Despite the nature of the sources as documents of Christian faith, something *is* salvageable from the Gospel records, namely a Jewish Jesus who can be placed and understood in the context of first-century Judaism.[27] This strikes many Jewish scholars as a far more sensible alternative than the direction taken by radical criticism. Thus Lapide writes:

> At a time when Christianity's Christ is being demoted by Paul Tillich to "essential manhood in existence"; when Gerhard Ebeling obfuscates him into "the basic situation of man as word-situation"; and when Rudolf Bultmann and his school seem bent on demythologizing him out of all reality, it is refreshing to see the Jesus of Judaism take on new substance and credibility in the literature of his native land.[28]

Vermes is convincing when he writes, against the outlook of radical Christian scholarship: "A theological interest [on the part of the Evangelists] is no more incompatible with a concern for history than is a political or philosophical conviction."[29]

Jewish scholars are of course aware that any historical reconstruction of Jesus remains only a partial one. At the end of his book on Jesus, Ben-Chorin calls his description of Jesus "piece-work," noting that "a full presentation is not possible because of the nature of the sources."[30] Nevertheless, much can be done. Despite the fact that the Gospels are primarily expressions of the Christian community, Baeck notes, "the history of Jesus, too, can be recovered from them and presented to the searching, critical eye."[31] According to Vermes, "notwithstanding all the redactional and editorial manipulation carried out by the primitive church and the evangelists, a concrete basis exists on which to reconstruct history."[32] Montefiore can write, "Yet, when all has been said, and when criticism has done its worst, it will probably remain true that

---

[27]Lapide wonders whether it is just this Jewishness and its incompatibility with the Christ of the Gentile church that have caused most researchers since Schweitzer to break off the quest for the Nazarene so unexpectedly. *RN*, 131.

[28]The closing sentence in "Jesus in Israeli Literature," *Christian Century* 87 (1970):1253.

[29]*GJJ*, 4. But Vermes cancels the positive effect of this observation later, when he writes that "our understanding of the real Jesus must derive basically from an analysis of the synoptic data relating to his actual ministry and teaching that are unaffected by accretions deriving from the creative imagination of nascent Christianity." *GJJ*, 7.

[30]*BJ*, 232.

[31]"The Gospel as a Document of the History of the Jewish Faith," 92.

[32]*GJJ*, 8.

it is, in large measure, the words ascribed to Jesus in the Synoptic Gospels which argue for the historical character of the man and of his life."[33]

Flusser, however, is the most optimistic of all and therefore at the opposite end of the spectrum from Sandmel. He begins his book on Jesus with these words: "The main purpose of this book is to show that it is possible to write the story of Jesus' life."[34] He continues, "The early Christian accounts about Jesus are not as untrustworthy as people today often think. The first three gospels . . . present a reasonably faithful picture of Jesus as a Jew of his own time." Indeed, Flusser goes so far as to say that "the only gospel that teaches a post-Easter Christology is the gospel according to St. John, and so it is of less historical value than the three synoptic gospels. . . . The Jesus portrayed in these gospels is, therefore, the historical Jesus, not the 'kerygmatic Christ.' "[35] Flusser, who in this conclusion parts radically with critical scholarship, explains the historical character of the synoptic Gospels as the result of their having been written after A.D. 70, when the influence of Paul had declined and therefore was less likely to have had an effect on the writing down of the tradition. Flusser, indeed, makes a valiant effort to interpret the synoptic Gospels as they are with almost no appeal to the church's alteration of the tradition. He succeeds to the extent that he does, however, only by ignoring much of the problematic material in the Gospels.

What must be emphasized is that the Jesus whom Jewish scholars regard as capable of reconstruction is by definition the Jewish Jesus— that is, Jesus as a Jewish personality fully at home in the context of first-century Judaism. It is presupposed, of course, that the historical Jesus must fit the contours of his Jewish environment and that he could not have broken out of the limited perspective of his contemporaries.[36] By definition, the Jewish Jesus is the Jesus of history. This method of reasoning is transparent in this statement by Flusser: "The picture of Jesus contained in them [the synoptic Gospels] is not so much of a redeemer of mankind as of a Jewish miracle worker and preacher. The

---

[33]*SG*, 1:xcix.

[34]D. Flusser, *Jesus*, ET by R. Walls (New York: Herder & Herder, 1969), 7.

[35]*Jesus*, 8–9. Yet a little later Flusser argues that "it is not so difficult for modern scholars to distinguish the work of editing from the original traditional material in the gospels" (10). Does Flusser mean that it is only the "original" tradition underlying the Synoptics that is nonkerygmatic? For the same optimism in Vermes, see *GJJ*, 8.

[36]Schonfield writes, "The exigencies of Christian missionary work among the heathen and polemic against the Jews have then succeeded in making him a far less credible megalomaniac, out of character and divorced from his native background." *FCS*, 91.

Jesus portrayed in these three Gospels *is, therefore, the historical Jesus*" (my italics).[37] This kind of Jewish Jesus is readily within reach of Jewish scholars, who indeed because of their background possess an intimate knowledge of the Jewish ethos and thus regard themselves as in a special position to ferret out the authentic from the inauthentic in the Gospel tradition. Ben-Chorin thus speaks of the role of Jewish intuition in separating history from fantasy,[38] and Klausner can write:

> We now know what in the Gospels to accept and what to reject, what is early and what is late, what the Evangelists unconsciously attributed to Jesus owing to their living under the influence of the post-Pauline church, and what, still unconsciously, they have preserved of Jesus' national Jewish features. Only after such a process of selection can we come to recognize the *historical* Jesus, the Jewish Jesus, the Jesus who could have arisen out of none other than Jewish surroundings.[39]

For Flusser, the Jewishness of Jesus, if not the key to determining the authentic material in the synoptic Gospels, is at least the key to correct interpretation: "In order to understand Jesus, we have to know about contemporary Judaism. The Jewish material is important, therefore, not just because it allows us to place Jesus in his own time, but because it allows us to interpret his sayings aright."[40] Vermes provides a good example of the same point:

> Instead of treating Jewish literature as an ancillary to the New Testament, the present approach will attempt the contrary, namely to fit Jesus and his movement into the greater context of first-century AD Palestine. If such an immersion in historical reality confers credibility on the Gospel picture, and the patchy portrait drawn by the evangelists begins suddenly to look, sound and feel true, this enquiry will have attained its primary objective.[41]

Enelow, noting the difficulty of establishing authenticity, says that the impartial student can nevertheless "sense" those sayings that genuinely represent the spirit of Jesus.[42] It is thus a very decidedly Jewish

---

[37]*EJ*, 10:10.

[38]*BJ*, 11.

[39]*JN*, 127. Cf. Maccoby, *RJ*, 95, and Ben-Chorin, "Jesus und Paulus in jüdischer Sicht," *Annual of the Swedish Theological Institute*, vol. 10, ed. B. Knutsson (Leiden: Brill, 1976), 23.

[40]*Jesus*, 10.

[41]*JJ*, 42.

[42]H. G. Enelow, *A Jewish View of Jesus* (New York: Macmillan, 1920), 65. Cf. Maccoby, who writes, "It is possible to recognize these earlier elements because they ring true to the conditions which actually existed in Jesus's lifetime." *RJ*, 95.

Jesus that is reconstructed on the basis of first-century Judaism, and all is assessed by what one must now regard as the final arbiter of authenticity—modern Jewish sensitivity.

There is, therefore, something of a paradox in the Jewish approach to the Gospels. There is, on the one hand, a moderate-to-strong emphasis on the historical unreliability of the Gospels, but then, on the other, a remarkable confidence about the reliability of the Gospel when anything "truly Jewish" is concerned.[43] Sandmel has in fact called attention to this paradox. "The paradox may be put this way: familiarity with Rabbinic Literature is the greatest persuader of the relative reliability of the Gospel accounts, but, on the other hand, an intimate acquaintance with the Gospels inevitably recalls the host of significant problems which constitute the nub of nineteenth-and twentieth-century Gospel study."[44] Elsewhere Sandmel expresses the same idea in these words: "What must be borne in mind is that already in the earliest of the written Gospels the embellishment of incidents about Jesus presents us with a contradiction: the portrayal of a believable background, but questionable or even unbelievable incidents."[45]

By and large, then, Jewish scholars have been more positive about the historical reliability of the Gospels than their radical Christian counterparts. Lapide, contrasting Graetz and Geiger with Strauss and Baur, writes, "In retrospect, the first Jewish researchers were prepared to accept greater parts of the Gospels as reliable than many Christian theologians of their epoch."[46] Sandmel had earlier made the same contrast, adding: "This phenomenon, of Jews being more retentive of Gospel reliability than Christians, was destined to recur."[47] He himself—and this is not a little surprising given his usual skepticism—can speak of the "good congruency" between the Gospels and contemporaneous materials and come to the conclusion that "however wrong this or that detail of the Gospels may be, the general, over-all impression of a conformity to the general facts is indisputable."[48]

One unusual aspect of this argument about the reliability of much within the Gospels is the notion held by a few Jewish scholars that an

---

[43]Lapide, for example, says that "Jewish scholars are convinced that the believable historical documentation concerning Jesus is much richer and more detailed than the historical findings concerning Abraham, Moses, David and the Prophets." *RN*, 131.

[44]*First Christian Century in Judaism and Christianity*, 90.

[45]*WJJ*, 123.

[46]*RN*, 95.

[47]*WJJ*, 66.

[48]Ibid., 65.

original, uncorrupted Gospel tradition—usually thought to be some kind of Hebrew Ur-Evangelium—underlay the present form of the Gospels. This view has of course been advocated by some Christian scholars.[49] Flusser puts great stock in this theory and indicates in his book on Jesus that "we shall often leave the separate gospels, and try to separate the original material from its editorial framework in all three gospels." He indicates what this means practically: "If, then, we can be sure that there is a Hebrew phrase behind the Greek text of the gospels, we translate that, and not the literal Greek."[50] In a recent article Flusser argues that the "old Hebrew stratum of the synoptic Gospels" reflects neither the christology of the church, nor the atoning significance of Jesus' death, nor the rejection of the Jewish people. These motifs are due to a Greek recension by a Gentile Christian, and Flusser goes so far as to say that passages expressing enmity against the Jews or rabbinic Judaism cannot be translated word for word back into Hebrew or Aramaic.[51] Ben-Chorin writes of his own book on Jesus that "the foundational thesis is that so to speak under the Greek overlay of the Gospels a Hebrew Ur-Tradition can be seen, because Jesus and his disciples were Jews, originally and only Jews."[52] Vermes has recourse frequently to an original Aramaic oral tradition that allegedly underlies the written Gospels.[53]

Sandmel again appears the maverick at this point. He comments disparagingly that "the 'original Aramaic' has beguiled a good many Jewish scholars," and describes H. P. Chajes's "far-fetched effort to demonstrate that a basic Hebrew gospel underlay Mark" as "deservedly completely ignored in the scholarship" on the Gospels.[54] In his

---

[49]E.g., C. F. Burney, *The Poetry of Our Lord* (Oxford: Clarendon, 1922); C. C. Torrey, *The Four Gospels: A New Translation* (New York: Harper, 1933); M. Black, *An Aramaic Approach to the Gospels and Acts* (Oxford: Clarendon, 1967[3]); R. Lindsey, *A Hebrew Translation of the Gospel of Mark* (Jerusalem: Dugith, n.d.).

[50]*Jesus*, 10ff. He regards Mark's Gospel as "a thorough revision of the original material" (10). See also *EJ*, 10:10.

[51]"Das Schisma zwischen Judentum und Christentum," *EvTheol.* 40 (1980): 219–20, 223, 239.

[52]*BJ*, 231.

[53]E.g., *JJ*, 29, 32–33, 128, 157. Vermes utilizes later Aramaic sources to throw light on the Gospel texts (cf. 19, 21, 53, 210–11).

[54]*First Christian Century in Judaism and Christianity*, 105, n.32. "While the earmarks of the results of translation are discernible in the four Gospels . . . the main line of modern scholarship holds that the Gospels, as we have them, are not translations, but Greek compositions. No documents in Aramaic are preserved, it suggests, probably because none were written." Sandmel, *A Jewish Understanding of the New Testament*, 14.

foreword to Lapide's book, Sandmel states that he regards as incorrect Lapide's excessive confidence that there was a Hebrew version of some of the gospel material.[55] Sandmel is also dubious about the confident assigning of authenticity on the basis of "Jewishness": "The broad congruency of some item in the Gospels with Jewish practice does not in itself establish historical reliability, and the circumstance that a Jew who has studied some Talmud sees a kindred atmosphere in the Gospels does not necessarily confirm the reliability of the Gospel item."[56]

It is not to be denied that the evangelists present history from a decidedly theological perspective—indeed, from a postresurrection perspective. But it is a long way from this fact to the conclusion that the Gospels contain little or no history. Radical Christian scholars regularly approach the Gospels with the a priori conclusion that the supernatural, the miraculous, or sometimes even the extraordinary cannot be regarded as historical. These elements are ruled out of court automatically as only the products of the postresurrection faith of the church. In a parallel way, Jewish scholars seem often to approach the Gospels with the a priori conclusion that whatever does not coincide with the modern Jewish estimate of first-century Judaism cannot be true of the Jesus of history. All that does not fit is relegated to alien influence, usually that of Paul and Hellenism. There is thus considerable overlap between the conclusions of radical Christian scholars and modern Jewish scholars.[57] To be sure, the latter are more conservative about much of the tradition, but in the end this is a rather insignificant difference.

Both groups are to be faulted for beginning with convictions that are hostile to the documents themselves and which are then pressed with a consistency that negates the message within them. More responsible critical scholars from the Christian side have issued a call for "openness to transcendence" wherein positivist historical criticism will not be allowed to "restrict our encounter with historical reality."[58] Moule

---

[55]Lapide, *Israelis, Jews and Jesus,* ix–x. For the work of Lapide in this general area, see his *Hebräisch in den Kirchen.* Forschungen zum jüdisch-christlichen Dialog 1 (Neukirchen-Vluyn, 1975).

[56]*WJJ,* 123.

[57]Martin Hengel, in a reference to the views of Jewish scholars, makes the same point when he writes that "it would be fascinating to trace further this *encounter between reformed Judaism and liberal Protestantism* in their criticism of christological dogma" (Hengel's italics). *The Son of God,* trans. John Bowden (Philadelphia: Fortress, 1976), 5–6.

[58]P. Stuhlmacher, *Historical Criticism and Theological Interpretation of Scripture,* trans. R. A. Harrisville (Philadelphia: Fortress, 1977), 90. See also M. Hengel, *Acts and the History of Earliest Christianity,* trans. J. Bowden (Philadelphia: Fortress, 1980), esp. 129–36.

similarly writes that "the nearer you push the inquiry back to the original Jesus, the more you find that you cannot have him without a transcendental element."[59] And Dodd stresses that "the whole point of the gospels is that the circumstances were far from ordinary. They were incidental to a quite peculiar situation, unprecedented and unrepeatable."[60] Many excellent scholars[61] have repudiated the "radical methodological skepticism"[62] of Bultmann and his followers.

Sandmel himself has appropriately criticized form criticism and "its supposedly objective method by which to differentiate between the historical and unhistorical." He found form criticism "to be very subjective, rather than completely objective. I found myself concluding that all too often the method argued in a circle, concluding from one layer a datum of where the church stood, let us say in A.D. 50, and then using that datum to identify other layers as coming from 50."[63] These criticisms are accurate and have been voiced by many Christian scholars. What deserves to be pointed out, however, is that they apply equally to the Jewish treatment of the Gospels. A high degree of subjectivity is involved in defining what is and what is not possible within the perimeters of first-century Judaism. Often that Judaism is defined only on the basis of the Judaism of the rabbinic literature without regard to the undeniable variety that characterized first-century Judaism. Even

---

[59]C. F. D. Moule, *The Phenomenon of the New Testament,* SBT 2.1 (London: SCM, 1967), 80. On the evangelists' faithfulness to the tradition concerning Jesus, see ibid., 78. See also Moule's *Origin of Christology* (Cambridge: Cambridge University Press, 1977), 1–10; 142–58.

[60]C. H. Dodd, *The Founder of Christianity* (New York: Macmillan, 1970), 32. Also appropriate to the subject of the present excursus is the following statement: "Thus the gospels record remembered facts, but record them as understood on the farther side of resurrection. There is no reason why this should be supposed to falsify or distort the record, unless, of course, it be assumed at the outset that such a belief *cannot* be true" (Dodd's italics). Ibid., 29.

[61]E.g., in addition to those already mentioned, L. Goppelt, J. Jeremias, T. W. Manson.

[62]The phrase is Hengel's. Such an approach, he argues, makes it "possible basically to utter only general commonplaces about the historical Jesus. This of course could have the grave consequence that we would lose altogether the criteria for differentiating Jesus from certain highly questionable religious figures of his age and environment." M. Hengel, *The Charismatic Leader and His Followers,* trans. James Greig (1968; ET, New York: Crossroads, 1981), 86.

[63]*The First Christian Century in Judaism and Christianity,* 153. The past tense is due to the fact that Sandmel writes autobiographically about how he has come to his high skepticism about the Gospels. But his point still stands. Cf. also his remark about the validity of form criticism, which he says, in his new (1974) preface to *A Jewish Understanding of the New Testament,* xxxi, he finds "all too often subjective and even capricious."

more serious, however, is the arbitrariness and circularity involved in beginning with a clear definition of Jesus as a Jew and then pressing that upon the Gospels and in turn deriving from them a correspondingly Jewish Jesus.[64]

It can only be regarded as strange, moreover, that the Gospel writers can have been so unfailingly accurate in the handing down of information about first-century Judaism and yet so consistently wrong where they present other (supposedly "un-Jewish") aspects of Jesus. The unusual consistency, rather, is that of the Jewish interpreters themselves, who designate as un-Jewish whatever does not fit their preconceptions. Schonfield reflects the practice of many Jewish scholars when he candidly writes, "To get as close as we can to the truth we have therefore to set aside everything said about Jesus and his teaching in the Gospels which is not in accord with his status as a devout Jew."[65] In the Gospels, according to Schonfield, "there is revealed on the one hand a Jesus who is wholly a Jew, and on the other hand a Jesus who is un-Jewish and at times anti-Jewish. They cannot be one and the same person."[66]

But what must be said as forcefully as possible is that *the kerygmatic Christ of the Gospels is fully Jewish*. Acceptance of the entire narrative of the Gospel tradition entails no denial of Jesus' Jewishness. The disciples and Paul himself were Jews and never for a moment believed that what they heard from Jesus, what they believed about him, or indeed even what they said about him involved moving away from Jewishness, either on their or Jesus' part. Jesus of course had some surprises for them. But given the larger framework of the fulfillment of God's purposes, these surprises were not seen as involving anything intrinsically alien to the faith of Israel.

In the approach taken in the chapters that follow, I do not intend to deny the influence of the church's theology on the historical narratives of the Gospels. What *is* denied, however, is that such influence automatically guarantees that any passage in question is unhistorical. I attempt in what follows only to make sense of the texts as they stand. This is not the place to attempt to argue the historicity of each passage. And it may be that some conclusions drawn here may need some revision or qualification on closer analysis. But even if this is true of some of the

---

[64]It is remarkable to find Jewish scholars claiming impartiality in this enterprise. Flusser presents his interpretation of Jesus "with no ax to grind" (*Jesus*, 12); Vermes gives "a historian's reading of the Gospels" (subtitle of *Jesus the Jew*).

[65]*FCS*, 54–55.

[66]Ibid., 27. "Where we find Jesus making statements which no Jewish Messiah could make, and where Jesus is presented in terms suggestive of deity, we can recognize these passages as contributions to what could readily be entertained by non-Jews" (21).

passages discussed, it could hardly be the case that the majority of these passages, let alone all of them, would have to be rejected. Our concern, in any event, must be with the totality of Jesus' teaching, and not simply isolated sayings,[67] for the whole matters greatly and from it emerge patterns that support the interpretation of the details.

But, it may be asked, does not this perspective begin with as much an a priori as that of the Jewish scholars here critiqued? Is this not simply to begin with the conclusion that Jesus of Nazareth is the supernatural, divine person—the incarnation of God—that the early church eventually believed him to be? It is of course clear that no one is capable of complete objectivity. The present work, furthermore, *is* written explicitly from a Christian perspective. Nevertheless, this standpoint of Christian faith is not imposed on the gospels, which after all are themselves very much the products of developed Christian faith. It is intrinsic to them.[68] My claim is simply that only such a view does justice to the Gospels as they stand. Only the evangelists' view of Jesus enables us to understand him and his teaching. Christian scholars do not come to the Gospels with an alien, a priori conclusion that they then impose on them. They deal with the documents as they are and attempt to let them speak for themselves. This is very different from beginning with a conclusion that requires consistent rejection of portions of these documents and results in a portrait of Jesus that is very unlike what the evangelists intended. If in the Gospels we find a Jewish Jesus, it is equally true that we find none other than a Jesus who in the kerygma is proclaimed Lord.

The chapters that follow should not be regarded as presupposing an uncritical stance toward the Gospel texts. To be sure, the approach is conservative and tries to do justice to the texts as they stand. It is assumed, rather than argued, that the sayings of Jesus have been handed down carefully and faithfully.[69] This approach, I believe, is compatible with a reasoned and reasonable criticism, i.e., a criticism that is not itself inimical to the very nature and content of the texts themselves.

---

[67]On this point, among Jewish scholars Montefiore has the soundest methodology. He does not overly concern himself with the question of *ipsissima verba,* but takes the Gospels as they stand. Since the Gospels exist as wholes, he reasons, one must reckon with their total teaching. See *SG* I: xcvii–xcviii; *RLGT,* xix; *RT,* 138.

[68]Thus Vermes' proposal to consider "the gospels without christology" can only lead us to conclusions far removed from those of the evangelists. The futility of such a pursuit has been shown by E. Hoskyns and N. Davey, *The Riddle of the New Testament* (London: Faber & Faber, 1931, with many reprints).

[69]For a cautious and eminently sensible approach to this subject, see B. Gerhardsson, *The Origins of the Gospel Traditions* (Philadelphia: Fortress, 1979). For an introductory discussion, see D. A. Hagner, "Interpreting the Gospels: the Landscape and the Quest." *JETS,* 24 (1981).

CHAPTER THREE

The Authority of Jesus:
His Relationship to the Law

THE NATURAL STARTING POINT in the study of Jesus' teaching as seen from the Jewish perspective is his attitude toward the Law, for the Jews are first and foremost the people of the Torah. In first-century Judaism, as in much of Judaism today, the Law was virtually synonymous with authority. The traditional view, still held by Orthodox Jews, is that God's revelation of the Torah to Moses on Mount Sinai included not only the written law (i.e., the Pentateuch) but also the oral law, the "traditions of the elders"—i.e., the interpretation of the written law now perpetuated in the rabbinic literature as found especially in the Mishna and its commentaries (which together make up the Talmud). Judaism is in the fullest sense founded on the Law. And since the Law constitutes the very essence of Judaism, it may be fairly said that one's view of the Law determines one's view of the validity of Judaism itself. The attitude of Jesus toward the Law is therefore of the greatest importance to the Jew, and the Jewish reclamation of Jesus depends to a large extent on this very question.

It is not surprising to note that in the Gospels it is clearly the Law that is the focal point of dispute between Jesus and the Jews.[1] Montefiore correctly remarks:

> The quarrels of Jesus with the Jews of his age, and more especially with the Pharisaic Rabbis, were not about the nature of God, His unity, His justice, His mercy; they were about the Law and its authority, and about the relation of outward ceremonial to morality, of ritual ordinances to spiritual religion.[2]

---

[1]Parkes, in his treatise on anti-Semitism, states that it is the Law that has been the basis of separation between Jews and Christians, not the crucifixion, as so commonly believed. *The Conflict of the Church and Synagogue* (London: Soncino, 1934), 45.

[2]"The Religious Teaching of the Synoptic Gospels in Relation to Judaism," *HJ* 20 (1921–22):437.

We now proceed to examine the Jewish understanding of Jesus' attitude to the Law—first generally, then with respect to specific problem passages, and concluding with an estimate of the extent of Jesus' break with tradition.

THE SPECTRUM OF THE JEWISH VIEWPOINT

The stance taken by Jesus with respect to the Law and its authority is not unambiguous.[3] Indeed, this is a question fraught with difficulty. At times Jesus speaks of the permanent validity of the Law (e.g., in Matt. 5:17–18); yet his actions and words often seem contrary to the Law (e.g., Mark 2:18–27). The majority of Jewish scholars, consistent with their affirmation of the Jewishness of Jesus, strongly emphasize Jesus' faithfulness to the Law. They are fond of compiling lists of the Jewish traits of Jesus in which they include the restriction of his and his disciples' ministry to Israel, due regard of the temple and its worship, the paying of the temple tax, the offering of sacrifice, the recitation of pharisaiclike prayers, the saying of grace at meals and the blessings over wine, the wearing of the *zizit* (the fringe or tassels attached to the four corners of a robe in fulfillment of the commandment in Numbers 15:37–41 and Deuteronomy 22:12), the regarding of dogs and swine as unholy, and other similar items that reflect Jesus' obedience to the Law and his agreement with social custom.[4] In the same way, the Jewishness of the teaching of Jesus contained in the Sermon on the Mount and elsewhere is repeatedly stressed.[5] Indeed, everything Jewish about Jesus in his

---

[3]B. H. Branscomb likens Jesus' attitude to a chromatic scale including all the notes between affirmation and rejection of the Law. *Jesus and the Law of Moses* (New York: Smith, 1930), 23; Oesterley and Box speak of the evidence as having a "two-fold character." *The Religion and Worship of the Synagogue* (London: Pitman, 1907), 146–47.

[4]Cf. Joseph Jacobs, "Jesus of Nazareth—In History," *JE* 7:162; Samuel Cohon, "The Place of Jesus in the Religious Life of His Day," *JBL* 48 (1929):94; Asher Finkel, *The Pharisees and the Teacher of Nazareth* (Leiden: Brill, 1964), 130ff.; J. Klausner, *JN*, 364; Vermes, *GJJ*, 38.

[5]Cf. especially G. Friedlander, *The Jewish Sources of the Sermon on the Mount*. Even Montefiore, against whom Friedlander's book is directed, is convinced that "the spirit of the Sermon is Jewish—in full accordance with the highest teachings of the Old Testament and of the Rabbis." *RLGT*, 161.

stance toward the Law is emphasized by Jewish scholarship in its persistent reclamation of Jesus for Judaism.

Jewish scholars, however, have not been completely successful in their attempt to portray Jesus as one who was fully faithful to the Law. Montefiore cogently remarks that the difference between the rabbis and Jesus in their attitude toward the Law cannot be denied, for it is basically this difference that led to the death of Jesus.[6] It is the paradox of Jesus' affirmation and denial of the Law that must be faced by Jewish scholarship (as well as Christian scholarship, it may be added) at the outset of any attempt to understand him and his relation to Judaism.[7]

The classification that follows is at best only approximate and obviously reflects some interpretation. The task is made even more difficult by the conflicting statements of certain authors— something that in itself reflects the perplexity caused by the data in the Gospels.

1. *A modest break with the Law.* Only a few Jewish scholars have been willing to speak of Jesus in terms of even a limited break with the Law. Most indeed only imply a break, and several who imply it make other statements that seem to contradict the implication. It should be noted, however, that where a break is spoken of or implied, it is always with the insistence that this in no way lessens Jesus' true Jewishness.

On this point Montefiore has perhaps been the most courageous. One of the few Jewish scholars willing to ascribe originality to Jesus, he boldly concludes that "Jesus was compelled to take up a certain attitude towards the Mosaic Law itself, and this attitude was novel and even revolutionary."[8] The new departure consisted in such things as the minimizing of the oral law; the careful differentiation of the moral and ceremonial laws, the former in every case taking precedence over the latter; the priority of the inward over the merely outward; and the stress on the surpassing importance of the higher law of love. Indeed, it is exactly in

---

[6]*RLGT,* 161; cf. Mark 3:6.

[7]"Jesus and the Law—this is one of the great problems of his life; and it is a problem in which we have to try our utmost to understand his opponents and our utmost to understand him." Montefiore, *SG* I, CXX.

[8]*RT,* 44.

these emphases that the genius of Jesus is said to consist.[9] Thus the teaching of Jesus regarding the Law "forms a new departure, and makes a break from the Judaism of his age."[10] In all of this, of course, Montefiore as a liberal Jew goes further than most other Jewish scholars are willing to go. According to Montefiore, however, in violating the Law in certain of his teachings and actions, Jesus contradicted his own assertion of the permanent validity of the Law. Thus it must be admitted that he falls short of the consistency of the rabbis.[11] "Logically and consistently, the right was on the side of the Rabbis; universally, ultimately, and religiously, the right was on the side of Jesus."[12]

Schonfield, too, is able to admit the radical stance taken by Jesus toward the Law, admitting that Jesus relaxed the rigid observance of the Sabbath, and even that he countermanded the dietary restrictions.[13] But Schonfield does not help us to understand how this is to be brought into harmony with his statements elsewhere that "Jesus taught his people that they must observe the Law in every particular,"[14] that loyalty to the Law was "a first essential of messianic policy" and therefore that Jesus' basic stance was one of affirmation of the authority of the Law.[15] These irreconcilable statements appear to reflect Schonfield's ambivalence as well as the inherent difficulty of the subject.

Sandmel is willing to admit a break with the Law if Jesus actually spoke the words of Mark 7:15: "There is nothing outside a man which by going into him can defile him." To say this is to repudiate the Mosaic food laws of Leviticus 11 and Deuteronomy

---

[9]C. G. Montefiore, *The Old Testament and After* (London: Macmillan, 1923), 231; cf. "The Religious Teaching of the Synoptic Gospels in Its Relation to Judaism," *HJ* 20 (1921–22):438.

[10]*HJ* 20 (1921–22):438.

[11]"The Originality of Jesus," *HJ* 28 (1929–30):102–3; cf. B. H. Branscomb's remark that ethical consistency rather than logical consistency was Jesus' test. "Jesus' Attitude to the Law of Moses," *JBL* 47 (1928):40.

[12]*RT*, 50.

[13]*PP*, 77, 205. The teaching of Jesus on these points, together with his eating and drinking, and his mixing with publicans and sinners, is discussed by Schonfield as marks of his turning away from the Nazirite tradition of his Galilean homeland.

[14]*FCS*, 50.

[15]*ANT*, xxxviii.

14.[16] According to Sandmel, however, we cannot be certain that Jesus did say these words;[17] they stand against the general picture given in the Gospels, which is one of basic agreement between the Jews and Jesus, with only occasional "hints" at any profound differences.[18] More recently Sandmel, speaking of the influence of Paulinism on the Gospel of Mark, has written of certain "presuppositions in Mark, namely, that the Laws of Moses are no longer valid, and that the new movement is quite separate from and independent of its parent, Judaism; the sacred Jewish calendar is no longer affirmed and confirmed."[19] Struggling with the overall difficulty of the evidence, Sandmel concludes about the Jesus of history: "The fact is that the Gospel materials do not provide a full, crystal-clear reflection of Jesus' attitude to the Law of Moses and to the oral law."[20]

In his article on Jesus in the *Jewish Encyclopedia,* Joseph Jacobs captures the tension between Jesus' affirmation of the Law on the one hand and his neglect and infraction of it on the other hand, "at least as it was interpreted by the Rabbis." Jesus, according to Jacobs, differs from John the Baptist in two ways: "(1) comparative neglect of the Mosaic or rabbinic law; and (2) personal attitude toward infractions of it." Yet Jacobs says a few lines later that Jesus was at the same time not essentially different from the Pharisees in his viewpoint. The paradoxical attitude of Jesus is explained by his conviction that "the Law should be obeyed unless a higher principle intervenes."[21] Jacobs appeals to the words of Luke 6:4 according to Codex Bezae as reflecting the

---

[16]*WJJ,* 136; cf. also Isaac Wise: "Jesus was against the Levitical Law." *Three Lectures on the Origin of Christianity* (Cincinnati, 1889), cited by Vorster, "Jewish Views on Jesus. An Assessment of the Jewish Answer to the Gospel of Jesus Christ" (doctoral dissertation, South Africa: University of Pretoria, 1975), 192.

[17]Sandmel, indeed, is very skeptical concerning the authenticity of the majority of sayings attributed to Jesus. Cf. S. Sandmel, *A Jewish Understanding of the New Testament* (Cincinnati: Hebrew Union College, 1956), 109.

[18]*WJJ,* 138.

[19]"Palestinian and Hellenistic Judaism and Christianity: The Question of the Comfortable Theory," *HUCA* 50 (1979):146. This issue is a memorial volume dedicated to Sandmel.

[20]*WJJ,* 136.

[21]*JE,* 7:162.

viewpoint of Jesus. There, seeing a man working on the Sabbath, and thus violating Torah, he says, "O man, blessed are you if you know what you are doing; but if you do not know cursed are you and a transgressor of the law."

2. *No break with the Law, but some (limited) differences with rabbinic Judaism.* Most Jewish scholars are inclined to understand Jesus as differing only mildly with the typical Jewish understanding of the Law in his day. Jesus is thus regarded as not essentially different from the Pharisaic rabbis of his day.

Israel Abrahams grapples with the problem of Jesus and the Law in his attempts to reconcile a high view of Pharisaic rabbinism with the teaching of Jesus. Since Jesus taught in a period of transition, during the development of different schools of exegesis, argues Abrahams, it was inevitable that there would be variant interpretations of the Law, and that these interpretations would eventually clash. Jesus, however, in taking advantage of a certain liberty in interpretation remains thoroughly Jewish. With the Pharisees he accepts the law of the Sabbath; he differs only in the exegesis of that law, i.e., concerning conditions that justify its abrogation.[22] Thus Abrahams is reluctant to go quite as far as his friend Montefiore in acknowledging a break with the Law on Jesus' part. Abrahams's position concerning Jesus and the Pharisees is neatly summed up in these sentences: "To treat morality as law, as on the whole the Pharisees did, spells neither self-delusion nor lack of spirituality. On the other hand to treat morality as an autonomous principle as Jesus on the whole did, spells neither license nor vacillation.[23]

For some, Jesus indeed is to be explained primarily in terms of his minimizing of the ceremonial law. Klausner is typical of this viewpoint. Quoting Luke 11:42 (especially the clause "these you ought to have done, without neglecting the others"), he insists that Jesus never annulled the Law, nor even the ceremonial laws contained in it.[24] At the same time, however, Jesus'

---

[22]*SP*, 1:134. Abrahams further suggests the possibility that the bitterness of the Sabbath controversy may be the result of its having taken place in Galilee where there may have been a special strictness. 131.

[23]Ibid., 2:vi.

[24]*JN*, 367.

teaching contained "suggestions of such a line of action"[25] and "a kernel of opposition to Judaism" that not he, but Paul, carried to its final conclusion.[26] Jesus himself is guilty only of an "*exaggerated* Judaism," which was ruinous to the national identity of Israel and which thus must ultimately be considered a "non-Judaism."[27] The "kernel of opposition" referred to evidently consists simply in the "little stress" placed on the ceremonial laws by Jesus who, says Klausner, was only "*unwittingly*" the founder of a new religion.[28] Elsewhere, Klausner says that both Jesus and Paul "set repentance and ethical deeds above the ceremonial laws."[29]

Jules Isaac similarly contends that Jesus did not stand against the Law, nor even against Pharisaism, but only against the elevation of the letter of the Law above the spirit of the Law.[30] Proposition 9 in his book *Jesus and Israel* reads as follows: "Jesus was born and lived 'under the [Jewish] Law.' Did he intend or announce its abrogation? Many writers hold that he did, but their statements exaggerate, distort, or contradict the most important passages in the Gospels."[31] The violation of the Sabbath was a violation of Pharisaic scruples, not of the Law itself. On the matter of dietary restrictions, Isaac is somewhat confusing. Jesus did not declare all foods clean, he says, despite the editorial interpolation of Mark 7:19. However, the regulations were "jostled in the scuffle" in the attempt of Jesus to

---

[25]Ibid., 276.

[26]Indeed, Paul could not have set aside ceremonial laws had not Jesus provided some precedent for doing so. *JN,* 369ff. Jesus only "hinted" at abolishment of the ceremonial laws. 275.

[27]*JN,* 374ff.; "Obviously, Jesus did not reckon with the fact that no people can, in daily life, retain its distinctiveness solely by means of abstract ethical views, and that, if Israel were to abandon the ceremonial laws peculiar to itself, it would be absorbed into the Gentiles and would disappear." "Christian and Jewish Ethics," *Judaism* 2 (1953):19.

[28]*JN,* 225; J. Klausner, *From Jesus to Paul,* ET by W. F. Stinespring (1943; reprint ed., New York: Beacon, 1961), 588.

[29]J. Klausner, "Christian and Jewish Ethics," *Judaism* 2 (1953):19.

[30]J. Isaac, *Jesus and Israel,* trans. Sally Gran (New York: Holt, Rinehart & Winston, 1971), 60.

[31]Ibid., 49. Isaac's twenty-one propositions are also found in an appendix to his book, *The Teaching of Contempt: Christian Roots of Anti-Semitism,* trans. Helen Weaver (New York: Holt, Rinehart & Winston, 1964).

"unshackle" Judaism. But this is not to be understood as a break with Judaism.[32]

A. Cohen and K. Kohler put the issue perhaps a little more sharply. Cohen also sees the difference between the Pharisees and Jesus to be the latter's emphasis on ethics at the occasional expense of Halakah (i.e., the specific laws of the Old Testament as interpreted by the Pharisees). "He isolated morality from the halachic framework in which it was embedded," and thus, for Cohen, he must be regarded as unorthodox in his attitude toward the Torah. Although the Pharisees were resentful of this, they never desired to be rid of Jesus.[33] Kohler, quoting Matthew 5:17–18, describes Jesus as a "perfect Jew" who was thoroughly loyal to the Law, and yet at the same time one who "did not heed slight transgressions against the Halakists."[34] Beyond this, however, Kohler is hesitant to go, since he regards the Gospels as generally untrustworthy.

Other Jewish scholars, somewhat more conservatively, appeal to differences of interpretation of the Law in explaining Jesus. Herbert Loewe maintains that Jesus was a faithful upholder of the Law all of his life; he repeats the common Jewish allegation that the portrayal of Jesus as one deliberately and consciously opposed to the Law is the reflection of the hostility between the early church and the synagogue.[35] Like Abrahams, Loewe understands the real differences between Jesus and the Pharisees to be in matters of halachic interpretation: other "differences" do not in fact exist, but are due to the misunderstanding of the Gospel data by modern readers.[36] Concerning Jesus, Loewe writes, "I regard him as a saintly artisan, of Hillel's type."[37] Asher Finkel also sees the hostility between Jesus and the Pharisees to center in matters of halachic interpretation. Jesus, who in his teaching resembles the school of Hillel, op-

---

[32]*Jesus and Israel,* 62–63.

[33]A. Cohen, *The Parting of the Ways* (London: Lincolns-Prager, 1954), 80.

[34]K. Kohler, *The Origin of the Synagogue and the Church* (New York: Macmillan, 1929), 218, 222.

[35]H. Loewe, "Pharisaism," *Judaism and Christianity,* 1:164.

[36]Ibid., 165, 178–79.

[37]Ibid., 160.

posed only those zealous Pharisees who were disciples of Shammai.[38] It is arguable that Loewe and Finkel should be classified under the heading that follows.

3. *No (essential) difference with rabbinic Judaism.* It is striking that the most recent Jewish writers on Jesus belong solidly under this heading, viz., Ben-Chorin, Flusser, Lapide, Maccoby, and Vermes. This trend indicates an increasingly ambitious Jewish reclamation of Jesus.

In his important book, Ben-Chorin puts Jesus clearly with the Tannaim of the first century. Although Jesus does speak with his own special authority ("But *I* say to you"), it is a mistake to regard this as a break with Judaism. Ben-Chorin does not account for this authority, but simply alleges that Jesus is rather sometimes to be put with Hillel and sometimes with Shammai in his interpretation of the Law.[39] Never does Jesus challenge the authority of Scripture. Instead he calls the attention of his listeners to the *intention* of the Law, something that is also an important concern within the rabbinic tradition.[40]

David Flusser has taken one of the strongest stands against the suggestion that Jesus violated the Law in any sense at all— whether written or oral: "The Gospels provide sufficient evidence to the effect that Jesus did not oppose any prescription of the Written or Oral Mosaic Law, and that he even performed Jewish religious commandments."[41] "Jesus did not seek to abrogate or even to reform the Jewish Law."[42] The mistaken impression that Jesus did counter the Law is in part due to the exaggerated wording contained in the Gospels; this wording reflects the later and growing rift between the synagogue and the church.[43] Flusser sees only one explicit violation of the Law attributed to Jesus in the Synoptics—the plucking of grain on the Sabbath.

---

[38]Finkel, *The Pharisees and the Teacher of Nazareth,* 134ff.

[39]*BJ,* 16–17. Cf. "Jesus und Paulus in jüdischer Sicht," *Annual of the Swedish Theological Institute,* vol. 10, ed. B. Knutsson (Leiden: Brill, 1976), 23.

[40]*BJ,* 75–76.

[41]D. Flusser, "Jesus," *EJ,* 10:13.

[42]D. Flusser, "The Son of Man: Jesus in the Context of History" in *The Crucible of Christianity,* ed. A. Toynbee (London: Thames and Hudson, 1969), 225.

[43]"Jesus," *EJ,* 10:12–13.

This, it is argued, however, is a contribution of the Greek translator who has added the plucking of the grain "to make the scene
more vivid."[44] What actually took place was only the rubbing of
grain in the hands, which was in fact allowed. Flusser elsewhere
stresses that it was the disciples who were guilty of the infraction,
and not Jesus.[45] In other instances of supposed violation, Jesus in
fact goes against the "tradition of the elders," which is to be
distinguished from the oral Law and where some degree of freedom was tolerated.[46]

Lapide's view of the matter is identical with Flusser's. According to Lapide, "Jesus was and remained a Torah-true Jew,
who never and nowhere (in Matthew, Mark, and Luke) transgressed against the Mosaic and rabbinic legislation."[47] Where
Jesus appears to go against the Law in the synoptic tradition,
closer examination reveals repeatedly that this is the result of
Christian misunderstanding or, as in the case of Mark 7:19, a
later tendentious interpolation.[48] The overwhelming evidence of
the Gospels is that Jesus upheld the authority of the Torah and the
Prophets. Jesus indeed fought against the deifying of law-observ-
ance (nomolatry) into the essence of Judaism.[49] But on this point
Jesus is in the good company of Hillel, Akiba, the Hasidim, and
the neoorthodox Jews. Thus Lapide is able to say: "Jesus was as
Torah-true as I, an orthodox Jew, am."[50]

Maccoby does not discuss the subject in sufficient detail. He
simply states that "the Gospels, despite the re-working they have
undergone, do not show Jesus as flouting or attacking a single
Biblical law."[51] Jesus also upheld the Pharisaic perspective, according to Maccoby, criticizing only the custom of hand-washing.

---

[44]D. Flusser, *Jesus*, ET by R. Walls (New York: Herder & Herder, 1969), 46.

[45]"The Son of Man," 225.

[46]Ibid.

[47]*RN*, 52. Cf. almost exactly the same statement in *ÖCJ*, 139: "Nowhere and never
does he condemn or reject one single Mosaic or rabbinic institution." The Gospel of John,
however, does, according to Lapide, present "Jesus as Torah-conqueror." *RN*, 55.

[48]*RN*, 51, 59; *ÖCJ*, 128.

[49]*RN*, 51, 60.

[50]P. Lapide, *Jesus im Widerstreit: Ein Jüdisch-Christlicher Dialog* (Munich, 1976),
26. The translation of these words in H. Küng, *Signposts for the Future* (Garden City,
N.Y.: Doubleday, 1978), 75, is slightly different.

[51]*RJ*, 108.

Although Geza Vermes's full view of the question of Jesus and the Law awaits the publication of his promised volume, *The Gospel of Jesus the Jew*, it is possible to anticipate his conclusions from his influential book *Jesus the Jew: A Historian's Reading of the Gospels*.[52] Vermes portrays Jesus as a Galilean Hasid whose teaching acquired authority, not because of his expertise in Law, but rather because of his exorcisms and healings.[53] Jesus' teaching is regarded as being in full accord with Jewish doctrine. In only one instance does Vermes regard a passage as seeming to indicate that Jesus went against the essentials of Judaism—in the matter of clean and unclean foods (Mark 7:19). Here, however, the redactor of the Greek Mark by a "deliberate twist" misrepresents a play on words in the Aramaic as meaning "thus he declared all foods clean." This is a reflection of the view of the redactor's church rather than an accurate account of what Jesus said.[54] There is no serious rift between Jesus and the Pharisees; what minor disagreements there were are properly understood as an "in-fighting" not untypical of the rabbinic tradition, which was itself in flux. What does set Jesus apart is his prophetic rhetorical stress of the ethical over the ritual, as must be expected from a preacher of repentance.[55] "Where the Law is concerned, the real distinction of Jesus' piety lies in his extraordinary emphasis on the real inner religious significance of the commandments."[56]

Most of the scholars who defend Jesus' absolute loyalty to the Law appeal to some extent to the influence of the later church on the Gospel narratives. Not all are willing to go as far as E. R. Trattner, who asserts that whereas Jesus himself never contemplated abolishing the Law, the evangelists "by putting their

---

[52](New York: Macmillan, 1973). This may now be supplemented by Vermes's Riddell Lectures, *The Gospel of Jesus the Jew* (University of Newcastle upon Tyne, 1981), an anticipation of the promised volume of the same title, and the Claude Montefiore Memorial Lecture of 1974 bearing the same title, "Jesus the Jew" (London: The Liberal Jewish Synagogue, 1974).

[53]*JJ*, 27.

[54]Ibid., 28–29. See below, p. 117.

[55]Vermes, "Jesus the Jew" (Montefiore Lecture), 12; *GJJ*, 40.

[56]*GJJ*, 40. "I believe it true to say that interiority, purity of intention, played a greater part in Jesus' thought." Ibid.

words into Jesus' mouth . . . made it appear that it was the Nazarene himself who undertook to tear down the whole fabric of Mosaic Legislation."[57] Thus for Trattner, as for Loewe, whenever Jesus appears to go against the Law, we encounter the opinion of the later church and not that of the historical Jesus. Other Jewish writers use this appeal at least to explain the interpolation of Mark 7:19.

Many Jewish scholars thus find considerable difficulty in understanding Jesus' stance toward the Law. Some sense that Jesus does not fit as readily into their Jewish perspective as they would like; others feel that he does indeed, when rightly understood, agree fully with the first-century Jewish climate. This same tension can be seen in the divergent opinions of two non-Jewish scholars who normally represent the Jewish viewpoint. In his definitive work on "normative Judaism," G. F. Moore is content to assert that Jesus' attitude toward the Law, indeed even the ceremonial law, was completely orthodox.[58] R. Travers Herford, on the other hand, notes that Jesus' teaching in places must be taken as superseding the Torah. The authority appealed to by Jesus is radically different from the authority appealed to by the Pharisees, and thus the ensuing conflict was inevitable. Moreover, because of its nature, the difference was irreconcilable.[59]

SPECIFIC PROBLEM PASSAGES

It is clear from the above survey of Jewish opinion that the problem of Jesus and the Law is difficult for Jewish scholars. Because they are intent on preserving the Jewishness of Jesus, they are reluctant to admit on his part any departure from the authority of the Torah. We must now consider the Jewish handling of the New Testament data relevant to the problem.

---

[57]E. R. Trattner, *As a Jew Sees Jesus* (New York: Scribner, 1931), 48.

[58]G. F. Moore, *Judaism* (Cambridge, Mass.: Harvard University Press, 1946) 2:9; cf. Moore's remark that Matthew 5:18–19 is thoroughly rabbinic in outlook. Ibid., 268–69.

[59]R. T. Herford, *The Pharisees* (London: Allen & Unwin, 1924), 67, 204.

The Authority of Jesus

The Antitheses of the Sermon on the Mount: Matthew 5:21–48

The antithesis that occurs no fewer than six times in these verses, "You have heard that it was said . . . but I say to you," poses no small problem for the Jewish reclamation of Jesus. To debate the meaning of Torah is one thing, but to assert one's own opinion with the egocentric authority of "but I say to you" is quite another.

It was Solomon Schechter who first suggested that these words were the result of the Greek translation of a common rabbinic formula used to indicate that some particular interpretation of a biblical passage may not have been valid in the fullest sense. A better translation for the formula would therefore be "one might hear so and so . . . but there is a teaching to say that the words must not be taken in such a sense."[60] Accordingly, Jesus is doing nothing extraordinary in this passage; he is merely following good rabbinic practice in his teaching. Jews have found this explanation helpful in explaining instances where the first element (the "you have heard" clause) includes material not found in the Torah (e.g., verses 21 and 43). This first element may include interpretative material as well as an actual statement of the Torah.[61]

However, Montefiore is quite correct in recognizing that it is the antithesis, or second element, that constitutes the real problem for Jewish scholars. According to him, Schechter's explanation fails to account for the un-Jewish character of the second element in each of the final two pericopes (verses 39–42; 44–48). For Montefiore, the antitheses are "definite and even vehement contrasts between old and new."[62] Since he finds it difficult to believe that Jesus uttered words so contrary to the Law, he thinks it not unlikely that these last two passages were

---

[60]Schechter, *JQR* 10 (1898):11, n. 3; 12 (1900):427.

[61]E.g., Abrahams, *SP*, 1:16; D. Daube, *The New Testament and Rabbinic Judaism* (London: Athlone, 1956), 56. Trattner takes the same position in his *As a Jew Sees Jesus*, 85–86.

[62]*RT*, 82.

added editorially by the early church.[63] While Montefiore recognizes the "sense of personal importance and personal authority" in Jesus' teaching, yet he concludes, "This especial emphasis of 'I say' as contrasted with what the Law says—the Law which Jesus too held to be divine—seems somewhat doubtful and difficult."[64]

David Daube follows Schechter in seeing a rabbinic formula behind these words of Jesus.[65] The first element in the original was "I might understand literally" and thus suggests the translation: "Ye have literally understood." This means that what follows is not necessarily to be understood as a strict quotation of the Torah. The second element of the rabbinic idiom, however, was "but thou must say," and included either a Scripture verse or some logical deduction (e.g., *a minori ad maius*) in support of the exhortation. What for the rabbis was an academic device used for practice in exegesis, became for Matthew a legislative device. Instead of "thou must say," there is the startling "I say to you," without logical or scriptural justification. Jesus is thus indeed denoted as "supreme authority." Yet, says Daube, the whole passage shows Jesus to be the upholder of the Law, since the second element never really contradicts the first. "On the contrary, wider and deeper though it may be, it is thought of as, in a sense, resulting from and certainly including the old rule, it is the revelation of a fuller meaning for a new age. The second member unfolds rather than sweeps away the first."[66] Most Jewish authors concur that Jesus was interested in deepening the meaning of the Torah and that this was in fact an enterprise close to the heart of many Pharisees.

Jewish scholars have had to agree that the antitheses represent something unusual so far as Jesus' contemporaries are concerned. Abrahams is content merely to say that the "I say to you" "introduces a personal element";[67] Ben-Chorin, however, notes that Jesus speaks out of his own special authority, and that

---

[63]SG, 2:498–99.
[64]RT, 81–82; cf. Kohler, *The Origins of the Synagogue and the Church*, 230.
[65]Daube, *The New Testament and Rabbinic Judaism*, 55–62.
[66]Ibid., 60; cf. "Concessions to Sinfulness in Jewish Law," *JJS* 10 (1959):11.
[67]SP, 1:16.

the "I say to you" constitutes the part of Jesus' teaching most different from that of the rabbis—a special note, although it does not represent a break with Judaism.[68] It is here that Jesus is most different from his contemporaries.[69] Klausner concludes that this personal authority represents "an exaggerated sense of nearness to God" that implied uniqueness and ultimately "confused Jesus' pure monotheism."[70] According to Schonfield, the "I say to you" simply reflects Jesus' own belief that exceptional authority had been conferred on him, and is therefore explained by his messianic consciousness.[71]

Lapide forthrightly admits that the "I say to you" "smacks of opposition" to the Torah and is therefore unrabbinic in tone. Since it "does not fit" with the picture of Jesus elsewhere in the Gospels, Lapide is inclined to deny that Jesus ever spoke in this way. Since the antithesis formula is not in Luke, it probably stems from the Matthean circle; what Jesus most probably said was either, "But I say to you who hear" (where the "but" signifies no opposition to the teaching of the Torah), as in Luke 6:27, or simply, "I say to you," as in Matthew 5:26.[72]

Samuel Cohon, on the other hand, skirts the problem rather too easily when, comparing Jesus' style of teaching in Matthew 5 to that of the Haggadists, he concludes that "no self-centeredness or undue individualism need have entered into his frequent use of the first person in his preaching. He but followed the form so abundantly illustrated in the Midrashim and in the Talmud."[73] The form and content of Jesus' teaching, however, seems to belie the characterization of Jesus as a typical Haggadist in Matthew 5.

By contrast, Orthodox Jews react strongly to the un-Jewishness of the antitheses. Ahad ha'Am puts it bluntly: "Israel cannot accept with religious enthusiasm, as the Word of God, the utterances of a man who speaks in his own name—not 'thus saith the

---

[68]*BJ*, 15–16.

[69]*BJ*, 77.

[70]*JN*, 378–79.

[71]*PP*, 70; "He dared to announce his conclusions with all the weight of a personal and independent authority." *ANT*, xli.

[72]*ÖCJ*, 132, following E. Stauffer.

[73]S. Cohon, "The Place of Jesus in the Religious Life of His Day," *JBL* 48 (1929):95.

Lord,' but '*I* say unto you.' This '*I*' is in itself sufficient to drive Judaism away from the Gentiles forever."[74] In this pointed remark, an Orthodox Jew shows his perception of the tone of authority encountered in the Sermon on the Mount.

One With Authority, and Not as Their Scribes: Matthew 7:29 (=Mark 1:22; cf. Luke 4:32)

When it is said explicitly by the evangelists that Jesus "taught them as one who had authority [*exousia*] and not as their scribes," thus separating him from the learned rabbis of his day, Jewish scholars are inclined to take exception. Thus the attempt has been made to escape the import of these words by postulating a corruption of the putative Hebrew text underlying the Gospel. The error, it is claimed, consisted in reading *kᵉmoshel* for *bᵉmashal*, thus reading "he taught them *with authority*" instead of the original "he taught them *by parable.*" But this conjecture, first put forward by H. P. Chajes,[75] necessitates Jesus' use of parables as the cause of great astonishment among his listeners (Matt. 7:28). Abrahams, however, has shown that teaching by means of parables was not a new phenomenon in Jesus' day and can hardly explain the astonishment he created.[76] At the same time, most Jewish scholars allow that Jesus' teaching was different in method from that of the rabbis of his day. Whereas Jesus taught simply and appealingly, the rabbis commonly used a specialized and rather technical kind of exegesis in their teaching. This in large measure accounts for the popularity of Jesus as a teacher. Kaminka, however, opposes Klausner on this matter.[77]

Daube regards the word *exousia* ("authority") in Mark 1:22 as authentic and as constituting a part of the earliest tradition.[78] Underlying this word in the first instance was the concept *reshuth*

---

[74]H. Kohn, ed., *Nationalism and the Jewish Ethic* (New York: Schocken, 1962), 298.

[75]*Markus-Studien* (1899), 11–12.

[76]*SP*, 1:95–96.

[77]Cf. G. F. Moore, "A Jewish Life of Jesus," *HTR* 16 (1923):102. Klausner himself suggests Chajes's theory as noteworthy. *JN*, 264.

[78]For the whole discussion, see Daube, *The New Testament and Rabbinic Judaism*, 205–23.

or "rabbinic authority," the mark of an ordained rabbi. It was this authority that specifically marked out the rabbis from the scribes. The latter in this context, says Daube, were not the learned rabbis, but simply the ordinary teachers of orthodox doctrine; the rabbis, however, had the authority to proclaim new *halachoth* and *horayoth* (decisions) that included novel doctrine. Thus the "authority" that came to the minds of the crowds who heard Jesus teach may at first have been the authority of an ordained rabbi. Indeed, this is what caused the difficulty: in actuality, Jesus was not an ordained rabbi. Therefore the question comes to him: "By what authority are you doing these things, or who gave you this authority to do them?" (Mark 11:28; cf. Matt. 21:23; Luke 20:2). Daube notes that Jesus' answer to this question imparts to the concept of *reshuth* the idea of "divine authority" or "almightiness," a concept that had its basis in Jesus' "mighty works and Messianic message."[79] Thus Daube is careful to allow for different levels of *reshuth*. He sums the matter up in these words:

> We need hardly mention that the wonderful ethical principles advocated by Jesus must have made a tremendous impression on his contemporaries. Thus, though we may find that in Mark 1:22 and 27 reference is made to *reshuth qua* Rabbinic authority, we are far from denying that Jesus' disciples, right from the beginning, considered his *exousia* to be of a very different kind. That these various shades in the meaning of the term could exist at the same time may easily be proved.[80]

Vermes, on the other hand, does not see as much significance in the reference to Jesus' authority as does Daube. For Vermes the authority of Jesus apparently does not reside in the teaching of Jesus itself (in contrast to that of the rabbis), but rather his teaching is accorded exceptional authority because of his exorcisms and healings (Vermes cites Mark 1:27 and Luke

---

[79]Ibid., 217–18; cf. Daube's discussion of the rhetorical form of the passages containing the questioning of Jesus' authority in the passages cited. He sees here evidence of the rabbinic adoption of Hellenistic rhetorical rules, in this instance reflecting a pattern of Socratic interrogation consisting of (1) a question by opponent, (2) a counterquestion, (3) the answer the enemy is forced to make, and (4) refutation. Ibid., 151–57.

[80]D. Daube, "*Exousia* in Mark 1:22 and 27," *JTS* 39 (1938):56.

4:36).[81] Vermes does note that Jesus "is said to have taught with
exousia, with authority, without feeling the need for a formal
justification of his words,"[82] while at the same time denying that
Jesus was any match in exegetical debate for "the luminaries of
Jerusalem Pharisaism."[83] This suggests that the authority of
Jesus was of a categorically different order than that of the Pharisees, a point that Vermes does not pursue. Undoubtedly there is
a connection between the authority of Jesus' words and his deeds.
Vermes' explanation, however, ignores the deliberate connection
made in other texts between the astonishment of the listeners at
his teaching and the authority of Jesus: "And when Jesus
finished these sayings, the crowds were astonished at his teaching, for he taught them as one who had authority, and not as their
scribes" (Matt. 7:28–29; cf. Mark 1:21–22); "And he was
teaching them on the sabbath; and they were astonished at his
teaching, for his word was with authority" (Luke 4:31–32).

Jacobs allows that certain passages in the Gospels (e.g.,
Matt. 11:29; 25:40; Mark 8:35) "indicate an assumption of
power which is certainly unique in Jewish history, and indeed
accounts for much of modern Jewish antipathy to Jesus, so far as
it exists." Jesus "emphasized his own authority apart from any
vicarious or deputed power from on high," and this involved a
tone that was "altogether novel in Jewish experience."[84] In a
similar way, Abrahams calls attention to the same extraordinary
fact: "Jesus spoke without reference to any mediate authority."[85] Montefiore says of Jesus' teaching: "Its touch of personal
authority is an element in its originality."[86]

Jewish scholars who do recognize the unusual nature of
Jesus' authority often make no attempt to explain it or to pursue
possible implications. Either that authority is regarded as somehow being possible within a rabbinic framework, or, if not, it is

---

[81]*JJ*, 27–28. Much earlier, Kohler argued similarly that Jesus gained fame not as a
teacher, but as a wonderworker. "Jesus of Nazareth—In Theology," *JE*, 7:167.
[82]*GJJ*, 20.
[83]*GJJ*, 19.
[84]J. Jacobs, "Jesus of Nazareth—In History," *JE*, 7:163.
[85]*SP*, 1:15.
[86]*RT*, 114. Cf. Jacobs, *JE*, 7:163.

regarded as the result of later theological tendencies read back into the Gospel narratives. Ben-Chorin is interesting in this regard. As we have seen, he calls attention to the special authority of Jesus in the Gospels. Having no real explanation of the authority, Ben-Chorin appeals to the impact of kergymatic tradition.[87] Similarly, it is "unthinkable" that Jesus could have said such words as those of Matthew 11:29–30: "Take my yoke upon you. . . ."[88] Ben-Chorin explains the healings performed by Jesus as faith healings, displaying the victory of spirit over matter, and as involving no exceptional authority on Jesus' part.[89] In the accounts of the raising of the dead, however, when Jesus accomplishes the deed immediately, without prayer (Mark 5:41; Luke 7:14), Ben-Chorin concludes an absolute authority is implied.[90] This prompts him to make the following frank admission, which could well apply to the entire subject of Jesus' authority in the Gospels. "The sense of the unique, absolute authority, that is evident from this way of acting, remains deeply problematic for the Jewish view of Jesus."[91]

Having looked into the subject of Jesus' authority generally, we may now turn to specific ways in which this authority manifests itself, so far as Jesus' stance toward the Law is concerned.

The Sabbath Controversy

Plucking Grain on the Sabbath: Mark 2:23–26 (=Matthew 12:1–7; Luke 6:1–4).
The Sabbath Logion: Mark 2:27–28 (cf. Matthew 12:8; Luke 6:5).
Healing on the Sabbath: Mark 3:1–6 (=Matthew 12:9–14; Luke 6:6–11).

These passages are extremely difficult for the Jewish reclamation of Jesus. In the first passage, when his disciples pluck

---

[87]*BJ*, 22.
[88]*BJ*, 52.
[89]So too Maccoby, *RJ*, 216.
[90]S. Ben-Chorin, *Jesus im Judentum* (Wuppertal, 1970), 41; cf. *BJ*, 16, 61.
[91]*Jesus im Judentum*, 41.

grain to eat on the sabbath, Jesus is asked by the Pharisees, "Why are they doing what is not lawful on the sabbath?" Reminding them that David and his companions once went counter to the Law without incurring God's displeasure, he answers with the famous Sabbath logion: "The sabbath was made for man; not man for the sabbath; so the Son of man is lord even of the sabbath." Thereupon in Mark follows the record of another Sabbath episode in which Jesus healed a man's withered hand, after he had asked his opponents, "Is it lawful on the sabbath to do good or to do harm?"

Jewish scholars have differing opinions concerning the extent to which Jesus violated the law of the Sabbath. We begin with those who see some infringement of the Sabbath in this material and work our way to those who see no countering of the Law here, but again some subjectivity is involved in this procedure.

In his commentary, Montefiore writes that Jesus "seems to concede that a breach of the Law [i.e., the written Law] has taken place" in the plucking of the grain, yet "it is an excusable and proper breach" since it is only illustrative of the higher principle underlying the Sabbath law.[92] Elsewhere Montefiore suggests the possibility that Jesus may have "not touched the validity of the *written* Pentateuchal Law" but rather countered only the casuistic interpretations of the Law by the rabbis. Montefiore's liberal convictions are reflected in his added remark: "Jesus probably realized the absurdity of many of the regulations about the Sabbath into which the Rabbis, in their mistaken zeal and too-eager legalism, had unfortunately been led."[93] Montefiore notes that the rabbis also said, "The Sabbath was made for you; you were not made for the Sabbath." Nevertheless, strict observance was required by the rabbis, with the only exceptions allowed being cases of sickness (but only the slightest infringements, not those involving healings), danger to life, and the suffering of animals.[94] In contrast, Jesus shows his insight into the "right princi-

---

[92]*SG*, 1:64.

[93]*RT*, 43.

[94]Mechilta on Exodus 31:14, cited by Montefiore, *RLGT*, 224; cf. Mark 2:27. The underlying principle was that "it is right to violate one Sabbath in order that many may be observed." *RLGT*, 243. See also BT, Yoma 86a.

ple," and "pays no heed to legal subtleties."[95] Yet Montefiore doubts that Jesus referred to himself as "lord of the Sabbath"; this idea is to be regarded as later than Jesus.[96]

Abrahams, a leading authority on the Pharisees, holds essentially the same position concerning Jesus and the Sabbath. He, too, notes that the Pharisees would have agreed that the Sabbath was made for humanity, but not vice versa.[97] But that there is a difference between Jesus and the Pharisees cannot be denied: "All things considered, it would seem that Jesus differed fundamentally from the Pharisees in that he asserted a general right to abrogate the Sabbath law for man's ordinary convenience, while the Rabbis limited the license to cases of danger to life."[98] The argument of the indignant ruler of the synagogue—"There are six days on which work ought to be done; come on those days and be healed, and not on the sabbath day" (Luke 13:14)—faithfully represents the Pharisaic viewpoint and, according to Abrahams, "remains unanswered."[99] Abrahams implies that the following of Jesus' precedent would have led to the ultimate destruction of the Sabbath and that the Pharisees were thus justified in their opposition to Jesus.[100] Although the schools of Hillel and Shammai were indeed debating *halachoth* concerning the Sabbath, they never contemplated radical ideas such as Jesus proposed. There is thus a clear departure from tradition on the part of Jesus and his disciples.[101]

Klausner, too, calls attention to the dangerous implications of Jesus' abrogation of the Sabbath. For the Pharisees the turning

---

[95]*RLGT*, 244.

[96]*SG*, 1:52.

[97]Cf. K. Kohler, *The Origins of the Synagogue and the Church* (New York: Macmillan, 1929), 216; Abrahams says: "If criticism be a science at all, then it seems to me that this Sabbatarian principle must be pushed back to the Maccabean age." I. Abrahams, "Rabbinic Aids to Exegesis," in *Cambridge Biblical Essays,* ed. H. B. Swete (London: Macmillan, 1909), 186.

[98]*SP*, 1:134.

[99]Ibid.

[100]Ibid.

[101]Samuel Cohon, however, says that Jesus was in essential agreement with the Hillelites concerning the Sabbath. "The Place of Jesus in the Religious Life of His Day," *JBL* 48 (1929):97; cf. Sandmel, "What is puzzling to Jewish students is that the Jewish attitude about the Sabbath as reflected in rabbinic Judaism is near to that ascribed to Jesus and remote from that ascribed to his opponents." *WJJ*, 152, n. 1.

point was Jesus' healing of the withered hand on the Sabbath. "From this stage they began to see that the man whom they had so far considered as nothing more than a Pharisaic 'Rab,' with his own views on certain religious questions (not a remarkable thing in the time of the Hillel and Shammai controversies), was, in real truth, a danger to religion and to ancestral tradition."[102] The crux of the matter was that, in this particular instance, Jesus could easily have waited until the following day to heal the man. "Jesus, on the Sabbath, heals diseases which are not dangerous." Further, "Jesus justifies his disciples when they pluck ears of corn on the Sabbath, thereby lightly esteeming the laws of Sabbath observance."[103] Klausner regards the Sabbath controversy as "an important landmark in Jesus' career," for from this time on his popularity with the people began to wane.[104]

A. Cohen also sees a significant break with the Law when Jesus healed on the Sabbath: Jesus "sanctioned the principle 'better the day, better the deed,' and himself performed as well as permitted his disciples to perform an act on the Sabbath which could equally well have been done on the next day."[105]

Some Jewish scholars, however, do not admit that Jesus broke with the Sabbath commandment of the written Torah in any real sense and prefer to describe the problem as involving only a break with the oral law of the Pharisees. Thus Jacobs, referring to the plucking of grain and the healings on the Sabbath, concludes that "at least" a break with Pharisaic traditions has occurred.[106] Schonfield sees a break with the Pharisees in Jesus' violation of their Sabbath injunctions. According to Schonfield, Jesus "relaxed the rigid Sabbath observance" of the Pharisees.[107] This, however, did not involve the actual breaking of the Sabbath: "He was accused by some of the Pharisees of violating the Sabbath laws; but in fact he had not done so."[108] Trattner concludes that the conflict between Jesus and the rabbis concerning the Sabbath

---

[102]*JN*, 279.

[103]Ibid., 369.

[104]Ibid., 279.

[105]A. Cohen, *The Parting of the Ways* (London: Lincolns-Prager, 1954), 80.

[106]*JE*, 7:162.

[107]*PP*, 77, 205.

[108]*FCS*, 50.

stemmed only from "those hairsplitting casuists among the Pharisees."[109]

Daube has called attention to the rabbinic form of the passage concerning the plucking of grain while also noting the clear difference between Jesus and the Pharisees. He notes the fact that the grain-plucking incident is set forth in a tripartite pattern consisting of (1) a revolutionary action, (2) a protest, and (3) the silencing of the remonstrants.[110] Here the second element, the question "Why do your disciples do what is unlawful on the Sabbath?" can be regarded as meaningful only if Jesus and his disciples were regarded as belonging to the same camp as the Pharisees. In the third element Jesus begins his answer in good rabbinic form by introducing a commonly accepted incident (the eating of the showbread by David and his companions) as the basis for his answer. But while there is basis for agreement in the incident itself, "where he [Jesus] differs from them is as to the interpretation of the teaching adduced."[111] Daube, along with other Jewish scholars, considers Jesus' reference to David's eating the showbread to be "anything but conclusive from the scholarly, legal point of view."[112] By this Daube means that in rabbinical exegesis a Halakah can be sustained only by the citation of a precept, not mere example, as in the present case; a historical event could not constitute the primary source of a Halakah. On the other hand, Matthew's addition of 12:5–6 introduced with the words "in the Law," is in strict accord with rabbinic procedure, as is the *a fortiori* argument used. If the priests are allowed to profane the Sabbath, how much more he who is greater than the temple. Says Daube, "The argument is of a kind which no student of *halakha* could lightly dismiss."[113]

Most of the recent Jewish writers on Jesus are insistent that

---

[109]Trattner, *As a Jew Sees Jesus,* 104.

[110]Daube, *The New Testament and Rabbinic Judaism,* 170ff.

[111]Ibid., 174; Daube finds the same pattern in seven different incidents in the synoptic Gospels. While the healing of the withered hand on the Sabbath is not one of these, the pattern is found in the healing of the infirm woman on the Sabbath (Luke 13:10ff.).

[112]Ibid., 68; cf. Montefiore, *SG,* 1:62; Abrahams, *SP* 1:134. Abrahams, however, adds the note that the Midrash understands David to have eaten the showbread on the Sabbath, thus making citation of that event somewhat less strained.

[113]Daube, *New Testament and Rabbinic Judaism,* 71.

Jesus broke neither with the written Law nor with the traditions of the Pharisees. Kohler anticipated this trend when he argued that Jesus' liberal attitude toward the Sabbath was the result of dependence on the teaching of the Hillelites.[114] Thus, like Kohler, Ben-Chorin calls attention to the fact that Mark 2:27–28 is "not without parallels in the rabbinic writings."[115] For Ben-Chorin, Jesus belongs with the Pharisees. His interpretation of the law is sometimes mild, with Hillel, sometimes more stringent, with Shammai.[116]

Sandmel, on the other hand, regards Mark 2:27–28 as much more significant than other Jewish scholars do:

> To declare that the Sabbath is made for man and not man for the Sabbath, and that the son of man is lord of the Sabbath, both denotes and connotes something quite different from the mere suspension of the Sabbath regulations by the rabbis in instances of emergency. Accordingly, it does not seem to me to be sound to regard somewhat analogous motifs either as identical or as common in origin.[117]

It is Flusser, however, who is the first Jewish scholar to deal with the specific passages that are difficult for the view that Jesus did not break with the traditions of the Pharisees. For Flusser, the introduction of "the one and only act of transgression of the Law recorded in the synoptic tradition" (i.e., the plucking of grain) is due to the Greek translation of an original Hebrew account thought by Flusser to underlie our present Gospel of Mark.[118] According to Flusser, it was permissible to pick up fallen grains and (in Galilee) to rub them in one's hand, and this is actually all that Jesus and his companions were doing. The idea of plucking grain was a detail added for vividness by a later translator unaware of the customs of that society.[119]

Flusser adds the observation that it is only the disciples who

---

[114]*JE*, 7:168.

[115]*BJ*, 61–62.

[116]Ibid., 17.

[117]S. Sandmel, *The First Christian Century in Judaism and Christianity* (New York: Oxford, 1969), 93.

[118]Flusser, *Jesus*, 46.

[119]Ibid.

are guilty of the violation, and not Jesus. He notes the same thing in the issue of neglecting to wash the hands before the eating of a meal (a "tradition of the elders," which Flusser distinguishes from the oral law)—only some of the disciples were guilty.[120] The relevance of this observation is difficult to see, however, if no infraction of Pharisaic law is entailed in either instance.

The episode of the Sabbath healing of the man with the withered hand constitutes no problem because, according to Flusser, such a healing—using only the instrumentality of words—was allowed on the Sabbath, even in matters where there was no immediate danger to life. So far as the Pharisaic traditions are concerned, therefore, "Jesus always conformed to these rules in all of his healings."[121] The impression given by the present Gospels is the result of later, tendentious emendations, but despite them, argues Flusser, "the Gospels provide sufficient evidence to the effect that Jesus did not oppose any prescription of the Written or Oral Mosaic Law."[122]

Lapide is similarly convinced of the fidelity of Jesus to Pharisaic tradition: Jesus, alleges Lapide, never went against the rabbinic legislation any more than he did the Law of Moses.[123] Lapide follows Flusser closely in his discussion of both the grain-plucking incident and the healing of the withered hand. He adds that the disciples had no need to pluck the grain, since at harvest time it lay on the ground; they merely rubbed the grain in their hands—something with which some Pharisees disagreed, but which others found acceptable. The way in which Jesus defends the action itself shows that he was serious about the keeping of the *halacha*.[124] Lapide similarly concludes that all four Sabbath healings (Matt. 12:9–13; Luke 13:10–17; 14:1–6; and even John 5:1–16) are in agreement with good rabbinic practice, though he does not adequately account for the several problematic aspects

---

[120]Ibid., 48; cf. "The Son of Man: Jesus in the Context of History," 225.

[121]Flusser, *Jesus,* 49. Flusser faults John 9:6 for suggesting that Jesus could have made use of the instrumentality of clay on the Sabbath in the healing of a blind man.

[122]*EJ,* 10:13.

[123]*RN,* 52. This point is said by Lapide to be "the best guarded secret of Christian biblical research."

[124]*ÖCJ,* 122–23.

of these passages.[125] The instances where Jesus can be shown to uphold Sabbath observance (Matt. 24:20; Mark 1:21; Luke 4:40) are noted by Lapide, as is Jesus' acceptability within the synagogue (Luke 4:16) and the inability of the council to find cause to put him to death (Mark 14:55), both of which would have been impossible had Jesus broken the Sabbath.[126]

Vermes does not discuss the grain-plucking incident other than to note that Jesus did not condemn his disciples for their activity.[127] Vermes concurs with Flusser that Jesus did not violate the Sabbath in the healing of the man with the withered hand, not even by the standard of the Pharisees' tradition, since the healing was by speech alone.[128] Yet Vermes calls attention to a point overlooked by Flusser (and Lapide, it may be noted): in the healing of the crippled woman on the Sabbath (Luke 13:13ff.) Jesus uses the laying on of hands, an act that does constitute a violation of the Sabbath by Pharisaic standards. Vermes reveals his own perspective when he notes the possibility that the reference to the laying on of hands could be construed as an addition by Luke in order to make more plausible the argument about the Sabbath, which follows in the narrative.

The Divorce Question

What God has joined together: Mark 10:2–9 (Matthew 19:3–8). When the Pharisees asked Jesus about the permissibility of divorce according to the Law, citing Moses' allowance of divorce (Deut. 24:1), he responded, ''For your hardness of heart he wrote you this commandment. But from the beginning of creation, 'God made them male and female.' '' It should be noted that in citing the creation account of Genesis Jesus appeals to Moses in his argument against Moses. Indeed, Jesus' implication is that he upholds the Law in a more fundamental way than does any appeal to Deuteronomy 24:1. Nevertheless, it is a mark of

---

[125]*RN*, 54.

[126]Ibid., 55–56.

[127]*JJ*, 35. Nor does he do so in his lectures, *The Gospel of Jesus the Jew* (The Riddell Memorial Lectures [Newcastle upon Tyne: University of Newcastle upon Tyne, 1981]).

[128]*JJ*, 25.

Jesus' authority that he can reject what Deuteronomy 24:1 does in fact allow. Interestingly, so far as rabbinic doctrine is concerned, Jesus at this point errs on the side of stringency rather than laxity: far from agreeing with Hillel, he outdoes even Shammai. Here, regardless of the reason and despite a heightening rather than a relaxing of the demands of Torah, Jesus does counter the explicit teaching of Moses. Most Jewish scholars, however, apparently do not regard this as a serious issue in the Jewish reclamation of Jesus and have not bothered to discuss it.

Abrahams sees little difference between Jesus and the Pharisees on this point. In his untiring defense of first-century Pharisaism, he writes the following: "'What the Lord hath joined, let no man put asunder' represented the spirit of the Pharisaic practice in the age of Jesus, at all events with regard to a man's first marriage."[129] Despite the allowance of divorce on various grounds, "the strongest moral objection" was felt against it.[130] Abrahams does not discuss the position taken by Jesus against divorce, other than to describe it as a "rigid attitude."[131]

Klausner similarly finds no great problem in Jesus' teaching on divorce. The key to a correct understanding of Jesus at this point is to be found in his answer to the question about Moses' commandment concerning a bill of divorcement. Jesus, says Klausner, "did not reply that he was come to take aught away from the Law of Moses," but rather justified Moses' commandment as necessary because of hardness of heart.[132] Klausner proceeds to liken Jesus' attitude concerning Moses' commandment to Maimonides' conception of the sacrificial system, and thus no ultimate contradiction of the Law is necessarily implied.

Montefiore and Sandmel, on the other hand, see the matter as much more serious in its implications. Montefiore considers Jesus' teaching on divorce to be "anti-Jewish."[133] Commenting on Mark 10:9, Montefiore writes, "Nowhere more than here

[129]SP, 1:68.

[130]Ibid., 69.

[131]Ibid., 71.

[132]JN, 364.

[133]C. G. Montefiore, "The Significance of Jesus for His Own Age," HJ 10 (1911–12):768.

does Jesus go nearer to denying the absolute divinity, permanence, and perfection of the Law: that is, if he forbade divorce
absolutely.''[134] According to Montefiore, Jesus reacted to rabbinic leniency on divorce and probably did go to the opposite
extreme of prohibiting divorce altogether.[135] Montefiore regards
the phrase added in Matthew 5:32, ''except on the ground of
unchastity,'' as a later, mitigating addition.[136]

Sandmel also stresses the importance of this passage from
the question of Jesus' attitude to the Law. For Sandmel, Jesus'
teaching on divorce in Mark 10 represents the ''nearest approach'' of Jesus to the Pauline conception of the Law as ''an
impediment to righteousness, and hence superseded.''[137]

The Food Laws

*Thus he declared all foods clean: Mark 7:14–23 (cf. Mat-
thew 15:10–20).* Jewish scholarship faces another, more serious
difficulty in Jesus' revolutionary utterance recorded in Mark 7:15
(cf. Matt. 15:11), ''There is nothing outside a man which by
going into him can defile him; but the things which come out of a
man are what defile him.'' These words themselves constitute a
break with the dietary regulations of the Torah even apart from
Mark's editorial comment: ''Thus he declared all foods clean''
(7:19).

Several Jewish scholars admit forthrightly that in this instance Jesus breaks with the written Torah. Yet they hesitate
somewhat to express the difference sharply and they insist on
Jesus' continuing Jewishness. As a liberal Jew, Montefiore regards Mark 7:1–23 as the most important passage in the Gospel
of Mark, and verse 15 as its key verse.[138] This verse, which

---

[134]*SG*, 1:232.

[135]*RT*, 45.

[136]*SG*, 2:66. Although Montefiore cannot bring himself to agree with Jesus' total
prohibition of divorce, he does conclude that Jesus made an incalculable contribution in
delivering women from their low status in Oriental society. *SG*, 2:67; cf. *RLGT*, 47.
Enelow, however, finds Jesus the cause of no change in the position of women. *A Jewish
View of Jesus*, 102.

[137]*WJJ*, 136.

[138]*SG*, 1:130; Liberal Judaism's attitude towards the ceremonial law is derived in the
first instance from the teachings of the eighth- and seventh-century prophets concerning
the things that affect God, and in the second instance from the teachings of Jesus concerning the things that affect man (Mark 7:15). Ibid.

Montefiore calls "one of the greatest sayings in the history of religion," denies the existence of ritual impurity in the material sense.[139] In so doing, however, Jesus is guilty of a grave inconsistency, for he "practically declares that the divine opinion was wrong."[140] "If Jesus' principle was true, then the Law was wrong," writes Montefiore.[141] Yet according to Montefiore, this was nevertheless a deduction that Jesus himself apparently did not realize; he was probably unaware of his own inconsistency.[142] As an analysis of Jesus' teachings, Mark's editorial comment that Jesus declared all foods clean is considered by Montefiore to be accurate only in the ultimate application of verse 15—something realized only much later. Montefiore thus finally shies away from the conclusion, already drawn, that Jesus' words are not compatible with the absolute authority of Torah: Jesus himself "did not deliberately intend to teach his disciples that the Pentateuchal dietary laws need no longer be obeyed."[143] Montefiore again finds his solution to the problem in Jesus' apparent inconsistency.

Klausner, too, notes the importance of Mark 7:15 for the whole of Judaism. With these words Jesus "would even permit (though he does this warily and only by hints) the foods forbidden in the Law of Moses." Klausner adds, "The breach between Jesus and the Pharisees was complete."[144]

Sandmel does not hesitate to draw this crisp deduction from the words of Mark 7:15: "The effect of this declaration is to repudiate the Mosaic food laws found in Leviticus 11 and Deuteronomy 14."[145]

Some Jewish scholars mention this passage but make little comment. Schonfield, for example, acknowledges that Jesus "held that nothing which enters a man's mouth defiles him" but

---

[139]SG, 1:153; "I am so keen about the great Logion that I cannot help hoping that Jesus really meant that outward uncleanness does not matter." Ibid., 16.

[140]SG, 1:160.

[141]RT, 48.

[142]SG, 1:156–57, 159; cf. C. G. Montefiore, "The Synoptic Gospels and the Jewish Consciousness," HJ 3 (1904–05):66.

[143]C. G. Montefiore, "The Originality of Jesus," HJ 28 (1929–30):102.

[144]JN, 291.

[145]WJJ, 136. Cf. J. Parkes, The Foundations of Judaism and Christianity (London: Vallentine, Mitchell, 1960), 170.

devotes little attention to the problem other than to suggest in the same paragraph that it was Jesus' "reading of his messianic mission" that led him to turn his back on much of the tradition in which he had been nurtured.[146] Similarly, Maccoby simply states with no examination of the Gospel texts that Jesus "makes no attempt, for example, to abolish the Jewish dietary laws or the laws of ritual impurity."[147] The strange silence of both Ben-Chorin and Flusser on the question of the food laws probably indicates that they find nothing problematic in the passage. In several places Flusser gives his opinion that in only one synoptic passage (the plucking of grain on the Sabbath) does Jesus appear to go against the Law, whether oral or written.[148] Almost certainly, both Ben-Chorin and Flusser would regard Mark's editorial comment "Thus he declared all foods clean" as a misunderstanding of the passage resulting from the special circumstances of the early Gentile church.

A few Jewish scholars have attempted to explain the passage in such a way as to deny altogether that Jesus' words meant the abrogation of the dietary rules. Thus for Kohler the logion of Mark 7:15, as it stands, could never have been said by Jesus, but is instead to be explained as originating in the antinomianism of Pauline (anti-Judean) circles.[149] Kohler conjectures that Mark 7:15 must originally have been "a principle which scarcely implied the Paulinian abrogation of the dietary laws, but was probably intended to convey the idea that 'the profane cannot defile the word of God' " (Ber. 22a).[150]

Denying the correctness of one's first impression from Mark 7:15 (i.e., that Jesus overthrew the dietary laws), Lapide argues that Jesus did not mean what he said to be taken literally. Since, in Lapide's view, Jesus elsewhere always upholds the Law, he must be understood to do so here too. The formula of Mark 7:14,

[146]*PP*, 205.

[147]*RJ*, 107. Cf. the same statement on p. 108: "He did not abrogate the dietary laws."

[148]Flusser, *Jesus*, 46; "The Son of Man: Jesus in the Context of History," 225; cf. Flusser's review of Wolfgang Pax; *In the Footsteps of Jesus*, in *Christian News from Israel*, N.S. 23.1 (1972):52.

[149]*JE*, 4:52.

[150]Ibid., 7:168.

"Hear and understand" points "unmistakably to a deeper sense."[151] Jesus means in this passage merely to stress the necessity of inner purity, without which ritual cleanliness counts for little (cf. Matt. 23:23). In this emphasis he is in perfect accord with the prophets of Israel.[152] According to Lapide, an "impertinent glossator" is responsible for the misinterpretation of the meaning of Jesus' words in Mark 7:19b.[153]

Vermes also disbelieves that Jesus actually rejected the dietary laws. As does Lapide, Vermes argues that the point Jesus wants to make in this passage is that external uncleanness is "trivial" when compared with moral uncleanness. This is more apparent in the Matthean account, which Vermes regards as "more original" than the Markan account. In the latter, "the text is so modified that it is scarcely possible to avoid the conclusion that Jesus rejected the basic Jewish dietary law."[154] This is due to a Greek translator, hypothesizes Vermes, who deliberately twisted what was a word-play in the original Aramaic. Following Matthew Black's suggestion that "food" in Mark 7:19b is used metaphorically for "excrement,"[155] Vermes conjectures that a polite term for latrine, "the place" (*dukha*) was connected with the verb "be clean" (*dekha*), so that the original read, "It does not enter into his heart but into his stomach, and so passes out into 'the place' where all excrement 'is purged away.'"[156] But by the time of the Greek redactor, concludes Vermes, "Gentile Christianity needed and welcomed a formal ratification in the teaching of the Gospel of the Church's abandonment of the laws and customs of Israel."[157]

It may be said fairly that the passages discussed above constitute important difficulties for the Jewish reclamation of Jesus. The majority of Jewish scholars have nevertheless done their best

---

[151]*ÖCJ*, 125–26; *RN*, 58–59.

[152]Ibid., 126–27.

[153]Ibid., 128.

[154]*JJ*, 28.

[155]Matthew Black, *An Aramaic Approach to the Gospels and Acts* (Oxford, 1967³), 217–18.

[156]*JJ*, 29. It may be noted with Vermes that this rendering of the passage does find support in the Sinaitic recension of the Syriac Gospel (4th to 5th century).

[157]Ibid.

to see Jesus as being solidly within the prophetic tradition. They repeatedly stressed that Jesus himself said, "Think not that I have come to abolish the law and the prophets; I have come not to abolish them but to fulfill them. For truly, I say to you, till heaven and earth pass away, not an iota, not a dot, will pass from the law until all is accomplished" (Matt. 5:17–18). As Hosea came with the message "I desire mercy, not sacrifice" (Hos. 6:6; quoted by Jesus in Matt. 9:13; 12:7), so Jesus came emphasizing the higher, spiritual aspects of the Law. But even as Hosea did not intend the abolition of the sacrifices, but rather their proper use, so also Jesus did not intend to annul the Law, nor even the ceremonial law: "These you ought to have done, without neglecting the others" (Matt. 23:23). These words, according to Abrahams, "might be fairly inscribed by Pharisaism as the motto on its banner."[158] Jesus came denouncing legalism, a perversion of the Law, even as most of the Pharisees themselves would have denounced it; he did not come to overthrow Judaism, to bring a new religion, or to set up a new law code. In spite of all this, however, it is only with considerable difficulty that Jewish scholars can deny that Jesus was different from any who preceded or followed him.

JESUS' BREAK WITH TRADITION

Jesus did break with tradition in an unprecedented manner. Although indeed he had not come to destroy the Law, it is at least quite clear that his presence was very significant so far as a right understanding of the Law is concerned. Viewed in context, his teaching can only be regarded as startling. He presents his teaching in the first person, with an unparalleled personal authority; as Lord of the Sabbath he allows his disciples to pluck grain and he himself heals on the Sabbath; he counters Mosaic teaching on divorce; and in principle he rescinds the dietary laws of the Pentateuch. To this list may be added such departures from tradition as his refusal to insist that his disciples fast (Matt. 9:14ff.; Mark

---

[158]*SP*, 2:31. Montefiore, however, wonders whether Jesus really said "without neglecting the others." Amos and Isaiah would not have said so, he writes. *RLGT*, 330.

2:18ff.; Luke 5:33ff.); his failure to wash hands before eating (Mark 7:1–2; Matt. 15:1ff.); and his eating with sinners, thereby disregarding ritual separatism (Matt. 9:11; Mark 2:16–7; Luke 5:30–31). Some of these items—the last three in particular—may, of course, involve allowable violation of traditions that, far from having binding force, were subject to free and continuing intramural debate. But this cannot serve to explain all the data that confront us in the Synoptic portrait of Jesus (not to mention that of the fourth Gospel).

The Jewish scholars who are most ambitious in the reclamation of Jesus for Judaism have often had to resort to extreme measures to make Jesus' teaching fit the mold. Not infrequently one encounters an ingenious conjecture, a clever emendation, a suggestion of word-play, or an appeal to a putative Hebrew gospel underlying the synoptic Gospels. These devices, however, are not convincing and point instead to the impossibility of the task.

As regards the Sabbath controversy, several Jewish scholars argue that it was the disciples and not Jesus who plucked grain on the Sabbath, just as it was the disciples who did not fast and who did not ritually wash their hands before eating.[159] The Jewish scholar David Daube, however, has shown that one cannot so easily separate Jesus from the disciples in these matters. Jesus shows no surprise when he is called to account for his disciples' conduct. Indeed, so close is the relationship between a master and his disciples that the master is considered responsible for the conduct of his disciples (and the disciples for their master's conduct). As Daube puts it, "So powerful is a master's position that an action he condones may be imputed to him just as much as one he initiates."[160] Jesus is to be considered as responsible for his disciples' plucking grain on the Sabbath as if he himself had done it.

Most frequently, however, Jewish scholars resort to a redaction-critical analysis of problematic passages, thereby denying

---

[159]E.g., S. Ben-Chorin, "Jesus and Paulus in jüdischer Sicht," *Annual of the Swedish Theological Institute,* vol. 10 (Leiden: Brill, 1967), 24; Flusser, *Jesus,* 48.

[160]David Daube, "Responsibilities of Master and Disciples in the Gospels," *NTS* 19 (1972–73):5.

their historical authenticity. Statements that suggest that Jesus possessed authority over the Law or in any sense broke with the Law are regarded as "anti-Jewish" and are said to mirror a clear tendency toward Pauline antinomianism and the growing rift between the synagogue and the church. Thus passages that do not fit with the Jewish conception of Jesus are dismissed from further consideration.

Jewish scholars, on the other hand, hold in high regard passages such as Matthew 5:17–20 and 23:1–3a, 23, where Jesus speaks positively of the Law and even upholds Pharisaic tradition, and Matthew 15:24 (cf. 10:5–6), where Jesus restricts his ministry to Israel. These passages are regarded by the vast majority of Jewish scholars as authentic elements of the most primitive tradition because of their apparent incongruity with the Pauline attitude toward the Law. Montefiore is a notable exception. He sides with Bultmann and other non-Jewish scholars in the view that Matthew 5:18–19 is "inconsistent with the attitude of Jesus to the Law taken as a whole," the reflection of certain anti-Pauline views in the early church, and hence most probably inauthentic.[161]

The Gospel of Matthew as it stands, however, holds these apparently different perspectives in tension: The mission of Jesus and his disciples is particularistic, yet also universalistic; the legitimacy of the Pharisees is recognized, yet they are denounced and their traditions disregarded; the Law is affirmed, yet apparently challenged. In short, this very Jewish Gospel can at times sound remarkably un-Jewish. Jewish scholars argue that the "un-Jewish" material reflects the impact on the Gospels of the era when the Pauline antinomian perspective had begun to dominate the church. The evangelists thus portray Jesus as at least an incipient antinomian. And yet for these scholars this later tendency has not managed to obscure totally the Jesus of history, who

---

[161]*SG*, 2:51; cf. Montefiore's description of verse 19 as "Rabbinism with a vengeance," *RLGT*, 38. Yet a few pages prior to this, Montefiore says, "Historically we can hardly expect to get any certain conclusion as to Jesus's theoretic attitude toward the Law, because he probably had not faced the question himself. He may have been inconsistent without being aware of it." Ibid., 48. Thus Montefiore, too, becomes tangled in the dilemma.

remained loyal to the Law and fully within the Jewish framework.

Some (non-Jewish) scholars, however, attribute Matthew's emphasis on Jesus' loyalty to the Law and Jewish tradition to the circumstances of Matthew's church rather than to an accurate portrayal of the Jesus of history.[162] That is, the church had not yet made the break with Judaism,[163] and the situation was one where the Law was affirmed in an effort to have an outreach among members of the synagogue. Thus for G. Barth a redaction-critical analysis yields this conclusion: "That the validity of the law was ended is precisely what Matthew contests."[164] Far from himself representing an antinomian tradition, "Matthew opposes a group who appeal in support of their libertinism to the fact that Christ has abolished the law."[165] Matthew 5:17–19 is accordingly not a part of the primitive tradition, but rather a product of the community.[166] It would follow that it is those passages where Jesus seems antinomian that actually represent the primitive tradition shining through the nomistic bias of Matthew and his church.[167] The Gospels (especially Matthew), in this view, may be said to contain a "re-judaizing" of the tradition about Jesus in order to conceal his truly radical perspective.[168]

---

[162]See most recently, R. Guelich, *The Sermon on the Mount* (Waco: Word, 1982), 134–74.

[163]G. Bornkamm, in G. Bornkamm, G. Barth, and H. J. Held, *Tradition and Interpretation in Matthew*, trans. Percy Scott (Philadelphia: Westminster, 1963), 39. This is forcefully countered by D. R. A. Hare, *The Theme of Jewish Persecution of Christians in the Gospel According to Matthew* (Cambridge: Cambridge University Press, 1967).

[164]In *Tradition and Interpretation in Matthew*, 70.

[165]G. Barth, in *Tradition and Interpretation in Matthew*, 164; cf. 159ff. See, however, W. D. Davies' refutation of the view that the Sermon on the Mount is a creation of Matthew to combat the influence of Paul on the church. *The Setting of the Sermon on the Mount* (Cambridge: Cambridge University Press, 1966), 316ff.

[166]R. Bultmann, *History of the Synoptic Tradition*, trans. John Marsh (New York: Harper & Row, 1968²), 138, 146.

[167]Cf. R. Bultmann, "The oldest material is clearly in the brief conflict sayings which express in parable-like form the attitude of Jesus to Jewish piety, e.g., Mark 7:15; 3:4; Matt. 23:16–19, 23f., 25f. In my view this is the first time that we have the right to talk of sayings of Jesus, both as to form and content." Ibid., 147.

[168]See, e.g., E. Stauffer, "Neue Wege der Jesusforschung" in *Gottes ist der Orient*, O. Eissfeldt Festschrift (Berlin, 1959), 185–86.

A fairer approach to the problem that faces us concerning Jesus and the Law is to avoid the forced choice between those passages where Jesus affirms the Law and those where he goes against the Law. Is it not conceivable that given the nature of his mission he can have said and done both? We may wonder whether real life is ever so uniform and uncomplicated as the absolutizing of a unitary strand of evidence seems to imply. Is it not fairer to hold these passages in tension and to try to understand that tension than to attribute one group (whichever) to the church and the other to Jesus?

We have seen one side of the tension in describing Jesus' break with the Law, and we must now turn our attention to the other side, i.e., the sense in which Jesus affirms the Law. Can the two sides be conceived as complementary rather than contradictory?

MATTHEW 5:17-20

No other passage in the New Testament is cited by Jewish writers more frequently and with more satisfaction in the Jewish reclamation of Jesus than Matthew 5:17-20. The argument is that if Jesus spoke the words recorded in these verses, he cannot be regarded as breaking with the Law in the way that has been described above. Jesus speaks in no uncertain terms of the permanency of the Law: he has not come to abolish the Law; neither an iota nor a dot will pass from it; the one who relaxes even the least of these commandments, teaching this to others, will be called least in the kingdom of heaven, whereas the one who keeps and teaches them will be called great.

Although this is not the place for a full exegesis of this difficult passage, some provisional exegetical comments are necessary. Verse 17 does obviously stress continuity between the mission of Jesus and the Law and the Prophets. The exact nuance of *plērōsai* ("to fulfill") is of course difficult to ascertain. Discussions of the word as it is found in verse 17 usually come to the conclusion that the meaning is "to establish,"[169] "to com-

---

[169]Thus David Hill, *The Gospel of Matthew*, NCB (London: Oliphants, 1972). "Jesus establishes the Law and the Prophets by realizing (or actualizing) them completely in his teaching and in his life." 117.

plete,"[170] "to fulfill,"[171] or "to perfect." Common to most, if not all, of these assessments is a teleological notion that suggests "to bring to its intended meaning." According to the Gospels, the continuity between the mission of Jesus and the Law and the Prophets is to be understood both in terms of his redemptive work and his ethical teaching. In our passage, as the context clearly shows, it is the latter that is in view.[172] Jesus brings the Law and the Prophets to their intended meaning by providing the correct interpretation of the Law, i.e., by expounding the true meaning of the commandments and therefore the true measure of righteousness.

According to verse 18, the Law remains fully authoritative as long as the present order exists ("till heaven and earth pass away"). This is expressed strongly so as to include even the minutiae (cf. "the least of these commandments," v. 19), indicating that the Law in its totality is in view. In the last clause, "until all is accomplished," Matthew calls attention to the final accomplishment of God's redemptive purposes.[173] But this

---

[170]J. Jeremias: "Jesus is not concerned with destroying the Law but with fulfilling it to its full eschatological measure." *New Testament Theology* (London: SCM, 1971), 207. Cf. W. D. Davies, who suggests that in its original context the word had an eschatological force. "Jesus brings the Law to its final end; he does this, as we stated, by utterly radicalizing it." *Christian Origins and Judaism* (London: Darton, Longman & Todd, 1962), 45.

[171]Thus Robert Banks, who concludes: "The word 'fulfill' in 5.17, then, includes not only an element of discontinuity (that which has now been realised *transcends* the Law) but an element of continuity as well (that which transcends the Law is nevertheless something to which the Law itself *pointed forward*)." *Jesus and the Law in the Synoptic Tradition* SNTSMS 28 (Cambridge: Cambridge University Press, 1975):210. For a similar perspective and a thorough, up-to-date discussion of the meaning of *plēroō,* see R. A. Guelich, *The Sermon on the Mount* (Waco: Word, 1982), 138–43.

[172]For the opposite conclusion, see Guelich, *The Sermon on the Mount,* 138–42.

[173]It is tempting to side with W. D. Davies in understanding the final clause of the verse ("until all is accomplished") as referring to the completion of Christ's work on the cross (as suggested in his article "Matthew 5:17,18," which first appeared in *Mélanges Bibliques en l'Honneur de' A. Robert,* and is now available in his *Christian Origins and Judaism*), since this fits nicely with the theology of the early church (especially, of course, Paul). However, not only does the passage have a futuristic eschatological ring to it, but this interpretation also seems to contradict the statement of Matt. 5:17 (i.e., the purpose of Jesus is *not* to destroy the law), as well as being difficult to reconcile with the words that follow. The second *heōs* clause, "until all is accomplished," may be tautologous with the first, "till heaven and earth pass away," but as an intentional emphasis on the eternal validity of the Law (and possibly by a conflation of originally separate dicta). More likely, however, is the interpretation that understands the *panta,* "all," as

serves as a reminder that for Matthew God's plan and purposes have hardly stood still since the giving of the Law through Moses. Through the ministry of Jesus, his death, and resurrection the kingdom of heaven has begun. To be sure, the consummation—eschatology proper—remains yet to occur, but this does not lessen the reality of fulfillment for Matthew. Indeed, there is a sense in which that fulfillment underlies the "fulfill" of verse 17. For Matthew, it is precisely the special identity and mission of Jesus that makes Jesus the finally authoritative interpreter of the Law.

In verse 19 "the least of these commandments" refers to the commandments of the Law. It must be remembered, however, that it is Jesus who expounds the true meaning of the commandments. It is precisely because the teaching that Jesus is about to give (especially the antitheses to follow) may *seem* to go against the Law, that Jesus speaks the words of 5:17ff. Although this teaching may sound new to the ears of his listeners, it is in fact the intended and completed meaning of the canonical Law. The person who obeys Jesus' teaching has obeyed "the least of these commandments," because through Jesus' teaching is perceived their real import.

Verse 20 supports this interpretation. The underlying question concerns the gaining of true righteousness—i.e., the righteousness toward which the Law is directed. The righteousness of the scribes and Pharisees falls short of the intended goal, primarily because (though not mentioned here) their understanding of the Law is misdirected. It is the teaching of Jesus, now to be given, that points to the real meaning of the Law and hence to the righteousness that alone is worthy of the kingdom.

This exegesis is, in fact, not very different from the common Jewish exegesis of the passage. Jewish scholars also commonly understand this passage to refer to a deepening of the Law, a fulfillment in the spiritual sense. Enelow describes this fulfillment as "a grasp of the full content and aim of the Law, an

---

referring to the demands of the Law. Cf. Robert Banks, "Matthew's Understanding of the Law," 236: "These are regarded not merely as imperatives but as signs which anticipate that which has now appeared in the teaching of Jesus. In it they can also be said now to have 'come to pass' (v. 18d) and to have been brought to 'fulfillment' (v. 17b)."

absorption and application of its spirit, an inward apprehension of its content, and the unfoldment of its purpose in actual life."[174] Daube argues that the Hebrew word underlying "to fulfill" is *qiyyam*, "to uphold," and that the remainder of the chapter proceeds along commonly accepted lines of rabbinic technique employed in the "upholding" of the Law.[175] Elsewhere he concludes that "the new demands promulgated by Jesus are conceived of as, in a way, already contained in the old ones laid down in Scripture."[176] However, at the same time, as we will see, the ethical teaching of Jesus is sufficiently different to be regarded by Jewish scholars as hopelessly idealistic and impractical for everyday living. The absoluteness of Jesus' ethic "means that Jesus brought the Law to its eschatological or ultimate fulfilment."[177]

As the last verse of the passage (v. 20) clearly indicates, it is true righteousness that above all concerns Matthew in this passage. This does not mean, however, that it is possible to put Jesus alongside the Pharisees as simply providing an alternate exegesis of the Law. As we have seen, the very authority with which Jesus interprets the Law puts him on an entirely different level. Jesus authoritatively brings the Law to its intended meaning not because he is a more able exegete than the Pharisees, but because of the fulfillment of God's promises that occurs in and through his ministry. That is, a salvation-historical reality is what finally accounts for the authoritative interpretation of the Law. The bringing to perfection of the Law as ethical teaching depends on the bringing of the Law to perfection in terms of salvation. The two cannot be separated.

Thus Jesus has not come to destroy the Law or the Prophets. He brings the Law to its deeper, intended meaning—something that can be done only because of the eschatological significance of his life and work. His final concern is indeed the establishment

---

[174]H. G. Enelow, *A Jewish View of Jesus* (New York: Macmillan, 1920), 68; cf. S. S. Cohon, "The Place of Jesus in the Religious Life of His Day," *JBL* 48 (1927):106.

[175]Daube, *The New Testament and Rabbinic Judaism*, 60–61.

[176]D. Daube, "Concessions to Sinfulness in Jewish Law," *JJS*, 10 (1959):10.

[177]W. D. Davies, *Christian Origins and Judaism* (Philadelphia: Westminster, 1962), 44; cf. C. H. Dodd, *History and the Gospel* (London: Nisbet, 1938), 126.

of that righteousness spoken of by the Torah and the Prophets. But he has the ability to penetrate beyond the letter of the biblical commandments to their true, inner significance so as to elucidate the ultimate, divine intent behind them.

Thus while Jesus does indeed at one level go against the letter of the text, transcending, for example, the Sabbath and dietary commandments, there is a deeper sense in which he at the same time upholds the Law. The key to this complexity lies in the identity of Jesus and the new era of salvation-history that dawns in and through his ministry. He alone therefore has the authority to give this definitive interpretation of Torah. The Jesus who says, "Till heaven and earth pass away, not an iota, not a dot, will pass from the law until all is accomplished" (Matt. 5:18) also says, "Heaven and earth will pass away, but my words will not pass away" (Matt. 24:35; Luke 21:33). It is Jesus' words that ultimately contain and preserve the eternal content of the Law and the Prophets. Again we are brought to the question of messianic authority, for "the attitude of Jesus to the Law implies his Messianic awareness or consciousness."[178]

MATTHEW 23

Another favorite passage among Jewish scholars in their reclamation of Jesus is Matthew 23:1–3, 23 (cf. Luke 11:42). Here Jesus says to the crowds and his disciples that the scribes and Pharisees sit on Moses' seat and that therefore it is right to "practice and observe whatever they tell you." Moreover, when Jesus faults the Pharisees for neglecting the weightier matters of the law, justice, mercy, and faith (Luke 11:42, "justice and the love of God"), he says, "These you ought to have done, without neglecting the others" (i.e., the tithing of dill, mint, and cumin—matters involving the Pharisaic extension of the Mosaic commandment concerning tithing).

How are we to reconcile these statements with the fact that, as we have seen, both Jesus and his disciples transgressed the teaching of the Pharisees (cf. Matt. 9:11, 14; 12:2)? How can

---

[178]Davies, *Christian Origins and Judaism*, 46.

Jesus say, "Practice and observe whatever they tell you" (23:3), when in the following sentence he indicates that the teachings of the Pharisees (especially in contrast of his, cf. 11:29–30) constituted heavy burdens and seems to rebuke the Pharisees for not making their demands lighter (23:4). Furthermore, in the criticism of the Pharisees that follows, it must be noted that Jesus criticizes not only their conduct but also their teaching (e.g., 23:16, 18). Indeed, earlier in the Gospel he has warned the disciples about "the leaven of the Pharisees and Sadducees," which is explicitly identified as their teachings (16:11–12). How are these apparently contradictory utterances to be reconciled?

The answer can only be that the Pharisees are to be honored simply because they concern themselves with the interpretation of the Law (they "sit on Moses' seat"). They are to be obeyed, but only to the extent that what they teach is not inconsistent with the true meaning of righteousness, which the disciples learned from Jesus, or—put positively—to the extent that their teaching is in accord with the true intention of the Mosaic Law.[179] In principle, the Pharisees are correct; in actuality, they are often wrong (cf. Luke 11:52: "You have taken away the key of knowledge"). The issue is again the real meaning of the Law and the nature of true righteousness. The knowledge of these things comes not from the rabbis, but from the "one teacher," the Christ (23:8, 10). So far as the minutiae were concerned, if the Pharisees wanted to tithe insignificant herbs, well and good, *as long as* they did not at the same time ignore the greater requirements, and hence the real meaning of Moses. The external is of little importance compared to the internal (23:25–28)—a motif already familiar to Matthew's readers from the Sermon on the Mount. Jesus again provides the true and final meaning of the Law, something the Pharisees were unable to do.

There is, then, first and foremost a strong continuity between the Law and the teaching of Jesus: Jesus brings the Law to its definitive interpretation. His fulfillment of the Law by bringing it to its intended meaning depends directly on his messianic

---

[179]Hill suggests that the point of 23:3 "may be to give the maximum force to the subsequent denunciation of the actions of the scribes." *Gospel of Matthew,* 310.

office and mission. Undeniably, therefore, we encounter a significant element of newness, and it is this newness that accounts for the authoritative manner in which Jesus expounds the meaning of Torah and the resultant aspect of discontinuity. This discontinuity does not cancel out the more basic continuity, but it is nevertheless there. Jesus does break with tradition while claiming that this break really involves fulfillment.[180] From the static perspective of the rabbis—i.e., the lack of movement in the history of salvation—such a conclusion was unthinkable. But given the dynamic of the presence of the kingdom, as Jesus announced it, this state of affairs is not beyond comprehension. Indeed, the coming of the Messianic Age would, according to much Jewish tradition, involve just some such restatement of the meaning of Torah as we find in the teaching of Jesus.[181] Jesus is the finally authoritative interpreter of the Torah: he penetrates in every instance beyond the letter of the Law to the will of God. The solution to the problem of Jesus and the Law is not simply to be found in the elevating of written Torah over the oral tradition of the Pharisees nor in the giving of primacy to the ethical over the ritual and ceremonial legislation, true though both of these observations are. It is to be found rather in the definitive (because eschatological) interpretation of the Law given by the bringer of the kingdom.[182]

To be sure, Jesus does not go as far as the early church and especially Paul in expressing the discontinuity in all clarity. Yet it is arguable that Paul makes explicit only what is already implicit in Jesus' words and deeds. Jesus necessarily leaves matters implicit because his view of the Law is bound up with his own identity and with his mission, which must come to its climax in

---

[180]Jules Isaac finds speaking in such a manner as this to be the result of "theological imagination," involving "subtleties" and "acrobatics." *Jesus and Israel*, 64. Is the problem found in the difficulty of conceiving of such complexity as a possibility, or is it a dislike for the possibility itself?

[181]See W. D. Davies, *Torah in the Messianic Age And/Or the Age to Come, JBLMS* 7 (Philadelphia: SBL, 1952); and the corrective article by R. Banks, "The Eschatological Role of Law in Pre- and Post-Christian Jewish Thought" in *Reconciliation and Hope*, Essays presented to L. Morris, ed. R. Banks (Exeter: Paternoster, 1974), 173–85.

[182]See H. J. Schoeps, "Jesus," in *Gottheit und Menschheit* (Stuttgart, 1950), 68.

his death and resurrection.[183] Only in this way can the new era come into existence.

Thus it was impossible for the full significance of Jesus' teaching about the Law to be immediately plain to the disciples even after the resurrection. That teaching was itself bound up with the complex newness of what had occurred in and through the total ministry of Jesus—the implications of which took some years to begin to be realized. We must, therefore, be prepared for a gradual understanding of the significance of Jesus' teaching concerning the Law on the part of the disciples. Furthermore, as long as the Christian community consisted solely of Jews, the issue of the Law was not likely to have been worked out. Indeed, only with Stephen, a Hellenistic Jew, do we find the beginning of a realization of the significance of Jesus as it bears on the temple and the Law (Acts 6:10–14). It is to be expected that the earliest Christians would continue in the Judaism in which they had been brought up. Thus it is understandable that Peter falls into difficulty at Antioch (Gal. 2:11–14) and that he must be enlightened by a vision before going to the house of Cornelius (Acts 10:9–16, 34–35). These incidents, often mentioned by Jewish scholars, do not necessitate the conclusion that Jesus did not speak and act with reference to the Law as the Gospels portray him doing. Again, we should note that Jesus spoke more implicitly than explicitly on these matters. It is for this reason, too, combined with his affirmation of Torah, that Jesus maintained a broad acceptability among the people, was allowed to preach in the synagogue, and was so difficult to find evidence against in his trial before the Jewish authorities.[184] It is also arguable that without a prior, though implicit, teaching of Jesus pertinent to the dietary restrictions Peter would *not* have eaten unclean food.

Similarly, the fact that no words of Jesus are cited in the Jerusalem Council of Acts 15—something often noted by Jewish

---

[183]Thus W. D. Davies writes: "Only when He had completed His service in death would He be justified in replacing the Old Torah by His own New Torah." *Christian Origins and Judaism*, 59; cf. 65.

[184]These points are set forth by Lapide, among other Jewish scholars, as evidence that Jesus did not break with the Law. *OCJ*, 139.

scholars—does not mean that Jesus could not have implicitly broken with the Law. The fact that Jesus spoke and acted as he did undoubtedly made the decision not to impose the Law on Gentiles much easier than it would have otherwise been, even if Jesus' words were not cited—which is not at all certain since Luke obviously gives a very telescoped account of the proceedings. It is important to note, furthermore, that the early church abandoned certain parts of Torah legislation without thinking that it was in any sense unfaithful to the teaching of Jesus.

We have seen that Jesus' break with tradition is very problematic for Jewish scholars. Most of those who admit the break find it necessary to appeal to a fundamental inconsistency deep within Jesus. Thus, for example, Montefiore writes concerning Matthew 15:11 that "in the heat of the conflict, and in the ardour of his ethical enthusiasm, Jesus probably did not realize the implications, the *Tragweite,* of his own saying."[185] Klausner calls Jesus' stance toward the Law "instinctive rather than conscious."[186] These statements sidestep the crucial issue in Jesus' break with tradition—his authority.

Only with considerable difficulty can Jewish scholars deny that something totally new is implied in Jesus' teaching, as well as in his deeds. Jesus taught with an unparalleled, independent, and self-conscious authority. The stance taken by Jesus toward the Law can therefore be understood only within the larger context of his ministry—that is, from a christological or kerygmatic perspective.[187] Robert Banks has expressed the radical shift caused by Jesus' perspective in these words:

> It, therefore, becomes apparent that it is not so much Jesus' stance towards the Law that he [Matthew] is concerned to depict; it is how the Law stands with regard to him, as the one who brings it to fulfillment, and to whom all attention must now be directed. For

---

[185]*RLGT,* 255.

[186]*JN,* 370.

[187]This is the strength of Guelich's treatment both of 5:17–20 and the entire sermon in which it occurs. Guelich, *The Sermon on the Mount.* Cf. too, for a similar approach, R. Banks, *Jesus and the Law in the Synoptic Tradition* (Cambridge: Cambridge University Press, 1975).

Matthew, then, it is not the question of Jesus' relation to the Law that is in doubt, but rather its relation to him![188]

The ministry of Jesus is, according to the Gospel narratives, a pivotal point in salvation history. Jesus, answering to protests concerning his failure to fast, says that "no one sews a piece of unshrunk cloth in an old garment" and "no one puts new wine into old wineskins . . . but new wine is for fresh skins" (Matt. 9:16–17; Mark 2:21–22; Luke 5:36ff.).[189] The new order has enormous consequences for what preceded. And when Matthew adds "and so both are preserved" he calls attention again to the fact that the change and the newness involve bringing the old to its intended meaning. Moreover, Jesus can say, "The law and the prophets were until John; since then the good news of the kingdom of God is preached" (Luke 16:16; Matt. 11:13). Newness is involved; continuity is implied. Without question, the coming of Jesus means something revolutionary for Judaism.[190] In the episode of the plucking of grain on the Sabbath Matthew records Jesus as saying, "I tell you, something greater than the temple is here" (12:6). This absolute authority of Jesus and this newness in viewpoint as it bears on the Law are correctly linked with the messianic claims of Jesus by Montefiore, Klausner, and Schoeps.[191] Thus in the last analysis, it is the Jewish scholars who stress the Jewishness of Jesus but who also accept the clear and striking uniqueness of Jesus that are the closest to the truth. Those at the other end of the spectrum, who deny any significant difference between Jesus and his contemporaries, cannot do justice to the teaching of Jesus generally, nor to his teaching concerning the Law specifically.

---

[188]Robert Banks, "Matthew's Understanding of the Law," *JBL* 93 (1974):242; cf. Banks, *Jesus and the Law in the Synoptic Tradition*, 251–52.

[189]Klausner clearly sees that a fundamental change is implied: "New matter must take on a completely new form." *JN,* 369; Montefiore quotes Klausner and seems to plead ignorance concerning the meaning of the words of the verse, *SG,* 1:60–61.

[190]For the clearest Jewish admission of this, see H. J. Schoeps, "Jesus und das jüdische Gesetz," in *Studien zur unbekannten Religions- und Geistegeschichte* (Göttingen, 1963), 59.

[191]Montefiore, *RT,* 120; Klausner, *JN,* 370; Schoeps, "Jesus und das jüdische Gesetz," 59.

There is, to sum up, no question but that it was Jesus' purpose to annul the rabbinic interpretations of the Law, interpretations that obscured its real meaning ("thus making void the word of God through your tradition which you hand on," Mark 7:13; Matt. 15:6). By his own authority Jesus thus set aside the oral interpretation that was held in such high esteem by the rabbis. Jesus, however, went beyond this. In principle, at least, he abrogated parts of the written Law itself, again solely on the basis of his own extraordinary authority.

Yet in the wake of this annulment Jesus does not propound a new law in place of the Mosaic Law. Instead, he proclaims the presence of the kingdom of God. His ethical teachings are not legislative, but descriptive of the righteousness of the kingdom,[192] and this righteousness is at the same time the true interpretation of the Mosaic Law. The conclusion of Jeremias is very appropriate:

> Thus it was Jesus himself who shook the foundations of the ancient people of God. His criticism of the *Torah*, coupled with his announcement of the end of the cult; his rejection of the *Halakah* and his claim to announce the final will of God, were the decisive occasion for the action of the leaders of the people against him, finally brought into action by the cleansing of the Temple. They took Jesus to be a false prophet. This accusation brought him to the cross.[193]

Clearly the problem of Jesus and the Law cannot be satisfactorily understood without coming to terms with his personal claims and his identity as the Messiah of Israel.

---

[192]See R. A. Guelich, "The Matthean Beatitudes: 'Entrance-Requirements' or Eschatological Blessings?" *JBL* 95 (1976):415–34; *The Sermon on the Mount*, 175–271. Cf. the earlier statements of Dibelius, *The Sermon on the Mount* (New York: Scribner, 1940), 77–78; J. Parkes, *Judaism and Christianity* (London: Victor Gollancz, 1948), 60; A. L. Williams, *The Doctrine of Modern Judaism Considered* (London: SPCK, 1939), 49.

[193]Jeremias, *New Testament Theology*, 211. Cf. G. E. Ladd: "On his own authority alone, Jesus set aside the principle of ceremonial purity embodied in much of the Mosaic legislation. This is a corollary of the fact that the righteousness of the Kingdom is to be no longer mediated by the law but by a new redemptive act of God, foreseen in the prophets, but now in process of being realized in the event of his own mission." *Jesus and the Kingdom* (New York: Harper & Row, 1964), 281; cf. 160.

CHAPTER FOUR

Eschatology and Ethics: The Kingdom of God

IN ITS ATTEMPT to understand Jesus within the framework of Judaism, modern Jewish scholarship has focused its attention on the teaching of Jesus. Jewish scholars have carefully and thoroughly searched the rabbinic literature to find teaching that parallels that of Jesus. The result of this comparative study has been the unanimous conclusion of Jewish scholarship that Jesus' teaching is essentially Jewish. This is regarded as true for nearly all of Jesus' teaching, but especially his ethical teaching. It is admitted by some, however, that at certain points Jesus does depart from what can be considered good Jewish teaching; yet in so doing, he is simply regarded as being in error. Thus Montefiore can say that the majority of Jews "insist that his teaching, where good, was not original, and where original was not Jewish or good."[1] We now turn to the teaching of Jesus as seen from the Jewish perspective, with special attention to the question of originality, and we begin with what is fundamental to all else: Jesus' preaching of the kingdom.

ESCHATOLOGY AND THE KINGDOM OF GOD

Jesus began his ministry with the preaching of the eschatological message of John the Baptist: "The time is fulfilled, and the kingdom of God is at hand; repent, and believe in the gospel" (Mark 1:15). This announcement indeed is at the heart of Jesus' ministry and teaching throughout the synoptic narratives. The disciples themselves are sent out by Jesus with the same

---

[1]C. G. Montefiore, "Jewish Conception of Christianity," *HJ* 28 (1929–30):249.

message: "The kingdom of God has come near to you" (Luke 10:9; cf. Matt. 10:7). Jesus, referring to his ministry of exorcism, says, "If it is by the finger of God that I cast out demons, then the kingdom of God has come upon you" (Luke 11:20; cf. Matt. 12:28). Jesus interprets his and his disciples' ministry in these words, spoken privately to the disciples: "Blessed are the eyes which see what you see! For I tell you that many prophets and kings desired to see what you see, and did not see it, and to hear what you hear, and did not hear it" (Luke 10:23–24; cf. Matt. 13:16–17). In response to the question of the Pharisees about when the kingdom was coming, Jesus replies, "The kingdom of God is not coming with signs to be observed; nor will they say 'Lo, here it is!' or 'There!' for behold, the kingdom of God is in the midst of you" (Luke 17:20–21). What is the Jewish understanding of this stress on the presence of the kingdom, so central to the purpose and message of Jesus?

The eschatological doctrine of a future coming of the kingdom of God is of course found in the Old Testament and among the rabbis.[2] It has not, however, been regarded by Jewish scholars as in any sense central or even very significant in rabbinic Judaism.[3] The tendency has been for Jewish scholars to ignore the apocalyptic literature as an aid to understanding first-century Judaism. Apocalypticism as a possible influence on the rabbis has often been minimized.[4] The rabbinic Judaism of the Talmud, on the other hand, has been designated as "normative" Judaism, although this assumption is under increasing criticism.[5] Sandmel, for example, stresses the existence of "varieties of Judaism" in

---

[2]For a full study of the rabbinic view of the kingdom (invisible, universal, and national), see S. Schechter, *Some Aspects of Rabbinic Theology* (London: Adam and Charles Black, 1909), 65–115.

[3]See S. Sandmel, *Judaism and Christian Beginnings* (New York: Oxford University Press, 1978), 206.

[4]E.g., C. G. Montefiore, "Jewish Scholarship and Christian Silence," *HJ* 1 (1902–3):341.

[5]See J. Neusner, "The Use of the Later Rabbinic Evidence for the Study of First-Century Pharisaism," in *Approaches to Ancient Judaism: Theory and Practice*, Brown Judaic Studies 1, ed. W. S. Green (Missoula, Mont.: Scholars, 1978), 215–28; R. A. Kraft, "The Multiform Jewish Heritage of Early Christianity" in J. Neusner, ed., *Christianity, Judaism and other Greco-Roman Cults*, Studies for Morton Smith, 4 vols. (Leiden: Brill, 1975), 3:174–99.

the first century, noting that "those who wrote apocalypses and those ancients who came to frown on those apocalypses came out of a common Judaism."[6] The dichotomy between Pharisaism and apocalypticism is a false one.[7] Pharisaism, based on the Old Testament, was not without its eschatological expectations; apocalypticism held the Torah in the same high regard that Pharisaism did. The eventual rejection of the apocalyptic literature from the Jewish canon of Scripture was due not so much to an anti-apocalyptic bias, but to a reaction against the rise of the Christian literature and the disillusionment with apocalyptic hopes after the disaster of A.D. 70. Some Jewish analyses of Jesus have nevertheless been inclined to separate Jesus from Pharisaic or prophetic Judaism and to explain him instead solely on the basis of contemporary apocalypticism.

Most Jewish scholars admit the centrality of the kingdom for Jesus, but argue that he taught only that the kingdom was imminent, not that it was already present in and through his ministry. In this belief in the imminence of the kingdom, Jesus was of course wrong, they say, but they regard this as an honorable error, since many other outstanding Jews since his day have been mistaken in a similar zeal. Indeed, the Jewish conviction is that the kingdom has not come in any real sense, and this forces Jews to reject the teaching of Christianity about Jesus. "No, there is still no kingdom, no peace, and no redemption. . . . Jesus of Nazareth was not the promised one because he did not redeem the world."[8] This sentiment, expressed here by Ben-Chorin, is universal in Judaism, although it seldom comes to such forthright expression.

It is agreed by Jewish scholars that Jesus held the typical Jewish expectation so far as the kingdom is concerned. Montefiore emphasizes that "almost invariably, if not always," Jesus meant by the kingdom of God something eschatological.[9] For

[6]Sandmel, *Judaism and Christian Beginnings,* 15.

[7]See W. D. Davies, "Apocalyptic and Pharisaism," in *Christian Origins and Judaism,* 19–30. Cf. also G. E. Ladd, "Why Not Prophetic-apocalyptic?" *JBL* 76 (1957):192–200, which discusses a related false dichotomy.

[8]S. Ben-Chorin, *Jesus im Judentum* (Wuppertal, 1970), 67–68. Further, "we know no enclave of redemption in the midst of an unredeemed world." Ibid.

[9]*RT,* 60; cf. Sandmel, *WJJ,* 84.

Klausner, Jesus expected a kingdom that was to be restored to Israel "in the political sense." "Jesus was, therefore, truly Jewish in everything pertaining to the belief in a worldly and even a political Messiah."[10] Klausner conceives Jesus' task to have been that of preparing his followers for the imminent arrival of the kingdom: "The real necessity was to stir up a great popular movement of penitents and well-doers; thus the kingdom of heaven would be brought still nearer and with it the occasion of Jesus' manifestation as Messiah."[11] According to Kohler, Jesus' ethics must be regarded as not for a world rejoicing in fulfillment, but "for a few of the elect and saintly ones who wait for the immediate downfall of this world and the rise of another."[12]

Vermes also interprets Jesus' message as the conviction "that God's rule over the world was imminent."[13] Vermes finds the Gospels "inconclusive" on the question of the time of the coming of the kingdom.[14] But the question of a past, present, or future kingdom is "irrelevant" because, according to Vermes, Jesus equates the kingdom with what is experienced through repentance. Thus the kingdom is interpreted as the subjective experience of those who repent. "It is in the surrender of the self to God's will that his sovereignty is realized on earth."[15] It is very doubtful, however, that Jesus' consciousness of the presence of the kingdom was the same as the rabbis' sense of the kingdom as present. If that is all Jesus meant, why did his message create such a stir? Certainly the point of Jesus' announcement is that the eschatological kingdom somehow becomes present in his deeds and words.

Other Jewish scholars admit that the explanation of Jesus' teaching about the kingdom as exclusively imminent does not tell the whole story. If for Jesus the full manifestation of the kingdom

---

[10]*JN*, 402; cf. Maccoby, *RJ*, 115–24, with the conviction that Jesus believed himself to be that Messiah.

[11]Ibid., 405; Maccoby holds the same perspective, see *RJ*, 113–14.

[12]K. Kohler, "Christianity in Its Relation to Judaism," *JE*, 4:51.

[13]*JJ*, 27; *GJJ*, 24. Vermes argues as "a methodological principle," that "the notion of a *parousia* is likely to reflect church apologetics and not Jesus' own ideas." Ibid.

[14]*GJJ*, 23.

[15]Ibid., 25.

lay in the future, it was at the same time, in some sense, also said to be present in his ministry. Thus, although Montefiore argues that Jesus "nearly always" spoke of an eschatological or future kingdom, he admits that the kingdom is also paradoxical in nature, being present as well as future.[16] He detects a similar double strain in the rabbinic concept of God's rule or reign. For the rabbis, God's kingship was experienced in the present, but also awaited a future consummation.[17] The rabbinic expectation of the Messianic Age, furthermore, included both material and spiritual elements, the latter being increasingly stressed with the rise of the doctrines of resurrection and immortality. With these Jewish conceptions of the kingdom Jesus would have been in essential agreement.[18]

Montefiore senses, however, that this does not do justice to the teaching of Jesus. Thus concerning Mark 1:15 he writes that even if the words "the time is fulfilled" are not actually authentic, "there is no reason to doubt that their sentiment was his."[19] Commenting on Matthew 12:28, Montefiore writes, "The Kingdom of God has already begun with the appearance of Jesus the Messiah. The rule of the devil and his agents is passing away; the rule of God, the new era, has begun."[20]

Klausner wrestles with the same paradox. Jesus' view of the kingdom "differed but little from that of his fellow Jews in the early Tannaitic period";[21] it involved a future reality quite unlike the present age—the so-called world to come—which Jesus mistakenly believed to be imminent. Nevertheless, for Jesus "in real fact, the kingdom of heaven had already begun: in a certain sense it had come."[22] Herein lies a radical difference: "The kingdom

---

[16]*SG*, 1:61; C. G. Montefiore, *The Old Testament and After* (London: Macmillan, 1923), 255; cf. *SG*, 2:161; *RLGT*, 131.

[17]*RLGT*, 131.

[18]*RT*, 61ff., 67. On the importance of resurrection to the Jews and Jesus, see also Schonfield (*PP*, 151–52) and P. Lapide, *Auferstehung: Ein jüdisches Glaubenserlebnis* (Munich, 1977).

[19]*SG*, 1:57.

[20]*SG*, 2:622.

[21]*JN*, 398.

[22]Ibid., 403; faced with this complexity, Friedlander writes, "We confess that we cannot reconcile the divergent views of the Gospels as to the Kingdom." *JSSM*, 143.

of heaven, according to Jesus, is in the present. The kingdom of heaven, according to Judaism, is to be 'in the latter days.' "[23]

Like Montefiore, Flusser notes that the rabbis believed in a present kingdom or rule of God as well as in the future, eschatological kingdom.[24] Jesus and the rabbis naturally shared common expectations about the age to come. They also agreed about the present to some extent, since for both the rabbis and Jesus the kingdom of heaven is to find expression on earth, and some individuals already live in the kingdom of God. Yet Flusser is aware of a difference: "There are individuals, therefore, who are already in the kingdom of heaven, not, as with the rabbis, because it was always so, but because at a specific point in time the kingdom has broken out upon earth." In the final analysis, Flusser speaks of the uniqueness of Jesus: "He is the only Jew of ancient times known to us, who preached not only that men were on the threshold of the end of time, but that the new age of salvation had already begun."[25] For Jesus, the kingdom of heaven is "the eschatological rule of God that has dawned already" and "a divinely willed movement that spreads among men over the earth."[26]

Of all Jewish writers on Jesus, Flusser has here given the most forthright and accurate statement about Jesus' teaching concerning the kingdom. There is a sharp contrast here between the viewpoint of the rabbis and Jesus. For the rabbis, as Flusser points out, "Israel must want to do only the will of God, then the kingdom of heaven will be revealed to them."[27] Abrahams, noting the connection between repentance and the Messianic Age, similarly captures the important difference between the rabbis and Jesus on this point: "The formula of John (or Jesus) was: Repent *for* the Kingdom is at hand. The Pharisaic formula was: Repent *and* the Kingdom is at hand."[28]

---

[23]*JN*, 406.

[24]D. Flusser, *Jesus* (New York: Herder & Herder, 1969), 85.

[25]Ibid., 88.

[26]Ibid., 91.

[27]Ibid., 87.

[28]*SP*, 1:34; cf. H. J. Schoeps, "Jesus," in *Gottheit und Menschheit* (Stuttgart, 1950), 62.

It is interesting to note the difference in the interpretation of Luke 17:21 among Jewish scholars. Those who insist that Jesus' view of the kingdom was consistently futuristic and that he never taught that the eschatological kingdom was making itself manifest in his person and ministry, explain the verse as a "spiritualizing" of the concept of the kingdom, something itself regarded as un-Jewish. The issue hinges on the meaning of *entos hymōn*: Is it to be translated "within you" or "among you"? Sandmel writes: "In at least one passage (Luke 17:21), 'the kingdom of God is within you,' the idea is 'spiritualized' through making it an individual matter."[29] Lapide notes that the kingdom of heaven stands at the center of Jesus' teaching, but that as his ministry proceeded, Jesus had necessarily to reformulate his teaching about the kingdom, removing it from objective reality and "interiorizing" it so that he began to announce that "the kingdom is within you."[30] This tactic, however, did not save Jesus from dying in disappointment and despair. The tendency to spiritualize the kingdom finds its logical outcome, according to Schonfield, in the eventual discarding by the church of the expectation of an earthly kingdom of God as being "insufficiently spiritual."[31]

It is Ben-Chorin, however, who has made the most of the spiritualizing of the kingdom supposedly indicated by Luke 17:21. He divides the ministry of Jesus into three stages: (1) eschatology, (2) introversion, and (3) passion. In the first stage Jesus announced the imminent coming of the kingdom. When, however, the kingdom failed to materialize (Matt. 10:23, "You will not have gone through all the towns of Israel before the Son of man comes"), Jesus had to revise his message and did so by introverting the kingdom message, which then became the kingdom of God "within you." This too, however, failed ultimately, leading to the crucifixion of Jesus and his cry of despair. Jesus proved to be, from the Jewish viewpoint, a tragic failure.[32]

---

[29]*WJJ*, 84.
[30]*ÖCJ*, 143.
[31]*PP*, 196.
[32]*BJ*, 26–27; *Jesus im Judentum* (Wuppertal, 1970), 44–45.

Montefiore is apparently uncertain about the meaning of Luke 17:21. He does say, however, that "there is no clear Rabbinic parallel to a conception of the Kingdom as 'a spiritual principle, which works unseen and regeneratively in the hearts of men.'"[33] As we have seen, he inclines to the view that Jesus' doctrine of the kingdom is almost always strictly eschatological. "How far it is ever a 'process' or an 'inward spiritual fact' is very much more doubtful."[34] Far more certain about the meaning of Luke 17:21 is Klausner, who says of the verse: "In other words, the Messiah is already *among you*—not as Tolstoy interpreted the saying, 'within man', but among such men as acted aright."[35] Schonfield too resists strongly any understanding of Luke 17:21 as an internalizing of the kingdom. The kingdom of God in the Synoptics "is a state of affairs on earth," to be "equated with the time when the Messianic Age will commence."[36]

We may summarize at this point by saying that the rabbis and Jesus share the expectation of a coming, eschatological kingdom of God to be realized on the earth. The nature of the kingdom would have been agreed on essentially, if not altogether, by the rabbis and Jesus. But despite this obvious and expected overlap of perspective, Jesus stands alone in proclaiming that the kingdom is present—not that of God's universal and timeless rule, but the promised eschatological kingdom, in advance of its fullest and final manifestation. This announcement is inseparable from Jesus' own identity, since the existence of the kingdom depends on his own appearance in the midst of history. Klausner correctly describes this relation between the kingdom and Jesus: "Jesus, from the moment of his baptism, looked upon himself as the Messiah; the Messiah was, therefore, already in the world, and so the kingdom of heaven, the kingdom of the Messiah, was likewise in existence in the world."[37] The idea of the existence of the eschatological kingdom in the present is intimately bound up with the person of Jesus and his messianic consciousness. This

---

[33]*RLGT*, 368; cf. *SG*, 2:1012–15.

[34]*SG*, 1:61.

[35]*JN*, 404.

[36]*FCS*, 68.

[37]*JN*, 403.

is allowed by Montefiore, even if indirectly: "The Kingdom of God which he announces is not only God's kingdom: it is also *his* kingdom."[38] The kingdom is present because the messianic King is present, and the kingdom is his gracious gift. For the rabbis, by contrast, the Torah stands as that which is of central importance in the present. By studying it and practicing it, the Jew brought nearer the eschatological advent of the kingdom.[39] From the Jewish perspective, then, as Klausner puts it, a "two-fold misapprehension of Jesus—the nearness of the kingdom of heaven and his Messiahship—perpetuated his memory and created Christianity."[40] Friedlander writes, "The Jews instinctively rejected the whole scheme of the Messianic Kingdom as expounded by Jesus."[41]

As regards other matters touching on eschatology, Jesus and the rabbis are in substantial agreement. Montefiore, reflecting his Liberal Judaism, is equally critical of the rabbis and Jesus so far as the doctrine of eternal punishment is concerned: "The views of Jesus about hell seem to have been no better and no worse than those of his contemporaries."[42] If the doctrine of future judgment was shared by Jesus and the rabbis, so also was the belief in a resurrection life their common possession.[43] Montefiore notes that the hope of immortality arose in the intertestamental period, and says that "by AD 20 it had already become, though not in the form in which the modern and liberal Jew clings to it, accepted dogma of the Pharisaic and Rabbinic synagogue."[44] In this one important point the Old Testament needed supplementing; in so doing, Jesus was only following the lead of those before him.[45]

---

[38]"The Significance of Jesus for His Own Age," *HJ* 10 (1911–12):776.

[39]*RLGT*, 254.

[40]*JN*, 405.

[41]*JSSM*, 162.

[42]*RLGT*, 332. Montefiore's criticism of the notion of eternal punishment is unsparing. Cf. *RLGT*, 82, 152, 244, 285–86; *The Old Testament and After*, 216, 288; "An Ancient Arraignment of Providence," *HJ* 17 (1918–19):271.

[43]C. G. Montefiore, "The Religious Teaching of the Synoptic Gospels in Its Relation to Judaism," *HJ* 20 (1921–22):436.

[44]C. G. Montefiore, "The Old Testament and the Modern Jew," 568; cf. Montefiore's own personal beliefs in "The Desire for Immortality," *JQR* 14 (1902):96–110.

[45]C. G. Montefiore, "The Old Testament and Its Ethical Teaching," *HJ* 16 (1917–18):238–39.

Jewish scholars, indeed, have generally not devoted much attention to Jesus' eschatological teaching. The reason for this is that the impetus for the modern Jewish study of Jesus comes almost exclusively from the Liberal wing of Judaism. But this perspective attaches little value to eschatology, which is regarded at best as speculation; only ethical teachings are relevant to the modern age. As we will see, however, there is a most important connection between the eschatological teaching of Jesus and his ethical teaching, so that the latter is understandable only in the light of the former.

THE ETHICAL TEACHINGS OF JESUS

To the Liberal Jewish scholars who have provided the impetus for the new Jewish understanding and appreciation of Jesus' teaching, nothing is more important than the ethical teachings of Jesus. Since in their view, ethics constitutes the very essence of religion and is the crowning achievement of Judaism,[46] it is here above all that the teachings of Jesus and Judaism must be compared. This preoccupation with ethics to the comparative neglect of other matters, as we have seen, is plainly the result of the rise of religious liberalism in the nineteenth century.[47] As in every area of Jesus' teaching, but here especially, Jewish scholars are concerned to stress the Jewishness of Jesus.

One of the most widely accepted conclusions of modern Jewish scholarship is that the ethical teachings of Jesus are fully Jewish. As we will see, this conclusion does not by any means apply to every aspect of Jesus' ethical teaching, but particularly to those elevated aspects that humanity as a whole has come to esteem. The Sermon on the Mount as a repository of the ethical teaching of Jesus is held in high regard by Jewish scholarship. Friedlander has taken the trouble to examine the Sermon on the

---

[46]See L. Baeck, *The Essence of Judaism,* ET by V. Grubenwieser and L. Pearl (London: Macmillan, 1936). "Judaism is not merely ethical, *but ethics constitutes its principle, its essence.*" 52; cf. C. G. Montefiore, "The Spirit of Judaism," in F. J. Foakes-Jackson and K. Lake, eds., *The Beginnings of Christianity* (London: Macmillan, 1920), 1:35–81.

[47]Cf. G. Lindeskog, "Jesus als Problem," *Judaica* 6 (1950):241; cf. Sandmel, *WJJ,* 95ff.

Mount in light of rabbinic and Jewish parallels and concludes that "four-fifths of the Sermon on the Mount is exclusively Jewish."[48] After his discussion of the Sermon on the Mount, Ben-Chorin draws an even stronger conclusion: the sermon is Jewish teaching material and contains "no originality." What is strewn about in Talmud and Midrash is concisely gathered together in the sermon, and therein lies its "eternal power."[49] Speaking of the ethical teaching of Judaism and the Gospels, Klausner's conclusion is typical (he mentions agreement with Geiger and Graetz) and given in italics: *"Throughout the Gospels there is not one item of ethical teaching which cannot be paralleled either in the Old Testament, the Apocrypha, or in the Talmudic and Midrashic literature of the period near to the time of Jesus."*[50] This general affirmation of the Jewishness of Jesus' ethical teaching finds expression in the following specific areas, some of which nevertheless involve considerable difficulty for Jewish scholars.

The Love Commandment

The natural place to begin this discussion of the ethical teaching of Jesus, viewed from the Jewish perspective, is with the answer of Jesus to the question concerning the "greatest commandment":

> You shall love the Lord your God with all your heart, and with all your soul, and with all your mind. This is the great and first commandment. And a second is like it, You shall love your neighbor as yourself. On these two commandments depend all the law and the prophets (Matt. 22:37–40; Mark 12:30–31; cf. Luke 10:27).

It is the conjoining of these two commands that provides the basis of Jesus' ethical teaching. Jewish scholars, however, are quick to point out that this particular conjunction was not novel with Jesus. Thus Daube says of the twofold law of love: "These were coupled as basic requirements already in pre-Christian Juda-

---

[48]*JSSM*, 266.
[49]*BJ*, 68; 83.
[50]*JN*, 384.

ism."[51] Concerning the connection between love for God and love for others, Abrahams' conclusion is to the same effect: "It therefore is not at all unlikely that such combinations as we find in the Synoptics were a common-place of Pharisaic teaching."[52] Jacobs refers to the answer of Jesus as "declaring the essential solidarity of his own views with those of the Old Testament and of current Judaism."[53] Schonfield mentions that although Christians ("including bishops") can be heard to say that Jesus' teaching of love for one's neighbor as for oneself is original, in fact it is but a combination of passages from Leviticus and Deuteronomy.[54] Flusser says of the double love commandment: "the fact that it does not appear in the rabbinical documents that have come down to us is probably a sheer accident."[55] Flusser takes note of some similarity, but also some difference, between Jesus and his contemporaries: "Those who listened to Jesus' preaching of love might well have been moved by it. Many in those days thought as he did. Nonetheless, in the clear purity of his love they must have detected something very special." Like the Hillelites, Jesus taught love, but Jesus "pointed the way further to unconditional love—even of one's enemies and of sinners."[56]

Loving One's Enemy

From the perspective of Jewish scholarship, one of the most significant and difficult sayings of Jesus is found in the Sermon on the Mount: "You have heard that it was said, 'You shall love your neighbor and hate your enemy.' But I say to you, Love your

---

[51]D. Daube, *The New Testament and Rabbinic Judaism* (London, 1956), 247. Cf. E. Rivkin, *A Hidden Revolution* (Nashville: Abingdon, 1978), 304ff. Daube proposes that Matthew's omission of the phrase "Hear, O Israel; the Lord our God, the Lord is one" (found in the Marcan parallel, 12:29) is the result of his desire to abide by the strict rules of rabbinic scholarship and thus have Jesus' answer a technically correct presentation of "precept." Ibid., 247ff.

[52]*SP*, 1:18.

[53]*JE*, 7:165; cf. similarly, J. B. Stern, "Jesus' Citation of Dt. 6,5 and Lv 19,18 in the Light of Jewish Tradition," *CBQ* 28 (1966):312–16.

[54]*FCS*, 109–10. Cf. Joseph Jacobs, "Jesus of Nazareth—In History," *JE*, 7:165.

[55]D. Flusser, *Jesus*, 71.

[56]Ibid., 74.

enemies and pray for those who persecute you'' (Matt. 5:43–44; cf. Luke 6:27–28, 35). In the first place, of course, it is objected that nowhere in the Old Testament is there an injunction to hate one's enemy. Ben-Chorin finds the suggestion ''most astonishing'' and refers the reader to Exodus 23:4–5, where one is commanded to help one's enemy.[57] Possibly, however, Jesus had in mind a viewpoint derived from passages such as Deuteronomy 23:3ff. and Psalm 139:21–22. But more important than this misrepresentation, according to Montefiore, the statement is misleading, since Jesus speaks only of relations between Israelites.[58]

This latter point is important to Jewish scholars because they do not see Jesus advancing the position held by the rabbis with respect to the Gentiles. Thus when Jesus speaks of loving one's neighbor, he does not mean to include non-Jews. The parable of the Good Samaritan is the one exception, but it is found only in the Gospel of Luke. And, according to Montefiore, if such a revolutionary idea had been in Jesus' mind, he would certainly have spelled it out in the Sermon on the Mount passage concerning enemies.[59] He writes, ''While I would predicate not merely nobility and beauty, but also originality of the parable of the Good Samaritan, it is going much too far to say that Jesus deliberately and consciously 'freed the conception of neighbor from its Jewish limitations.' ''[60] Jacobs is constrained (apparently by its strangeness) to speculate that ''the Good Samaritan'' was originally ''the Good Israelite''; the change is reckoned to anti-Semitic influence on the New Testament.[61] Jewish scholars do not find much, if anything, that is new in what Jesus or the Gospel writers have to say about the Gentiles.

There is always an understandable interest on the part of Jews in demonstrating that the rabbis do not make a bad showing

---

[57]*BJ*, 79; cf. G. Friedlander, who calls it ''a fine example of deliberate invention,'' *JSSM*, 69–70; cf. P. Lapide, *ÖCJ*, 137. Lapide resists any explanation of Jesus' words about hating one's enemy as deriving from the Qumran community. Ibid., 138, n. 29.

[58]C. G. Montefiore, ''The Old Testament and Its Ethical Teaching,'' *HJ* 16 (1917–18):241.

[59]*RLGT*, 345; cf. Montefiore's skepticism concerning the parable. *SG*, 2:84.

[60]C. G. Montefiore, ''The Originality of Jesus,'' *HJ* 28 (1929–30):108.

[61]*JE*, 7:162.

when compared with the Gospels. Abrahams writes, "It is indeed remarkable how many stories are to be found in the Rabbinic sources of conduct very like that of the Good Samaritan."[62] Commenting on the parable of the Good Samaritan, Ben-Chorin notes that love for brother and neighbor is also found in the Old Testament.[63] The Pharisee too insisted that his neighbor was any man in need;[64] hatred was generally condemned by the rabbis.[65] Any "hatred" for the non-Israelite was justified only insofar as he was connected with idolatry.[66] This, however, is a rather theoretical truth, since in fact nearly all Gentiles were regarded as idolatrous.[67] Montefiore admits that the rabbis were rather equivocal in their attitude toward the Gentiles. Thus, although it is unfair to say that hatred of the Gentiles was considered correct, it is also unfair to say that the non-Jew was loved as much as the fellow Jew.[68]

Montefiore further points out that although the legal relations existing between Jews were inapplicable to non-Jews, the latter were included in the teachings of the *moral* law, which knew no limitations of nationality.[69] Billerbeck concludes from a Talmudic saying (Jer. Megillah iii §2, 74a) that the rabbis did teach the hatred of enemies. Montefiore answers that the question involved is a specifically legal matter and that the passage does not reflect typical rabbinic morality.[70] Montefiore's candid con-

---

[62]*SP*, 2:39.

[63]*BJ*, 101.

[64]Abrahams, *SP*, 2:35.

[65]Montefiore, *RLGT*, 88–89.

[66]*RLGT*, 86–87.

[67]Cf. Montefiore's concession that every non-Jew seemed an enemy at times. *RLGT*, 69–70; see also G. Friedlander's severe criticism of Montefiore at this point. *JSSM*, 70–71.

[68]*RLGT*, 68. See also J. Piper, *"Love Your Enemies,"* SNTSM 38 (Cambridge: Cambridge University Press, 1979):48.

[69]*RLGT*, 65.

[70]Ibid., 102; Montefiore says the words may have been quoted "as a mere joke, or for a hundred possible reasons." Ibid. The explanation of difficult rabbinic sayings as mere humor is a common one in Jewish scholarship. Cf. C. G. Montefiore and H. Loewe, eds., *A Rabbinic Anthology* (London: Macmillan, 1938), xlvi. Longenecker, realizing that he may be classed "a humorless fool," remarks that "there are light touches in the Talmud, but the work is a basically serious one. And it was meant to be taken seriously." Richard N. Longenecker, *Paul: Apostle of Liberty* (New York: Harper & Row, 1964), 75, n. 48.

clusion on the whole matter, however, is that particularism did constitute the prevailing mood of the rabbis and that "Rabbinic teaching *was* defective about love of the foreigner and the idolater."[71] Despite their conception of God as the creator of all, it must be admitted that "any idea of universal love to all men, Gentile and Jew, was very far from the Rabbinic mind."[72]

David Flusser has detected a noticeable shift in perspective among certain Jews of the pre-Christian era.[73] Moving away from a simplistic notion of compensatory justice, these Jews began to speak of serving God out of love rather than compulsion. The way one treated one's neighbor who was ultimately, before God, "like yourself,"[74] was the way one could expect to be treated by God. This is the background to the teaching of Jesus in the double commandment to love God and neighbor. A new sense of human solidarity began to emerge and the distance between the righteous and sinners was no longer regarded as absolute. From this it is not far to conclude, as did the rabbis before Jesus, that the Golden Rule in negative form ("Do not do to others what is hateful to yourself") is applicable even to one's enemies. Even at Qumran, where hatred of one's enemies (who were also, by definition, God's enemies) was encouraged (IQS 1:9–11; 10:17–20), the members of the community were not actually to render evil to anyone.[75] Vengeance is God's, and granted the imminence of eschatology (from their perspective) one must be content to leave matters with God.[76] Ben-Chorin nevertheless points out the difference between Jesus and Qumran at this point, though elsewhere he finds that Jesus' teaching parallels that of the Qumran community.[77] While this new sensitivity

---

[71]*RLGT*, 62–63.

[72]*RLGT*, 70. The abstract doctrine of the common creaturehood of man was obscured by the concrete division of men into Jews and non-Jews. Ibid., 74.

[73]See D. Flusser, "A New Sensitivity in Judaism and the Christian Message," *HTR* 61 (1968): 107–27; Flusser, *Jesus*, 65–83.

[74]Flusser understands the words "Love your neighbor as yourself" to mean "Love your neighbor, a fellowman like yourself." "A New Sensitivity," 116.

[75]See K. Stendahl, "Hate, Non-Retaliation, and Love. IQS x. 17–20 and Rom. 12:19–21," *HTR* 55 (1962):343–55.

[76]K. Stendahl aptly remarks, "Why walk around with a little shotgun when the atomic blast is imminent?" *HTR* 55 (1962):344–45.

[77]*BJ*, 79–80.

provides the environment in which Jesus preached, Flusser regards the teaching of Jesus as "unique and incomparable," especially in its exhortation of *love* toward one's enemies.[78]
"Christianity surpasses Judaism, at least theoretically, in its approach of love to all men."[79] A similar conclusion is drawn by
Lapide, who notes that while Judaism knows no hatred of the
enemy, it also knows no love of the enemy, and therefore the
command to love one's enemy is new—indeed, in Lapide's view,
it is "the only new thing in the Sermon on the Mount."[80] This,
however, is denied by Friedlander who, after citing some passages that exhort kindness to an enemy (but which hardly prove
Friedlander's point), concludes, "Jesus then was not teaching his
contemporaries anything new in saying 'Love your enemies and
pray for them who persecute you.'"[81] Abrahams, by contrast,
noting some partial parallels in Jewish literature, still frankly
concludes, "We do not find in the Rabbinic literature a parallel
to the striking paradox, *Love your enemies.*"[82]

Some Jewish scholars see an ulterior motive in the Christian
evaluation and limitation of the Old Testament command "You
shall love your neighbor as yourself" (Lev. 19:18). Inevitably, it
is claimed, Christian scholars minimize its value in order to enhance the originality of Jesus' statements.[83] Montefiore, who
holds a consistently high view of Old Testament and rabbinic
morality, is at the same time able to say, "I would not cavil with
the view that Jesus is to be regarded as the first great Jewish
teacher to frame such a sentence as: 'Love your enemies, do good
to them who hate you, bless them that curse you, and pray for
them who ill-treat you' (Luke vi, 27, 28)."[84] In contrast to the
common Jewish opinion, Montefiore places the exhortation to

---

[78]"In Judaism hatred is practically forbidden but love to the enemy is not pre-
scribed." Flusser, "A New Sensitivity," 126. Cf. *Jesus,* 70; "Jesus," *EJ,* 10:13; cf.
Stendahl, "Hate, Non-Retaliation, and Love," 355.

[79]Flusser, "A New Sensitivity," 127.

[80]*ÖCJ,* 138.

[81]*JSSM,* 73.

[82]*SP,* 1:164.

[83]Cf. Montefiore, "The Old Testament and Its Ethical Teaching," 244. Such a
statement coming from Montefiore is all the more significant because he is one of the few
Jewish scholars who claim originality for Jesus.

[84]*RLGT,* 103.

love one's enemies "among the noblest specimens of human ethics, among the finest of human ideals and commands."[85] This appreciation of the teaching is clearly made possible by the interpretation put on it by Montefiore. First, as we have already noted, Jesus must not be thought of as referring to either the public enemy or the non-Jew.[86] Indeed, the verse must be regarded as neither including nor excluding them, for they were simply not in Jesus' mind at the time. By the term *enemy* he meant nothing more than the "private enemy of the individual."[87] Moreover, by *love* he did not mean the conjuring up of emotional feelings, but simply (1) the eradication of hatred and revenge, (2) praying for their conversion and welfare, and (3) doing good for them at every opportunity. In all of this, "Jesus unites himself with the *very* best Rabbinic teaching of his own and later times. It is, perhaps, only in trenchantness and eager insistency that he goes beyond it."[88]

When Jewish scholars hear "Love your enemies" from the lips of Jesus, however, their minds seem automatically to turn to Matthew 23. Montefiore writes, "How much more telling his injunction would have been if we had had *a single story* about his doing good to, and praying for, a single Rabbi or Pharisee! One grain of practice is worth a pound of theory."[89] Far from keeping his own teaching in the Sermon on the Mount, Jesus castigates his enemies with such phrases as "vipers" and "children of hell," and says to them, "Depart from me, you cursed, into the eternal fire" (Matt. 25:41). These, says Montefiore, are Jesus' worst teachings, and in the utterance of them Jesus demonstrates a grave inconsistency.[90] "To the hardest excellence of all [i.e., loving one's enemies] even Jesus could not attain."[91] Moreover,

---

[85]Montefiore, "The Old Testament and Its Ethical Teaching," 242.

[86]*RLGT*, 61.

[87]Montefiore, "The Old Testament and Its Ethical Teaching," 242.

[88]*RLGT*, 85.

[89]Ibid., 103. Montefiore regards Jesus' prayer of forgiveness on the cross as of doubtful authenticity.

[90]Ibid., 55. "In his language towards his opponents—if its authenticity be assumed—we can convict him of inconsistency out of his own mouth." *RT*, 54.

[91]Montefiore, *RT*, 53. Cf. Klausner, *JN*, 394; S. S. Cohon, "The Place of Jesus in the Religious Life of His Day," *JBL* 48 (1927): 93; Ben-Chorin, *BJ*, 79; Friedlander, *JSSM*, 72.

Jesus never indicates that God loves the Pharisees "in spite of their obstinacy and unbelief," but instead "he indicates pretty clearly that his own hatred of these persons is shared by God."[92] Klausner calls attention to the same problem with these words: "Christianity is the faith of mercy, the religion of love. But even Jesus himself could not remain true to his own teaching."[93] Abrahams, as well, calling attention to the inconsistency, says that we are here "faced by a real paradox in the Gospel criticism of the Pharisees; it excludes *them* from the gracious message which Jesus brought."[94] Sandmel is puzzled that Christians can read Matthew 23 "and still speak of Jesus as a kindly man."[95] Thus, in the end, for Jesus and the Christian, "Love your enemies" became "Love the fellow-believer."[96]

It may be worth noting, however, that the harsh words of Jesus are not uttered for their own sake, but have a positive didactic purpose for his own disciples. The purpose of Matthew 23 is not to vent the anger of Jesus but to reveal as forcefully as possible the serious wrongness of the Pharisees. It would be a mistake to conclude that these harsh words exclude the possibility of an underlying love of Jesus for the Pharisees. Note the words of Matthew 23:37 where at the end of a scathing denunciation Jesus says, "How often would I have gathered your children together as a hen gathers her brood under her wings, and you would not!" Indeed, it is arguable that the severity of Jesus' words is caused by the fact that the Pharisees are, or should be by their own principles, so close to the truth. Concerning the unfaithfulness of the church to the love commandment of Jesus, however, especially in its relationship with the Jewish people through the centuries and up into the modern era, nothing need be said,[97] and no excuses are allowable.

---

[92]Montefiore, *The Old Testament and After,* 250.

[93]J. Klausner, "Christian and Jewish Ethics," *Judaism* 2 (1953):22. Cf. S. Zeitlin, *The Rise and Fall of the Judaean State* (Philadelphia: Jewish Publication Society of America, 1967), 2:159.

[94]*SP,* 2:37.

[95]*WJJ,* 125; Sandmel does not regard Matthew 23 as authentic words of Jesus. Ibid.

[96]C. G. Montefiore, "The Significance of Jesus for His Own Age," *HJ* 10 (1911–12):778.

[97]Cf. C. G. Montefiore, "Anti-Semitism in England," *HJ* 19 (1920–21):337–46.

Forgiving Others

Obviously included in the concept of "loving one's enemy" is the forgiving of sins others have committed against oneself. The words of forgiveness spoken by Jesus from the cross (Luke 23:34) indicate that he may have been more consistent with his own teaching than Jewish scholars usually admit. Montefiore questions the authenticity of the saying, but regards it as "a religious gem without which the religious literature of the world would be the poorer."[98] There is, strictly speaking, no comparable rabbinic utterance, i.e., from the lips of a martyr. The rabbis do, however, know the meaning of forgiveness and teach it. Abrahams writes, "The Pharisaic theory consistently was that the unforgiving injured party became the *sinner* through his implacability."[99] The rabbis, however, thought not only of the sinned against, but also the sinner. In contrast, Montefiore notes, "Jesus seems always to think of the receiver, not of the doer, of the wrong."[100] Jewish scholarship is convinced that along this line Jesus has little to contribute to the teaching of the rabbis. As Abrahams proudly says, "The teaching of Judaism on the subject of forgiveness is in fact the brightest and strongest link in its golden chain."[101]

The Golden Rule

It is well known, of course, that Hillel, a contemporary of Jesus, had formulated the Golden Rule in its negative form: "What is hateful to thyself do not do unto thy neighbor."[102] Friedlander argues that the Golden Rule as expressed by Jesus is a Targum of Leviticus 19:18: "Love thy neighbor as thyself." He finds "parallels" to the positive form of the commandment (e.g., Aboth ii.15, 17; *Aboth de Rabbi Nathan* xv, xvi; Ecclus. 31:13), but despite his claims, these are hardly the equivalent of

---

[98]*RLGT*, 372.

[99]*SP*, 1:152.

[100]*RLGT*, 135; cf. 51–52.

[101]*SP*, 1:156.

[102]BT, *Shab.* 31a. The negative formulation is also found in the Apocrypha, Tobit 4:15.

Jesus' formulation. Then, however, Friedlander, as though apparently not quite convinced himself, proceeds to argue for the superiority of the negative form over the positive form, since the former is "much more practical" while the latter "takes us into the region of generosity."[103] Abrahams, refusing to agree with Jewish scholars who claim there is no difference between the negative and positive formulations, suggests that "the negative form is the more fundamental of the two, though the positive form is the fuller expression of practical morality."[104] According to Abrahams, the latter, which has wrought incalculable good to humanity, is a deduction from the former, which "goes deeper into the heart of the problem."[105] Ben-Chorin also notes the similarity between Hillel and Jesus, but adds that love has a decisive importance for Jesus, and it is this that makes his teaching more radical than Hillel's. Nevertheless, there is nothing new in the Golden Rule, according to Ben-Chorin.[106]

Service and Humility

Jesus' emphasis on service and humility seems to be somewhat different from the teaching of the rabbis. Montefiore regards "the lowly or devoted service of others" as comparatively new and without parallels in the rabbinic literature.[107] He further indicates that a distinct class-consciousness existed among the rabbis, who prided themselves on their learned profession, concluding that "the idea that 'he who is greatest among you shall be your servant' [Matt. 20:26; Mark 10:43; cf. Luke 22:26] was, I think, a novel one."[108] Yet, at the same time, Montefiore is

---

[103]*JSSM*, 232ff.

[104]*SP*, 1:22. G. B. King has discussed this issue in "The 'Negative' Golden Rule," *JR* 8 (1928): 268–79, concluding that "basically they are the same, in idea as in origin" (277).

[105]Ibid. Montefiore, however, agreeing with Kittel, concludes that the difference between the negative and positive formulations is so slight as to make it of no importance. *RLGT*, 151.

[106]*BJ*, 17, 80–81.

[107]*RLGT*, 299.

[108]Ibid., 324–25.

constrained to say that the spirit of this great saying "was not really alien or unknown to the Rabbis."[109]

Nonretaliation

One ethical teaching that is problematic for Jewish scholars is Jesus' conception of nonretaliation embodied in his injunction "If any one strikes you on the right cheek, turn to him the other also" (Matt. 5:39; Luke 6:29). As Montefiore notes, most Jewish scholars find this saying to be in contrast with rabbinic teaching and thus regard it unfavorably.[110] Montefiore admits that "tit for tat" is very important in Jewish ethics and religion, and indeed confesses that it occupies "a larger place than the facts of life or our highest ethical and religious conception can fully justify and approve."[111] However, he finds no antithesis between the spirit of the rabbis and the teaching of Jesus found in Matthew 5:38ff.[112] "Here it may not unjustly be said that he follows the best Jewish Teaching, both of the Old Testament and of the Rabbis; follows it and deepens it by his categorical and un-qualified injunctions."[113] At the same time, there is a certain originality involved, but it is an originality of degree rather than kind: "It is the same spirit which inspired the best teaching of the Rabbis, carried to an extreme."[114] Montefiore notes, further, that the law of requital is not abandoned in the synoptic Gospels, but "seems used for higher purposes, and looked at in its higher aspects."[115] Sandmel, too, concentrates on the common spirit of the rabbis and Jesus, in spite of acknowledged but unimportant differences: "I know nothing in Judaism which parallels the Christian counsel to turn the other cheek. Yet if there is some

[109]Ibid., 328.

[110]Ibid., 50.

[111]C. G. Montefiore, "The Synoptic Gospels and the Jewish Consciousness," *HJ* 3 (1904–05):622.

[112]*RLGT*, 54.

[113]Montefiore, "The Originality of Jesus," 107.

[114]*RLGT*, 52; the rabbis, in contrast, are "cooler and calmer," characterized by common sense and realism. Ibid.

[115]Montefiore, "The Synoptic Gospels and the Jewish Consciousness," 663.

slight difference in emphasis at this one point, the social ideals are nevertheless synonymous."[116]

One of the most important questions concerning this particular teaching of Jesus, viewed from the Jewish perspective, is its applicability. Thus Zeitlin appears willing to recognize the moral excellence of the teaching, but asks, "Could a society really function on such principles?"[117] This objection, however, is based on the presupposition that Jesus taught that evil should not be resisted at all under any circumstances. Some Jewish scholars have attacked this presupposition in defense of the Jewishness of Jesus' teaching. Thus Montefiore writes, "The maxims are not intended to be laws supplanting the civil and the criminal code: allowance must be made for oriental exaggeration, for the picturesque and vivid illustration, in order to make the principle more clear."[118] Daube has argued that Matthew 5:38ff. was not meant to oppose literal retaliation, since by the first century this had been replaced by money penalties. Thus what is in the mind of Jesus is not mutilation, but insult; what is at stake is not physical abuse, but personal rights and honor. Jesus' teaching was, accordingly, that "a man should be meek under an insult" and not insist on the redress he might rightfully claim. "It advocates . . . a humility which cannot be wounded, giving of yourself to your brother which will achieve more than can be achieved by narrow justice."[119] Along with this, attention must be called to the fact that for the rabbis one of the most grievous sins against one's neighbor was putting him to shame in public.[120]

Other Jewish writers see a stronger difference here between Jesus and the rabbis. Friedlander argues against Montefiore that Jesus meant his doctrine of nonresistance of evil to be a new principle of society: "He revolutionized the spirit of all law by teaching non-resistance," something that if followed would have meant the destruction of society.[121] According to Flusser, Jesus

---

[116]*WJJ*, 132.

[117]S. Zeitlin, "The Pharisees: A Historical Study," *JQR* 52 (1961–62):121.

[118]Montefiore, *The Old Testament and After*, 247.

[119]Daube, *The New Testament and Rabbinic Judaism*, 257, 259; for the whole discussion, see 254–65. Daube regards the passage as a rare presentation of "a pre-Talmudic stage of Jewish private law." Ibid., 265.

[120]Montefiore, "The Spirit of Judaism."

[121]*JSSM*, 66.

took his doctrine of not resisting one who is evil from "the Essene fringe," which held to a notion of passive resistance to evil, and it was this concept that Jesus developed into his command to love one's enemy.[122] Thus, although Jewish in spirit, the doctrine of "turning the other cheek" is regarded by Flusser as something "indeed revolutionary, subversive."[123] Ben-Chorin too regards nonresistance to evil as a radical doctrine that is to be explained by Jesus' expectancy of an imminent end of the present age.[124]

Jewish scholars again press the charge that Jesus himself failed in that which he enjoined on others. Klausner, referring to the cleansing of the temple (Mark 11:15ff.), expresses this opinion: "In contradiction to his familiar law . . . Jesus 'resisted evil' in active and violent fashion."[125] Montefiore raises a similar complaint: "That the same Jesus who said 'Resist not evil, or the evil-doer,' was ready enough that blows should be given where they are in place may be gathered from many of the parables."[126] Referring to John 18:23, Ben-Chorin also charges that Jesus did not fulfill his own ethic.[127]

Maccoby, on the other hand, regarding Jesus as a self-confessed messiah primarily concerned with the overthrow of the Romans, denies that Jesus ever taught nonretaliation: "The saying 'Resist not evil' is a negation of everything the Jews stood for. . . . Only the forlorn circumstances of the post–70 A.D. Christian Church could have led to the ascription of this saying to Jesus."[128]

Self-renunciation and Asceticism

Also to be noted as off the rabbinic line is "a kind of passionate glorification of renunciation and adversity as works of

---

[122]*Jesus,* 80ff.

[123]Ibid., 89.

[124]*BJ,* 79.

[125]*JN,* 315.

[126]Montefiore, *The Old Testament and After,* 251.

[127]*BJ,* 79.

[128]*RJ,* 110. Maccoby notes that Jesus did not shy away from driving out the money-changers from the temple with a whip (109).

true discipleship, and as the one sure passport to heaven."[129] For
the rabbis, adversity and martyrdom are not gloried in, but regarded as tragic necessities.

Thus Friedlander responds critically to the notion of Christian discipleship: "The spirit of abnegation and self-denial that
sacrifices individual and personal freedom is alien to Jewish
teaching."[130] Klausner, on the other hand, has criticized Jesus'
ethical teaching for being overly individualistic, concerned only
with the salvation of one's own soul. For Klausner the result
seems to be that "he who wishes to save his soul and to live
according to the ethics of Jesus has no choice but to withdraw to
the wilderness or shut himself up in a monastery."[131] Montefiore, however, seems to have grasped Jesus' teaching more
clearly at this point. Self-sacrifice as he points out, is not solely
for one's own sake, but for the sake of others as well; the Christian virtues are not passive, but active, reaching out to the salvation of others.[132] The salvation of one's own soul always implies
a new love towards others.[133] Or, to put it the other way around,
"To save others is also to save yourself."[134] Montefiore, however, also criticizes the doctrine of self-renunciation: "Deliberate,
voluntary, and complete renunciation is not put forward as an
ideal by the Rabbis."[135] The idea of a self-renunciation either for
the sake of a cause or for the sake of others is foreign to the
rabbis.

Some Jewish scholars see not only a tendency to selfish
individualism in Jesus' teaching, but also the inclination to a false
other-worldliness. This comes to light, it is claimed, in Jesus'
attitude toward material joys, wherein says Montefiore, "lies a
real difference between Jesus and the Rabbis."[136] Jesus, for

---

[129]Montefiore, "The Synoptic Gospels and the Jewish Consciousness," 664.

[130]*JSSM*, 67.

[131]Klausner, "Christian and Jewish Ethics," 21.

[132]"The Synoptic Gospels and the Jewish Consciousness," 665. According to
Walker, repentance leads not so much to the state of being saved, but "into a state of
being filled with the saving spirit as regards others." T. Walker, *What Jesus Read*
(London: Allen & Unwin, 1925), 62.

[133]*RLGT*, 285; cf. *RT*, 79.

[134]Montefiore, *The Old Testament and After*, 255.

[135]*RLGT*, 355.

[136]Ibid., 16.

example, was very much opposed to the possession of material wealth, sensing in it a danger that the rabbis, for all their excellence, did not see.[137] "The Rabbis looked at wealth and poverty from a more realistic and common-sense point of view than Jesus. In this matter they were less paradoxical, if you will, less idealistic, than he."[138] The injunction "Sell all that you have and distribute to the poor, and you will have treasure in heaven" (Luke 18:22) is quite unrabbinic in tone.

G. Friedlander, in his book *The Jewish Sources of the Sermon on the Mount,* devotes an entire chapter to the subject "The Un-Jewish Asceticism in the Gospels." In it he also calls attention to the unusual character of Jesus' negativism toward wealth, connecting it with the importance of entering the kingdom. Among the rabbis "there was no genuine desire to renounce money, or to refuse to utilize it in a good and proper manner. Herein Judaism rejects the Gospel teaching."[139] Commenting on the first beatitude ("Blessed are the poor," Luke 6:20), Ben-Chorin mentions the possibility of a connection between the teaching of Jesus and the teaching at Qumran, where poverty was regarded as an encouragement to walk in the way of the Spirit.[140] Friedlander had much earlier theorized about Jesus' dependence on Essene teaching in his denigration of wealth. Jewish scholars, indeed, refer not infrequently to the Essenes in explaining the ethical teaching of Jesus as well as other aspects of the Gospels.[141]

A further area regarded as "undoubtedly off the rabbinic line" is that of voluntary celibacy, as for example in Matthew 19:12: "There are eunuchs who have made themselves eunuchs for the sake of the kingdom of heaven." In the words that follow, "He who is able to receive this, let him receive it," Jewish scholars understand the implications of a double morality. Daube says, "Matthew represents it as not designed for all members

---

[137]Ibid., 140, 281.

[138]Ibid., 274.

[139]*JSSM,* 180.

[140]*BJ,* 70.

[141]Cf. K. Kohler, "Jesus of Nazareth—In theology," *JE,* 7:169; J. Isaac, *Jesus and Israel,* ET by Sally Gran (New York: Holt, Rinehart & Winston, 1971), 83.

even of the new community, but for a select circle only."[142] In contrast to this teaching, "Judaism has consistently deprecated and depreciated celibacy; it has required its saints to show their sanctity *in* the world and amid the ties and obligations of family life."[143] Friedlander describes Matthew 19:12 as "a strange un-Jewish strain" that, together with Luke 14:26 (renouncing wife and children to become a disciple), was responsible for the tradition of Christian monasticism. Jesus "was a celibate and despised marriage."[144] Ben-Chorin, on the other hand, finds this entire strand of teaching to be impossible in the mouth of Jesus. According to Ben-Chorin, Jesus, like every rabbi in Israel, was himself married and taught no doctrine of celibacy.[145]

Even for the married, however, Jesus has an impossibly high standard; for another teaching of Jesus that is given as an absolute is the prohibition of divorce. This also is cited by Montefiore as a mark of Jesus' originality. Indeed, his teaching on divorce, and additionally his association with women and the mercy and compassion shown them in the Gospels, are indications of the greatness of Jesus as a teacher.[146] Jesus went beyond Shammai in the strictness of his teaching on divorce, according to Montefiore, for "he may even have deliberately wished to put women on a footing of greater equality with man."[147] This as-

---

[142]D. Daube, "Concessions to Sinfulness in Jewish Law," *JJS* 10 (1959):11; Daube notes that the New Testament is not averse to such measures that play "an important part in resolving the tension between a standard unattainable by and indeed destructive of society and the normal needs of continuing civilised life." Ibid.

[143]*SG*, 2:265; thus Ahad ha'Am writes with some acerbity: "The Catholic Church, correctly understanding the Gospel teachings has built countless houses of refuge for celibates of both sexes." "Judaism and the Gospels," 313; cf. Klausner, "Had there been no ascetic and monastic element in Jesus' teaching, monasticism would not have become a peculiarity of Roman and Orthodox Christianity." *JN*, 395.

[144]*JSSM*, 52, 55, 175.

[145]*BJ*, 128ff., citing Wellhausen on Jesus and celibacy. See the similar view of a Protestant scholar, W. E. Phipps, *Was Jesus Married?* (New York: Harper & Row, 1970).

[146]Ibid., 46–47; cf. Ahad ha'Am's animosity toward Montefiore: "As he [Montefiore] repeatedly pours out the vials of his wrath in harsh and crude denunciations of the Jewish law of divorce, his tone is that of a monk just emerging, Gospel in hand, from his retreat, who has no desire to know anything whatever as to the views which prevail at the present day in the world around him." "Judaism and the Gospels," 315.

[147]C. G. Montefiore, "The Originality of Jesus," *HJ* 28 (1929–30):107.

sessment, however, is challenged by G. Friedlander, who finds no advance for women in Jesus' teaching and who argues that the rabbinic viewpoint has the advantage of taking into account "human nature as it exists in every-day life."[148]

It is evident, then, that Jewish scholars perceive in the teaching of Jesus a certain strain of asceticism that goes counter to the rabbinic mentality.[149] "The occasional ascetic touches in the Gospels are, speaking generally, off the Rabbinic line."[150] By way of contrast, Abrahams notes, the Pharisees steered a middle course between the extremes of luxury and asceticism.[151] An important feature of rabbinic Judaism is that "the conception of holiness is positive: the actions of the natural man must be hallowed."[152] Therefore Judaism has "persistently rejected asceticism."[153]

ABSOLUTENESS AND IMPRACTICABILITY

The radical and absolute character of Jesus' ethical teachings is highly problematic for Jewish scholarship. "A main characteristic of the teaching of Jesus is its absoluteness, and hence its paradoxicalness."[154] Indeed, this characteristic of his teaching is to no small extent a part of Jesus' originality. Montefiore writes of this uncompromising absoluteness: "In examples of it, Jesus seems to be original, in that he tends to go off the Jewish line and not merely to develop Jewish teaching or to 'fulfill' it."[155] In some instances the absoluteness of the teaching is intimately bound up with Jesus himself. Thus he says, "If any man would come after me; let him deny himself and take up his cross and follow me" (Mark 8:34; cf. Matt. 16:24; Luke 9:23). Concerning these words Montefiore perceptively remarks, "Here we have

---

[148]*JSSM*, 57.
[149]Montefiore, *The Old Testament and After*, 243.
[150]Montefiore, *RLGT*, 138.
[151]*SP*, 1:121.
[152]Montefiore, *RLGT*, 139.
[153]Friedlander, *JSSM*, 171.
[154]Montefiore, *RLGT*, 230.
[155]Montefiore, "The Originality of Jesus," 106.

not only teaching of the highest originality, but also pregnant with the most astonishing issues."[156] Another discipleship saying that is difficult for Jewish scholars is, as we have seen, Luke 14:26: "If any one comes to me and does not hate his own father and mother and wife and children and brothers and sisters, yes, and even his own life, he cannot be my disciple" (cf. also the saying in its positive form in Matthew 10:37). This, too, is original and "has an anti-Rabbinic ring."[157] Klausner repeatedly refers to Jesus' ethical teaching as "extremist," and Ben-Chorin concludes that the way of Jesus "is so radical that it surpasses the human dimension."[158] When Montefiore describes the teaching of Jesus, he refers to "its passion, its enthusiasm, its tremendous thoroughness."[159] Judaism, moreover, as we have seen, has no room for this absolutism and the doctrine of total renunciation.

This absoluteness of Jesus' ethical teachings has called forth criticism of what Jewish scholars consider its most serious weakness: its impracticability. Jewish scholars maintain that Jesus' ethic is, above all, unrealistic and unattainable.[160] In the first place, it is said, no society based on the ethical teachings of Jesus could function properly; and this criticism must be understood in light of the importance of the community in the Jewish viewpoint. Klausner has been one of the severest critics of Jesus' teaching along this line. He writes:

> Jesus' moral teaching ceased to provide a firm basis for the life of human society. True Christianity, the Christianity of the Sermon on the Mount, cannot be practiced in an organized Society or State, where there must be law and justice, there must be family life, there must be security of life and property.[161]

Zionist and Orthodox Jews inevitably see Jesus' teaching in the light of national Israel. Klausner accordingly writes, "Nothing is more dangerous to national Judaism than this exaggerated Juda-

---

[156]Ibid., 105.

[157]RLGT, 230.

[158]BJ, 78.

[159]C. G. Montefiore, *Liberal Judaism and Hellenism* (London: Macmillan, 1918), 100.

[160]"The teachings of the Gospels are so hopelessly impossible of accomplishment," writes Paul Goodman. *The Synagogue and the Church* (London: Routledge, 1908), 282.

[161]"Christian and Jewish Ethics," 23; cf. *JN*, 393.

ism; it is the ruin of national culture, the national state, and national life.''[162] The new individualism one encounters in the teaching of Jesus seems to impoverish necessary social standards. Social considerations as such never seem to have had much place in Jesus' teaching.[163] Montefiore also recognizes that the teachings of Jesus cannot serve as the laws of a state,[164] but he departs considerably from his Jewish brethren when he observes that if those teachings are not suited to society, ''this is rather the society's fault than theirs. . . . They seem to point to a higher law than can as yet be put into practice, but which is not, for that reason, to be ridiculed as unpractical and absurd.''[165]

Not only, however, are Jesus' teachings inapplicable for society as a whole, they are also unrealistic for the individual. Jesus' commands transcend the powers of human nature, whereas Judaism has always taken into consideration the limitations of that nature. According to Klausner, ''Herein lies the superiority of Judaism: it takes account of man's evil inclinations no less than his good inclinations.''[166] As we have seen, Jewish scholars contend that Jesus' teaching was so idealistic that not even he himself was able to abide by it. And if Jesus himself could not, how much less those who profess to follow him. The contradiction in Jesus himself ''between precept and practice cannot but prove that this extreme ethical teaching cannot possibly be carried out in practice in everyday life, even by so exceptional a man for whom society was naught and the individual soul everything.''[167]

Having been commanded to do the impossible, his followers in frustration seem to have neglected his ethical teaching altogether.[168] The rabbis, however, do not present an ethical teach-

---

[162]*JN*, 374; cf. Ahad ha'Am, ''Judaism and the Gospels,'' in H. Kohn, ed., *Nationalism and the Jewish Ethic* (New York: Schocken, 1962), 309.

[163]H. J. Cadbury, *The Peril of Modernizing Jesus* (1927; reprint ed.: Naperville, Ill.: Allenson, 1962), 95.

[164]*RT*, 105.

[165]Montefiore, ''The Synoptic Gospels and the Jewish Consciousness,'' 661.

[166]Klausner, ''Christian and Jewish Ethics,'' 23.

[167]*JN*, 395.

[168]This fact is regarded by Jewish scholars as proven alone by the centuries of persecution Jews have experienced from Christians.

ing that is humanly impossible, but one that is realistic, with the result that paradoxically the Jews have come closer to fulfilling the ethical teachings of Jesus than have the Christians.[169] For Klausner the absoluteness of Jesus' teachings explains the Jewish rejection of Christianity. The Jew instinctively perceives that Christianity provides "not a *creed* of life like Judaism, but an abstract and irrational creed, which runs counter to the course of human life, and which men do not attempt to put into practice because it is incapable of being put into practice."[170] Thus for Klausner, although "Jesus surpassed Hillel in his ethical ideas" and "concerned himself more with ethical teaching than did Hillel," all of this is negated because "his teaching has not proved possible in practice."[171]

Montefiore, however, is much more positive in his view of Jesus' ethical teaching than the majority of Jewish scholars. For him the "heroic" character of Jesus' teaching provides a goal that people must ever strive for. Thus he writes, "So far from its being a reproach against an ethical teaching or ideal that it is suited for saints and angels, and not for average working-men and women, it is, on the contrary, a right and necessary quality."[172] The commands of the Sermon on the Mount are not meant to be understood as impossibilities. At the same time, however, they are not to be taken literally, but rather as principles that can be adapted to everyday life. "The *letter* of even this prophet's teaching may kill; here too we must sometimes look only to the *spirit*."[173] Thus, in the command to "love one's enemies," Montefiore says, "Jesus, I am sure, was thinking of something which *is* practicable."[174]

Vermes' handling of this problem is similar to that of Montefiore. Referring to the command to love one's enemies and to turn the other cheek, he writes, "This is his usual custom: to opt for a maximum of exaggeration in order to underline what he is

---

[169]Klausner, "Christian and Jewish Ethics," 26.

[170]Ibid., 28.

[171]*JN*, 397.

[172]Montefiore, *The Old Testament and After*, 244. He adds that "the Old Testament contains its unfulfillable demands no less than the New." Ibid., 245.

[173]*RT*, 104. Cf. Montefiore's appreciation of Windisch at this point. *RLGT*, 55.

[174]Montefiore, "The Old Testament and Its Ethical Teaching," 242.

attempting to convey." The command to love one's enemies, Vermes says, is to be taken no more literally than is that to hate one's family members (Luke 14:26). The hyperbolic nature of the commands is borne out by Jesus' own failure literally to turn the other cheek (John 18:23).[175]

ETHICS AND THE KINGDOM OF GOD

It is obvious that in addition to the general Jewishness of Jesus' ethical teaching there is also something very unusual and new about this teaching, especially when one considers its radical character and absoluteness. Jewish scholars are unanimous in the conclusion that the peculiar nature of Jesus' ethical teaching is the result of his eschatological expectations. Jesus came preaching that the kingdom of God was imminent. It is this conviction that controls all that he had to say and do. Jesus is said to have had an "eschatological temper," which accounts for his preoccupation with the human soul and the call to an absolute righteousness. Since the end of the present world order was close at hand, the salvation of the individual alone was of importance.[176] Jesus' ethical demands are of an eschatological character because he was convinced that the totally other, the "second aeon," was about to be revealed.[177] Thus Montefiore writes, "Much of the moral teaching of the gospel is relative to that one overmastering idea [the End], even when the idea itself is not definitely expressed."[178] Commenting on Jesus' teaching of nonviolence, Schonfield also correctly relates Jesus' teaching to the announcement of the kingdom: "It was incumbent on the Children of the Kingdom to display already the qualities of the Age to Come, what Jesus called its perfections, as the Law of Moses instructed."[179]

Utilizing the doctrine of the imminence of the kingdom as an interpretative key, virtually all Jewish scholars take a stance simi-

---

[175]*GJJ*, 44.
[176]Montefiore, *The Old Testament and After*, 268; *RLGT*, 281.
[177]Montefiore, "The Originality of Jesus," 110.
[178]*RT*, 77.
[179]*FCS*, 70–71.

lar to that of Albert Schweitzer in explaining the absoluteness of Jesus' teaching as an "interim" ethic—that is, a radical ethic to be followed in the brief period of time remaining before the arrival of the eschatological kingdom. Abrahams, for example, refers explicitly to an "interim" ethic as a possible explanation of Jesus' extreme utterance on divorce.[180] Friedlander characterizes Jesus as a teacher "whose vision was that of an apocalyptic dreamer, whose message was eschatological and therefore of little practical value for everyday life."[181] Klausner too traces the absoluteness of Jesus' ethical teachings to his conviction that the kingdom of God was near, adding that Jesus believed himself to be the Messiah. He writes:

> Now, if the Kingdom of God, which is the same as the Kingdom of the Messiah, "is at hand" because "the time is fulfilled," it follows that the Messiah cannot attach any importance to the life of the actual present: his gaze is fixed on the life of "future days," the life of "the days of the Messiah."[182]

For Klausner it is this conviction of the imminence of the end of this age that "explains the extremist ascetic ethical system of Jesus." And in Klausner's view, indeed, it is just here that we are to look for the origins of Christianity: "This two-fold misapprehension of Jesus—the nearness of the kingdom of heaven and his Messiahship—perpetuated his memory and created Christianity."[183] Trattner writes in a similar vein: "Jesus actually and literally believed that the Kingdom was at hand and for this reason it is safe to assume that his teaching was in part colored by this fanciful expectation."[184]

Ben-Chorin, as we have seen, appeals to Jesus' expectancy of the end as the explanation of the command not to resist evil.[185] Similarly, Lapide notes the significance of the expectation of the

---

[180]*SP*, 1:68; Abrahams thinks it more likely that the teaching was meant only for the disciples.

[181]*JSSM*, 262–63.

[182]Klausner, "Christian and Jewish Ethics," 22.

[183]*JN*, 405.

[184]Trattner, *As a Jew Sees Jesus*, 65.

[185]*BJ*, 79.

kingdom for Jesus' ethical teaching: "The high torah-morality has everything to do with this."[186]

. Nevertheless, some Jewish scholars admit that much of Jesus' ethical teaching is unrelated to, or can be detached from, a belief in the imminent end of the age,[187] or is even "clearly inconsistent" with such a view.[188] Montefiore may be mentioned as an example of this perspective. Jesus, unlike the rabbis, according to Montefiore, certainly believed that this world order was rapidly coming to its end. "Jesus believed that the end of the old world order was at hand. There was no time for half-measures, and no need to prepare for the morrow."[189] "The idea that he [Jesus] merely intended and suited for this short intervening period—an 'interim' ethic—is exaggerated, but it is not without its element of truth."[190] This, indeed, provides Montefiore with an explanation of many of the un-Jewish elements of Jesus' teaching. He writes, "It does not follow that Jesus, had he supposed that the 'age' was going to last and that the Messianic era and transformation were not near at hand, would have taken the exact line which he did on various social questions, such as riches and property, family ties, or marriage."[191] Still, when all is said, because of Montefiore's "spiritual" (as opposed to "literal") interpretation of Jesus' ethical teachings and his high valuation of them from the perspective of Liberal Judaism, he counts much of Jesus' ethics worthy even when separated from their original framework.[192] This too, for Montefiore, bears on the question of the impracticability of the ethical teaching of Jesus. Thus he writes:

> Righteousness was to be the keynote of the new Kingdom, as well as the passport of admission within its gates. Like many another

---

[186]*ÖCJ*, 141.

[187]Montefiore, *SG*, 1:25, 58–59.

[188]Abrahams, *SP*, 1:101, speaking of the parables of Jesus, and in particular the Parable of the Talents (Matt. 25:4–30; Luke 19:12–27).

[189]C. G. Montefiore, "The Religious Teaching of the Synoptic Gospels in Its Relation to Judaism," *HJ* 20 (1921–22):442.

[190]Montefiore, *The Old Testament and After*, 243; cf. *SG*, 2:54.

[191]Montefiore, "The Significance of Jesus for His Own Age," 768.

[192]*SG*, 1:25; 2:114.

religious teacher, Jesus did not ask himself the question how far
the virtues upon which he laid such great stress would be needless,
or incapable of being realized and practiced, in the renovated
world. He was keen about them for their own sake, apart from
their immediate effects.[193]

Trattner is in agreement with Montefiore on this point. He writes,
"It is true that his [Jesus'] message was set in an apocalyptic
framework but it is also true that this framework may be removed
without damage to the permanent element of his preachment."[194]

Schoeps, however, is much nearer the truth when he emphasizes the inextricable connection between the ethical teaching of
Jesus and his announcement about the kingdom. According to
Schoeps, the purpose of the Sermon on the Mount is "to announce (as the introductory beatitudes also do), *how* the true
realization of the Law must appear and how it *will* appear—*when*
the Kingdom comes." The question of the realizability of this
ethic is not considered at all in the Sermon "because the 'nova
lex Christi' is not placed before men in order that the Kingdom
may come, but because it is coming."[195] Schoeps goes on to note
the connection between the Sermon on the Mount and the self-
consciousness of Jesus as the promised Son of Man.

It is understandable that Jewish scholarship desires to separate Jesus' ethical teaching from his eschatological teaching
(which is in turn bound up with his self-consciousness). Jesus'
eschatology is for all Jews self-evidently wrong, and for Liberal
Jews irrelevant in any case. To the extent that the ethical teaching
of Jesus strikes Jewish scholars as authentically Jewish, it will be
argued that that teaching possesses an on-going validity. But
from the perspective of the Gospels the ethical teaching of Jesus
and the proclamation of the kingdom of God belong together and
the former can be understood only in light of the latter.

In this discussion of the Jewish understanding of Jesus' ethical teaching, the tension between continuity and discontinuity is

---

[193]Ibid., 1:16; for the entire discussion, see 13ff.
[194]Trattner, *As a Jew Sees Jesus*, 93.
[195]H. J. Schoeps, "Jesus," in *Gottheit und Menschheit* (Stuttgart, 1950), 62.

again readily apparent. On the one hand Jewish scholars are intent on stressing the Jewishness of Jesus. His teachings epitomize the best of rabbinical Judaism; in spirit, if not in letter, Jesus and the rabbis stand together. On the other hand, however, Jesus, in his ethical teachings, seems to go far beyond anything the rabbis ever taught. And it is precisely this aspect of Jesus' teaching that causes difficulty for the Jewish scholar.

Flusser sums up the surprising newness of Jesus when he says:

> The germ of revolution—if we may speak thus—in Jesus' preaching does not emerge from a criticism of the Jewish law, but from other premises altogether. Jesus was not the first to provide these: his attack proceeded from attitudes already established before his time. Revolution broke through at three points: the radical commandment of love, the call for a new morality, the idea of the kingdom of heaven.[196]

The question is whether Flusser's final analysis of Jesus is sufficient to account for the revolutionary character of Jesus' teaching.

Klausner also faces the combination of old and new in the ethical teaching of Jesus, further illustrating the dilemma of Jewish scholarship, in these words:

> Christian ethics are so closely derived from the Old Testament and the Talmud [sic] that, as Geiger and Graetz have both rightly concluded, there is not a single ethical sentence in the whole of the New Testament which cannot be paralleled either in the Old Testament, in the literature of the Apocrypha and Pseudepigrapha, or in the Talmudic and Midrashic literature of the era of Jesus and Paul. Nevertheless, there is something distinctive and specific in the moral law of Christianity which is not found in the moral law of Judaism.[197]

Klausner's solution, as we have seen, is to understand that while Jesus' ethics were essentially Jewish, he overemphasized and exaggerated them to the extent that they became un-Jewish and led to a "non-Judaism."[198] This exaggeration, as we saw earlier

---

[196]Flusser, *Jesus*, 65.
[197]Klausner, "Christian and Jewish Ethics," 16; cf. *JN*, 384.
[198]*JN*, 393.

(p. 164), is attributed by Klausner to Jesus' mistaken belief that the kingdom was about to arrive.

Montefiore sums up what is "novel and noteworthy" about Jesus' ethical teachings from a Jewish viewpoint under four points: (1) it is a heroic teaching, (2) it is an ethic of activity, (3) it remarkably blends a "higher selfishness" and the "highest unselfishness," and (4) it contains the germ of a double ethic. Yet despite these new aspects in Jesus' ethical teaching, nothing is totally new; his teaching only carries forth and deepens the teaching of the Old Testament.[199]

Jewish scholars thus find little difficulty in appreciating the ethical teaching of Jesus. Much of that teaching is regarded as a reflection of the best of rabbinic Judaism and is therefore counted admirable and worthy. Montefiore confessedly goes beyond the mainstream of Jewish opinion when he ascribes "a degree of excellence" even to the more extreme of Jesus' teachings such as "resist not wickedness" and "love your enemies."[200] But generally the ethical teaching of Jesus has been the easiest of Jesus' words to reclaim for Judaism. Klausner has expressed what has become the widespread opinion of Jewish scholarship in the following oft-quoted words, which appear at the very end of his book on Jesus: "If ever the day should come and this ethical code be stripped of its wrappings of miracles and mysticism, the Book of the Ethics of Jesus will be one of the choicest treasures in the literature of Israel for all time."[201]

But can this be done, given the very nature of that teaching and its context in the ministry of Jesus? Kaminka, with Montefiore and Klausner in mind, voices the opinion of an Orthodox Jew when he insists that "the Gospels are far from being merely a compendium of ethics: and even considered in that light, the Jew, who had precepts and examples of the Law and the Prophets and the Writings, above all the Book of Psalms, had no need of such a handbook."[202] The perceptivity of these words is evident.

---

[199]Montefiore, *The Old Testament and After,* 240ff.; cf. "Anti-Semitism in England," *HJ* 19 (1920–21):324–25.

[200]Montefiore, "The Originality of Jesus," 107.

[201]*JN,* 414; cf. p. 381. For a somewhat similar statement, see Vermes, *GJJ,* 47.

[202]Quoted by G. F. Moore, "A Jewish Life of Jesus," *HTR* 16 (1923):102.

Some serious questions remain. Can the ethical teachings of Jesus be taken out of their eschatological context, stripped of their christological implications, and made into an ethical code-book without spiritualizing away their absoluteness and thereby nullifying their original intention? Moreover, given rabbinic Judaism's lofty ethics, why did Jesus deem it necessary to proclaim a new ethic that is admittedly impracticable? Still further, how is the centrality Jesus assigns to himself in his ethical teachings to be understood?

Certainly Jesus' ethical teaching is to a large degree Jewish and can be paralleled in the rabbinic literature. At the same time, however, as we have seen, it repeatedly goes beyond what is feasible within the rabbinic perspective. Jesus calls his disciples to an unconditional love of others, including their enemies; to the positive action of the Golden Rule; to a new concept of service and humility; to nonretaliation in the face of evil; to self-renunciation and to a lifestyle that opposes the materialism of this world. And his call to discipleship involves an absoluteness that is incomprehensible if taken on its own terms, apart from the good news Jesus brings.

Jesus revolutionized the ethical tradition he inherited and held in common with the rabbis; he "took over the traditional ethic, and yet in doing so transformed it into something new."[203] The new dynamic that enables Jesus to transform the Jewish ethical tradition is the message of the kingdom of God that he has come to inaugurate. Only with this new proclamation of the kingdom—not its imminence, but its presence—can the ethical teaching of Jesus, with all its idealism, be understood. Jesus' ethics, in short, are not "interim" ethics, nor are they merely hyperbolical: they are the ethics of the present kingdom.[204] The dawning of the kingdom of God in the person of Jesus makes possible a new order of life and a new relationship with the Father. The perfection of that new order is exemplified in the absoluteness of Jesus' ethical teachings. These teachings do not constitute a new code of ethics to be substituted for the Law, but

---

[203]E. F. Scott, "The Originality of Jesus' Ethical Teaching," *JBL* 48 (1929):112.
[204]C. H. Dodd, *History and the Gospel* (London: Nisbet, 1938), 125.

are rather a description of kingdom righteousness.[205] They are eschatological ethics, but brought to the present in advance of the final consummation of the age. Jesus' ethical teachings are not legislative, but descriptive. Accordingly they are relevant only to the person who has experienced the new order of life—the reign of God, which is a gift—and they constitute for that person an ideal toward which he or she strives in the present. The ethics are not followed in order to gain acceptance with God or to bring the kingdom into existence. Instead, the followers of Jesus *begin* with that acceptance and the reality of the kingdom, receiving through it a transformed nature, which, though not enabling them to arrive fully at the ideal in the present, enables them to achieve it in greater measure than had ever before been possible.[206] T. W. Manson is thus correct when he writes that "what Jesus offers in his ethical teaching is not a set of rules of conduct, but a number of illustrations of the way in which a transformed character will express itself in conduct."[207]

If the ethical teaching of Jesus cannot be understood apart from his proclamation of the kingdom, neither can the latter be understood apart from the person of Jesus. Thus in the last analysis the understanding of Jesus' ethical teaching depends on one's interpretation of the person of Jesus.

---

[205]T. W. Manson, *The Teaching of Jesus* (Cambridge: Cambridge University Press, 1963²), 301.

[206]Cf. G. E. Ladd, *Jesus and the Kingdom* (Waco: Word, 1969), 286.

[207]Manson, *The Teaching of Jesus,* 300.

First-Century Pharisaism

IT IS REGRETTABLE, but true, that the Gospels are responsible for the consistently negative view of the Pharisees that has become so widespread among Christians, a view in which "Pharisee" has become synonymous with "hypocrite."[1] Understandably, therefore, Jewish scholars have persistently challenged the accuracy of the Gospel portrayal of the Pharisees, judging it prejudiced and unfair. Sandmel well reflects the Jewish resentment when he remarks: "No group in history has had a greater injustice done to its fine qualities and positive virtues than have the Pharisees through parts of the Gospels."[2]

The importance of a correct understanding of first-century Judaism for understanding the Gospels cannot be overemphasized.[3] Neither the nature of Jesus' mission nor the sense of his teaching can be grasped apart from an adequate knowledge of the religious life of his day. It is primarily Jewish scholars who are responsible for a new and more adequate knowledge of the Pharisees and their doctrine. "We owe a real debt to Jewish scholarship for correcting many long-established views about Pharisaism."[4] This new, enlightened appreciation of Pharisaism has been championed by several non-Jewish writers as well, among whom G. F. Moore, T. Herford, and James Parkes deserve special mention. The results of this labor have begun to take effect, and Vermes can now write that what he calls academic anti-Judaism "has largely disappeared, and we have now a more open, positive and constructive approach by New Testament scholars towards post-biblical Judaism."[5] Yet, as Vermes points out, two major tools used by New

[1]Cf. S. Zeitlin, "The Pharisees," *JQR* 52 (1961–62):119.

[2]S. Sandmel, *A Jewish Understanding of the New Testament* (Cincinnati: Hebrew Union College, 1956), 24.

[3]Cf. G. Vermes, "Jewish Studies and New Testament Interpretation," *JJS* 31 (1980):1–17.

[4]J. Jocz, *JPJC*, 17.

[5]"Jewish Studies and New Testament Interpretation," 9–10. Cf. Montefiore's remark: "When everybody who was not a Jew joined in believing that both Jesus and Paul were necessarily right, and that, both theoretically and actually, all the Scribes and Pharisees, as lovers of the Law, were hypocritical, proud, cruel and all the rest of it, it was quite exciting to try to prove that Jesus and Paul were wrong. But now . . . the interest and piquancy of the controversy are enormously diminished." *SG,* 1:291.

Testament scholars to gain knowledge about first-century Judaism—the Strack-Billerbeck *Kommentar* and Kittel's *Theological Dictionary*—continue to provide a negatively biased perspective.

A proper understanding of the Pharisees must begin with their earnest quest for righteousness.[6] It was this in turn that led them to the development of the oral law as a kind of "hedge" about the written Law. Obedience to this oral law, which was soon said to have originated along with the written Law through the mediation of Moses, would ensure obedience to the written Law because of its more elaborate definition of the commandments. It was thus a thirst for true righteousness that led the Pharisees to their passionate zeal for the minutiae of the oral law. Through the Pharisees the strict holiness of the priests and the temple was to be brought to the common people in their everyday life, producing of the nation itself a kingdom of priests and a holy people.[7]

Jewish scholars take strong exception to the statements of the New Testament that the Law, written or oral, was in any sense a burden, let alone an insufferable one (cf. Acts 15:10). Jesus' words about the Pharisees cannot be accepted: "They bind heavy burdens, hard to bear, and lay them on men's shoulders; but they themselves will not move them with their finger" (Matt. 23:4; cf. Luke 11:46). On the contrary, Jewish scholars insist, the Law was never a burden in first-century Judaism. Montefiore writes, "To those within there was no bondage, but freedom. The Rabbis said, 'There is no liberty except through the Torah.' "[8]

In order to appreciate the Jewish attitude toward the Law, it must be remembered that Judaism in one sense owed its existence to the Torah. It was the Torah that set Israel apart as unique among the nations. God's goodness brought the Torah to Israel, and Israel's possession of the Law was not only a mark of her election but also a source of joy and pride to the individual Jew. In the words of Israel Abrahams, for the Pharisee, "the Torah became ever more the object of Israel's affection. On Israel's side, service was the token of love, on God's side the opportunity of service was a precious gift, bestowed as a loving privilege."[9] The fulfilling of the Law was thus considered a privilege, and, as Sandmel notes, "what is a privilege to carry never seems a

---

[6]For a more comprehensive discussion of the Pharisees than can be given here, see D. A. Hagner, "Pharisees," in M. C. Tenney, ed., *Zondervan Pictorial Encyclopedia of the Bible* (Grand Rapids: Zondervan, 1975), 4:745–52.

[7]See the many writings of J. Neusner, e.g., *From Politics to Piety: The Emergence of Pharisaic Judaism* (Englewood Cliffs, N.J.: Prentice-Hall, 1973); *Early Rabbinic Judaism* (Leiden: Brill, 1975).

[8]*RT*, 31.

[9]*SP*, 1:13.

burden to those who bear it.''[10] Thus the Law that stands over him in its stringent requirement is at the same time dearest of all things to the Jew. "His glory and his duty, his happiness and his obligation, lie alike in fulfilling God's declared will.''[11] To the Jew of the first century the Law was a delight rather than a burden.[12]

Accordingly, Abrahams argues that it is not fair to interpret Jesus' words "My yoke is easy, and my burden is light" (Matt. 11:29–30) as an attack against the Pharisees. With Chrysostom he prefers to understand the things referred to, not as the rabbinic law and the teaching of Christ, but simply virtue and vice. Christ's yoke is the yoke of virtue rather than the more burdensome yoke of vice.[13] While it is true, of course, that submission to the Torah was regarded as taking upon oneself the "yoke of the kingdom," or the "yoke of the Law," yet it "was never a yoke that galled.''[14] Abrahams admits that Matthew 23:4 refers to rabbinic laws but, finding it impossible to believe that the verse refers to the Pharisees as a whole, he restricts it to certain Pharisees.[15] Montefiore, commenting on the Matthew 11 passage, captures well the Jewish perspective: "But the real Rabbinic feeling is that the Law is a delight. The more laws, the more honour to Israel; the more laws, the more grace of God.''[16] A transformation of the meaning of Matthew 11:28ff. is accomplished by Lapide, who understands the yoke of Jesus to be the yoke of Torah, and argues that "Jesus himself preached, as did all the Pharisees, the welcome, saving yoke of Torah.''[17]

Although the rabbis were aware of the distinction between the moral and ceremonial laws of the Torah, they held both in equally high regard. Similarly, the interpretative oral law made no distinction between the two, and this accounts in large measure for its strange character. Danby writes:

> Granted the acceptance of the written Law as God's will for Israel, Israel's teachers had not the right to determine the relative importance of this or

---

[10]*WJJ*, 80.

[11]*RLGT*, 193–94.

[12]Ibid., 239–40. "The *one* section of the ceremonial Law which caused some trouble was the observance of the Sabbath. And yet note the customary paradox—the Sabbath was pre-eminently the day of delight and feasting, the day of joy and peace and sunshine, for all the harassed communities of Israel." Ibid., 241.

[13]*SP*, 2:4ff. Montefiore, however, understands the burdensome yoke as the rabbinic laws, but with only "a limited justification." *SG*, 2:177–78.

[14]*SP*, 2:14.

[15]Ibid., 10.

[16]*RLGT*, 240.

[17]*RN*, 68.

that injunction. Therefore the Oral Law preserves with equal piety customs and decisions arising out of the "lightest" as out of the "weightiest" precepts of the Law revealed to Israel at Sinai.[18]

Yet with their acknowledged stringency, and in spite of the Gospel contention that they would not move a finger to lighten the burden, the rabbis were concerned to ease the demands as much as possible. Abrahams writes, "At every period we find the Rabbis relieving burdens." Decrees were always subject to the ability of the majority to endure them; historically the Hillelites triumphed over the stricter Shammaites.[19] Indeed, Jesus in his more liberal attitude is often likened to Hillel by Jewish scholars, over against the more stringent Shammai.[20]

The rabbis were in fact concerned to make life under the Law liveable. An example of accommodation can be seen in the allowance of divorce. According to David Daube, when Jesus referred to Moses' write of divorcement as the result of the people's "hardness of heart" (Matt. 19:8; Mark 10:5), he was using a well-established category in rabbinic thought. The category reflected the rabbinic preference for the lesser of two evils. Thus concessions were made and lower standards of piety were accepted in order to lessen the probability of conscious misconduct on the part of the weaker members, who composed the majority of the community. Daube sees the origin of this special category in the confrontation of the pietistic sects. "Apparently it was in solving the tension between the undeniable holiness of sectarian life and its impracticability for ordinary folk that the Rabbis coined the principle under discussion."[21]

A further example of adjustment of the Law is Hillel's introduction of *prozbul*, i.e., a certificate deposited in court, enabling debts to be maintained beyond the beginning of the seventh year, when, according to biblical law, all debts were to be annulled (M. *Shebi* 10:3–4). The closer the seventh year came, the more difficult it obviously became for the needy to find lenders. The *prozbul* thus provided a useful way around the letter of the Law.[22] This and other accommodating measures

---

[18]*The Mishnah*, xvii; cf. Montefiore, *RLGT*, 240–41.

[19]*SP*, 2:12; cf. W. D. Davies. "Contemporary Jewish Religion," in *Peake's Commentary on the Bible*, ed. M. Black and H. H. Rowley (London: Nelson, 1962), 708.

[20]E.g., Lapide, *RN*, 63–64.

[21]D. Daube, "Concessions to Sinfulness in Jewish Law," *JJS* 10 (1959):8.

[22]Neusner notes that Hillel may not have originated the *prozbul*. J. Neusner, *From Politics to Piety* (Englewood Cliffs, N.J.: Prentice-Hall, 1973), 16–17. Neusner also notes this later development: "It was Aqiba and his associates of Yavneh who so enriched the exegetical tradition of the rabbis that they could find whatever they wanted in Scripture" (17).

were introduced "for the better order of the world."[23] "The Rabbis were progressive, forward looking men; and they insisted upon the necessity of an Oral Law to make the written Law adaptable to the facts of daily existence."[24] Klausner also notes the reality of the adaptation of the Law for the needs of daily life: "The Pharisees tried to adapt religion to life: it was immaterial whether this induced new stringencies or new leniencies."[25]

Thus the rabbis were not insensitive to the realities of life, nor did they subjugate the people to burdens that were too difficult to bear. "We do not impose on the community a hardship which the majority cannot endure" (BT Baba Bathra 60b). Moreover, as Jewish scholars are not slow to point out, Jesus himself offered a yoke to his disciples that could hardly be called light—as, for example, in his Sermon on the Mount and in his strict prohibition of divorce.

Jewish scholars are also impelled to refute the notion that in the first century the masses neglected the Law because it was found to be too burdensome or required a learning that was beyond their reach. The problem arises out of an apparent antagonism between Hillel (a leading rabbi, c. 50 B.C.–A.D. 10) and the 'Am Ha-'Areṣ (the "people of the land," or ordinary peasants). The latter refused to take upon themselves the Pharisaic yoke of the Law and thus could not attain to piety according to Hillel's standard. Non-Jewish scholars have been prone to identify the 'Am Ha-'Areṣ with those of whom the Pharisees say, "But this crowd, who do not know the law are accursed" (John 7:49); they similarly find them to be the "publicans and sinners" with whom Jesus so frequently associated, and who found his teaching with its "easy yoke" so attractive. Jewish scholars strenuously object to the contention that a majority of the population disregarded the Law, were alienated from the rabbis, and regarded themselves as spiritually disinherited. The 'Am Ha-'Areṣ was not simply the man without knowledge, or always and only the poor man.[26] Says Montefiore, "On the contrary, the masses were the champions of the Law, and the Law was *their* inheritance; while sprung from the masses, their friends and spokes-

---

[23]Cf. N. H. Glatzer, "Hillel the Elder in the Light of the Dead Sea Scrolls," in K. Stendahl, ed., *The Scrolls and the New Testament* (New York: Harper, 1957), 240. Glatzer sets forth the possibility that Hillel's reform measures were an attempt "to reform Pharisaic Judaism as an answer to the challenge of the sectarian movement" (244).

[24]A. Cohen, "Jewish History in the First Century," in *Judaism and the Beginnings of Christianity* (no ed.) (London: Routledge, 1923), 22.

[25]*JN*, 221.

[26]Montefiore contra Strack-Billerbeck, *RLGT*, 315; *RT*, 30ff.; cf. Abrahams, "'Am Ha-'Areç" in Montefiore, *SG*, 2:647–69.

men, were the great majority of the Rabbis.''[27] The Law was always the prized possession of the common people, not exclusively of the rich and learned. The most that Montefiore will concede is the probable existence of a ''submerged tenth'' who violated the Law and were thus despised.[28] This small fraction of the population did find Jesus attractive since he did not separate himself from them as did the Pharisees. Jesus' success with the *'Am Ha-'Areṣ* has led some to conclude that his teaching differed in content from that of the Pharisees.[29]

S. Cohon says that ''the testimony of the Synoptic Gospels makes Jesus an *'Am Ha-Aretz Hasid*,'' since he ''refused to subject himself to Pharisaic innovations.''[30] Solomon Zeitlin, however, discards the whole notion of a breach between the Pharisees and the *'Am Ha-'Areṣ* as being historically untrue. ''No reference is made in the entire tannaitic literature of antagonism between the *Perushim* and the *Ame ha'aretz*.''[31] And Sandmel cautions against taking Jesus himself to be an *'Am Ha-'Areṣ*, asserting that ''the rabbinic literature gives too little data for any firm knowledge of the *Am Ha-Arez*.''[32] Aharon Oppenheimer's recent major study concludes that the *'Am Ha-'Areṣ* were desirous of keeping the Torah, though not to the same punctilious degree as the Pharisees; were not ''on opposite sides of the barricade'' from the Pharisees; and were not connected with the Christians.[33] Ellis Rivkin has also recently denied that the Pharisees' preoccupation with the Law was intended to separate them from the *'Am ha-'Areṣ*. ''The Pharisees thus did not make the Laws of ritual purity rigorous for themselves but for the priests.''[34]

Jewish scholars thus insist that the Jews of the first century (and later) did not think of themselves as ''under'' the Law in any oppressive

[27]*RT*, 30–31.

[28]Ibid., 38; elsewhere Montefiore says, ''It was a *small* tenth and no more.'' *SG*, 1:cix.

[29]M. Smith, ''A Comparison of Early Christian and Early Rabbinic Tradition,'' *JBL* 82 (1963):172.

[30]S. Cohon, ''The Place of Jesus in the Religious Life of His Day,'' *JBL* 48 (1929):104.

[31]S. Zeitlin, ''The Pharisees,'' *JQR* 52 (1961–62):97. The erroneous argument is based on the supposed equivalence of *Perushim* with *Haberim*, according to Zeitlin. Ibid.

[32]*WJJ*, 113, n. 12; cf. Montefiore's reference to the ''thick mist'' hanging over the subject. *RLGT*, 11.

[33]A. Oppenheimer, *The 'Am Ha-'Aretz. A Study in the Social History of the Jewish People in the Hellenistic-Roman Period* (Leiden: Brill, 1977), see esp. 224–29.

[34]E. Rivkin, *A Hidden Revolution* (Nashville: Abingdon, 1978), 161; see too his article ''Pharisees'' in *IDB* supplementary volume, 657–63.

sense.[35] Quite the contrary, the Law, including the oral Law for the Pharisees, was regarded as a joy and delight, a privilege to perform, and the distinctive mark of Israel as God's people.

But a second major area of debate involves something about which Jewish scholars are, if anything, even more demonstrative in their denial. Because Jesus repeatedly calls the Pharisees hypocrites (e.g., Matt. 23 passim), accusing them of pretense and externalism, one of the most common allegations made by non-Jews has been that the Pharisees knew nothing of true, inward religion. This is vehemently denied by all Jewish scholars without exception. Abrahams, who wrote his two-volume work on Pharisaism to correct precisely this common misconception, flatly states, "Pharisaism was not ritualism."[36] A book such as Solomon Schechter's *Aspects of Rabbinic Theology* (1909) shows beyond question that early Judaism was in fact a deeply spiritual religion[37] and should long ago have put to an end the common negative stereotype. Because first-century Judaism was the heir of the prophets, acquaintance with the prophetic tradition and all that it stood for must be allowed.[38] Walker correctly argues that the ancestral religion of Jesus "required an *inward, as well as an outward,* righteousness."[39] Far from being the victims of formalism, hypocrisy, and self-righteousness, as Abrahams puts it, the Pharisees "were marked by often quaint and sometimes charming delicacies of feeling and thought, by a pervading attraction to the sincere, the simple, the non-ostentatious."[40] Jacobs writes, "The Prophets and Rabbis had continuously and consistently insisted upon the inner motive with which pious deeds should be performed."[41]

The emphasis of rabbinic Judaism falls naturally on the importance of doing the Law. Abrahams has justly characterized Pharisaism as "a system of morality expressed as law."[42] A legalism or nomism—i.e., a religion centered on the obedience to commandments—*can* of course

---

[35]Note the change of title for §28 in the new edition of E. Schürer, *History of the Jewish People in the Age of Jesus Christ,* 3 vols. (Edinburgh, T. & T. Clark, 1979–) from "Life Under the Law" to "Life and the Law."

[36]*SP,* 1:88.

[37]Cf. S. Schechter, *Some Aspects of Rabbinic Theology* (London: Black, 1909), 21ff.; idem, *Studies in Judaism* (London: Black, 1896), 173.

[38]See W. D. Davies, "Contemporary Jewish Religion," 710.

[39]T. Walker, *What Jesus Read* (London: Allen & Unwin, 1925), 41–42.

[40]*SP,* 2:109.

[41]J. Jacobs, "Jesus of Nazareth in History," *JE,* 7:163.

[42]*SP,* 2:113.

lead to externalism, pride, and hypocrisy. But surely Montefiore is correct when he says that "there is no necessary or essential connection of formalism and hypocrisy with a legal religion."[43] Conscious of the dangers inherent in the emphasis on deeds of the Law, many rabbis insisted on the fulfillment of *kawwanah,* "devotion" in heart in the fulfilling of a commandment, doing it with "full and deliberate intention," and they stressed the importance of *lishmah,* the doing of the deed "for its own sake,"[44] Some examples of evasive casuistry and instances of so-called acting cleverly can of course be found in the Talmudic literature. But these aberrations are so few and insignificant that they do not bother Jewish scholars. As Loewe puts it, "We are quite content to say, 'Well, yes, they are unpleasant cases in the highest degree, but not one Jew in a thousand has heard of them, not one in ten thousand moulds his life on them, what then do they amount to?' "[45] Along with intense effort, the need for repentance, forgiveness, and grace were also recognized. In short, the spiritual was combined with the legal in what may appear to be a rather incongruous whole. But it was the reality of this combination that made the Law the joy of the Israelite.

A religion that stresses deeds of the Law—especially one that is as punctilious as rabbinic Judaism is—of course *may* lead to a self-righteousness and an exaggerated emphasis on merit. By its nature nomism may encourage an individual to count himself acceptable before God on the basis of his own fulfillment of the various external requirements of the Law. It is, however, a gross misconception to regard the rabbinic devotion to the Law as necessarily a "justification by works." Jewish scholars are very sensitive to what they regard as a Protestant, or more specifically, Pauline polemic against the Law. Thus Schoeps argues that "the rabbinic praises of the law can be understood only in this sense of fulfilling God's will, and never in the sense of some ethics of merit, no matter how fashioned."[46]

Montefiore particularly takes Strack-Billerbeck to task on this point. In differentiating between the righteousness of the rabbis and that of Jesus, Billerbeck "misinterprets the inner meaning of the Rabbinic

---

[43]"The Synoptic Gospels and the Jewish Consciousness," *HJ* 3 (1904–05):667.

[44]For *kawwanah,* see Montefiore, *RLGT,* 183–84; for *lishmah,* ibid., 188–89, and Schechter, *Some Aspects of Rabbinic Theology,* 159ff.

[45]H. Loewe, "On Acting Cleverly," Appendix II (380–89) in Montefiore, *RLGT,* 383.

[46]H. J. Schoeps, *The Jewish-Christian Argument* (London: Faber & Faber, 1965), 41.

legalism."[47] Montefiore willingly admits that some of the evidence lends a *prima facie* credibility to Billerbeck's argument that the rabbis trust in their own achieved righteousness for salvation. Yet simultaneously the rabbis throw themselves on the mercy and the grace of God. The plain truth is that they are not consistent in this matter. But when the whole picture is seen, according to Montefiore, "the alleged sharp opposition between the soteriology of Jesus and the soteriology of the Rabbis" cannot be maintained.[48] Abrahams, in full agreement with Montefiore, similarly concludes, "The Pharisaic position will never be understood by those who fail to realize that it tried to hold the balance between man's duty to *strive* to earn pardon, and his *inability* to attain it without God's gracious gift of it."[49]

Rabbinic Judaism is clearly a legal religion. But the fact that its center involves a nomism or legalism can be seriously misleading. At this point Sandmel's words are appropriate: "The lawyer's library by no means exhausts the literature of the Jews, for Jews have their prayer book and they have the Psalms and the Prophets. And, above all, the legalistic literature itself contains copious passages of an edifying character."[50] E. P. Sanders has demonstrated that the nomism of rabbinic Judaism is a "covenantal nomism" that begins with and presupposes the election of Israel and the covenant relationship with God. The stress on obedience to the Law in rabbinic Judaism, therefore, is a matter of response to the salvation already provided by the mercy of God rather than an attempt to accumulate merit before a remote and hostile God whose favor must be won.[51]

With this deservedly high view of Pharisaic Judaism before us, what are we to make of the Gospel portrayal of the Pharisees? Jewish scholars are understandably disturbed by the many passages in the New Testament that derogate the religious life of the Jews of the first century. To these scholars it is inconceivable that the Pharisees as a whole could be guilty of the accusations made against them in the Gospels. Thus Montefiore calls the picture of the Pharisee in Jesus' parable (Luke 18:9ff.) "a ludicrous caricature of the Pharisaic ideal."[52] Abrahams

---

[47]*SG*, 2:161.

[48]*RLGT*, 195. For the whole discussion see pages 154–201, where Billerbeck is quoted *in extenso*. See also Abrahams on "God's Forgiveness" in *SP*, 1:139–49. Cf. Montefiore, "Rabbinic Judaism and the Epistles of St. Paul," *JQR* 13 (1901):174.

[49]*SP*, 1:147. For further discussion of this subject, see below, pp. 191–99.

[50]*WJJ*, 79.

[51]See E. P. Sanders, *Paul and Palestinian Judaism* (Philadelphia: Fortress, 1977).

[52]*RT*, 37.

calls him "an exceptional case, one of the weeds of ritualism, not one of its ordinary or natural fruits."[53] Similarly, it is frequently argued by Jewish scholars that the view of the Pharisees in Matthew 23 is in fact diametrically opposite to true Pharisaic piety.

The solution to the problem is a simple one according to many Jewish scholars. The most common explanation is that Jesus' remarks refer only to the few weeds among the many flowers. Since Jesus cannot have been referring to the Pharisees in general, he must have had in mind a very small minority, the exception to the rule, who may in fact have been as he describes them. Montefiore says that we must interpret the denunciatory passages "historically to mean that there were *some* very bad Scribes and *some* very bad Pharisees."[54] It is admitted that Pharisaism had its "weeds," and its "black sheep,"[55] but the Jewish objection is that the whole class is condemned without qualification, "as if *all* the Rabbis of the age of Jesus were hypocrites and vipers, or as if all Rabbis were *necessarily* hypocrites and vipers."[56] Matthew 23 "tars the whole class of Rabbis and Pharisees with the same bitter and undifferentiating brush."[57] As Abrahams commented, "The danger always lies in the tendency to confuse a system with its abuses."[58]

It is pointed out by Jewish scholars that the rabbis attacked the selfsame sins that Jesus did. Montefiore notes that "the Rabbis denounce hypocrisy no less hotly than Jesus."[59] Seven kinds of Pharisees are listed in the Talmud (BT Sot. 22b; PT Ber. ix. 14b)[60] in what

---

[53]*SP*, 1:57.

[54]*RT*, 22.

[55]Abrahams, *SP*, 2:vii, 119; Montefiore, *RLGT*, 322.

[56]Montefiore, *RLGT*, 322. Cf. S. Sandmel, *A Jewish Understanding of the New Testament* (1956; reprint ed., New York: Ktav, 1974), 24–25. A. Lukyn Williams attempts to construe *hypokritēs* to mean not hypocrite, but "play-actor," thus making the fault of the Pharisees mere superficiality rather than purposeful chicanery. *Talmudic Judaism and Christianity* (London: SPCK, 1933), 63ff. The contexts in which the word is used (cf. Matt. 23:33), however, would seem to argue against Williams's theory.

[57]Montefiore, *SG*, 2:296.

[58]*SP*, 1:85, 87.

[59]*RLGT*, 118, 322. Yet elsewhere Montefiore says the following: "It does seem to me that his denunciation of formalism and pride, his contrasted pictures of the lowly Publican and the scrupulous Pharisee, were new and permanent contributions to morality and religion. As the Jewish reader meets them in the Synoptic Gospels, he recognizes this new contribution; and if he is adequately open-minded, he does homage and is grateful." "The Synoptic Gospels and the Jewish Consciousness," *HJ* 3 (1904–05):666.

[60]A. Guttmann translates the passage from the Palestinian Talmud as follows: "There are seven kinds of Pharisees: 1. The shoulder Pharisee. 2. The wait-a-while

Flusser calls "a fivefold variation on the theme of hypocrisy—the last two kinds of hypocrisy are replaced by two positive kinds of Pharisee."[61] Flusser goes on to suggest that this explains the seven "woes" against the Pharisees in Matthew 23. The first type of Pharisee is the "shoulder-Pharisee who lays commandments upon men's shoulders."[62] According to Klausner, the Talmud refers to the "Pharisaic plague," and both Klausner and Flusser note the similar vitriolic criticism of hypocrisy to be found in the *Assumption of Moses* (7:3–10), where the Pharisees are referred to as "pernicious and criminal men, who claim to be righteous . . . pleasing themselves, hypocritical in all their ways . . . their hands and hearts are all corrupt, and their mouths are full of boasting—and yet they complain: do not touch me lest you make me unclean."[63] Similar criticism of the Pharisees comes from another Jewish quarter, the Essenes, who describe them as "slippery exponents" who lead the people astray by "their deceitful doctrine, lying tongues and false lips" (4QpNah 2:7–10). "False teachers, they lead astray, and blindly they are heading for a fall, for their works are done in deceit" (1QH 4:6–8). "They closed up the fountain of knowledge to the thirsty and gave them vinegar with which to quench their thirst" (IQH 4:11; cf. Matt. 23:13 and Luke 11:52).[64] Jews, therefore, were not uncritical of the Pharisees, and with the Talmudic evidence in mind, Abrahams declaims, "The Pharisees were themselves the most severe critics of the possible abuses of their own system."[65]

One way, then, of explaining the Gospel passages that criticize the Pharisees is to conclude that they apply only to the exceptional weeds among the flowers. Another common way of accounting for the problematic passages is to deny that Jesus actually spoke at all about the

---

Pharisee. 3. The balance Pharisee. 4. The deducting Pharisee. 5. The 'I want to know my guilt and shall compensate for it' Pharisee. 6. The fearing Pharisee. 7. The loving Pharisee." The amoraic explanation that follows points to (1) ostentation, (2) procrastination, (3) care to keep sinning and doing good deeds in equal proportions, (4) justification of minimal performance of good deeds, and (5) desire to compensate a sin with a good deed. The sixth and seventh categories are likened to Job and Abraham. *Rabbinic Judaism in the Making* (Detroit: Wayne State University, 1970), 166.

[61]D. Flusser, *Jesus* (New York: Herder & Herder, 1969), 54. Cf. Sandmel, *A Jewish Understanding of the New Testament*, 24.

[62]Quoted by Flusser (*Jesus,* 54) from *Ber.* 14b.

[63]As cited by Flusser, *Jesus,* 47; cf. *JN,* 227.

[64]These passages are quoted by Flusser, *Jesus,* 54–55.

[65]*SP,* 1:80, 159. Cf. Ben-Chorin, "Jesus und Paulus in jüdischer Sicht," *Annual of the Swedish Theological Institute,* X, ed. B. Knutsson (Leiden: Brill, 1976) 22; Maccoby, *RJ,* 229.

Pharisees in this negative way, and to attribute such passages instead to the later hostility between the church and the synagogue. In some instances, for example, the historicity or accuracy of a reported controversy can be repudiated. Thus Zeitlin regards the hand-washing dispute as anachronistic and concludes, "We have the right to maintain that some controversies between the Pharisees and Jesus and his disciples could not have occurred during their lifetime."[66] Montefiore considers the *corban* passage (Matt. 15:5–6; Mark 7:11–12) to be so full of difficulty in the light of Mishnaic evidence that he thinks it best to regard it as inauthentic.[67] To Montefiore and most Jewish scholars, it is because of the later controversies between the synagogue and the church that Jesus in the Gospels appears as always necessarily right, and his opponents as always necessarily wrong.[68] "Hence the Gospels' picture of the Pharisees as the leading opponents of Jesus reflects the situation of the nascent church, which found in the Pharisees a major competitive force preventing conversion of Jews to faith in Jesus as messiah."[69]

From the Christian side an attempt was made by F. C. Burkitt to reconcile a high view of Pharisaic religion with the negative statements of Jesus by positing a fundamental difference between pre–A.D. 70 and post–A.D. 70 Judaism, with the former as Jesus describes it and the latter as the Talmudic literature describes it.[70] This explanation is rightly rejected by Montefiore.[71] But it does raise a question that bears on any discussion of the Pharisees and the Gospel narratives, namely the extent to which the rabbinic literature of A.D. 200 (the Mishna, codified by Rabbi Judah the Patriarch) and later (the Talmudic commentaries of the fifth and sixth centuries) accurately reflects the character of first-century Judaism.

Many Jewish scholars oppose the suggestion that there was any marked difference in spirit between the Judaism of A.D. 600 and that of A.D. 30. In defending the position of Law in early Judaism, Montefiore

---

[66]"The Pharisees," *JQR* 52 (1961–62):121. Cf. Lapide, *RN*, 51; Maccoby, *RJ*, 97.

[67]*SG*, 1:148ff.; cf. C. G. Montefiore, "Jewish Scholarship and Christian Silence," *HJ* 1 (1902–03):342–43.

[68]"What a Jew Thinks About Jesus," *HJ* 33 (1934–35):517. Cf. H. G. Enelow, *A Jewish View of Jesus* (New York: Macmillan, 1920), 136.

[69]Neusner, *From Politics to Piety*, 68. Cf. Vermes, who writes: "The proposal advanced by the form critics that many of the scholastic debates and arguments between Jesus and the Pharisees should be postdated and identified as exchanges between the leaders of the Jerusalem church, the 'Judaizing' circles of Palestinian Christianity, and their Pharisee opponents, appears in consequence very persuasive." *GJJ*, 20.

[70]F. C. Burkitt, *The Gospel History and Its Transmission* (Edinburgh, 1907²), 170ff.

[71]*SG*, 2:627.

remarks that even if there were a considerable difference, that difference would have to be due to some factor other than the Law, since, if anything, the Law was more developed and a more dominant influence and thus would have been more "burdensome" (which, in fact, it was not) in the Middle Ages than it was in A.D. 30. Montefiore admits a slight amount of evidence that there may have been a greater percentage of bad rabbis in the earlier period, yet this would hardly be enough to justify the "sweeping statement" of the Gospels.[72] Answering Strack-Billerbeck's claim that the catastrophic judgment of A.D. 70 profoundly modified the Pharisaic reliance upon legal righteousness for justification before God, Montefiore objects,

> But, historically, there is no reason to believe that the Rabbis thought more of God's "grace" and of human "weakness" after 70 than before it, or again, that they insisted more on man's responsibility and on his capacity (within limits) to fulfill the Law before 70 than after it.[73]

Nor, insists Montefiore, this time against Burkitt, can one take the ill-fated Hadrianic Revolt as a turning point in the Jewish religion. We know enough about men before Hadrian, such as Hillel, Jochanan ben Zakkai, and Akiba to make such a theory unwarranted.[74] Most Jewish scholars have agreed with this viewpoint that the Judaism of the rabbinic literature is not essentially different from that of Jesus' Pharisaic contemporaries. They have been supported by many non-Jewish scholars such as G. F. Moore, who describes what he calls "normative Judaism," and A. Lukyn Williams, who concludes, "The outlook and attitude of Talmudic Judaism is identical with that of Palestinian Rabbinic Judaism of the first century."[75] Danby, in his introduction to the Mishna, notes the difficulty of intimating the historical value of the Mishnaic material, due to the lapse of time, political upheavals, and the absence of Sadducean doctrine. Yet he sees "no trace of a tendency to effect reforms," but instead, "a veneration for the letter of tradition remarkable for pedantic insistence on verbal exactitude."[76] More recently this conservative attitude toward the continuity of the tradition

---

[72]*RT*, 32–33.

[73]*RLGT*, 200. "The main elements of the Rabbinic religion underwent little change from 50 to 500 A.D." "Rabbinic Judaism and the Epistles of St. Paul," *JQR* 13 (1901):164.

[74]*SG*, 2:226.

[75]*Talmudic Judaism and Christianity* (London: SPCK, 1933), 55. Cf. J. Parkes, *Judaism and Christianity* (London: Gollancz, 1948), 45; S. Cohon, "The Place of Jesus in the Religious Life of His Day," *JBL* 48 (1927):83.

[76]*The Mishnah*, xiv–xv.

has found expression in such Jewish scholars as E. E. Urbach and A. Guttmann.[77]

At the same time, however, a few Jewish scholars have begun to challenge this conclusion. Sandmel distinguishes between Pharisaism and Rabbinism, noting that "the hostility in the Gospels is directed to Pharisaism, not Rabbinism, and this may well provide us with a clue to the circumstance that in the age of Jesus, Rabbinism had as yet not come to its triumph."[78] Sandmel is very pessimistic about using the rabbinic literature in determining the nature of first-century Judaism: "Since it is possible only to a limited extent to associate the teaching attributed to some sage with a given age, and since 90 and 70 stand as curtains obscuring our vision, then it follows that we will always be in some area of great uncertainty as to the stage at which the Rabbinic tradition stood prior to 70."[79] Since only "stray bits" of pre-A.D. 70 material are preserved in the rabbinic literature, even a nonpartisan use of that literature leaves us with a high degree of uncertainty.[80] Jacob Neusner is, if anything, even more skeptical about the possibility of obtaining a knowledge of pre-70 Pharisaism from the rabbinic literature. To be sure, Neusner argues for a kind of continuity: "We shall have to regard the Yavnean rabbis as successors of the pre-70 Pharisees and treat the two as a single sect, or kind, of Judaism."[81] Yet the rabbinic literature must be used "only with very great reserve" as evidence of the character of first-century Judaism.[82] "Much that we are told about the Pharisees reflects the situation, interests and viewpoint of the teller, not of the historical Pharisees."[83] At the end of his study,

---

[77]E. E. Urbach, *The Sages, Their Concepts and Beliefs,* trans. I. Abrahams (Jerusalem: Magnes, Hebrew University, 1975); Guttmann, *Rabbinic Judaism in the Making:* "The termination of the sacrificial cult, the centralized sanctuary, the high-priesthood and many other laws and institutions due to the destruction of the Temple in Jerusalem, resulted in significant changes in the forms and ways of religious life of Palestinian and Diaspora Jewry. However, these changes did not cause an essential modification of the character of 'mainstream' Judaism" (xi).

[78]S. Sandmel, *The First Christian Century In Judaism and Christianity. Certainties and Uncertainties* (New York: Oxford, 1969), 101, n. 15; cf. 70–71.

[79]Ibid., 62–63. We may also note here E. P. Sanders' skepticism about pre-70 Judaism and his refusal to equate the post-70 rabbis with the earlier Pharisees. *Paul and Palestinian Judaism.*

[80]Sandmel, *A Jewish Understanding of the New Testament,* 200–201.

[81]J. Neusner, "Emergent Rabbinic Judaism in a Time of Crisis," in the collected essays, *Early Rabbinic Judaism* (Leiden: Brill, 1975), 43.

[82]"The Use of the Later Rabbinic Evidence for the Study of First Century Pharisaism," in W. S. Green, ed., *Approaches to Ancient Judaism: Theory and Practice,* (Missoula, Mont.: Scholars, 1978), 219.

[83]Neusner, *From Politics to Piety,* 2.

Neusner concludes: "The historical Pharisees of the period before 70 A.D. have eluded us."[84] Thus, regarding the problem of the Gospel portrayal of the Pharisees, Neusner's skepticism wins out: "Since we cannot truly know whether the Pharisees were hypocrites or sincere, we might as well not wonder about it."[85] Indeed, Neusner is altogether unhappy that the sources are approached with questions set by Christian scholars and criticizes the recent trend whereby apologetic motives have encouraged an uncritical use of the sources on both sides.[86] Neusner has also repeatedly insisted on the variegated nature of pre-70 Judaism as a fact to be remembered[87] and, with E. Rivkin, he has thrown a question mark over the continuity between Pharisaism and the religion of the Bible.[88]

Interestingly, some similar points had been made long ago by Christian scholars in response to Montefiore. Burkitt, for example, argued that the diversity of first-century Judaism must adequately be taken into account in any consideration of the subject. His conclusion was that the practices of the Pharisees in the Gospels "are not to be identified *en bloc* with Jewish orthodoxy of Talmudic times."[89] A. Menzies, in another rejoinder to Montefiore, went somewhat further when he argued that the Gospels rather than the Mishna must remain the principal sources of information about first-century Judaism, for, in addition to the different religious climates in the two periods, one must reckon with the possibility of intentional omission of objectionable material from the Mishna as well as the possibility of Christian influence during the intervening period.[90]

Without question the discussion of first-century Pharisaism has been made more difficult because of apologetic concerns—on the one hand, of conservative Christians in wanting to defend the authenticity of Jesus' words in the Gospels, and, on the other hand, of the Jews in their desire to keep Jesus and the Pharisees as close together as possible. The

---

[84]Ibid., 143.

[85]Ibid., xxiii.

[86]Ibid., 6; cf. "The Use of the Later Rabbinic Evidence for the Study of First Century Pharisaism," 217–18.

[87]See Neusner, *Early Rabbinic Judaism* (esp. "The Demise of 'Normative Judaism,'" 138–51); "The Use of the Later Rabbinic Evidence"; and especially "'Judaism' after Moore: A Programmatic Statement," *JJS* 31 (1980):141–56.

[88]See Rivkin, *A Hidden Revolution*.

[89]F. C. Burkitt, "Jesus and the 'Pharisees,'" *JTS*, 28 (1927):397; cf. M. S. Enslin in prolegomenon to reprint of I. Abrahams, *Studies in Pharisaism and the Gospels* (New York: Ktav, 1967), XXII.

[90]A. Menzies, "A Rejoinder" [to Montefiore's "Jewish Scholarship and Christian Silence"], *HJ* 1 (1902–3):83.

existence of a clear Jewish polemic is acknowledged by Sandmel: "At least some of the adulation for the Pharisees by modern Jewish scholars represents a defensive reaction, not only to shield the Pharisees from Gospel slurs, but to go on to exalt them."[91] True though this may be, a few Jewish scholars have been willing to allow the existence of certain defects within Pharisaism. These defects are of course relative and not absolute. Montefiore has been among the most frank in this regard. He admits, for example, that the Law, with all its good and noble points, is also the source of all the weaknesses of rabbinic religion.[92] He candidly sums up the defects of first-century Judaism under three headings: (1) "the putting of ritual in the place of morality," (2) "self-righteousness or pride," and (3) "a certain ill-directed intellectualism."[93] Klausner similarly admits that in every system matters of secondary importance eventually displace those of primary importance and the best of ideas become distorted and transformed. For Klausner, the main defect of the Pharisees was their placing of the ceremonial legislation on a par with the moral law. Indeed, the outcome of this is that "the casuistry and immense theoretical care devoted to every one of the slightest religious ordinances left them open to the misconception that the ceremonial laws were the main principle and the ethical laws were only secondary."[94] In the more recent Jewish writing on Jesus it becomes more difficult to find such statements. Flusser, however, allows that "the general truth that strict observation of ritual purity can itself encourage moral laxity, was applicable even in Jesus' day." He adds that "obviously, there were some petty minds among the Pharisees—such people are found in all societies."[95] Schonfield writes that "sometimes in their zeal, as is often the way, they lost sight of the spirit of an institution in stressing its strict observance, but their intentions were good."[96] The new edition of Schürer, purged of much anti-Judaism, is still able to conclude in a passage that shows Vermes' influence:

---

[91]Sandmel, *The First Century in Judaism and Christianity*, 101, n. 15. But the distortion occurs on both sides (cf. 66). See also S. Sandmel, "The Jewish Scholar and Early Christianity," *The Seventy-Fifth Anniversary Volume of the Jewish Quarterly Review*, ed. A. A. Neumann and S. Zeitlin (New York: Ktav, 1967), 474ff.

[92]*RLGT*, 15.

[93]C. G. Montefiore, "Rabbinic Judaism and the Epistles of St. Paul," *JQR* 13 (1901):168.

[94]*JN*, 216.

[95]Flusser, *Jesus*, 56. He quickly adds that the leaders of Jesus' day, though "not without faults," were "far from being petty-minded."

[96]*PP*, 77.

The religious life of Palestinian Judaism outlined in these pages aimed at the sanctification of the individual and the nation. In practice, however, the great accumulation of commandments and obligations could lead also to pettiness, formalism, and an emphasis on outward observance rather than true integrity. Even though rhetorically exaggerated and representing the standpoint of a Galilean charismatic, a number of sayings attributed to Jesus by Matthew and Luke undoubtedly expose the excesses and abuses to which a legally motivated religion tended to lead.[97]

Neusner has recently criticized Moore's treatment of Judaism for neglecting the central importance of Halakah in its own right and, quoting F. C. Porter's 1927 review of Moore's work, for focusing attention on the piety and ethics of prophetic religion to the virtual exclusion of the significance of the ritual, cultus, and law that compose the Mishna.[98] The insistence on the equal importance of the ceremonial and moral parts of the Law is in itself, if not necessarily, at least potentially dangerous. If, as Loewe says, it is "natural and inevitable" that the mass of commandments in the Torah "clog the simplicity of prophetic teaching,"[99] how much more is this likely where an elaborately articulated oral tradition is accepted as having authority comparable to that of the written Law. Jewish scholars in their admission of these problems are thus not far from the contention of Jesus that the oral Law, and perhaps an undue stress on the ceremonial parts of the written Law, had—for some, if not for all—in effect obscured the real message of the Law (Matt. 15:6; Mark 7:13).

That there is something problematic about the nature of legalism itself is allowed by Montefiore, albeit hesitatingly: "It may be that the fact that a few distinguished Rabbis seem really to have believed that they had fulfilled all the demands of the Law, and that they were therefore completely righteous, shows that there was something lacking in the whole Rabbinic conception of righteousness and in the legalism which was the root of it."[100] This may account for Jesus' whole bearing toward the religious perspective of the Pharisees. Jesus' attack on the

---

[97]E. Schürer, *The History of the Jewish People in the Age of Jesus Christ,* 3 vols. (Edinburgh: T. & T. Clark (1979–), 2:486. Some Gospel passages from Matthew 23 follow (vv. 24–25, 27–28).

[98]J. Neusner, "'Judaism' after Moore: A Programmatic Statement," *JJS* 31 (1980):141–56.

[99]H. Loewe, "The Place of Law in Modern Jewish Teaching," in G. Yates, ed., *In Spirit and Truth* (London: Hodder & Stoughton, 1934), 253.

[100]*RLGT,* 171. He wistfully adds, "I do not feel wholly clear about this point."

abuses of Pharisaism, writes Montefiore, may have "led him half-unconsciously to an attack, or at all events to an *implied* attack, upon the system itself."[101]

The arguments of modern Jewish scholarship on behalf of the Pharisees cannot be ignored. We have every reason to believe that Pharisaism ideally—and in the actual lives of many Pharisees—was the expression of truly prophetic religion. Indeed, the New Testament itself affords evidence for the existence of admirable Pharisees. One need only think of a seeker of truth (John 3:1ff.) and an advocate for justice (John 7:50), or of the scribe to whom Jesus said, "You are not far from the kingdom of God" (Mark 12:34), of those who showed hospitality to Jesus (Luke 7:36; 11:37; 14:1), of those who warned Jesus of the attempt on his life (Luke 13:31), or of the fairness and restraint of Gamaliel (Acts 5:34–39). Formalistic piety and inward spirituality,[102] nomism and prophetic morality, are not mutually exclusive. There were, of course, bad Pharisees, and there are some potential weaknesses in Pharisaism. The piety reflected in the rabbinic literature has its low points as well as its high points and is plainly and admittedly inconsistent. But it behooves Christians to take a positive attitude toward Pharisaism. Klausner is obviously correct when he writes, "A religion and a sect should be judged by the principles it expounds and by the best of its teachers rather than by its unworthy members: it should be judged by the best that it contains and not by the worst."[103] The fact is that the Pharisees and Jesus would have seen eye to eye on many of the essential elements of true religion. Indeed, the Pharisees may have been as sensitive as they were to Jesus' unorthodoxies just because they may have thought of him as a Pharisee.[104] On the other hand, as Ben-Chorin suggests, Jesus' grave concern with the Pharisees was due to the fact that in some ways they were so close to the truth: "Just this closeness explains the great tension between them."[105]

---

[101]*RT*, 40.

[102]Cf. R. N. Longenecker, *Paul, Apostle of Liberty* (New York: Harper, 1964), 79. Longenecker's whole discussion in chapter 3, "The Piety of Hebraic Judaism," is to be commended for its fairness toward the findings of Jewish scholarship.

[103]*JN*, 215.

[104]H. J. Cadbury, *The Peril of Modernizing Jesus* (1927; reprint ed., Naperville, Ill.: Allenson, 1962), 69; cf. H. G. Enelow, *A Jewish View of Jesus* (New York: Macmillan, 1920), 39.

[105]S. Ben-Chorin, *Jesus im Judentum* (Wuppertal, 1970), 43. Cf. J. Parkes, *Judaism and Christianity* (London: Gollancz, 1940), 59; cf. Newsham: "This concern of Jesus for the Pharisees is, in reality, the mark of His appreciation of their great possibilities." "Why Jesus Feared the Pharisees," *ExpT* 63 (1951–52):67.

In the final analysis, there is no necessity of a forced choice between the positive view of Pharisaism from the rabbinic literature and the (mainly) negative view from the Gospels. As Montefiore long ago pointed out,[106] if we assume on the one hand the existence of a "fair number" of bad Jews in the time of Jesus—and, we may add, the intrinsic potential for abuse in any legalism—and on the other hand that Jesus and the Gospel writers engaged in some degree of hyperbole in statements about the Pharisees (e.g., making it appear as though Pharisaism universally was corrupt), the problem all but disappears. Pharisaism was at heart a movement for righteousness, admirable in its attempt to bring every area of life in subjection to the Law. It was the longing for a righteous Israel and the hope of the coming messianic kingdom that motivated the Pharisees. The piety and expectant tone of the Pharisaic Psalms of Solomon is virtually indistinguishable from that, so highly honored by Christians, which appears in the poetic utterances of Luke 1 and 2. God was about to do a great work for his people, and in preparation it was necessary for the people to turn to the Law anew. The scribes and the Pharisees accordingly made the Law an influence in the lives of the masses that it had never before been.

Strange though it may at first seem, the real quarrel between Jesus and the Pharisees was not in any fundamental way about righteousness. Indeed, to discuss the problem of Jesus and the Pharisees on this level alone can only be misleading. Thus Montefiore is more wrong than right when, contrasting Jesus with Paul, he writes, "The Jesus of the Synoptic Gospels *was* a critic and pathologist of Judaism. His criticisms are real: they are flesh and blood. . . . Jesus put his finger upon some real sore places: upon actual dangers, limitations, shortcomings."[107] Of course Jesus did accuse the Pharisees (i.e., many of them) of failing to keep the Law that they professed. Indeed, he did argue that their teaching tended to annul rather than to fulfill the Law and warned his disciples about "the leaven of the Pharisees" (Matt. 16:6ff.). And in his critical teaching he did give an exposition of the true meaning of the Law.

The fundamental disagreement between the Pharisees and Jesus, however, is altogether of another order. Indeed, the real quarrel lay much deeper. Jesus came announcing the presence of the kingdom of God in and through his own person and ministry. This dawning of the

---

[106]*SG*, 2:626–27.

[107]C. G. Montefiore, "Rabbinic Judaism and the Epistles of St. Paul," *JQR* 13 (1901), 167; cf. idem, "The Religious Teaching of the Synoptic Gospels in Its Relation to Judaism," *HJ* 20 (1921–22):445.

kingdom of God involves a newness that breaks out of the constrictive boundaries set by the Pharisees of Jesus' day and Jewish scholarship of today. Thus, as we have seen, Jesus' attitude toward the Law makes it difficult to understand him as a first-century Jew concerned simply with the preservation of Pharisaic ideals. Jesus goes too far in his claims of authority to satisfy such an interpretation. It is at bottom the question of personal authority that caused the clash with the Pharisees and it is this same question that troubles present-day Jewish scholarship.[108] Here Jesus is completely out of line with Jewish tradition. "He bids men to come to Him, learn of Him, listen to Him, obey Him, as if all other authority was at an end."[109] The real quarrel between the Pharisees and Jesus centers finally on the personal claims of Jesus and the centrality of these claims to his message. Jesus, in fact, put his own person in that central place previously held by the Torah as God's revelation to humanity.

---

[108]See above, pp. 99–105.

[109]F. Lofthouse, "The Old Testament and Christianity," in Wheeler Robinson, ed., *Record and Revelation* (Oxford: Clarendon, 1938), 467.

CHAPTER FIVE

The Religious Teaching of Jesus: Humanity's Relationship to God

THE RELIGION OF JESUS is regarded by Jewish scholars as thoroughly Jewish. The words of Wellhausen are frequently cited with approval: "Jesus was not a Christian: he was a Jew. He did not proclaim a new faith, but taught men to do the will of God."[1] It is, of course, to be expected that Jesus would share the religious perspective of his people. The Scriptures of the Hebrew Bible were authoritative for Jesus as they were for the Jews. There was no need for him to define or defend the basic doctrines of the Jewish faith; they were, rather, assumed and built upon. Frequently, however, a mistaken and unfortunate polarity has been imposed on the data by Christian writers, and this polarity results in a caricature of Judaism and an exaggeration of the uniqueness of Christianity.

To be sure, given the primary message of Jesus—the announcement of the presence of the kingdom—we must be prepared for a degree of unusualness in the teaching of Jesus about God and humanity, involving at least a sharpened clarity, if nothing more. The extent of the newness involved has been the subject of Jewish comment, and to this we now turn our attention.

GRACE AND WORKS

We have noticed in the preceding chapter the centrality of the Torah in the religious life of the Jew. Judaism can be de-

---

[1]*Einleitung in die drei ersten Evangelien* (Berlin, 1905), 113. Quoted, e.g., by Klausner, *JN*, 95; Lapide, *ÖCJ*, 90; Ben-Chorin, *Jesus im Judentum* (Wuppertal, 1970), 7; cf. Vermes, *GJJ*, 3.

scribed as essentially a "covenantal nomism,"[2] a legal religion emphasizing the deeds of the Law and giving pride of place to what is appropriately termed orthopraxy as contrasted with orthodoxy.[3] In this emphasis Jewish scholars see no difference between Jesus and the rabbis. Jesus too stresses the necessity and importance of good deeds (cf. Matt. 7:21ff.), the only difference being that he stresses *hearing* and doing, while the rabbis stress *learning* and doing.[4] As we have also seen, Jewish scholars strongly oppose any suggestion that the Law may have been a burden to the first-century Jew. On the contrary, as for the psalmist of old (e.g., Ps. 119), the Law was his delight, and his desire to obey the Law was motivated by his love for God.[5] Unquestionably a religion that stresses law always has its inherent dangers. Jewish scholars, however, contend that true Judaism is self-correcting at this point. The Jewish argument is that while a legal religion *can* deteriorate into a mechanical and hypocritical externalism, it need not *necessarily* do so. A legal religion can be deadening, but ideally it can encourage the kind of spirituality championed by Jesus. Montefiore describes Judaism as follows:

> "A legal religion." Yes, but a religion which culminated in the view that for God's sake and His law's sake, for the pure love of God and for the pure love of His law, must all commands be fulfilled, that the intention is even greater than the deed, and that thoughts of sin are even more serious than the sin itself.[6]

The resemblance to the perspective of Jesus in these words is intentional.

---

[2]The description is that of E. P. Sanders in *Paul and Palestinian Judaism* (Philadelphia: Fortress, 1977).

[3]Cf. R. T. Herford, "What they [the rabbis] imparted was not a *doctrine* but a *discipline,* which required the doing of right actions and the refraining from wrong ones." "Repentance and Forgiveness in the Talmud With Some Reference to the Teaching of the Gospels," *HJ* 40 (1941–42):56.

[4]Montefiore, *RLGT,* 153–54.

[5]Cf. Schechter, *Some Aspects of Rabbinic Theology* (London: Black, 1909), 68.

[6]C. G. Montefiore, "The Spirit of Judaism," in F. J. Foakes-Jackson and K. Lake, eds., *The Beginnings of Christianity* (London: Macmillan, 1920), 1:80. A similar conclusion is voiced by Oesterley: "It would have been impossible, at any rate among the bulk of the people, for a mere external legalism to have quenched the love and trust which the individual Jew felt for and in his God." "Judaism in the Days of the Christ," in F. J. Foakes-Jackson, ed., *The Parting of the Roads* (London: Edward Arnold, 1912), 94.

Thus the Jewish contention is that the Gospels have little, if anything, to offer first-century Judaism. "The Beatitudes have undoubtedly a lofty tone," writes G. Friedlander, "but let us not forget that all that they teach can be found in Isaiah and the Psalms. Israel finds nothing new here."[7] If Jesus came emphasizing the "moral" as more fundamentally important than the "ceremonial," the rabbis would "on the whole" have done the same.[8] If Jesus stressed the importance of thought and intention as well as deed, so also did the rabbis.[9] If Jesus came repeating Hosea's cry for "mercy and not sacrifice," that too was rabbinic doctrine, "doubtless Rabbinic doctrine at its best, but Rabbinic doctrine nonetheless, and not very unusual Rabbinic doctrine either."[10] Even the admittedly revolutionary statement of Mark 7:15 can be seen, as Montefiore sees it, as "only an application of a principle which runs on all fours with theirs [i.e., the rabbis]."[11]

Nor, according to Jewish scholars, did Jesus come offering a new and different way of salvation. We have already called attention to Montefiore's feud with Billerbeck over the question of soteriology. The latter's contrast of the law-righteousness of the rabbis with the new righteousness proclaimed by Jesus is regarded by Montefiore as a "false antithesis."[12] The rabbis did not depend on their righteous deeds for acceptance with God, but rather on His grace and mercy. Humanity's relationship with God, for them, was not in the last analysis based on merit, but on grace. In this connection, Montefiore quotes the daily prayer of the early rabbinic Jew: "Not because of our righteous acts do we lay our supplications before thee, but because of thine abundant mercies. What are we? What is our piety? What our righteousness?"[13]

Sandmel, however, has correctly noted that while there is agreement that God has a will for man that he can know, "it is in

---

[7]*JSSM*, 23.
[8]Montefiore, *RLGT*, 316.
[9]*RLGT*, 42.
[10]Ibid., 242.
[11]Ibid., 254.
[12]Ibid., 161.
[13]Cf. ibid., 19.

answering the question *how* can man fulfill the will of God that a strand in Christianity is the antithesis of the Jewish way."[14] Indeed, there is a basic difference here that cannot be explained away. Self-effort in doing the deeds of the Law and thereby attaining righteousness is vitally important. According to Vermes, "in the inter-Testamental period . . . relation with the Father grows to be less of a privilege conferred on Israel as a people, and increasingly dependent on merit."[15] "If man tries, God aids. Man *must* and *can* try."[16] Montefiore does finally concede to Billerbeck that this difference exists in Judaism's righteousness: "It is *not* all grace. It *is* partly man's own effort."[17] Yet simultaneously Montefiore can say, "No words, indeed, could more aptly and succinctly describe the Rabbinic frame of mind and religious position than to say that 'man depends absolutely and at every stage on God,' and that he is 'continually accepting, or believing, or corresponding, or obeying.' "[18]

In a similar vein, Ben-Chorin stresses the necessity of grace: the free grace of God is already found in the Old Testament (Exod. 33:19).[19] He notes that the Jews have long since given up trying to imitate God's holiness. Yet he adds, "The Law was given to all Israel, in order that we might fulfill it . . . I myself must do it. Since no one else can take my place—I myself must fulfill it in the probationary test of this life."[20]

Abrahams likens Judaism to "the *synergism* of Erasmus," setting it, as do all Jewish scholars, in complete contrast to Pauline Christianity.[21] At the same time, however, "nothing that man, with his small powers and finite opportunities, can do constitutes a *claim* on the favour of the Almighty and the Infinite. In

---

[14]*WJJ*, 132.

[15]*GJJ*, 25.

[16]Montefiore, *RLGT*, 271.

[17]*RLGT*, 201; thus, although there are some parallels of free grace in the rabbinic literature, Jesus' teaching may be regarded as "comparatively new and original." *RT*, 98.

[18]C. G. Montefiore, "Rabbinic Judaism and the Epistles of St. Paul," *JQR* 13 (1901):214.

[19]*BJ*, 100.

[20]Ben-Chorin, *Jesus im Judentum*, 71.

[21]*SP*, 1:146.

the final resort all that men receive from the divine hand is an act of grace."[22] For the Jew there is a tension between our action and God's gift, and this tension must always be preserved. Abrahams writes, "The Pharisaic position will never be understood by those who fail to realize that it tried to hold the balance between man's duty to *strive* to earn pardon, and his *inability* to attain to it without God's gracious gift of it."[23] Citing Akiba's dictum, "The world is judged by grace, yet all is according to the amount of work" (Aboth 3.20), Abrahams concludes, "The antinomy is the ultimate doctrine of Pharisaism."[24]

Rabbinic religion, then, consists of both works and grace, and "the works are never adequate without the grace."[25] Montefiore writes, "God expects a man to be and do good, and He ascribes merit to, and rewards the man, and more especially the Israelite, who does good and fulfills the Commandments, but beyond all human merit and deed are His compassion and His grace."[26] Thus Montefiore disagrees with Billerbeck that rabbinic religion is a religion of self-redemption solely on the basis of one's own efforts. Fortunately, he says, the rabbis were satisfied with inconsistency at this point and maintained propositions not capable of harmonization.[27] Moreover, according to Montefiore, Billerbeck's contention that the fourth Beatitude ("Blessed are those who hunger and thirst for righteousness, for they shall be satisfied" [Matt. 5:6]) speaks of those who are aware that they can produce no righteousness on their own power, is a Lutheran misreading of the verse. Such a concept of righteousness apart from good deeds would have been foreign both to Jesus and the compiler of Matthew.[28] For although among the rabbis it was

---

[22]I. Abrahams, *Daily Prayer Book* (London: Eyre and Spottiswoode, 1914), xxi.

[23]*SP*, 1:147.

[24]Ibid., p. 146.

[25]Montefiore, *RLGT*, 196; cf. G. H. Dalman, "It is quite correct to say: Christianity is the religion of faith, Judaism a religion of works. But it is necessary in this matter to guard against misunderstanding. Christian religion also speaks of works, while Judaism is not without faith." *Christianity and Judaism*, trans. G. H. Box (London: Williams and Norgate, 1901), 49–50.

[26]C. G. Montefiore and H. Loewe, *A Rabbinic Anthology* (London: Macmillan, 1938), 88–89.

[27]*RLGT*, 163.

[28]Ibid., 17.

"often repeated that man has no claim upon God because of his virtues,"[29] righteousness was apparently of *some* avail.[30]

Judaism is thus a religion that calls people to observance of the Law, but in the context of grace. The giving of the Law itself rests on the foundation of God's gracious covenant with Israel. Obeying the Law is therefore the response of those who know themselves to be the elect people of God. Both grace and the necessity of works are affirmed in Judaism.

Without denying the importance of righteousness for Jesus— i.e., the obedience of the Law according to his definitive interpretation—it does seem that grace holds a more dominant position in his perspective than it does in Judaism.[31] This has been noticed by several Jewish scholars. According to Klausner, in the Jewish view God requires justice and "will by no means acquit the guilty" (Nah. 1:3). But for Jesus, "sinners and non-sinners, evil and good, ungodly and righteous, all alike are of the same worth in God's sight."[32]

Flusser draws attention to the same point by his comments on Matthew 20:1–16, where the vineyard owner pays all the workers in the vineyard the same wage, ignoring the actual amount of time they had worked. This passage, like that of Luke 13:1–5 in a negative way, is regarded by Flusser as undermining the concept of the justice of God: "All the norms of the usual concepts of the righteousness of God are abrogated."[33] Flusser concludes that

> Jesus' concept of the righteousness of God is incommensurable to reason: man cannot measure it. . . . It leads to the preaching of

---

[29]C. G. Montefiore, "The Spirit of Judaism," in F. J. Foakes-Jackson and K. Lake, eds., *The Beginnings of Christianity* (London: Macmillan, 1920), 69; cf. *RLGT,* 365.

[30]Walker's conclusion is that "Works were not thought at any time to buy the mercy of God, but the presence of works in some measure made the situation hopeful enough to warrant God, who is just, in showing mercy to the supplicant." T. Walker, *What Jesus Read* (London: Allen & Unwin, 1925), 49.

[31]See the helpful article by C. F. D. Moule, which discusses the subject in terms of Judaism and Christianity: "'. . . As we forgive . . .': a Note on the Distinction between Deserts and Capacity in the Understanding of Forgiveness," in E. Bammel, C. K. Barrett, and W. D. Davies, eds. *Donum Gentilicium: Studies in Honour of David Daube* (Oxford: Clarendon, 1978), 68–77.

[32]*JN,* 379–80.

[33]D. Flusser, *Jesus*, ET by R. Walls (New York: Herder & Herder, 1969), 82.

the kingdom in which the last will be first, and the first last. . . . It is at once profoundly moral and yet beyond good and evil. In this demonic view, all the "important" customary virtues and the well-knit personality, worldly dignity and the proud insistence upon the formal fulfillment of the law, are fragmentary and empty.[34]

Flusser also argues that the notion of just compensation had already begun to weaken in the second-century B.C.E. He cites Antigonos of Sokho (Aboth 1:3) as an indication of this: "Be not like servants who serve the master on condition of receiving a reward, but be like servants who serve the master not on condition of receiving a reward." More than a century after Antigonos some Pharisees in opposition to the established Pharisees stressed love for its own sake. This new emphasis "irrespective of any compensation, would indicate a relaxation of the compensatory doctrine" and reflected "the new Jewish sensitivity concerning divine justice as manifested in the world."[35] According to Flusser, this new sensitivity prepared the way for the radical viewpoint found in the teaching of Jesus. Whether this is correct or not, it remains evident that the perspective of Jesus stands in sharp contrast to that of mainstream Judaism not yet penetrated by this new sensitivity.

Montefiore views the parable of the workers in the vineyard (Matt. 20:1–16) as providing "a corrective to a frequent element" of rabbinic teaching by pointing to "the higher justice of grace and love upon which God acts."[36] At the same time, however, he shows that grace is not absent from the teaching of the rabbis, on the one hand, and that Jesus does not altogether deny the justice of God and the doctrine of measure for measure, on the other. For Jesus, however, grace is more prominent and thus "the balance is better kept by him than by the Rabbis."[37]

The centrality of grace in the perspective of Jesus is reflected in his parables, particularly the superlative parables that

---

[34]Ibid., 83.

[35]D. Flusser, "A New Sensitivity in Judaism and the Christian Message," *HTR* 61 (1968):111; cf. 119; *Jesus,* 65ff.

[36]*SG,* 2:702.

[37]*RLGT,* 286.

emphasize grace (e.g., Luke 15). It is widely admitted that Jesus used parables more extensively and more effectively than the rabbis. Ben-Chorin notes that there are parallels to Jesus' parables, but admits that with their "paradoxical dialectic" the parables of Jesus are a high point.[38] Unlike the rabbinic parables, those of Jesus "all breathe the spirit of *one* personality," writes Ben-Chorin, "a personality which is not altogether unproblematic."[39] Abrahams also calls attention to the similarity and dissimilarity between the rabbinic parables and the parables of Jesus and agrees that "the Gospel Parables are marked by characteristic features which testify to an original and exalted personality in their authorship, or at least in their adaptation."[40]

The central significance of grace in the ministry of Jesus is also seen in the fact that he continually moves among sinners in order to bring to them the good news he proclaims. "For the Son of man came to seek and to save the lost" (Luke 19:10); "For I came not to call the righteous, but sinners" (Matt. 9:13). Here Jesus admittedly transcends the rabbinic attitude of separation and isolationism. Vermes describes the attitude of Jesus by which he came to be called sarcastically "friend of tax-collectors and sinners," one of the marks of "the piety peculiar to Jesus the religious man."[41] To the rabbis, the sinners with whom Jesus mingled were "persons of immoral life," and they "would have been chary of intercourse with such men at all times."[42] In Jesus' free association with sinners, says Montefiore, "we meet a new and gracious characteristic of Jesus, and to it there are no parallels in the Rabbinic literature."[43]

> The summons not to wait till they meet you in your sheltered and orderly path, but to go forth and seek out and redeem the sinner and the fallen, the passion to heal and bring back to God the

---

[38]*BJ*, 96.

[39]Ben-Chorin, *Jesus im Judentum*, 40.

[40]*SP*, 1:91.

[41]*GJJ*, 44.

[42]Abrahams, *SP*, 1:55; cf. Daube's interesting remarks concerning the gravity of Jesus' association with the Samaritan woman in John 4. D. Daube, *The New Testament and Rabbinic Judaism* (London: Athlone, 1956), 373.

[43]*RLGT*, 221; cf. Walker, *What Jesus Read*, 66.

wretched and the outcast—all this I do not find in Rabbinism; *that* form of love seems lacking.[44]

Indeed, Montefiore is anything but sparing in his praise of Jesus' teaching at this point: It is "something both great and new,"[45] "a new and great departure,"[46] and "a fresh and original teaching, which has produced fruit to be ever-reckoned among the distinctive glories of Christianity."[47] Among the rabbis, says Montefiore, "we do not, I think, find the same passionate eagerness to *cause* repentance, to save the lost, to redeem the sinner."[48]

The exceptional stress on grace in the teaching of Jesus is to be explained as a part of the eschatological message of Jesus. It is the grace of the kingdom of God that now begins to make its appearance in the person of Jesus.

REPENTANCE

Repentance is "the corner-stone of Jewish piety,"[49] and its importance in Judaism through the centuries is abundantly evident. What the Law with its commandments cannot do, repentance—the turning of the sinner to God—accomplishes within the inner person. Thus Montefiore concludes, "The Rabbinic teaching about repentance is perhaps the brightest jewel in the Rabbinic crown."[50] For the rabbis, as much as for Jesus, repentance is never impossible for the sinner.[51] Montefiore writes that in first-century Judaism "the relation of men to God was kept permanently hopeful by the progressive stress laid upon the doctrine

[44]Montefiore, "The Spirit of Judaism, 79.

[45]*RLGT*, 372.

[46]C. G. Montefiore, *The Old Testament and After* (London: Macmillan, 1923), 252.

[47]C. G. Montefiore, "The Synoptic Gospels and the Jewish Consciousness," *HJ* 3 (1904–5), 665.

[48]Ibid.

[49]*RLGT*, 273.

[50]Ibid., 260.

[51]Ibid., 343. Herford, "Repentance and Forgiveness in the Talmud," 59; Abrahams, however, is not sure of the universal possibility of repentance in the Gospels. Cf. *SP*, 1:142.

of repentance."[52] The sense of God's stern justice, sometimes gained from the rabbinic writings, is only meant to counteract the possible abuse of the affirmation of God's lovingkindness.[53] Montefiore considers it very difficult to decide whether the rabbis or Jesus had a more forgiving conception of God. "Nothing that Jesus says about it [repentance] beats, or goes beyond, what the Rabbis say about it. In fact, the Rabbinic teachings about repentance are more fully worked out."[54] According to Maccoby, "the characteristic voice" of Jesus is to be heard in his preaching on repentance: "In a wonderful series of parables Jesus expressed Pharisaic themes of God's mercy and the efficacy of repentance in a manner hardly rivalled in the Pharisaic literature."[55]

There is, nevertheless, some difference between the rabbis and Jesus on the doctrine of repentance, and a few Jewish scholars have called attention to it. This difference involves the priority of grace in the teaching of Jesus—something pointed out in the preceding section. In Judaism, the stress on the possibility of repentance and the nature of God as forgiving is counterbalanced by the fact that repentance is left entirely to the sinner's own initiative. Montefiore writes, "What is new and striking in the teaching of Jesus is that this process of repentance takes an *active* turn."[56] Abrahams can say that although Pharisaism desired to make repentance easy, "it was inclined to leave the initiative to the sinner, except that it always maintained *God's* readiness to take the first step. Jesus in his attitude towards sin and sinners was more inclined to take the initiative."[57] Beyond this admission, Jewish scholars see no advancement in Jesus' conception of repentance. It should be pointed out, however, that Jesus' stress on repentance is again related to his announcement of the kingdom (Mark 1:15). Repentance in this instance brings a person to a new reality and does not restore that person to something pre-

---

[52]Montefiore, "The Spirit of Judaism," 53.

[53]Montefiore and Loewe, *Rabbinic Anthology*, 315.

[54]*RLGT*, 260.

[55]*RJ*, 117. "These parables are so redolent of the spiritual atmosphere of Pharisaism that they are the strongest proof that Jesus really existed, and was a Pharisee teacher of original power." Ibid.

[56]*SG*, 2:249.

[57]*SP*, 1:58.

viously enjoyed.[58] It is this that accounts for the dynamic of grace in the teaching of Jesus.

Basic to the rabbinic viewpoint on repentance is human free will and man's inherent capability of repentance. Although first-century Judaism recognized the existence of *yeṣer ha-ra'*—the evil inclination within us—by no means was it thought to cripple human beings to the extent that they became incapable of self-help. Thus Loewe writes that among the rabbis "original sin is not quite unknown, but it is not allowed to upset the Jewish scheme of salvation by man's own efforts, helped by the divine mercy and grace."[59] The evil *yeṣer* was indeed responsible for the human condition, yet it was put there by God with the specific intention that we struggle with it, trying always to subdue it. "The Rabbis did not propound any theory as to the corruption of man's heart or the incapacity of man to be good without a preliminary regeneration."[60] The evil inclination can effectively be overcome only by the study and practice of the Law.[61] Sandmel, to be sure, can refer to the existence of the notion of human limitation in Judaism but adds that "it has the distinctive difference of not negating nearly as completely man's capacity to achieve."[62]

One aspect of Jesus' teaching concerning man's relationship to God is difficult for Jewish scholars—the notion of particularism or election. Thus Montefiore describes the statement of Jesus that "many are called, but few are chosen" (Matt. 22:14) as a "gloomy pessimism" outdoing the particularism of the rabbis.[63] For the rabbis, "repentance was conceived as possible for a Gentile no less than for a Jew."[64] In Matthew 11:25–26, Jesus

---

[58]"For Jesus, repentance did not so much bring one back again to what one had left, as drive one on to what one had not been hitherto." Walker, *What Jesus Read*, 81.

[59]Quoted by Montefiore, *RLGT*, 25; cf. G. H. Dalman, *Christianity and Judaism*, ET by G. H. Box (London: Williams and Norgate, 1901), 53.

[60]Montefiore and Loewe, *Rabbinic Anthology*, 306.

[61]Ibid., 302.

[62]*WJJ*, 97.

[63]*RLGT*, 311; Montefiore says of the fourth Gospel: "All the love which God and the Logos, God's son, bear the world is only to an elect portion and the sinner is wholly and necessarily wanting." "The Religious Value of the Fourth Gospel," 43.

[64]*RLGT*, 337.

thanks the Father that the things of the kingdom have been hidden from the wise and revealed to babes, thus directly countering the position of the rabbis. To the latter it would have been inconceivable to praise God for such a sad turn of events. Montefiore's conclusion concerning Jesus' words is significant: "The verse, whether authentic or not, shows Jesus in antagonism to the Rabbis, not merely on the score of some particular question (e.g., the observance of the Sabbath), but absolutely and altogether."[65] Friedlander summarizes the difference between Judaism and Jesus on the matter of election and grace in these words: "The initiative [for Jesus] is at every point taken by God, and no question can be entertained of precedent merit on the part of the recipients of the blessings." On the other hand, "Judaism teaches that 'the *righteous* of all races inherit the future bliss' (Tosephta *Synhedrin,* xiii, 2)."[66]

Jesus, according to Jewish scholars, would have made use of parables, just as did the rabbis, not to conceal the truth from outsiders, as Mark 4:11–12 teaches, but as a teaching device in order to make the truth understandable to all. Montefiore therefore regards Mark 4:11–12 as inauthentic.[67] Abrahams is of the same opinion, arguing that it is "preposterous" to suppose "that Jesus taught in parables *in order* that men might misunderstand."[68] Vermes similarly concludes, "That he employed them to conceal the meaning of his message is a contorted and tendentious explanation."[69]

Inasmuch as God is responsible for human nature, including the evil inclination, Judaism conceived of God as being in some sense under obligation to be lenient and forgiving.[70] Thus, according to Abrahams, "divine pardon is the logical correlative of human frailty."[71] Moreover, "God owes it, as it were, to his

---

[65]Ibid., 237.

[66]*JSSM,* 248ff.

[67]*RLGT,* 252; cf. *SG,* 1:102. Cf. Klausner, *JN,* 265.

[68]*SP,* 1:106; Abrahams continues: "This is to mistake an Oriental process of thought by which consequences are often confused with motives."

[69]*JJ,* 27.

[70]Cf. Dalman, *Christianity and Judaism,* 53.

[71]*SP,* 1:139.

own nature to forgive."[72] In spite of this fact, however, even after a person has repented, he or she has no *right* to demand forgiveness; that is still, in the last analysis, a matter of grace.[73] In a similar vein, Montefiore writes, "One might almost say that man was created in order to give opportunity for God to display His forgiveness, His lovingkindness, His mercy, His grace—the last three words translating indifferently the one Hebrew word ḥesed."[74]

ATONEMENT

There is a certain gravity about human evil inclination in the perspective of Jesus that is lacking in the rabbinic perspective. This becomes evident in the nature of the remedy offered for this evil inclination. As we have seen, the rabbinic antidote for the evil inclination is to be found in the Law: "The study of the Law is the sovereign remedy against the evil *yetzer*."[75] For Jesus, however, the overcoming of evil is a part of the dawning of the kingdom and both are dependent on his death (cf. Mark 10:45). The great difference here between Judaism and Christianity has been noted by Jewish scholars. Montefiore observes that in Judaism the results of the evil inclination rather than its origin constitute the important factor.[76] Klausner indicates that the Christian view is ultimately derived from the Jewish concept of "the sin of this first man."[77] Sandmel describes the difference in terms of how sin is viewed: for Jews sin is "an act or action"; for Christians it is "a state, a condition of man."[78] The difference can be described in terms of divine and human perspectives on the problem of evil. Herford puts the difference in these terms, noting that rabbinic Judaism regards the evil inclination from the

---

[72]Ibid., p. 143.

[73]Herford, "Repentance and Forgiveness in the Talmud," 62.

[74]Montefiore and Loewe, *Rabbinic Anthology*, 88.

[75]Ibid., 302.

[76]Montefiore, "The Spirit of Judaism," 54.

[77]J. Klausner, "Christian and Jewish Ethics," *Judaism* 2 (1953):18.

[78]*WJJ*, 45.

human end and treats it "as a factor indeed in every individual, but not as a core of cosmic evil needing a divine act and special divine agent to deal with it."[79] In the Christian view of sin, according to Sandmel, "atonement implies a change in man's nature. Man cannot unaided work this transformation; in other words, man himself cannot atone." Herein lies the difference between Judaism and Christianity: "We believe that man must make his own atonement, not have atonement wrought for him."[80] Schoeps similarly writes, "Israel does not need to be redeemed by an atoning sacrifice, because it has already been elected by God."[81]

Atonement for sin has held an important place in Judaism as exemplified in the sacrificial cultus of the Old Testament and the continuing central place of the Day of Atonement. But since the destruction of the temple and the cessation of the sacrifices, "Israel's united devotion to the Law has the atoning power of sacrifices."[82] Indeed, as Montefiore points out, "the two ideas of atonement and forgiveness tended to run and merge into one another."[83] The result is that for rabbinic Judaism repentance and prayer take center stage in human relationship to God. Each can be said by Judaism to atone for sins, that is, to bring about forgiveness: "Far more powerful and wide-reaching [than sacrifice] as an agency for the cancellation of sin is repentance."[84] "Sincere prayer brought forgiveness for sin."[85] Thus no further means of atonement is needed. Humans have within themselves the ability to repent and thereby to assure forgiveness and restoration. The notions of a special atoning sacrifice and a redeemer or

---

[79]R. T. Herford, "The Fundamentals of Religion as Interpreted by Christianity and Rabbinic Judaism," *HJ* 21 (1922–23):323.

[80]*WJJ*, 46–47.

[81]H. J. Schoeps, *The Jewish-Christian Argument*, trans. D. E. Green (London: Faber & Faber, 1965), 163.

[82]Montefiore and Loewe, *Rabbinic Anthology*, 225. The study of Law also has power to atone. Ibid., 230.

[83]Ibid., 229.

[84]Ibid., 225; cf. Maimonides, cited by Montefiore as correctly summarizing the rabbinic view: "There is nothing left us but repentance, which, however, atones for all transgressions." See Montefiore's article, "On Repentance," which appears as Appendix III in *RLGT*, 390–422, first published in *JQR* 16 (1904): 211ff.

[85]Montefiore and Loewe, *Rabbinic Anthology*, 342.

savior who suffers for the sins of his people are superfluous. Thus again, as we have seen, central to the religious life in Judaism is a basic optimism concerning man and his ability (but always with God's assistance) to do God's will. For this reason, Jewish scholars regard what they call "Pauline" theology (i.e., the doctrine of humanity as trapped by sin and in need of a savior) as un-Jewish. Man *can* do God's will, and if they fail, there is always the possibility of repentance and pardon.[86]

Jewish scholars admit the Jewishness of the general idea of a vicarious suffering of the righteous on behalf of sinful Israel. Daube, for example, notes that "by the time of the New Testament, the idea of a just man giving his life as *kopher, lytron,* 'ransom' or 'expiation,' for the community or the sinners was common in Judaism."[87] Nevertheless, of those Jewish scholars who accept the fact that Jesus foretold his death, most deny that Jesus understood his own suffering and death as an expiatory sacrifice. Thus Flusser allows the idea in first-century Judaism, but argues that "Jesus did not intend to die in order to expiate the sins of others by his own brief passion."[88] Flusser, however, can elsewhere note that "if as Christians believe, the martyr was at the same time the Messiah, then his death has a cosmic importance."[89] The connection between Jesus and the Suffering Servant of Isaiah was first made by the church after the Crucifixion. The idea belongs, according to Flusser, to a later "Greek stage" of the Gospel development.[90] Similarly, Montefiore notes that "in the Rabbinic literature the death of the righteous is often stated to be an atonement of the sins of the wicked."[91] Nevertheless, Montefiore finds it very difficult to believe that Jesus spoke

[86]Cf. C. G. Montefiore, "Rabbinic Judaism and the Epistles of St. Paul," *JQR* 13 (1901):204; Herford, "The Fundamentals of Religion," 321–22.

[87]*The New Testament and Rabbinic Judaism,* 11. See also Montefiore and Loewe, *Rabbinic Anthology,* 230.

[88]Flusser, *Jesus,* 98. Flusser depends on Morna Hooker, *Jesus and the Servant* (London, 1959). As to the meaning of Jesus' death, Flusser asks: "At the end, had he realized that his execution was the crown of his transvaluation of all the usual values?" Ibid., 104.

[89]*EJ,* 10:14.

[90]"Das Schisma zwischen Judentum und Christentum," *EvTheol* 40 (1980):219.

[91]*SG,* 2:277; cf. *RLGT,* 300–301.

the words of Mark 10:45, "For the Son of man also came not to be served but to serve, and to give his life as a ransom for many." The first part of the verse may well be authentic and original, but the second half of the verse, concerning the giving of Jesus' life as a ransom for many, is to be regarded as Pauline terminology and hence as deriving from a time later than Jesus.[92] Kaminka notes that the soteriology of Christianity even more than its antinomianism makes Christianity unacceptable to the Jews.[93] The doctrine of Jesus' atoning death, despite Old Testament antecedents seen by the early church, is generally attributed to the influence of Hellenistic religious concepts.

Ben-Chorin, on the other hand, does not regard it as impossible that Jesus combined the image of the Son of Man (Dan. 7) with that of the Suffering Servant of God (Isa. 53). Noting the existence of the tradition of a suffering Messiah before the time of Jesus, Ben-Chorin concludes that Jesus may well have seen his death as an inevitability and have thought of his death as "a kind of offering."[94] Flusser doubts that Jesus himself thought of his death as expiatory, yet he is able to write: "The most important motifs in the Church's conception of Christ already existed independently in pre-Christian Judaism. The same is also true of the expiatory death of Jesus."[95] Schonfield also admits that in the time of Jesus the Davidic Messiah and the Suffering Just One of Isaiah were combined into one composite picture, at least in Galilee. Jesus accepted the combination and, according to Schonfield's own unusual hypothesis, it played a significant role in his deliberate staging of his own death.[96] So far as atonement is concerned, however, Schonfield writes, "The Jews, of course, believed also in sacrifice as an atonement for sin; but this was not associated with the death and resurrection of anyone whether human or divine." Here we encounter instead the influence of the

[92]SG, 1:260.

[93]Quoted in G. F. Moore, "A Jewish Life of Jesus," HTR 16 (1923):95.

[94]BJ, 158; cf. S. Ben-Chorin, Jesus im Judentum (Wuppertal, 1970), 42–43.

[95]D. Flusser, "The Son of Man: Jesus in the Context of History," in The Crucible of Christianity, ed. A. Toynbee (London: Thames & Hudson, 1969), 233.

[96]PP, 212, 151, 177.

mystery religions.[97] The new revision of Schürer cautiously allows the idea of a suffering Messiah in Judaism, but adds that "it did not become a dominant notion." The literature analyzed does not contain "the slightest allusion to an expiatory suffering of the Messiah."[98] Thus although the individual ideas may have been present in Judaism, there is no evidence of their conjunction, and hence the New Testament evidence is discounted.

There is an obvious tendency, then, for Jewish scholarship to deny that Jesus viewed his own death as a vicarious atonement. Verses such as Mark 10:45 and Matthew 26:28 ("for this is my blood of the covenant, which is poured out for many for the forgiveness of sins") are either ignored or relegated to postresurrection theology read back into the narrative. There is, of course, a decided preference among Jewish scholars to interpret the death of Jesus in political rather than in religious terms, let alone in terms of a definitive atonement for humanity.

PRAYER

Prayer is an important component in the rabbinic concept of humanity's relationship to God. That the rabbis could rise to great heights in their doctrine of prayer is plainly evident from Abrahams' excellent article on the subject.[99] Montefiore reflects the general opinion of Jewish scholarship when he says that "on the subject of prayer Jesus spoke as a child of his age. Or we may say that he spoke on the lines of the Rabbis . . . he expressed the best current Rabbinic ideas with beauty and vividness."[100] Jewish scholars have been particularly interested in pointing out the rabbinic parallels and fully Jewish content of the well-known Lord's Prayer (Matt. 6:9–13). Trattner points out that "sentence

---

[97]*FCS*, 77. "The death of no man could be accepted by God as a substitutionary sacrifice for the sins of another." Ibid., 90.

[98]E. Schürer, *The History of the Jewish People in the Age of Jesus Christ*, new rev. ed. by G. Vermes, F. Millar, M. Black, vol. 2 (Edinburgh: T. & T. Clark, 1979), 549 (Appendix on "The Suffering Messiah").

[99]*SP*, 2:72–93; at its best, "it is an attitude of mind, a constant element of the religious life, independent of the exigencies of specific needs or desires." Ibid., 80.

[100]*RLGT*, 146–47.

for sentence, phrase for phrase, and word for word'' the prayer can be matched in Jewish sources, and he therefore describes it as ''a bouquet of Hebraic flowers sprung from Jewish soil.''[101] The Jewish parallels to the prayer, as well as to the Matthean beatitudes (5:3–11), are traced out carefully by Ben-Chorin and by G. Friedlander. Friedlander indeed examines the Jewish basis of the entire Sermon on the Mount. Ben-Chorin concludes that although there is nothing original in the prayer—''the elements are altogether from the synagogue''—''in its simplicity and completeness, this prayer is actually a high point,'' even in a sense ''timeless.''[102] A similar conclusion, noted approvingly by Abrahams,[103] is drawn by Montefiore, who went so far as to describe the prayer as ''original in the choice of ideas, and in their grouping.''[104] Friedlander, however, finds the prayer lacking in originality: ''All the phrases and petitions are *borrowed* from Jewish sources.'' Further, ''there is not a single idea or expression which cannot be found in pre-Christian literature of Israel.'' He takes issue even with Montefiore's assertion of originality in choice and grouping of ideas, regarding the prayer as simply an adaptation of Ezekiel 36:23–31.[105] Joseph Jacobs argues that the prayer is an abbreviation of parts of the Eighteen Benedictions.[106]

Thus, although some Jewish scholars sense a freshness and conciseness about Jesus' prayer, it remains for them a distillation of the best of Jewish prayer, and in the final analysis Jewish opinion is that the rabbis would have had little to learn from Jesus concerning prayer.[107]

---

[101]E. R. Trattner, *As a Jew Sees Jesus* (New York: Scribner, 1931), 74.

[102] Ben-Chorin, *Jesus im Judentum,* 41–42; *BJ,* 119.

[103]*SP,* 2:98.

[104]*SG,* 2:536; Montefiore appears to have substituted ''felicitous'' for ''original'' in his second edition. *SG,* 2:100.

[105]*JSSM,* 125, 163–64; cf. Abrahams, *SP,* 2:94–108, who agrees with Wellhausen that the parallels do not justify the conclusion that the prayer is only a ''cento.'' See especially 98.

[106]*JE,* 7:162.

[107]See the recent symposium by Jewish and Christian scholars: J. J. Petuchowski and M. Brocke, eds., *The Lord's Prayer and Jewish Liturgy* (New York: Seabury, 1978), which incorporates material from an earlier publication *Das Vaterunser: Gemeinsames im Beten von Juden und Christen* (Freiburg im Breisgau: Herder, 1974).

GOD AS FATHER

One aspect of Jesus' teaching about God needs further examination at this point. What is the Jewish perception of Jesus' repeated reference to God as his Father, even as *Abba*?

We may begin with the Jewish rejection of the common supposition that for the first-century Jew, God was remote and inaccessible—One who was to be feared rather than loved. This is regarded by Jewish scholars as a caricature of the truth. The fear and love of God are not mutually exclusive; indeed, the two are juxtaposed in the Old Testament itself.[108] Moreover, it is argued, the rabbinic conception of God is not essentially different from that of the synoptic Gospels.[109] Most important of all, Jesus was not the first to affirm the fatherhood of God. On the whole, the teaching of Jesus concerning the fatherhood of God is not different from the best of rabbinic teaching.[110] It was not uncommon in first-century Judaism for God to be addressed as "Father."[111] Montefiore writes concerning this high conception of God, including His lovingkindness and fatherhood (both nationally and individually), that "to the Rabbinic, mediaeval and modern Jew, it was the ABC of his religion."[112] Jewish scholars therefore insist that Jesus did not originate the concept of God as Father.

Concerning the nature of God, then, there was little difference between the view of the first-century Jew and the Christian. God was regarded by both as the omnipotent Creator and Ruler of all that exists, and humanity was regarded as having been created in His image.[113] For the Jew as well as the Christian, God's nearness was as important as His transcendence. Both

---

[108]Montefiore, "The Spirit of Judaism," 61.

[109]Montefiore, *The Old Testament and After*, 201.

[110]Cf. Montefiore, *RLGT*, 109; cf. idem, "The Spirit of Judaism," 48; H. G. Enelow, *A Jewish View of Jesus* (New York: Macmillan, 1920), 88.

[111]For the use of "Father" in the Rabbinic literature, see G. F. Moore, *Judaism*, 3 vols. (Cambridge, Mass.: Harvard University Press, 1946), 2:201ff.

[112]C. G. Montefiore, "The Synoptic Gospels and the Jewish Consciousness," *HJ* 3 (1904–05):255. Cf. E. Rivkin, *A Hidden Revolution* (Nashville: Abingdon, 1978), 304ff.; J. Jacobs, "Jesus of Nazareth—In History," *JE*, 7:162.

[113]Montefiore, "The Spirit of Judaism," 38–39.

Jew and Christian emphasized God's justice and His mercy, His demand for obedience, and His lovingkindness. Even the loving, seeking character of God as portrayed in the parable of the Prodigal Son, is at bottom "thoroughly Jewish and Rabbinic," although always it must be added, "at their best."[114] Montefiore sums up the matter from the Jewish viewpoint in these words: "What the Jewish reader feels in reading the Gospels is no new doctrine as regards the divine fatherhood, but an old familiar doctrine in (very frequently, not always) a high degree of purity, warmth, and concentration."[115]

While Jewish scholars deny that Jesus taught anything concerning God as Father that was totally new, some do admit that he nevertheless made a certain contribution to the subject. Montefiore, for example, notes that in Jesus' conception of the fatherhood of God, "the element of race and nationality seemed to fade away."[116] Jesus adds to an already existent national and communal piety a dimension of personal intimacy between God and man hitherto unattained. This deepened sense of intimacy is new, according to Montefiore, as is Jesus' continual emphasis on the fatherhood of God, in contrast to the merely occasional rabbinic reference. Klausner, too, refers to the frequency of Jesus' use of "Father" as compared with the rabbis, concluding that it is an "*excessive* emphasis" on the part of Jesus.[117] Montefiore concludes, "This regular conception of God as Father, in proportion to the intensity and vividness of the feeling which suggested it, was something which may fitly be called original."[118]

Although Jesus may have transferred the concept of the fatherhood of God from the national to the personal level, Jewish scholars reject any suggestion that the individual Jew did not at the same time refer to God as "*my* Father." "The intensely intimate and close relation of God to Israel extends to his relationship with every individual Israelite. Nothing in the language

114Montefiore, *RT*, 94–95.

115Ibid., 93.

116Ibid., 92.

117*JN*, 378.

118C. G. Montefiore, "The Originality of Jesus," *HJ* 27 (1929–30):104.

or in the terminology used by Jesus would have seemed novel to any Rabbinic Jew.''[119] While Montefiore grants that ''Jesus felt and realised God to be his father, himself to be His son, with vivid intensity,'' this differed only in degree not in kind, from the experience of the average Jew.[120] Friedlander refuses to consent even to this mild a difference in the concept: ''We deny that the Fatherhood of God is expounded by Jesus with more depth and intensity than by the great prophets and teachers of Israel who lived before the age of Jesus.''[121]

Nevertheless, it is important to note, as Jeremias has pointed out, that Jesus appears to be unique in addressing God as ''my Father'' (rather than ''our Father'') and in using the intimate term *Abba* (Mark 14:36 and parallels).[122] Flusser and Vermes are aware of the evidence at this point, but do not find it convincing. Both refer to the passage in the Babylonian Talmud (*Taanit,* 23b) where Hanan, grandson of Honi the Circle-Drawer, refers to God as ''the *Abba* who gives rain,'' but they do not comment on the fact that the passage is oblique at best, involving only an indirect reference to God as *abba,* prompted by the lighthearted cry of children, and that God is actually addressed by Hanan as ''Master of the world.''[123] Both Flusser and Vermes liken Jesus to contemporary charismatic miracle workers in first-century Judaism and earlier. Flusser notes Honi's reference to God as Father and Hanina's being addressed by God as ''My son.'' Nevertheless, Flusser seems conscious that these examples are not as convincing as they could be when he writes concerning Jeremias's argument: ''Considering the scarcity of rabbinic mate-

---

[119]*RLGT,* 114.

[120]*RT,* 93.

[121]*JSSM,* 126–27.

[122]See especially J. Jeremias, *The Central Message of the New Testament* (London: SCM, 1965), 9–30; idem, *The Prayers of Jesus, SBT* 2.6 (London: SCM, 1967), 11–65. ''To date nobody has produced one single instance in Palestinian Judaism where God is addressed as 'my Father' by an individual person'' (*Central Message,* 16). ''Nowhere in the literature of the prayers of ancient Judaism—an immense treasure all too little explored—is this invocation of God as *Abba* to be found, neither in the liturgical nor in the informal prayers.'' Ibid., 19.

[123]These points about the Talmudic passage are noted by Jeremias, *Central Message,* 19.

rial on charismatic prayer, this does not tell us very much."[124]
Vermes, referring to the argument about Jesus' use of *Abba* and
the implication drawn from this, can only ask, "Do these positive and summary theological assertions take sufficient notice of
the facts of Jewish history?"[125] Yet what Vermes offers hardly
seems to establish his conviction that Jesus' use of *Abba* was not
unique.

Thus, although it is clear that God was referred to as "Father" in first-century Judaism, Jesus differed from his contemporaries in (1) his frequent and consistent use of "Father" in addressing God, (2) his use of the first personal pronoun "*my*
Father," and (3) in his use of *Abba*. There is a uniqueness here
that cannot be overlooked. Klausner thus refers to Jesus' use of
"Father" as a sign of his messianic consciousness. "Jesus
looked upon himself as the Messiah, and as the Messiah he was
closer to God than was any other human being."[126] It was the
"overemphasis of the divine Fatherhood in relation to himself,"
according to Klausner, that ultimately caused his exaltation in the
christology of Paul and his contemporaries.[127] Jesus, in short,
was conscious of the fatherhood of God in a unique way, and the
intimate relationship with God presupposed by Jesus points inevitably beyond the ordinary, and again to the question of Jesus'
own person.[128]

THE PLACE OF JESUS

Thus, although Jewish scholars have little difficulty in finding numerous and important similarities between the religious
teaching of Jesus and that of the rabbis, there are, as we have
seen, some striking differences in the areas we have discussed,
and all of these interestingly cluster around the person of Jesus
himself. Both Orthodox and Liberal Jews find the central position

---

[124]Flusser, *Jesus*, 145, n. 159; quoted by Vermes, *GJJ*, 27. See too Sandmel's
criticism of Jeremias's argument, S. Sandmel, *The First Christian Century in Judaism
and Christianity* (New York: Oxford, 1969), 201–2, n. 11.

[125]*JJ*, 210. See also the discussion in *GJJ*, 27.

[126]*JN*, 378.

[127]Ibid., 392.

[128]Cf. A. Lukyn Williams, "'My Father' in Jewish Thought of the First Century,"
JTS 31 (1930):47.

of Jesus in the synoptic Gospels problematic. Friedlander, from the perspective of an Orthodox Jew, calls attention to the problem in these words: "The Gospel introduces the idea of one divine son, apart from all men, becoming a mediator between God and humanity (Matthew 11:27; Luke 10:22; Mark 10:45)."[129] Even Montefiore is troubled by the centrality of Jesus, as reflected, for example, in Matthew 11:27: "All things have been delivered to me by my Father; and no one knows the Son except the Father, and no one knows the Father except the Son and anyone to whom the Son chooses to reveal him." Montefiore, although elsewhere able to ascribe originality to Jesus, finds it difficult to believe that Jesus uttered these words. "There is no sure parallel for his speaking of himself as 'the Son' in a special sense. The exclusiveness of the saying that 'no one knows the Father except the Son' is painful; one can only hope that Jesus never uttered it."[130] For Flusser, the passage may well be authentic, but is to be regarded, together with parallels in the hymns of Qumran, as reflecting "the mentality of the charismatic apocalyptic who has access to the mysteries of God, through which he is able 'to enlighten the minds of many.'"[131] But this explanation hardly seems adequate to account for Jesus' words, especially considering them in the total context of Jesus' ministry and alongside other sayings of a similar type.

Abrahams, on the other hand, readily admits the uniqueness of Jesus and at the same time points to the crux of the problem from the Jewish perspective: "Jesus indeed was animated by a strong, one may even say a unique, sense of his own relation to and unbroken intercourse with God. But this sense of nearness is weakened for all other men when the intercourse with God is broken by the intrusion between them and God of the person of Jesus."[132] The possibility that Jesus claimed a mediatorial role in man's relationship to God has important consequences for the Jewish estimate of Jesus. Kohler writes, "Judaism recognizes in

---

[129]*JSSM*, 82.
[130]*SG*, 2:173.
[131]Flusser, *Jesus*, 96.
[132]*SP*, 1:142.

principle no mediatorship between God and man.''[133] For the Jews, ''no mediation is necessary between God and man. No mediator intervenes or introduces.''[134] Similarly, Klausner declares, ''Judaism does not associate the Messiah with the Godhead, nor attribute to the Messiah a deciding role in the day of redemption: Judaism knows nothing of redemption through an intermediary or intercessor between God and man.''[135] This, too, is the view of Montefiore, who writes, ''The ordinary Rabbinic Jew approached God directly and felt his answers in the heart. So far as there was any mediation at all, the mediator was not an angel, but the Law.''[136] The Hebrew Christian Jakob Jocz, however, rightly maintains that mediation, far from interfering in the direct relationship between human beings and God, as argued so frequently by Jewish scholars, mends the broken relationship that exists between them.[137] Elsewhere he notes that mediation is an important part of the religion of the Old Testament and that the emphasis of Judaism on directness of approach to God ''is a definite departure from the Old Testament position. It is here, if nowhere else, that we recognize the difference between the Synagogue and the Old Testament religion.''[138]

It remains clear that there are a number of passages in the synoptic Gospels that, because of the central position assumed by Jesus in the relationship between man and God, remain an obstacle to the Jewish reclamation of Jesus. Matthew 11:25–27 has already been mentioned. When Jesus exhorts people to take up their cross and follow him (Matt. 10:38; Mark 8:34; Luke 9:23), Montefiore, though finding the spirit of the verse to be rabbinic, immediately adds that ''for 'Jesus' must be substituted 'God and his Law.' ''[139] And presumably he would require the same sub-

---

[133]*JE*, 8:406.

[134]Montefiore, ''Jewish Conceptions of Christianity,'' 260.

[135]*JN*, 406.

[136]Montefiore, ''The Spirit of Judaism,'' 48.

[137]Jocz concludes that ''behind the Jewish objection to mediation is human hybris which makes man misunderstand his true position, namely that he is estranged from God.'' ''The Son of God,'' *Judaica* 13 (1957): 139.

[138]*JPJC*, 279.

[139]*RLGT*, 231; cf. R. T. Herford, ''The Fundamentals of Religion as Interpreted by Christianity and Rabbinical Judaism,'' *HJ* 21 (1922–23): 316.

stitution in the verses that precede and follow that one: "He who loves father or mother more than me is not worthy of me; and he who loves son or daughter more than me is not worthy of me . . . he who finds his life will lose it, and he who loses his life for my sake will find it." When Ben-Chorin encounters the similar "on my account" in the beatitude of Matthew 5:11 ("Blessed are you when men revile you and persecute you and utter all kinds of evil against you falsely on my account"), he regards it as indeed "new," but relegates it to the influence of the kerygmatic tradition.[140] Friedlander calls attention to the centrality of Jesus in the Synoptics with these words: "Several times in Matthew, and once in Mark, we are told that the people 'worshiped' Jesus. In no case did he reject the worship, or rebuke those who offered it to him. This aspect of prayer and worship is indeed, both new and un-Jewish."[141]

Unquestionably, Jesus' teaching about humanity's relationship to God and his own central role in that relationship contains elements sharply divergent from rabbinic Judaism. Accordingly, Jewish scholars have little to say about verses such as Matthew 10:32–33 (Luke 12:8–9): "So everyone who acknowledges me before men, I also will acknowledge before my Father who is in heaven, but whoever denies me before men, I also will deny before my Father who is in heaven"; Matthew 10:40 (cf. Luke 9:48): "He who receives you receives me, and he who receives me receives him who sent me"; Luke 10:16: "He who hears you hears me, and he who rejects you rejects me, and he who rejects me rejects him who sent me." In Jewish discussions of Jesus, passages of this kind are given little attention. That there is indeed something unique about Jesus' words concerning himself is sensed by many Jewish scholars. Yet it is characteristic of most of these scholars to discount such passages as inauthentic and as creations of the early church, reflecting its postresurrection perspective.[142]

---

[140]*BJ*, 74.

[141]*JSSM*, 118.

[142]E.g., Klausner says that "in spite of himself" Jesus became "in the thought of the next Christian generation," the "Son of God" and a "ransom for many." *JN*, 405.

In the religious teaching of Jesus we have again encountered a newness that presents a difficulty for the Jewish reclamation of Jesus. We find in Jesus' teaching an extraordinary emphasis on grace that is to be understood as a part of the eschatological message of Jesus concerning the arrival of the kingdom of God. The new era of the grace of the kingdom depends in turn on the atoning death of Jesus, who stands in a special mediatorial relationship between God and humanity, offering not only the forgiveness of sins through repentance but an altogether new existence in the kingdom of God. Repentance in the synoptic Gospels constitutes not so much a way *out* when one has failed, but a way *in* to a new, incomparable relationship with the Father. Central to all of this is the personal significance of Jesus as the unique Son. Jesus forgives sins and is criticized by the scribes for usurping the prerogative of God (Matt. 9:2ff.; Mark 2:5ff.; Luke 5:20ff.; 7:48–49). Jesus' sense of intimacy with his Father involves not simply enormous significance so far as his personal identity is concerned but also makes him and his work of pivotal importance for the relationship between humanity and God.

In all of this—as in his unparalleled stance of authority vis-à-vis the established religious institutions of Israel—Jesus presents an unprecedented claim of personal significance and a deliberate advance on anything that Judaism had previously known. While the material or the imagery of Jesus' teaching is not original or unparalleled in rabbinic Judaism, the essential content remains by its nature new, original, and of definitive importance.

Jesus' announcement of the arrival of the kingdom of God, his authoritative interpretation and fulfillment of the Law, his heightened ethical imperatives, together with his unique consciousness of the surpassing importance of his person and mission, indicate a pivotal turning point in history that involves a new conception of humanity's relationship with God.

EXCURSUS

The Question of Originality

IN THE PRECEDING CHAPTERS we have explored the similarities and differences between the ethical and religious teaching of Jesus and that of the rabbis. We have seen repeatedly that despite the extensive overlapping of common material, there is an undeniable newness in the teaching of Jesus. It is this newness or originality that is problematic for Jewish scholars in their reclamation of Jesus. Nevertheless, by regarding this newness as an "extension" of rabbinic teaching or by attributing it to the kerygmatic interests of the early church, Jewish scholars tend with few exceptions to deny any real originality on Jesus' part. Thus it is not uncommon to encounter the *nihil novi* dictum: "What is good in the Gospels is nothing new; what is new is nothing good." The new can be nothing good because it is regarded *ex hypothesi* as un-Jewish. In his survey of Jewish scholarship on Jesus, Lapide has traced three stages of development in the brief history of the affirmation of Jesus' Jewishness. In the first, the emphasis was that "Jesus was a Jew"; in the second, that "Jesus was thoroughly Jewish"; in the third, that "Jesus was nothing but Jewish." The third stage, according to Lapide, "set out to prove—with a certain intensity, if not vehemence—that his teaching was not Christian and his concerns not broadly humanitarian, that his activity was meant for Israel and not the world, and least of all the Church."[1]

It is a fact that the question of originality has seldom been looked at without considerable bias on one side or the other. Thus Enelow writes:

Jewish writers have tried to prove that anything taught by Jesus may be found in Jewish literature, and that therefore he could not be called original; while Christians have deemed it necessary to defend Jesus against the charge of borrowing or reproducing from Jewish sources, lest his originality be impugned.[2]

---

[1]*Israelis, Jews and Jesus,* trans. P. Heinegg (New York: Doubleday, 1979), 130. In the original German, the categories are that Jesus was (1) *Jude,* (2) *Ur-Jude,* and (3) *Nur-Jude* (140–41).

[2]H. G. Enelow, *A Jewish View of Jesus* (New York: Macmillan, 1920), 14; cf. the same in D. Daube, *The New Testament and Rabbinic Judaism* (London: Athlone, 1956), 256.

Montefiore calls attention to the same fact in these words: "Both Jews and Christians have sometimes been a little unfair as regards this question, the former in unduly depreciating the originality of Jesus, the latter in unduly exalting it."[3] Walker sums up the matter well when he writes:

> The one rejoices, and rightly so, that Jesus after all is acknowledged to have been in so much just a very good Jew of his day; the other is harassed with the suspicion that the outcome of investigation may be that there may be found little more in Jesus than could be found in good contemporary Judaism.[4]

Montefiore is very sensitive to the resultant distortions caused by Christian scholars. In the first place, the excellence of Old Testament morality is often wrongfully attacked in order to enhance the originality of Jesus.[5] More serious, however, is the fact that many Christian scholars regard that which agrees with their conception of Christianity as automatically un-Jewish, and that which disagrees with it as automatically constituting the very essence of Judaism.[6]

Accordingly, as we have seen, an important motive in the Jewish discussion of Jesus' teaching is the defense of first-century Judaism. Only when the latter is shown to exhibit a high religious and ethical teaching, can Jesus be reclaimed for Judaism. It is for this reason that Jewish scholars place such great emphasis on the common elements in the rabbinic literature and the teaching of Jesus. This indeed is one of the most familiar themes encountered in modern Jewish scholarship. Montefiore, despite certain admissions of originality in the Sermon on the Mount, is convinced that "the spirit of the Sermon is Jewish—in full accordance with the highest teachings of the Old Testament and of the Rabbis."[7] Jesus' teaching for the most part does not go beyond that of the *best* rabbis.[8] Goodman presents a typical conclusion: "It is the Jewish view that Jesus added no important original element to the

---

[3]*RT*, 85. Montefiore writes critically of Christian and Jewish extremists who "live in corners" and miss the "large, simple facts of the matter." C. G. Montefiore, "Judaism and Europe," *HJ* 21 (1922–23):730.

[4]T. Walker, *What Jesus Read* (London: Allen & Unwin, 1925), 58.

[5]C. G. Montefiore, "The Old Testament and Its Ethical Teaching," *HJ* 16 (1917–18): 240.

[6]C. G. Montefiore, "On Some Misconceptions of Judaism and Christianity by Each Other," *JQR* 7 (1896): 198.

[7]*RLGT*, 161; cf., however, G. Friedlander's criticism of Montefiore's wholehearted acceptance of the Sermon on the Mount. *JSSM*, 262.

[8]*RT*, 112.

religious and moral assets which had been accumulated by the Jewish prophets and sages."[9] Sandmel comes to a similar, though more cautious, conclusion: "The differences between the rabbis and the total New Testament are not nearly so extreme as partisan scholarship, on both sides, has supposed."[10]

The fundamental elements in the teaching of the rabbis and Jesus are the same, and hence Jesus must in the end "find his place in the development of Judaism, and not be regarded as the founder of a new and separate religion."[11] Not even in the "selected excellencies of the Johannine writings" is there anything contrary to the spirit of Judaism and "the main drift and current of its teachings."[12] For in the rabbinic literature, too, there was "from the first century onwards a passionate love for God, a passionate love for His Law, and a very real love of neighbor."[13] Christian and Jew were children of the same Father, and thus it is not surprising that, in spite of the differences, there should be a striking identity in ethical standards between the two.[14] Indeed, one may go so far as to say that "Christianity is the most Jewish of all non-Jewish religions."[15] Montefiore similarly concludes, "The doctrine of Jesus may be regarded either as pure Christianity or pure Judaism. Either way of looking at it contains a truth."[16]

Thus, for the most part, it is argued, a Jew familiar with rabbinic Judaism who turns to read the Gospels encounters little that is unfamiliar to him. Even as the first-century Jew would have been largely in agreement with Jesus' teaching, so also a third-century Jew hearing the Gospel story (apart from names) would not have considered anything to be "very novel or very extravagant."[17] The modern Jew finds

---

[9]P. Goodman, *The Synagogue and the Church* (London: Routledge, 1908), 233.

[10]S. Sandmel, *A Jewish Understanding of the New Testament* (1956; reprint ed., New York: Ktav, 1974), 313.

[11]C. G. Montefiore, "Mr. Smith: A Possibility," *JQR* 6 (1894): 109.

[12]C. G. Montefiore, "The Religious Value of the Fourth Gospel," 71.

[13]C. G. Montefiore, "The Spirit of Judaism," in F. J. Foakes-Jackson and K. Lake, eds., *The Beginnings of Christianity* (London: Macmillan, 1920), 79.

[14]Sandmel, *A Jewish Understanding of the New Testament*, 312; cf. R. T. Herford, "The Fundamentals of Religion as Interpreted by Christianity and Rabbinical Judaism," *HJ* 21 (1922–23): 326.

[15]M. Eisendrath and J. Parkes, *Jewry and Jesus of Nazareth* (Royston: Parkes Library, 1964), 21.

[16]Montefiore, "The Religious Value of the Fourth Gospel," 60.

[17]Montefiore, *RLGT*, 32; idem, *The Old Testament and After* (London: Macmillan, 1923), 202.

that much of the New Testament reads like "an old Rabbinic homily."[18] Montefiore well sums up the Jewish conclusion when he writes:

> Apart from this conflict about the Law (and apart from the question of Jesus himself, his powers, his authority, and his claims), an average Rabbinic Jew of, say, 200 A.D. could, I fancy, have read the Synoptic Gospels without often saying to himself, "I wholly disagree with this teaching," or, again saying, "I like this teaching, but I find it very strange." He might have said that a few times, but I do not fancy he would have said it often.[19]

For this reason, Montefiore, together indeed with all Jewish writers, regards Christian attempts to convert the Jews as unjustifiable.[20]

We have seen that one of the most common methods Jewish scholars use in the denial of any originality in Jesus' teaching is the citation of rabbinic parallels. Such citation of parallels, however, is done with little, if any, attention to the date of the rabbinic material—a procedure that may be regarded as of questionable value in answering the question of originality. As we have seen, recent studies have raised again the problem of reading later rabbinic texts as though they actually reflected the situation of the first century, and the priority of making them address questions that were at best on the fringe of their interests.[21] This, however, is no obstacle to many Jewish scholars. Only a few, such as Sandmel, have called attention to this problem:

> Some Jewish scholars seem to believe that since some of this material is demonstrably older than Jesus, potentially all of it is; and some Christian scholars, overlooking the fact that later collections contain quite ancient materials, declare that the true priority and hence the inherent value of originality belong to Jesus. But since controlling criteria are absent, these quarrels about priority are as useful, and truly as relevant, as that about the chicken and the egg.[22]

---

[18]S. Schechter, "Some Rabbinic Parallels to the New Testament," *JQR* 12 (1900): 418.

[19]C. G. Montefiore, "The Religious Teaching of the Synoptic Gospels in Its Relation to Judaism," *HJ* 20 (1921–22): 437.

[20]C. G. Montefiore, "The Attempted Conversion of the Jews," *HJ* 27 (1928–29): 429.

[21]See J. Neusner, "The Use of the Later Rabbinic Evidence for the Study of First-Century Pharisaism," in *Approaches to Ancient Judaism: Theory and Practice*, ed. W. S. Green (Missoula, Mont.: Scholars, 1978), 219. Cf. G. W. Buchanan, "The Use of Rabbinic Literature for New Testament Research," *Biblical Theology Bulletin* 7 (1977): 112ff.

[22]Sandmel, *A Jewish Understanding of the New Testament*, 200. Cf. E. F. Scott, "The Originality of Jesus' Ethical Teaching," *JBL* 48 (1929): 109.

Basic to the Jewish position is Montefiore's statement that "Rabbinic religion and Rabbinic morality developed in their own way: they were wholly unaffected by the teaching of Jesus."[23] "Though most of them [the rabbinic parallels] are later than the Gospels, they are not borrowed from the Gospels. They are independent creations and developments."[24] Questions of priority and date are also regarded by Montefiore as comparatively unimportant. Indeed, he considers the question of temporal priority to be of relatively little interest. What is significant and important for Montefiore is whether or not a particular rabbinic teaching, regardless of date, is a native and independent development. If in fact it is, then to Montefiore the temporal priority or "originality" of Jesus is a "secondary, and a comparatively unimportant originality."[25] It is as though one must hold judgment in abeyance until the whole of the rabbinic tradition has had its say.

Another fact, however, that makes the value of parallels questionable is the kaleidoscopic nature of the rabbinic literature.[26] The latter admittedly "contains almost every conceivable variety of opinion,"[27] and accordingly, "from the Talmudic sea you can fish out what suits your purpose."[28] Further, because of the vastness of this literature, parallels can be found to almost every utterance of Jesus, regardless of whether or not the saying truly represents the prevailing rabbinic spirit.[29] As to the misleading nature of "stray quotations," Abrahams remarks, "It is not possible to understand a system in this way, to judge the architecture of a building by inspecting an odd brick or two detached from one of its walls."[30] To know what rabbinic religion really is

---

[23]*SG*, 1:cxxxix; cf. *RLGT*, 72.

[24]C. G. Montefiore, "The Synoptic Gospels and the Jewish Consciousness," *HJ* 3 (1904–05): 653; cf. "Judaism and Europe," 730.

[25]C. G. Montefiore, "The Originality of Jesus," *HJ* 28 (1929–30): 99; "The Religious Teaching of the Synoptic Gospels in Its Relationship to Judaism," *HJ* 20 (1921–22): 436; *SG*, 1:cxxxix; *RLGT*, XVII; "The priority in date is almost always on the side of Jesus," *RLGT*, 162.

[26]"It is necessary to demonstrate rather than assume the antiquity of a given tradition, and rabbinic texts cannot be taken, as on the Maimonidean view, to represent the entirety, or even necessarily the mainstream, of pre-rabbinic Judaism." W. Horbury, "Rabbinics," *ET* 91.8 (1980): 238.

[27]C. G. Montefiore, "Rabbinic Judaism and the Epistles of St. Paul," *JQR* 13 (1901), 192.

[28]Montefiore, *RLGT*, 51.

[29]Montefiore, *RT*, 110–11.

[30]I. Abrahams, "Rabbinic Aids to Exegesis," in *Cambridge Biblical Essays*, ed. H. B. Swete (London: Macmillan, 1909), 167; cf. R. T. Herford, "Repentance and Forgiveness in the Talmud," *HJ* 40 (1941–42): 55.

requires not only "familiarity with the subject, but . . . also impartiality and a certain tact or *flair*."[31]

Enelow similarly finds it unprofitable "to debate as to whether those several teachings of Jesus were duplicated or anticipated by other Jewish teachers."[32] According to Abrahams, "too much stress is laid on indebtedness. We are, and long shall be, unable to analyse the contents of the Gospels into old and new, to separate in the teaching of Jesus the absolutely original from what was, more or less, already in the possession of the best Jewish minds."[33] But the most concerted attack against the misuse of parallels comes from Sandmel, who says that even should true parallels be found, they are not significant unless they are distinctive in comparison with the broad areas of common agreement in all the Jewish literature of the early period. Sandmel argues against the facile manner in which scholars detect borrowing, in one direction or another, on the basis of "parallels" that in fact are the common property of many Jewish movements.[34] He accuses Billerbeck of excerpting without genuinely comprehending the tone and import of the rabbinic literature, and of often substituting quantity for quality in his compilations.[35] Montefiore says of Strack-Billerbeck that while they doubtless possess the knowledge of the rabbinic literature, they are not always impartial, nor do they possess enough "flair" for understanding what is truly rabbinic in spirit.[36]

A major source of confusion concerning the question of Jesus' originality is the difficulty of defining the word *originality*. Montefiore, who is unquestionably the foremost Jewish exponent of an "originality" in the teaching of Jesus, helps by delineating the following categories. Five kinds of sayings are attributed to Jesus in the Gospels: (1) rabbinic; (2) at bottom rabbinic, yet carried forward; (3) unusual to the rabbis, but not opposed; (4) an intensification of the unusual, and (5) opposed to rabbinic doctrine and spirit.[37] The number of sayings allo-

---

[31]Montefiore, *SG*, 1:cxxxix; *RLGT*, 265.

[32]Enelow, *A Jewish View of Jesus*, 176.

[33]Abrahams, "Rabbinic Aids to Exegesis," 182.

[34]S. Sandmel, "Parallelomania," *JBL* 81 (1962): 3–4. "Parallelomania" is defined as "that extravagance among scholars which first overdoes the supposed similarity in passages and then proceeds to describe source and derivation as if implying literary connection flowing in an inevitable or predetermined direction" (1).

[35]Ibid., 9ff. The crowning sin of Strack-Billerbeck is that on the one hand they employ the rabbinic literature to elucidate the New Testament but, on the other, refuse to allow that rabbinic teaching was as fine as that of Jesus, even when the teaching is identical. Ibid., 10.

[36]*RLGT*, 265.

[37]*RLGT*, xix.

cated by Montefiore to the fifth category would be few indeed. This fact sheds new light on Montefiore's conception of "originality"—that word encountered so frequently in his discussions of Jesus' teaching. For Montefiore, Jesus' originality, to collect some words and phrases, consists in such things as "smoothing," "developments and fillings out," "additions," "legitimate expansions," "magnificent supplements and expansions," a spirit that is "eager, passionate, forthgoing," an "enthusiasm and passion," "a white heat of intensity," and a "fire and passion."[38] Vermes seems also to find originality in the "added dimension of effectiveness and power" in Jesus' teaching about righteousness. Although many rabbis stressed inwardness, "interiority, purity of intention, played a greater part in Jesus' thought."[39] As Montefiore puts it, "There is much more filling out to be found in the New Testament than actual and entire novelty."[40] Jesus' originality consists as much in what he did *not* say, as in what he did say. "The originality of Jesus lies in this, that he felt and picked out what was true and eternal amid the chaos and the rubbish, and that he enunciated and emphasized it with the greatest possible insistence and stress."[41] That the teaching of one man contained so much excellence in such concentrated form is, for Montefiore, originality.[42] Nonetheless, for the Jew, there is always more that is fundamentally great in the Old Testament than in all that Jesus said: "Great as are the supplements, the fundamentals seem to him greater still."[43]

Thus we frequently encounter paradoxical statements in Jewish writers on the question of originality—statements that themselves point to the Jewish dilemma. A typical expression of Montefiore's view is the following: "Jesus was a Jew, and his religious teaching will, I fully believe, have to be regarded as fundamentally Jewish upon the one hand, but as showing developments and originality upon the other."[44] These words, however, taken by themselves are somewhat misleading, for by "original" Montefiore means merely an extension of that which is Jewish: "It was quite possible for him to be both original *and* Jewish,

---

[38]Collected at random from Montefiore's writings.

[39]*GJJ*, 40.

[40]Montefiore, *The Old Testament and After*, 286.

[41]Montefiore, "The Synoptic Gospels and the Jewish Consciousness," 659. This statement is made in reply to Wellhausen, who sardonically remarked, "Yes, the rabbinic literature contains all that Jesus taught, and a great deal more."

[42]*RLGT*, xviii, 162; Montefiore, "The Originality of Jesus," 104.

[43]C. G. Montefiore, "The Old Testament and the Modern Jew," *HJ* 30 (1931–32): 569; cf. idem, "The Significance of Jesus for His Own Age," *HJ* 10 (1911–12): 768.

[44]C. G. Montefiore, "Judaism and Europe," 730.

so that even his very originality was, in nine cases out of ten, Jewish and not anti-Jewish."[45] Thus in the last analysis, Montefiore may be said to differ little from the mainstream of Jewish scholarship. He repeats a version of the old dictum: Jesus' teaching "does not, for the most part, contain what we, from our liberal Jewish point of view, can regard as *completely new* doctrine which is also *true* doctrine."[46] Elsewhere, however, Montefiore seems to say the exact opposite: "I most assuredly do not mean that there was nothing new in the teaching of Jesus, and nothing original, or nothing which was not both new and true, both good and original."[47] Montefiore's dilemma is the dilemma of Jewish scholarship. The total reclamation of Jesus' teaching by Jewish scholarship cannot be accomplished without ignoring or dismissing certain data.

Other Jewish scholars reflect the same dilemma in varying degrees. Enelow, for example, differs little from Montefiore. Speaking of the Jewishness of Jesus' teachings, he writes, "The merit of Jesus lay in giving those traditions and ideals a new expression, a new emphasis; and in endowing them with the perennial appeal of a fascinating personality."[48] Jesus' originality lay in making religion a "personal matter"; "religion and personality with him became one."[49] Sandmel's view, however, seems to be the view of Jewish scholarship. Because of the candid expression, his view seems to differ considerably from Montefiore's, but in reality the difference is slight:

> I own to seeing no originality in the teachings of Jesus, for I hold that those passages which deal with his supernatural role reflect not his authentic words but the piety of the developing Church. As to those teachings which are conceivably his, they seem to me to be of a piece with Jewish teaching, and that they range from the commonplace of that Jewish teaching through a sporadic flash of insight that other Jewish teachers also achieved.[50]

Jewish scholars thus attempt to recognize some difference, some degree of "originality" in the teaching of Jesus. Yet in the last analysis the originality that is admitted is of little consequence. Not uncommonly, as we have seen, it is expressed as a matter of Jesus' selection of

[45]Ibid.

[46]Montefiore, *The Old Testament and After*, 286; cf. Sandmel, *WJJ*, 90.

[47]Montefiore, "The Significance of Jesus for His Own Age," 768.

[48]H. G. Enelow, *A Jewish View of Jesus* (New York: Macmillan, 1920), 82.

[49]Ibid.

[50]*WJJ*, 109.

the best of the rabbinic traditional materials together with an ingenious combination of items, the "extending" of some of these, the placing of a prophetic emphasis on them, and the infusion of the lot with an infectious enthusiasm.

> A religious teacher might, I suppose, be called original who combined and collected together the best elements of religion existing in his time, emphasized those most important and fruitful, developed them, drew out their implications, and rejected or ignored other elements which did not harmonize with the first, or which, though he and his contemporaries may have been unaware of it, belonged in reality to a lower level and an outgrown age. I am inclined to believe that herein to a great extent lay the originality of Jesus.[51]

But it is a serious question whether such an analysis does justice to the remarkable newness that emerges in the teaching of Jesus. A key problem in the typical approach to the question of originality was pointed out long ago by Lindeskog, who suggested that an atomistic approach—i.e., a saying-by-saying assessment of originality—was incapable of arriving at the truth. The new, he argues, "lies finally in the shaping of a new organic wholeness."[52] Sandmel comes to a similar conclusion: "The uniqueness of Jesus would lie not in single particulars, but in the combination of facets, in the totality of what we may perhaps glimpse of him, and not in any one isolated way."[53] It is, indeed, in the totality of Jesus' teaching that we confront a newness that cannot be explained away. His ethical and religious teachings are, as we have seen, given in the context of his proclamation of the presence of the kingdom of God and his sense of his own central position in the coming of that kingdom. Individual sayings of Jesus may often find their parallels in the rabbinic literature, but even then we have often encountered the unusual and the exceptional. Taken together and set in the context of the dawning kingdom of God, as they must be if they are to be understood correctly, the sayings of Jesus entail a degree of originality that is far beyond what is usually admitted by Jewish scholars.

This originality of Jesus has, for the most part, been given insufficient attention by Jewish scholars. The "harmonizing method," by

---

[51]Montefiore, *RT*, 85; cf. Klausner, *JN*, 389.
[52]G. Lindeskog, *Die Jesusfrage im neuzeitlichen Judentum* (Uppsala: Almquist & Wiksells, 1938), 236.
[53]*WJJ*, 109–10.

which Jesus' teaching is paralleled with that of rabbinic Judaism, saying by saying (with varying degrees of success), may have the effect of obscuring to some extent the revolutionary newness of what Jesus proclaims. But, as we have seen, it does not and cannot succeed altogether.

Modern Jewish scholarship has reclaimed Jesus largely through the plainly evident Jewishness of his teaching, but also by ignoring or failing to explain what does not fit the rabbinic Jewish framework. This trend, whereby the teaching of Jesus is seen only as a continuation of the traditions of Judaism, is a relatively new one. For although Judaism has always been tolerant of varieties of doctrine, Jews in the past have nearly always regarded the teaching of Jesus as subversive.[54] It may be that the earlier Jewish reaction to the teaching of Jesus was more accurate in its sense of the degree to which Jesus departed from Judaism and the extent to which Jesus' teaching is fundamentally inseparable from his own personal claims.

When all has been said, we are driven again to the question of the person of Jesus. For in any investigation of the teaching of Jesus the pivotal question that always emerges is, indeed, the personal identity of this teacher who with his teaching announces the fulfillment of the promises and offers through his life and death the kingdom of God as the gift of God's grace.

---

[54]E. F. Scott, "The Originality of Jesus' Ethical Teaching," *JBL* 48 (1929): 110–11.

CHAPTER SIX

The Person of Jesus: His Mission

JEWISH SCHOLARS have occupied themselves much more with the teaching of Jesus in the synoptic Gospels than with the personal claims he makes in those same documents. The reason for this is plain: the teaching of Jesus is more readily reclaimable; the personal claims of Jesus to a great extent remain problematic. And yet, of course, despite the difficulty of the subject for Jews, the teaching of Jesus is ultimately inseparable from the person of Jesus. The difficulty occasionally experienced by Jewish scholars in understanding and explaining the teaching of Jesus itself reflects this fact. The problem of the person of Jesus, therefore, must eventually be faced head-on if a true estimate of the teaching of Jesus in the Gospels is to be attained. Schoeps has correctly seen this as "the most decisive point": "the unique *self-understanding* of Jesus, the messianic son-of-man consciousness, which contains the key to the understanding of his character."[1]

Sandmel has noted that generally the modern Jewish discussion of Jesus comes to two conclusions: (1) "that those Christian views which regard Jesus as more than a man are inconsistent with Judaism and uncongenial to Jews" and (2) "that those virtues ascribed to Jesus the man, the 'Jewish Jesus,' are characteristic Jewish virtues, expressed in Judaism and integrally a part of it."[2] Jewish scholarship has dwelt primarily on the latter conclusion; the former involves a more difficult and disagreeable subject and is usually dispatched with quickly. A true understanding of Jesus is not possible, however, if the sole concern of

---

[1]H. J. Schoeps, "Jesus," in *Gottheit und Menschheit* (Stuttgart, 1950), 70.
[2]*WJJ*, vii.

the investigation is to demonstrate the Jewishness of Jesus. The Jesus of the Gospels in fact resists being squeezed into a rabbinic mold. Neither the Jewishness of Jesus nor the considerable overlap between his teaching and that of the rabbis is to be doubted. But Jesus cannot be seen simply as another, albeit exceptional, Pharisaic Jew. Such a view of Jesus makes the Gospel narrative especially difficult to understand. If, as William Temple said, it is a mystery why anyone troubled himself to crucify the Christ of liberal Protestantism,[3] how much more a mystery it would be that the Jesus of Liberal Judaism was crucified. As Hans Küng has noted, if Jesus had been a liberal Jew, he would have had as little difficulty as the liberal Hillel.[4]

CATEGORIZING JESUS

The Jewish assessment of Jesus, as we have seen, regularly accords with the conclusion that his teaching is fully Jewish. Whatever description is accepted must be compatible with the Jewish reclamation of Jesus, or at least incompatible with Christian claims about Jesus. The discussion itself is carried on, it is claimed, in the domain of historical research rather than dogmatics; it is the Jesus of history who is being described, fairly and objectively, by the commonly recognized canons of critical historiography.

A wide variety of designations is available, of course, and little agreement exists among Jewish scholars as to which is the most appropriate. Some of these designations overlap and more than one may apply at the same time. Most of the designations to be considered are flexible in meaning, making possible a Jewish interpretation even of titles favored by the church. The various possible designations may be broadly classified, for convenience, as "more acceptable" and "less acceptable."

MORE ACCEPTABLE DESIGNATIONS

More acceptable, from the Jewish perspective, are those designations that place Jesus most securely into his Jewish con-

---

[3]William Temple, *Readings in St. John's Gospel* (reprint ed., London: Macmillan, 1961), xxvii.

[4]H. Küng, *Signposts for the Future* (Garden City, N. Y.: Doubleday, 1978), 76.

text. To a varying degree these designations may allow that Jesus was remarkable and exceptional among his contemporaries, but not that he was unique in any significant sense. The titles are decided on primarily by means of an analysis of the teaching and ministry of Jesus rather than from his claims about himself, which are almost always attributed to the faith of the postresurrection church. The teaching and ministry of Jesus, understood on their own terms, are capable of a variety of interpretations. This accounts for the lack of agreement among Jewish scholars concerning the designation that is most appropriate to describe him. There is, however, fairly widespread agreement about which of these designations are more acceptable and which are less acceptable.

Pharisee

In light of the controversies and growing hostility between Jesus and the Pharisees in the Gospel narratives, it may at first seem unlikely that Jesus would be identified as a Pharisee. Yet, at the same time, it is clear that Jesus and the Pharisees have much in common. Jewish scholars, as we have seen, have been effective in pointing out the large extent to which the teaching of Jesus may be paralleled in rabbinic sources. The bulk, certainly, of Jesus' teaching is not innovative but shares the perspective of much of first-century Judaism.

The question here depends on the interpretation of Jesus' teaching and his mission, with the focus being on Jesus' own stance toward the Law. Since Jesus is regarded by Jewish scholars as affirming the Law, debating its practical application to everyday living, and striving toward an ideal righteousness, he is almost always acknowledged as sharing in the spirit of Pharisaism, even by those who do not accept the designation "Pharisee" as appropriate in describing him. Jesus and the Pharisees have much more in common than they have differences, it is argued; and where there are differences, they are not of fundamental significance.

Abrahams, more than any other Jewish scholar, has examined Pharisaism in relation to the Gospels, rescuing it from the negative stereotyping it tends to receive in the Gospel narratives.

Abrahams, however, does not regard Jesus as a Pharisee. He is aware of a number of differences (e.g., concerning the Sabbath, human access to God), but these do not negate the fact that for the most part Jesus and the best representatives of the Pharisees stood on common ground.

Most Jewish scholars take a position similar to Abrahams'. Montefiore sees frequent similarity between the best Pharisees and Jesus, but in his own ambivalent manner he is more willing to see somewhat of a break with the Pharisees in Jesus' own originality. Klausner also finds "certain fundamental differences between Jesus and the Pharisees." (1) Jesus stressed the nearness of the Messiah and his kingdom; (2) he stressed the moral law; (3) he taught mainly in parables; and (4) his miracles were as important as his teaching.[5] Yet at the same time, despite undeniable and important differences, Jesus ultimately belongs with the Pharisees, rather than against them.

> The Pharisees objected to Jesus' behavior—his disparagement of many ceremonial laws, his contempt of the words of the "sages" and his consorting with publicans and ignorant folk and doubtful women. They considered his miracles sorcery and his messianic claims effrontery. Yet for all that, *he was one of themselves* (italics his).[6]

Rabbi Samuel Umen uses such terms as *spiritual, heavenly, mysterious,* and *mystical* to describe the teachings of Jesus and regards this tone of the teaching together with the concern for the individual rather than the nation and Jesus' own messianic claims as major differences from the teachings and attitude of the Pharisees.[7] Nevertheless, "Jesus' approach to the law was Pharisaic"[8] and "the spirit of Jesus is Pharisaic."[9] Asher Finkel

    [5]*JN,* 255.

    [6]Ibid., 335.

    [7]S. Umen, *Pharisaism and Jesus* (New York: Philosophical Library, 1963), 121; cf. 128–29.

    [8]Ibid., 126. Cf. also the statement by Loewe: "In general he followed the Pharisaic line." H. Loewe, "Pharisaism" in *Judaism and Christianity,* vol. 1, ed. W. O. E. Oesterley (London: Sheldon, 1937), 181.

    [9]Umen, *Pharisaism and Jesus,* 125. A similar position is expounded by J. Parkes, *Jesus, Paul and the Jews* (London: SCM, 1936), 78, who further argues that Jesus had as his purpose the reformation of certain abuses in Pharisaism.

adopts a similar stance, but is more specific when he dissociates Jesus from the strict school of Shammai, against which Jesus' castigations were directed, and likens him instead to the school of Hillel: "The Pharisaic approach adopted by the disciples of Hillel's school—their humbleness, restraint, clear argumentative reasoning and liberal stand—was close in spirit to that of the teacher of Nazareth."[10]

Only a few Jewish scholars are willing specifically to designate Jesus a "Pharisee." Klausner does so, but with sufficient qualification to indicate that the designation must be understood with some care.[11] One of the earliest attributions of this title to Jesus by a Jewish scholar comes from Abraham Geiger, a pioneer in the modern Jewish study of Jesus. Geiger saw little difference between Jesus and the Pharisees and described Jesus as a Pharisee "with Galilean coloring" who in no way uttered a new thought and never destroyed national barriers.[12] Not much later, Daniel Chwolsohn also described Jesus as one who consistently conducted himself as a Pharisee.[13]

Martin Buber also described the historical Jesus, much of whose teaching is shown to be parallel with that of the Pharisees, as belonging to Pharisaic Judaism.[14] Paul Winter too identifies Jesus as a Pharisee. He is rather emphatic in stating that Jesus never differed with the Pharisees; where the Gospels indicate controversy, they reflect the later hostility that came to exist between the synagogue and the church. Even Jesus' eschatological orientation is said to have been shared by the Pharisees in the pre−A.D. 70 period. Thus, *"in historical reality, Jesus was a Pharisee. His teaching was Pharisaic teaching, Pharisaic from*

---

[10]Asher Finkel, *The Pharisees and the Teacher of Nazareth* (Leiden/Köln: Brill, 1964), 134.

[11]To a considerable extent "Jesus remained a true Pharisaic Jew." His answer to the question about the greatest commandment reveals that "Jesus is thus still a Pharisee." *JN,* 319.

[12]Abraham Geiger, *Das Judentum und seine Geschichte* (Breslau, 1864), 111–12. Cited by J. Jocz, *JPJC,* 28; and S. Sandmel, *WJJ,* 64.

[13]Daniel Chwolsohn, *Das letzte Passamahl Christi und der Tag seines Todes* (St. Petersburg, 1892). See Klausner's summary, *JN,* 121ff.; cf. Jocz, *JPJC,* 325, n. 62.

[14]Martin Buber, *Two Types of Faith,* trans. N. P. Goldhawk (London: Routledge and Kegan Paul, 1951), 137; cf. 79, 92, 159–60.

the period before the conflagration with Roman military might" (italics his).[15] Ben-Chorin also argues that Jesus was a Pharisee: he was called "rabbi," his teaching both in form (e.g., parables, use of Scripture) and in content was that of a Pharisee, and he was faithful to the Law. Those who called Jesus a prophet were only the uneducated *'Am Ha-'Aretz.*[16]

One of the most forceful assertions that Jesus was a Pharisee comes from Maccoby: "Jesus was not only educated as a Pharisee; he remained a Pharisee all his life. . . . As a Rabbi, Jesus was a typical Pharisee teacher. Both in style and content, his religious teachings show an unmistakable affinity to Pharisaism, and especially to the teachings of the great apostle of Pharisaism, Hillel."[17]

Mention may be made here, too, of Lapide's article "Two Famous Rabbis" in which he finds "a spiritual kinship" between "two Rabbinic reformers," Rabbi Jeshua of Nazareth and the eighteenth-century Rabbi Israel of Mezibezh, the "Besht." Lapide places their sayings side by side and concludes, "Humble and full of compassion for human frailty, aflame with a burning sense of the inherent holiness of God's universe, *both Rabbis* have but one desire: To release Israel from sin and the world from its bonds in order to usher in at long last the Kingdom of Heaven" (italics his).[18]

Some Jewish scholars, however, deny that Jesus can be correctly described as a Pharisee. Vermes notes some similarities, but concludes, "It would be a gross overstatement to portray him as a Pharisee himself."[19] Schonfield denies that Jesus was brought up in Pharisaic Judaism,[20] although similarity

---

[15]*On the Trial of Jesus,* 2nd ed., rev. and ed. T. A. Burkill and Geza Vermes (Berlin/N.Y.: De Gruyter, 1974), 186; cf. 171.

[16]See *BJ,* and "Jesus und Paulus in jüdischer Sicht," *Annual of the Swedish Theological Institute,* vol. 10, ed. B. Knutsson (Leiden: Brill, 1976), 20ff.

[17]*RJ,* 106–7.

[18]P. Lapide, "Two Famous Rabbis," *Annual of the Swedish Theological Institute,* vol. 10, ed. B. Knutsson (Leiden: Brill, 1976), 109.

[19]*JJ,* 35; compared to the Pharisees, with their exegetical skills, "Jesus was an amateur in the field" (*GJJ,* 19).

[20]*PP,* 29.

at points is allowed. Sandmel says of the historical Jesus, "I simply do not know enough about him to have an opinion, and I simply do not have enough to set him, as it were, in some one single category."[21] A little later, however, he concludes, "We are unable to see any clear picture of any profound distance between Jesus and his fellow Jews."[22]

The thesis that Jesus was a Pharisee goes further than the Gospel evidence allows. It cannot be denied that Jesus resembles the Pharisees surprisingly often. But this overlap is hardly sufficient to warrant identifying him as a Pharisee.[23] Does Jesus intend merely a reformation of certain segments of Pharisaism? Does he simply present an alternative oral Torah that enables us to put him alongside Hillel and Shammai as offering a third rabbinic route? A careful analysis of the full sweep of Jesus' teaching as contained in the synoptic Gospels indicates that in actuality he departs radically and fundamentally from the Pharisaic perspective. As we have seen, Jesus not only at several specific points inclines away from Pharisaic tradition (e.g., in the neglect of ritual hand washing and fasting; and in his association with sinners), but with unparalleled authority (*exousia*) departs from the literal teaching of the written Torah (in the relaxing of Sabbath injunctions and implicitly the dietary law and in his prohibition of divorce) in order to bring its ultimate intention to light, whether directly (by redefining) or indirectly (by not allowing the lesser to obscure the greater). Despite legitimate parallels that exist between Jesus and the Pharisees, Jesus himself cannot be understood when pressed into the Pharisaic mold.

---

[21]*WJJ*, 108.

[22]Ibid., 138.

[23]Recently William E. Phipps, a Protestant scholar, has energetically argued that Jesus was a Pharisee. Phipps demonstrates that Jesus does share in two important Pharisaic doctrines: the compatibility of human freedom and divine providence, and belief in the resurrection of the dead. He also shows some similarities between the teaching of Jesus and that of the Pharisees. Phipps, however, fails to give sufficient heed to the centrally important controversies with the Pharisees. And although he admits a further dimension to Jesus wherein he is said to resemble the prophets, Phipps does not grasp the uniqueness of Jesus that marks him off from the Pharisees and all other Jewish parallels. "Jesus the Prophetic Pharisee," *JES* 14 (1977):17–31.

Essene

One of the few Jewish scholars to regard Jesus as an Essene was also one of the earliest to write on the subject of Jesus. Heinrich Graetz in the middle of the nineteenth century argued that the "unworldly" perspective of Christianity made it similar most of all to the teaching of the Essenes. Jesus, like the Essenes, displayed decidedly ascetic tendencies, and "although it cannot be proved that Jesus was admitted into the order of the Essenes, much of his life and work can only be explained by the supposition that he had adopted their fundamental principles."[24] Other Jewish scholars see much similarity between Jesus and the Essenes, especially in his social teachings, caused by direct or indirect influence, but do not go so far as to categorize Jesus himself as an Essene.[25] Kohler is perhaps closest to Graetz, yet without calling Jesus an Essene. Kohler does describe him as "the acme and the highest type of Essenism."[26] Abrahams writes, "It is undeniable that certain features of his teaching are Essenic."[27]

The discovery of the Dead Sea scrolls encouraged other scholars, including some Jewish scholars, to see Jesus and Christianity as influenced to some extent by the Qumran community, whether or not that community itself is correctly described as Essene.[28] Other Jewish scholars, however, strongly dissent from associating Jesus with the Essenes.[29]

---

[24]Heinrich Graetz, *History of the Jews* (ET, London, 1891–92), 11:150. Cited in Jocz, *JPJC*, 137. Cf. Sandmel, *WJJ*, 61ff.; S. Grayzel, *A History of the Jews* (13th ed.; Philadelphia, 1962). See also U. C. Ewing, *The Essene Christ* (New York, 1961).

[25]A. Finkel, *The Pharisees and the Teacher of Nazareth* (Leiden: Brill, 1964), 133; Klausner, *JN*, 211. Flusser regards most of Jesus' moral teaching as from "the Essene fringe." D. Flusser, *Jesus*, ET by R. Walls (New York: Herder & Herder, 1969), 76ff.; cf. *EJ* 10:13.

[26]K. Kohler, "Jesus of Nazareth—In Theology," *JE*, 7:169. "In him the Essene ideal reached its culmination," idem, "Christianity in Its Relation to Judaism," *JE*, 4:52; cf. idem, *The Origins of the Synagogue and the Church* (New York: Macmillan, 1929), 238.

[27]*SP*, 1:16.

[28]Cf. S. Ben-Chorin, *BJ*, 70–71; Flusser, *Jesus*, 76ff. Cf. also, from a non-Jewish perspective, A. Dupont-Sommer, who identifies the Qumran community with the Essenes and likens Jesus to the community's Teacher of Righteousness. *The Essene Writings from Qumran* (Oxford: Blackwell, 1961). Cf. also Ewing, *The Essene Christ*.

[29]J. Carmichael, *The Death of Jesus* (New York: Macmillan, 1962), 109–10; M. Mansoor, *The Dead Sea Scrolls* (Leiden: Brill, 1964), 160ff.; Sandmel, *WJJ*, 106.

Zealot

Robert Eisler, following the earlier argument of H. S. Reimarus, described Jesus as a political revolutionary who gathered about himself others of a like mind in order to bring about a rebellion against the Roman occupation.[30] Other Jewish scholars have pursued this line of analysis. Joel Carmichael, for example, follows Eisler in determining Jesus' purpose to be a "final onslaught on the citadels of the powers of this world." He came to Jerusalem, Carmichael continues, "like the Herald of the Kingdom bringing it about in power."[31] Lapide describes Jesus as an *Heilspolitiker* whose goal was to overthrow Roman rule and establish a messianic kingdom of God in its place.[32]

Most Jewish scholars who would not directly associate Jesus with the Zealots regard him as at least sympathetic to the Zealot desire for national independence (cf. the Zealot among Jesus' disciples, Matt. 10:4; Mark 3:18; Luke 6:15). Although denying that he was a Zealot, Maccoby sums up the perspective of Jesus as "a revolutionary vision, involving the overthrow of Roman power."[33]

Moreover, it is commonly agreed among Jewish scholars that Jesus was condemned and executed not for any religious reason but because he was regarded as being potentially, if not actually, seditious. Galilee after all was a hotbed of rebellion. "Zealot or not," writes Vermes, "Jesus was certainly charged, prosecuted and sentenced as one, and that this was due to his country of origin, and that of his disciples, is more than likely."[34]

---

[30]Robert Eisler, *Iesous Basileus Ou Basileusas. Die messianische Unabhängigkeitsbewegung vom Auftreten Johannes des Taufers bis zum Untergang Jakobs des Gerechten nach der neuerschlossenen Eroberung von Jerusalem des Flavius Josephus und der christlichen Quellen.* 2 vols. (Heidelberg, 1929–30). ET: *The Messiah Jesus and John the Baptist* (London, 1931).

[31]Joel Carmichael, *The Death of Jesus,* 182.

[32]*RN,* see especially "Zionismus im Neuen Testament" and "Jesus der Heilspolitiker," pp. 25–40. Lapide quotes approvingly S. G. F. Brandon, *Jesus and the Zealots* (Manchester, 1966). See also Lapide in H. Küng, *Signposts for the Future* (Garden City, N.Y.: Doubleday, 1979), 80ff.

[33]*RJ,* 120. Jesus was not a Zealot, but an apocalyptist who looked for miraculous deliverance. Ibid.

[34]*JJ,* 50. In his lectures, *The Gospel of Jesus the Jew,* Vermes is more insistent that Jesus was not a Zealot: "He was not a social reformer or a nationalistic revolutionary, notwithstanding recent claims to the contrary." 42.

Hasid (Miracle Worker)

Kohler attributes the impact of Jesus on his contemporaries not to his teaching but to his wonder-working. A true estimate of Jesus can be formed, according to Kohler, only by careful attention to the thaumaturgic and eschatological climate of that time. Jesus can then be seen to be genuinely historical and genuinely Jewish, paralleling other famous Jewish healers and wonder-workers, such as Hanina ben Dosa.[35]

Vermes, the author of the most potent Jewish analysis of Jesus to be published in recent years, presents a schema similar to Kohler's. Vermes stresses Jesus' role as healer and exorcist and places him fully within charismatic Judaism. He is more precisely described as "the paramount example of the early Hasidim or Devout."[36] Parallels to Jesus are found in other charismatic miracle workers such as the first-century B.C. saint Honi the Circle-Drawer (=Onias the Righteous in Josephus) or even more convincingly the Galilean Hanina ben Dosa of the first century A.D. Vermes presents a number of interesting similarities between these Hasidim and Jesus. Galilee, important to Vermes' reconstruction, is shown to be independent in spirit and rebellious against Rome (a major cause for the political suspicions that brought Jesus to his death). Galilee is further seen to be a breeding ground for Jewish charismatics. Whether the roots of charismatic Judaism were exclusively Northern or not, according to Vermes, "it is, in any case, safe and justifiable to conclude that the sophisticated religious ambiance of Galilee was apt to produce holy men of the Hasidic type."[37]

Flusser's view of Jesus is similar to that of Vermes. The picture of Jesus derived from the Gospels, read impartially, "is not so much of a redeemer of mankind as of a Jewish miracle-worker and preacher."[38] The view of Jesus as charismatic miracle-worker, teacher, prophet, and Messiah was more important to

---

[35]K. Kohler, "Jesus of Nazareth—In Theology," *JE*, 7:167.

[36]*JJ*, 79.

[37]Ibid., 79–80.

[38]Flusser, *Jesus*, 8; and "Jesus," *EJ*, 10:10. Unlike Vermes, Flusser also regards Jesus as "Pharisaic in general outlook." *Jesus*, 13.

Jewish Christianity, even in later centuries, than the kerygmatic Lord.[39] Flusser, like Vermes, draws parallels between Hanina ben Dosa and Jesus.[40]

Samuel S. Cohon also regards Jesus as a Galilean Hasid, adding that he comes from the *'Am Ha-'Areṣ*. That is, Jesus engaged in charismatic healing and prayer by the power of the Holy Spirit, but the emphasis of his teaching places him with the "people of the land" and "in the teaching company of the Hasidim who stood outside of Pharisaism."[41]

Schonfield too finds the explanation of Jesus in his Galilean origins. Jesus was not brought up in Pharisaic Judaism, but amidst North Palestinian sectarianism, which had the reputation of being "the natural home of heresy," and especially of messianic pretenders.[42] Schonfield's emphasis, however, is less on the charismatic dimension of Jesus as miracle-worker (although this is to be expected in a saint),[43] and more on Jesus as the self-convinced messianic king and political liberator of his people.

Prophet

With the category of prophet, it should immediately be noted, we move away from various Jewish sects and groups of the first century[44] to a higher level of individuality, wherein Jesus is recognized as not readily comparable to his own contemporaries. This fact is underlined by the prevailing sentiment that prophecy was dead and that its renewal awaited the eschatological era. It is this prophetic silence that accounts for the stir caused by John the Baptist (whose style intentionally recalled the image

---

[39]Flusser, *Jesus*, 8–9.

[40]Ibid., 69–70, 93, 95.

[41]Samuel S. Cohon, "The Place of Jesus in the Religious Life of His Day," *JBL* 8 (1927): 108. Article available in reprinted form in J. B. Agus, ed., *Judaism and Christianity* (New York: Arno, 1973), 82–108. J. Jacobs also classifies Jesus with the *'am ha-'areṣ, JE*, 7:163.

[42]*PP*, 201; cf. 30. For Essene influence on Jesus, see 56.

[43]Ibid., 263.

[44]To round out our discussion of sects, mention should be made of the eccentric views of R. Leszynsky who sees important affinity between Jesus and the Sadducees (*Die Sadduzäer* [Berlin, 1912]) and J. Jacobs who puts Jesus with the Ebionim or "the poor" (*Jesus as Others Saw Him* [New York: B. G. Richards, 1925], 52).

of Elijah) and Jesus, both of whom inevitably raised nationalistic hopes for a messiah, as well as provoking fear and opposition in those whose position depended on the preservation of the relatively peaceful status quo. To describe Jesus as a prophet or even as "prophetic" in this sense is, importantly, to consider him unique among his contemporaries.

Thus at first glance it may seem surprising that one of the more popular designations of Jesus by modern scholars is that of "prophet." At the same time the advantage of such a designation is that it is in keeping with the Jewishness of Jesus and yet allows in him a certain freedom with respect to the religious life of his day. To affirm that Jesus was a prophet is, needless to say, not necessarily the same as agreeing that he was *the* eschatological prophet (i.e., of Deut. 18:15ff.).

Montefiore, the champion of Jesus as prophet, sums up the religion of the prophets in these words: "the knowledge and worship of the one true God, justice and compassion rather than sacrifices and outward ceremonial."[45] Jesus' teachings are "of the same lineage and spirit" as the teachings of the prophets.[46] Indeed, the teaching of Jesus resembled that of the prophets in practically every detail. In his stress on the inward, as opposed to the outward; the spirit, rather than the letter; the motive, rather than the deed; in his warring against externalism and formalism; in his summons to a true spirituality; in all of these, Jesus stands with the prophets.[47] With them he announced the immediate denouement, and with them he stressed the consequent necessity of spiritual preparation.[48] Jesus possessed the prophetic temper of mind; he was convinced of his divine inspiration. Along with the inwardness and the intense spirituality of his teaching, he exhibited the prophetic tendency to magnify issues and to speak in absolutes.[49] Like any great prophet, he tended to imagine the

---

[45]*RT*, 101; cf. the same description in C. G. Montefiore, *The Old Testament and After* (London: Macmillan, 1923), 230.

[46]Montefiore, *The Old Testament and After*, 234.

[47]Cf. *RT*, 102; C. G. Montefiore, "The Religious Teaching of the Synoptic Gospels in Its Relation to Judaism," *HJ* 20 (1921–22): 437; *SG*, passim.

[48]*RT*, 16–17, 20–21.

[49]Montefiore, "Religious Teaching," 436.

perversion of a few as characteristic of all, and his own doctrine as the "real, true, old, and original doctrine." For Montefiore, Jesus is "one of the greatest and most original of our Jewish prophets," "a sort of eighth-century prophet born out of season."[50] "Jesus occupies the remarkable position of resuming the work and role of the prophets. He is in the genuine succession to Amos and Isaiah. It is most just that the title of prophet is, in Luke, repeatedly ascribed to him."[51]

We may parenthetically note, however, that these words of Montefiore are objectionable to some Jews. Thus G. Friedlander voices the opinion of an Orthodox Jew when he writes, "Mr. Montefiore's attempt to inscribe Jesus in the role of the prophets of Israel cannot be permitted to pass without a protest."[52] "The Jews," says Friedlander, "have refused steadfastly to see in the hero of the Gospels either a God, or an inspired prophet, or a qualified lawgiver, or a teacher in Israel with a new message for his people."[53] This provides a good illustration of the stance of most of Orthodox Judaism in the whole matter of the Jewish reclamation of Jesus.

Enelow agrees closely with Montefiore's assessment of Jesus. He writes, "In his own way Jesus did what the Prophets had done: He gave a fresh interpretation of the laws governing the spiritual life, a fresh message concerning the meaning and the purpose of religion, a new illumination of the sense and the object of the old prophetic utterances. Here lay his genius and originality."[54] Similarly, L. J. Edgar writes, "Not only was Jesus a prophet but there is good ground for believing that he was a prophet true to the essentials of Judaism."[55] Again we see an allowance for distinctiveness in Jesus.

According to Maccoby, "It is quite clear from the Gospels that Jesus's first appearance as a public figure was as a *proph-*

---

[50]C. G. Montefiore, "What a Jew Thinks About Jesus," *HJ* 33 (1934–35): 516.
[51]Montefiore, *The Old Testament and After*, 229.
[52]*JSSM*, xxiii.
[53]Ibid.
[54]H. G. Enelow, *A Jewish View of Jesus* (New York: Macmillan, 1920), 17.
[55]L. J. Edgar, *A Jewish View of Jesus* (London: The Liberal Jewish Synagogue, 1940), 6. Cf. G. Cornfeld, *Daniel to Paul* (London, 1962), 259.

et."[56] By "prophet" Maccoby understands a political leader who proclaims to the nation deliverance from the Roman oppression through the arrival of the kingdom of God.

For Vermes, Jesus the charismatic Hasid is automatically associated with the prophetic tradition of the Old Testament (and particularly with Elijah and Elisha). "Prophet" as used here must be understood, according to Vermes, specifically as "miracle-worker" rather than in the classical sense. The usage in which Jesus is understood to be a prophet is thus not associated with any eschatological significance.[57] The understanding of Jesus as *the eschatological prophet* is the result of later theologizing in the Gospel of John and the Acts of the Apostles.[58]

Without committing themselves to any conclusion, a few Jewish scholars argue that Jesus certainly at least regarded himself as a prophet (cf. Matt. 13:57). Flusser, for example, is not convinced regarding a messianic-consciousness in Jesus but sees throughout the New Testament "indications that Jesus had seen himself as a prophet."[59] Flusser, however, carefully differentiates this from the idea of eschatological prophet, which he denies was in the mind of Jesus.[60] Schonfield, on the other hand, indicates that Jesus regarded himself as not simply *a* prophet, but as *the* Prophet like Moses, with all the messianic overtones of that title in first-century Judaism.[61] Of course, as events were to demonstrate, he says, Jesus was wrong in this conviction.

Other Jewish scholars, although finding some similarity between Jesus and the prophets, regard the designation *prophet* as improper for Jesus. Klausner, for example, rejects the notion that Jesus was a prophet. He admits that Jesus in his teaching borrowed heavily from prophetic Judaism and that his two extremes

---

[56]*RJ*, 111.

[57]*JJ*, 89–90.

[58]Ibid., 96. The relevant New Testament passages are Matt. 21:11, 46; Mark 6:15; Luke 7:16, 39; 9:8, 19; 24:19; John 4:19; 6:14; 7:40; 9:17; Acts 3:22; 7:37. Vermes also notes the confusion concerning the Jewish expectation of Elijah; he comes as the agent of restoration or the herald of the beginning of the messianic age. Ibid., 95.

[59]*EJ*, 10:14. Cf. D. Flusser, "The Son of Man: Jesus in the Context of History," in A. Toynbee, ed., *The Crucible of Christianity* (London: Thames & Hudson, 1969), 228.

[60]Flusser, *Jesus*, 99.

[61]*PP*, 87; cf. 173, 209.

of "kindliness of heart and the most violent passion, show in him a character akin to that of the Prophet."[62] Klausner is nonetheless reluctant to speak of him as a prophet. The reason given, which incidentally reflects Klausner's Zionist convictions, is that Jews cannot regard Jesus as a prophet because "he lacks the Prophet's political perception and the Prophet's spirit of national consolation in the political-national sense."[63]

S. Cohon also argues that while Jesus was clearly in sympathy with the prophets, neither he nor his disciples made the claim that he was a prophet. Indeed, to Cohon the term seems inappropriate, since Jesus "moves on a wholly different plane." His concern was not with the present world, but with that which was to come, and thus he is best classified with the apocalyptic rather than the prophetic tradition. He is a prophet only insofar as that designation may be regarded as an attribute of messianism.[64]

Some Jewish scholars, finally, disallow that in any sense Jesus can be regarded as a prophet, because he speaks in a way that is utterly foreign to the prophetic style. Ben-Chorin regards it as inadmissible to say that Jesus was a prophet, since he does not use the stereotyped prophetic formulae (e.g., "Thus says the Lord").[65] Kohler denies the title of prophet to Jesus because of his egocentric manner.[66] Jacobs notes a confidence equal with the prophets', but calls attention to Jesus' divergent sense of autonomous authority.[67]

It is clear from this survey that in the perspective of Jewish scholarship Jesus shows striking similarities to the prophets. He repeats and carries forth their teachings and yet at the same time cannot satisfactorily be subsumed under the title of *prophet*. In comparison even with the prophets, Jesus' sense of personal authority and significance seems obtrusive. Montefiore recognizes

---

[62]*JN*, 410.

[63]Ibid., 414.

[64]S. S. Cohon, "The Place of Jesus in the Religious Life of His Day," *JBL* 48 (1927): 86.

[65]*BJ*, 15.

[66]K. Kohler, *The Origins of the Synagogue and the Church* (New York: Macmillan, 1929), 230.

[67]*JE*, 7:163.

the truth that "more than a prophet is here."[68] Thus he writes that "the personal claim was, in truth, partly prophetic—belonging to Jesus as a prophet—but partly, and still more, Messianic, belonging to him in virtue of his belief that he was or would be the Messiah."[69] To that question we must now turn.

LESS ACCEPTABLE DESIGNATIONS

In our discussion of the title *prophet* we have begun to approach the uniqueness of Jesus and thus already have reached the realm of the controversial. It is problematic for some Jews to classify Jesus with the prophets. It is much more difficult if by prophet we mean *the* eschatological "Prophet like Moses," with the clear messianic connotations of that designation. Yet since it is clear that the time of Jesus was one of revolutionary ferment, and apocalyptic enthusiasts were not uncommon (cf. within the New Testament itself Theudas and Judas the Galilean, Acts 5:36–37), Jesus may also have understood his mission in the same terms and thought of himself as the eschatological Prophet, as well as the Messiah. Some Jewish scholars accept these titles at least, and possibly others when rightly understood (as we will see), as historical (used by Jesus and his disciples), if it is kept very clear that they designate in the contemporary context only a human agent in God's eschatological program and not a superhuman or divine being. Of course it follows immediately that since the Roman rule in Palestine was not overturned and the messianic kingdom was not established for Israel, the Jewish conclusion is that Jesus and his disciples were wrong in attributing these titles to Jesus. But even in their error they remained loyal, dedicated Jews who nonetheless shared the aspirations of their nation, albeit in too zealous and exaggerated a fashion.

In what follows we will see that Jewish scholars generally take a much more conservative stance toward the historicity of the synoptic Gospels than does radical Protestant scholarship. This is at least true insofar as the matter in question can be fitted

---

[68]*RT*, 115; cf. Friedlander's strong objection, *JSSM*, xxiii.
[69]Ibid., 119–20.

comfortably into the contemporary historical context as perceived by them. Where it cannot, as we have seen, the text may be understood as unhistorical and taken, with radical critical scholarship, as reflecting the faith of the postresurrection church read back into the Gospel narrative. The general conservatism of Jewish scholars toward the text is largely explained by their correct sense of its authentically Jewish tone and their willingness to allow what is outrageous from their perspective to be counted as simple error. The designations now to be considered are acceptable at all only to the extent that they are understood as *not* meaning what the church takes them to mean.

Messiah

It is quite remarkable that the majority of modern Jewish scholars conclude that Jesus believed himself to be the Messiah. Without exception, of course, it is held that on this point Jesus was deluded. For Jews the question of Jesus' personal and messianic consciousness is of purely historical and scientific, and not religious, interest. As we have seen, however, that does not prevent many of them from admiring much of Jesus' moral and religious teaching.

We begin with Montefiore, who writes of Jesus:

> At some period of his career the conviction seems to have come to him that he was yet more than a prophet, that he was in fact none other than he of whom prophets had spoken and for whose coming so many generations had yearned, the Anointed One, the Messiah.[70]

It was this that caused the severe conflict between Jesus and the Jewish authorities, says Montefiore. Moreover, it is this fact that presents "the biggest problem of the gospel story" for the modern scholar.[71]

What was Jesus' own conception of his messiahship? Montefiore recognizes the difficulty of the question, but tends to

---

[70]*SG*, 1:cxxii.
[71]Ibid. Cf. the seemingly interminable list of questions drawn up by Montefiore.

believe that Jesus' concept of Messiah would have differed little from that of the first-century Jew. But this simply raises a second question, for which "adequate material for an adequate answer is, unfortunately, lacking."[72] Yet, according to Montefiore, some things can be said. Very likely Jesus was influenced by the apocalyptic writers so that he conceived of the Messiah as being something greater than the description of him in Isaiah 11. He was not a mere man inaugurating a new earthly kingdom, but the proclaimer and a leading character of the imminent kingdom of God, which would replace the old order. Thus, although Jesus was not deliberately unnational in outlook, political and national issues were not considered important by him. Still, the view of Messiah held by Jesus was not un-Jewish. Apocalypticism influenced the rabbis and Pharisees so that many believed in a more than human Messiah. "Though less than and distinct from God, he was conceived by some as more divine than the ordinary man."[73] Further, "Jesus as the Messiah *in posse* felt that he possessed greater power, and claimed a more personal allegiance, than any prophet before him."[74] Here, of course, Montefiore characteristically goes well beyond his Jewish colleagues.

Montefiore sternly resists the idea that Jesus' conception of the kingdom of God was wholly spiritual and in that sense un-Jewish. In the first place, the Jewish conception was never without its spiritual aspects. Second, if Jesus' conception was without material and national significance, he asks, why did he allow the people to continue believing in a Messiah delineated along the lines of Isaiah 11? Accordingly, Montefiore regards the exhortation to secrecy concerning Jesus' messiahship in Mark 8:30 as historical, attributing it either to Jesus' sense of the political danger involved, or his reluctance to anticipate the divine denouement.[75]

Montefiore thinks it likely that Jesus went to Jerusalem to inaugurate the kingdom; yet the possibility of "temporary defeat

---

[72]*SG*, 1:15.
[73]*RT*, 127.
[74]Ibid., 120.
[75]*SG*, 1:184.

and death may well have crossed his mind."[76] In the days of Jesus, the very idea of a dying and rising Messiah who would only afterward inaugurate the kingdom and be glorified, was entirely foreign. The conception of the Messiah's work as a lowly service culminating in death "may have been the special development made by Jesus to the conception of the Messiah."[77] Moreover, "any idea of his [the Messiah's] *death* as an atonement or as a 'ransom' was unknown to the Rabbis," although in later rabbinic literature the idea of the Messiah *suffering* for his people is not unknown.[78] For Montefiore, the import of Jesus' messianic consciousness, as far as his teaching is concerned, is that it gave to it "a special added touch of fervour and enthusiasm."[79]

Enelow evaluates Jesus' messianic self-consciousness along lines similar to Montefiore's understanding. The kingdom he desired to establish was spiritual in nature. Jesus was misunderstood to be a political Messiah and he sadly disappointed and embittered his followers when it finally became evident that he was not that kind of Messiah. "Was he thinking of one thing when he spoke of the Kingdom of Heaven, and was the multitude thinking of another? That is what formed the tragedy."[80] Other Jewish writers who accept that Jesus claimed to be the Messiah minimize the national-political element. Thus, Klausner, noting that Jesus was "obsessed by his idea that he was the Messiah," argues that although Jesus must, "like every Jewish messiah," have had thoughts of rebellion against the Romans, at the end he rejected this because "his dreamy, spiritual nature was not fitted for such methods."[81] Elsewhere, Klausner characterizes Jesus as "the most Jewish of Jews" whose *exaggerated* Judaism con-

---

[76]*RT*, 135; *SG*, 1:190–91.

[77]*SG*, 1:17; *RT*, 135; Montefiore also suggests on this line a possible connection with the Man of Daniel 7:13, who he says Jesus may have expected to be in his glory. *SG*, 1:17.

[78]*RLGT*, 305; cf. T. Walker, *What Jesus Read* (London: Allen & Unwin, 1925), 68–69.

[79]*RT*, 132.

[80]Enelow, *A Jewish View of Jesus*, 139.

[81]*JN*, 253.

stituted the most serious danger to national Judaism, bringing
with it "the ruin of national culture, the national state, and national life."[82] Klausner finds the notion of a suffering Messiah in
Israel; yet, to him, Jesus did not anticipate his own suffering, nor
did he attribute any atoning significance to it.[83] When all is said,
however, it is Jesus' messianic consciousness that best explains
his apparent eccentricities. Klausner finds this solution the most
helpful in seeing Jesus from the Jewish perspective. It is this very
messianic conviction of Jesus that accounts for the un-Jewishness
of his teaching.[84] Apart from some such explanation, Jesus remains an enigma.

Cohon makes a similar appeal to explain what occurred. He
argues that "in view of the persistence of the testimony," Jesus'
messianic consciousness cannot be denied. From that self-consciousness on Jesus' part "sprang his entire mode of conduct, his
sense of special authority in healing and teaching, his peculiar
attitude towards sinners and his apocalyptic teaching."[85] But
while this consciousness "presents a psychological puzzle to
moderns," it best explains the phenomenon of Christianity.[86]
Schoeps is also insistent that Jesus can be understood only as
claiming to be the Messiah/Son-of-Man. Referring to Matthew
11:27, Schoeps writes, "Here Jesus affirms an entirely unique
union with God and a knowledge of God's will, as that which
could be had only by the one sent by God, the Messiah himself."[87] This, continues Schoeps, is the explanation of his absolute power and authority and his call to discipleship.

It is interesting that Sandmel, who as a critical scholar holds
an agnostic position with regard to the Jesus of history, can, at
the same time, venture the following opinion: "I believe that he
believed himself to be the Messiah, and that those scholars who

---

[82]Ibid., 347. "His *overemphasis* was *not* Judaism, and, in fact, brought about *non-*Judaism." *JN*, 393.

[83]Cf. J. Klausner, *The Messianic Idea in Israel* (London: Allen & Unwin, 1956); *JN*, 405–6.

[84]*JN*, 405.

[85]Cohon, "The Place of Jesus," 86.

[86]Ibid.

[87]Schoeps, "Jesus," 73.

deny this are incorrect."[88] Sandmel points to the diversity of messianic expectations in the first century and notes that common to all was the expectation that God would bring judgment on the Romans on Israel's behalf through his agent, the Messiah. Only much later was the idea of the Messiah "transformed from something involving specific and temporal characteristics into something involving more suprahuman abstractions."[89] So far as the New Testament is concerned, however, there are "only the dimmest associations of Jesus' messiahship with Jewish national hopes."[90] The idea that the death of the Messiah could atone for sins is regarded by Sandmel as decidedly un-Jewish.[91]

Zeitlin is more consistently agnostic at this point than Sandmel. Zeitlin raises the question and examines some of the Gospel data, including the messianic-secret motif, but concludes that as far as any claim to messiahship by Jesus is concerned, "no historical explanation can be advanced." Jesus' motives "remain a mystery."[92]

Perhaps the most common analysis among Jewish scholars who conclude that Jesus thought himself to be the Messiah is that which stresses the political nature of the messianic expectation, whether in terms of an intended literal revolt or an apocalyptic inbreaking. Of course, those Jewish scholars who were presented earlier as designating Jesus a Zealot may also be mentioned here. Thus Eisler, Carmichael, and Lapide allow that Jesus perceived himself as a kind of political messiah, a person who was to be instrumental in the defeat of the Romans and the establishment of the kingdom of God.

Schonfield finds the explanation of Jesus in his messianic consciousness: "Yet, surely, the entitlement of Jesus to speak and act as he did arose from his Christ-consciousness. His ministry among the Jews was directly related to the Messianic philosophy, the Divine Plan for bringing about the Kingdom of God on

---

[88]*WJJ*, 109.

[89]Ibid., 33.

[90]Ibid., 36.

[91]Ibid., 45–46. Cf. J. Jacobs, "Jesus of Nazareth—In History," *JE*, 7:163.

[92]S. Zeitlin, *The Rise and Fall of the Judaean State*, 2 vols. (Philadelphia: Jewish Publication Society of America, 1967), 2:160.

earth heralded by the Hebrew Prophets."[93] Schonfield further-more accepts the existence of the concept of a suffering Messiah in the day of Jesus.[94] "A Messianic view did exist which en-visaged the persecution of the Messiah and designs on his life; but not one held that his foes would succeed in killing him, for this would have meant the triumph of the forces of evil."[95] Schonfield's reconstruction, unusual for a Jewish scholar, de-pends much on the Northern (i.e., Galilean) associations of Jesus—associations that enabled Jesus to put together as compati-ble the concepts of Righteous King, Suffering Just One, and Son of Man.[96]

Maccoby stresses the apocalyptic character of Jesus' expec-tations. Although Jesus began as a rabbi and prophet, the day came when "he became convinced that the Messiah and deliverer whose advent he had been prophesying was none other than himself."[97] Thus Jesus announced himself, from Caesarea Phi-lippi onward (Mark 8:27–29), as "the final King-Messiah whose advent was the culmination of human history."[98]

As further representatives of the clearly apocalyptic view of Jesus' own messianic consciousness, we may briefly mention E. R. Trattner[99] and A. H. Silver.[100] For both writers Jesus was to some extent forced to his position by the circumstances that confronted him. Only the apocalyptic action of God through his

---

[93]*FCS*, 17; cf. 25, 52. Schonfield boldly asserts that "the right understanding of Jesus commences with the realization that he identified himself with the fulfillment of the messianic hope . . . no one could be more sure of his vocation than was Jesus, and not even the threat of imminent death by the horrible torture of crucifixion could make him deny his messiahship" (*PP*, 33). Schonfield goes so far as to make the following remark-able statement: "It is needful to emphasize that neither before nor since Jesus has there been anyone whose experiences from first to last have been so pin-pointed as tallying with what were held to be prophetic intimations concerning the Messiah" (*PP*, 36). Schon-field's argument is that Jesus carefully calculated all such correspondences, including the suffering, in order to demonstrate his messiahship.

[94]*PP*, 212.

[95]*FCS*, 87–88.

[96]*PP*, 32.

[97]*RJ*, 114.

[98]*RJ*, 123. In entering Jerusalem, Jesus, according to Maccoby, "was making a bid for power as a literal, not metaphorical or 'spiritual,' King of the Jews." 132.

[99]E. R. Trattner, *As a Jew Sees Jesus* (New York: Scribner, 1931).

[100]A. H. Silver, *Where Judaism Differed* (New York: Macmillan, 1956).

messianic agent could bring the historical resolution that faithful Jews awaited.

Flusser appears ambivalent about the question of Jesus' own claim to be Messiah. "The early Christian Church believed Jesus to be the expected Messiah of Israel, and he is described as such in the New Testament; but whether Jesus thought himself to be the Messiah is by no means clear."[101] Nonetheless, argues Flusser, "he must surely have seen himself as being more than a herald of the Kingdom of Heaven and more than a healer and wonder-worker."[102] Flusser regards the continual reference to the coming Son of Man in the third person as evidence that "Jesus actually did not believe himself to be the Messiah." Yet elsewhere Jesus identifies himself with the Son of Man. Flusser's conclusion: "Thus Jesus' understanding of himself as the Messiah was probably inconsistent, or at first he was waiting for the Messiah, but at the end, he held the conviction that he himself was the Messiah."[103] More recently Flusser has written that "on the basis of the statements of Jesus in the synoptic Gospels it is possible to ascertain that the strong self-consciousness of Jesus, the concept of sonship, and very probably his messianic mission are authentic and go back to the 'historical' Jesus."[104] Jesus, however, made no association between his messianic role and his death as an expiation of sins.[105] Kohler argues similarly that whereas Jesus made no claim to be the Messiah prior to his entry into Jerusalem, he did so later, especially in his action of casting the money-changers out of the temple.[106]

Some Jewish scholars remain unconvinced that Jesus ever claimed to be the Messiah. Ben-Chorin considers Jesus' messianic self-consciousness in the Gospels to be unhistorical; it is rather to be explained by the impact of the kerygmatic tradition.

[101]*EJ*, 10:13–14.

[102]Flusser, "The Son of Man," 228.

[103]*EJ*, 10:13–14. Cf. Flusser, *Jesus*, 103–4; idem, "The Son of Man," 228, 230.

[104]D. Flusser, "Das Schisma zwischen Judentum und Christentum," *EvTheol* 40 (1980): 219.

[105]Flusser, "The Son of Man," 233; idem, *Jesus*, 103–4. Flusser attributes this to a later Greek recension of the Gospels. Idem, "Das Schisma zwischen Judentum und Christentum," 219.

[106]Kohler, "Jesus of Nazareth—In Theology," 169.

Historical reconstruction of the story of Jesus must be freed from Christian overpainting.[107] Included in that overpainting is the suggestion that Jesus regarded himself as the Messiah. In this Ben-Chorin agrees with a common perspective of radical Protestant scholarship.[108]

We turn finally to Vermes, who notes that the affirmation of Jesus as the Messiah was an essential belief of earliest Christianity. All the same, argues Vermes, the Synoptic portrait of Jesus critically interpreted gives "every reason to wonder if he really thought of himself as such."[109] Only when Jesus' enemies failed to find a nonpolitical cause, did they seize upon the Galilean's potential for revolution as the means to condemn him.[110] Vermes thus denies that Jesus conceived of his role along any of the lines of contemporary messianic speculation, whether as the Priest Messiah, the Prophet Messiah, preexisting heavenly Messiah, or slain Messiah (this last concept he dates from the martyrdom of Simeon ben Kosiba in A.D. 135). The only meaningful understanding of the title for Jesus' audience would have been that of a Davidic King Messiah, which was the common expectation, but which is exactly the designation Jesus refused to accept. His followers, however, would not accept that he was not the Messiah, transferred the reign of Messiah to the post-Easter interval, and produced a theological synthesis utilizing several strands of messianic speculation. Ultimately the title was preserved in the Gentile church, not for its own content, but for "psychological and polemical value in the Jewish-Christian debate."[111]

Two points emerge from this survey of Jewish opinion on the question of Jesus' messiahship. First, it is clear that for the many Jewish scholars who are not unwilling to allow that Jesus may have claimed to be the Messiah, in no case is it allowed that he was correct in his belief. Sandmel well sums up the Jewish attitude at this point:

---

[107]*BJ*, 13.

[108]It is surprising that on this question Sandmel does not side with radical Protestant scholarship as he usually does, but it must be remembered that he admitted to being in the realm of speculation when he affirmed Jesus' messianic self-consciousness.

[109]*JJ*, 149.

[110]Ibid., 144.

[111]Ibid., 153ff.

Any claims made during the lifetime of Jesus, that he was the Messiah whom the Jews had awaited, were rendered poorly defensible by his crucifixion and by the collapse of any political aspect of his movement, and by the sad actuality that Palestine was still not liberated from Roman dominion.[112]

L. Edgar writes to the same effect: "History has proved that Jesus was not the Messiah whom the Jews were eagerly waiting. He did not deliver them from the yoke of Rome and the Perfect Age most certainly did not come."[113]

Second, Jewish scholars, when speaking of Jesus' messianic consciousness, are very careful to point out that the Messiah was always regarded as distinct from God. In no sense can it be said that the Messiah is a manifestation of God. This can be seen in the Orthodox Jew Ahad ha'Am who, however, at this point reflects the virtually unanimous view of Jewish scholarship when he writes of the Messiah: "His importance lies not in himself, but in his being *the messenger of God* for the bringing of redemption to Israel and the world."[114]

We have now come as far as most Jewish scholars are willing to go in their analysis of the Jesus of the Gospels. To many of them it is conceivable that Jesus may have claimed to be the Messiah—as understood in contemporary Jewish expectation—and that he was deluded, though with the best of Jewish intentions. Again the pattern is clear: to the extent that the Jesus of the Gospels is reclaimable, or at least not fundamentally incompatible with Judaism, the Gospel accounts are given credence; to the extent that he appears not to be reclaimable, the evidence is attributed to the theologizing of the postresurrection church. Thus other possible designations of Jesus such as Lord, Son of Man, Son of God—since they move decidedly away from traditional Jewish acceptability—are ordinarily not considered at all. These titles are quite readily understood as reflecting the faith of the

---

[112]S. Sandmel, *A Jewish Understanding of the New Testament* (1956; reprint ed., New York: Ktav, 1974), 33.

[113]Edgar, *A Jewish View of Jesus* (pamphlet published by the Liberal Jewish Synagogue), 5.

[114]Ahad ha'Am, "Judaism and the Gospels," in H. Kohn, ed., *Nationalism and the Jewish Ethic* (New York: Schocken, 1962), 297. But see Flusser's remarks below, p. 266.

church and are accordingly counted as having no historical value. And Jewish scholars are quite happy to point out that in this conclusion they are simply following what Protestant critical scholarship has demonstrated.

Vermes proves to be the exception at this point. He gives full consideration to these so-called christological titles and as a historian "salvages" them from kerygmatic mutation. In numerous instances indeed he must appeal to the faith of the church as being read back into the life of Jesus. But he attempts to show that frequently such an expedient is unnecessary, as the titles are often capable of another interpretation. This approach of Vermes is significant and deserves a brief summary at this point.

Lord

By a thorough investigation of the philological background of the word *lord* in the Aramaic spoken by Jews in the New Testament era, Vermes concludes that "the designation '(the) lord,' is appropriate in connection with God, or a secular dignitary, or an authoritative teacher, or a person renowned for his spiritual or supernatural force. The field in fact—and contrary to the opinion generally held by New Testament experts—is entirely open."[115] A survey of the Gospels with "fresh eyes" shows that the use of the appellation "lord" is historically authentic. In Mark and Matthew it is used as an address to a miracle-worker; in Matthew the use is extended to apply to a teacher or a religious leader, and this becomes the predominant usage in Luke.[116] Even in the fourth Gospel this meaning of "lord" is found, although we also find here the evolutionary apex of "Lord" as it came to be used in a Hellenistic milieu.

Son of Man

Vermes' argument on the meaning of *Son of Man* is well known from his oft-cited article that appears as an appendix to the

---

[115]*JJ*, 121.
[116]Ibid., 126–27.

third edition of Matthew Black's *Aramaic Approach to the Gospels and Acts*.[117] The discussion of this difficult subject in *Jesus the Jew*,[118] a scholarly *tour de force*, is based on and extends the earlier discussion. In brief, Vermes' conclusions remain that "son of man" is Aramaic and not Hellenic in derivation and that the expression is never used as an autonomous title but is primarily a circumlocution for the first personal pronoun. The use of the expression in Daniel 7:13 is to be understood as a collective for "the saints of the Most High" and not as a reference to an individual. Only in speculative exegesis of this passage is "son of man" regarded as having acquired eschatological and messianic connotations. Despite this, as even in the 1 Enoch passages, without some kind of explanation or qualification the expression "son of man" is "neither clear, nor distinctive enough to act as an autonomous title."[119] As for the Gospel evidence, the "son of man" references not connected with Daniel 7:13 are taken by Vermes as circumlocutory. But those connected with Daniel 7:13 directly (Mark 13:26; 14:62) or indirectly (Mark 8:38; Luke 12:8; *parousia* passages), since they do not fit in with the reconstructed historical background, are not explainable and hence are regarded necessarily as "the product of Christianity" or "timid early 'post-crucifixion' hints at the exaltation and imminent glorious revelation of the Messiah." It cannot be proved, concludes Vermes, that these references go back to Jesus.[120] If they did, "the necessary prerequisite of full Messianic con-

---

[117](Oxford, 1967) Appendix E, 310–28. Vermes indicates in *Jesus the Jew: A Historian's Reading of the Gospels* (New York: Macmillan, 1973), 189, his surprise that Black added his own criticism to the appendix in which he reiterated his own conclusion that the phrase includes "eschatological overtones."

[118]Pages 160–91. Vermes describes the designation as "a cross-road of paradoxes," enumerating three basic paradoxes: (1) the lack of the use of "son of man" outside the Gospels, and never in Paul and the other epistles; (2) the use of "son of man" only by Jesus in the Gospels, and never by others in addressing him; and (3) "the serious lack of impact made by the expression on the contemporaries of Jesus." *JJ*, 160–61. See now his latest full discussion, "The Present State of the 'Son of Man' Debate," *JJS* 29 (1978): 123–34.

[119]*JJ*, 175. Vermes also cautions that the post–A.D. 70 dating of 4 Ezra and 1 Enoch (Section 2, chapters 37–71, the so-called "son of man" book) makes it impossible to use this material to shed light on the time of Jesus.

[120]Ibid., 183ff.

sciousness on the part of the speaker'' would have to be accepted.[121] Needless to say, this is thought to be unacceptable. Thus Vermes defends the historical authenticity of the expression in the Gospels, as far as his presuppositions will allow him to, finding it necessary in the last analysis to appeal to the pressure of kerygmatic tradition of the early church.

Flusser is one of the few Jewish scholars to allow the possibility that Jesus did speak of himself as ''Son of Man,'' understood as a messianic title. Although Jesus sometimes appears not to be convinced of his messianic identity, ''yet other apparently authentic sayings of Jesus can be understood only if it is assumed that Jesus thought himself to be the Son of Man.''[122] Again, Jesus is regarded by Flusser as either inconsistent or as coming to self-consciousness only toward the end. Thus Flusser writes that ''those present correctly understood this [the statement of Luke 22:69, ''But from now on the Son of man shall be seated at the right hand of the power of God''] as Jesus' indirect admission of his Messianic dignity. . . . In the end, the conviction gained strength that he himself was the coming Son of man.''[123] As we will see, Flusser goes so far as to admit that this title had a divine connotation for Jesus and his disciples.

Son of God

Vermes also defends the historical authenticity of the title Son of God as applied to Jesus. Beginning with the Old Testament meaning of Son of God as applied to heavenly or angelic beings, Israel or individual Israelites, and kings of Israel, Vermes traces the title as it becomes associated with messianic expectation in the intertestamental writings and in the literature of Qumran. A survey of the entire context, Jewish and Hellenistic, yields the following conclusion: ''All in all, it would appear that a first-century A.D. Palestinian Jew, hearing the phrase *son of*

---

[121]In circular fashion, Vermes refers to his negative conclusions about Jesus' messianic self-consciousness as evidence why such a prerequisite cannot be accepted. Ibid., 183.

[122]*EJ*, 10:14.

[123]Flusser, *Jesus,* 103.

God, would have thought first of all of an angelic or celestial being; and secondly, when the human connection was clear, of a just and saintly man.''[124] Of the Gospel testimony Vermes concludes, ''It is impossible to prove and unwise to suppose that Jesus defined himself as *the son of God.*''[125] Passages such as Mark 13:32 and Matthew 11:27 are attributed to the faith of the primitive church.[126] Jesus *is* addressed as Son of God in the sense of Messiah, but this means nothing more than divine appointment and adoption. In the majority of cases, however, Jesus is addressed (by demons, men, and the heavenly Voice) as the Son of God in the sense of miracle-worker, or charismatic exorcist. Importantly, Vermes establishes that the title is authentically Semitic and not a Hellenistic importation. The data of the Synoptics concerning the divine worship of Jesus conform ''exactly to the image of the Galilean miracle-working Hasid.''[127] Jesus could well have been conscious of this kind of divine sonship. Vermes further challenges the argument that Jesus' use of *abba* is unique, citing some parallels in the Hasidic piety of rabbinic literature.[128] Thus Vermes argues that the earliest historical stratum of Son of God in the Gospels refers to the miracle-worker exorcist. From this initial derivation these later developments follow in succession: Son of God as Messiah by adoption, preexistent Son of God, and ultimately Son of God by nature (especially in the fourth Gospel), thus producing ''the final amalgam.''[129] Never, however, in the Jewish context does one move beyond the office of the messianic agent to the actual notion of divinity. That derives, according to Vermes and virtually all Jewish scholars, from a Gentile-Christian context in the larger environment of pagan Hellenism.

Vermes in his valuable study has given us an individualistic

---

[124]*JJ,* 200.

[125]Ibid., 201.

[126]In his lectures *The Gospel of Jesus the Jew,* Vermes allows that Matthew 11:27 is ''probably representative of Jesus' thought,'' but that all the verse suggests is ''an ideal reciprocity between Father and son'' that does not entail equality. *GJJ,* 40–41.

[127]*JJ,* 209.

[128]Ibid., 210ff.; cf. *GJJ,* 27.

[129]*JJ,* 212; cf. *GJJ,* 46.

interpretation of the designations of Jesus, but this interpretation, though plausible in its own way, is not satisfactory. The problem is not altogether in the interpretation of the data (although at several points exception may be taken), since for the most part Vermes' analysis is a possible one. This is not the place to attempt to answer Vermes' arguments one by one, although this needs to be done.[130] The weakness of Vermes' conclusions lies not simply in the improbability of single items, but in the implausibility of his hypothesis *in toto*. The more serious problem with Vermes' analysis is whether or not it does justice to the full sweep of the Gospel data and not simply to the various specific designations of Jesus. Again, we observe the weakness of an atomistic approach that ignores the pattern of data as a whole. In short, it remains very questionable whether the Jesus of the Gospels can be adequately contained within the single description of him as a charismatic Hasid. The reduction of the data to this one category at every point, together with the need at numerous important passages to appeal to the creative faith of the early church as having been interjected into the Gospel narratives, leaves the impression that a predetermined conclusion has been successfully reached. Vermes has moved beyond most Jewish scholars in the very fact that he discusses the titles of Jesus, but the final result is not significantly different.

It cannot be doubted that the possible categorizations of Jesus thus far surveyed contain their own fair amount of truth. Certainly Jesus in his teaching closely resembles the prophets of the Old Testament. Yet the category of "prophet" does not in itself adequately serve to classify either Jesus or his teaching. The category of "Messiah" takes one a good way further in its appropriateness. Jesus professed both to be the Messiah and to inaugurate in himself the Messianic Age. He came not to reform Judaism, but to bring God's reign to earth anew. Thus his teaching is strikingly messianic in character, describing the righteousness of the kingdom in its absoluteness. Yet even the category "Mes-

---

[130]On the Son of Man question, see J. A. Fitzmyer, "The New Testament Title 'Son of Man' Philologically Considered" in *A Wandering Aramean. Collected Aramaic Essays, SBLMS* 25 (Missoula, Mont.: Scholars, 1979), 143–60; idem, "Another View of the 'Son of Man' Debate," *JSNT* 4 (1979): 58–68.

siah," as understood by the Jew, fails to portray Jesus and his
teaching adequately. Thus, not infrequently the Jewish scholar is
frustrated in his understanding of Jesus, and Jesus and his teaching remain a mystery. When all is said and done, there remains a
uniqueness about Jesus that bars restricting him within the limits
and boundaries established by modern Jewish scholarship.

THE UNIQUENESS OF JESUS

There is, then, an obvious natural reluctance among Jewish
scholars to admit any uniqueness in Jesus and his teaching. They
look for and find in Jesus only that which can be characterized as
"Jewish." "The possibility that Jesus made unusual claims for
himself is from the start ruled out as improbable."[131] And yet the
careful Jewish scholar in his discussion of the Jewishness of
Jesus' teaching, as we have seen, must continually use qualifying
words and phrases such as "generally," "usually," "for the
most part," etc. There are conjectures, suggestions of translation
errors, and ultimately appeals to the theological creativity of the
early church. Of course, it is part and parcel of the method of
scientific historiography that one's own conclusions are always
tentative and that at many points the scholar must engage in
speculation to arrive at a plausible reconstruction. Nevertheless it
seems that Jewish scholarship in its thoroughgoing attempt to
reclaim Jesus for Judaism has been unduly influenced by dog-
matic concerns. It can hardly claim to depend strictly on objective
or scientific scholarship, when it must make use of such strained
explanations to reach the desired result.[132] Only with great difficulty and determination, however, can the Jesus of the Gospels
be made to fit the preconceived mold.

1. To begin with, Jewish scholars deny that Jesus ever
taught his disciples to put their faith in him. Thus, according to

---

[131]This is the analysis of the Hebrew Christian J. Jocz. *JPJC*, 38.

[132]This applies also to Vermes, whose book is subtitled *A Historian's Reading of the
Gospels* and who writes in his preface that the book "is decidedly not intended to depict a
'Jewish' Jesus as a denominational counterpart of the Jesus of the various churches, sects
and parties that claim allegiance to him." *JJ*, 9; cf. *GJJ*, 1.

Enelow, his desire was to reproduce in his disciples the intensely personal relationship he enjoyed with God. "His message was not, Make me, or my words, the means of your religion."[133] While Jesus may be said to have "interpreted, transmitted, and transformed his Jewish heritage,"[134] he did nothing to transmute it. Montefiore also contends that the faith Jesus demanded was faith not in himself but in God. "The faith which Jesus demanded was only faith in himself so far as to recognize that he was the prophet and messenger of God."[135] Faith for Jesus was trust in the goodness and power of God. This was only good rabbinic doctrine, though Jesus in his emphasis of faith makes it more central. Loewe, however, admits that in the miracle passages, at any rate, a totally new and unrabbinic notion is introduced in that "faith means faith in Jesus."[136] This is inconceivable to Montefiore, who writes, "The strong claims which he made for love and surrender to his personal leadership did not, for him, I feel sure, involve any confusion of thought or feeling between himself and the divine object of worship."[137] Still, continues Montefiore, there was enough of a germ in this to become the full-blown christological doctrine of later centuries.

As we have seen, however, Jesus does place himself in a strategic place as far as the relationship between humanity and God is concerned. For Jesus, what is important is not simply having faith in God, but believing and receiving the message of the coming of the kingdom of God, which in turn demands a right relationship to Jesus. This is true regardless of the absence of the exact language "have faith in me." *It is the centrality of Jesus in all that God is doing and will do that must be faced.* Jesus is to be "confessed before men," to be "received," to be "followed."

---

[133]Enelow, *A Jewish View of Jesus,* 27.

[134]Ibid.

[135]Montefiore, *The Old Testament and After,* 225; cf. *RLGT,* 201; idem, "The Religious Teaching of the Synoptic Gospels in Its Relation to Judaism," 445.

[136]Quoted by Montefiore in *RLGT,* 206; Montefiore immediately adds the note: "I do not agree: to Jesus at least, as *he* spoke them, they usually meant faith in God."

[137]C. G. Montefiore, "The Significance of Jesus for His Own Age," *HJ* 10 (1911–12): 778.

Humanity is called to relationship with him and *thereby* to relationship with the Father.

2. Jewish scholars deny that Jesus intended to found a new religion. "Jesus taught Judaism: in his own eyes, and according to his own intention, he taught no new religion, but, at most, only a corrected, and developed version of the old religion of his fathers. And he was not deceived."[138] This, of course, is a repetition of the "Jewishness of Jesus" theme. Enelow says that whatever his self-consciousness may have been, it was that he was a *Jew*.[139] It was Paul who founded the Christian religion, for Jesus himself "died a Jew, having no idea that he was destined to be called the founder of a new faith, to supersede or destroy his own."[140]

The argument of Jewish scholarship at this point presupposes that Christianity is a "new" religion. Jesus certainly did not conceive his task to be the establishment of a new religion. Nor did the Jews who composed the primitive church ever believe that they had transferred from the faith of their fathers to a new religion. Not even Paul, universally regarded by Jewish scholarship as the creator of Christianity, conceived his task as departing from the Jewish faith in which he had been brought up. On the contrary, all these Jews believed that what they preached was nothing other than the fulfillment of Judaism's hope. They hardly denied that an eschatological denouement was yet to come, yet they insisted that a new and critically important stage of development had been reached. What was believed in was *true Judaism,* true to the intent of Torah and the promise of the prophets.

3. Jewish scholars are increasingly able to acclaim Jesus in very exalted language. Only a few, however, allow themselves to speak of any kind of uniqueness in Jesus. Montefiore rightly points out that Jesus possessed a unique sense of authority:

---

[138]C. G. Montefiore, "Modern Judaism," *HJ,* 17 (1918–19):646; cf. idem, "The Religious Teaching," 439–40.

[139]Enelow, *A Jewish View of Jesus,* 13.

[140]Ibid., 156; cf. R. T. Herford, "The Fundamentals of Religion As Interpreted by Christianity and Rabbinic Judaism," *HJ* 21 (1922–23): 324.

> It must include for me the "Messianic consciousness of Jesus," his power and prerogative to forgive sin, the whole conception of his "Messianic" office and mission, and of his peculiar and divine Sonship; it must include the doctrines of the Ransom (Mark 10:45), and of the vicarious and redemptive sacrifice upon the cross; it must include also that part of his conception of his office which prompted or enabled him to say, "This is my body; this is my blood of the covenant which is shed for many."[141]

In view of Montefiore's high appreciation for Jesus, some have wondered what hindered him from moving over to Christian Unitarianism. In his reply, Montefiore stated that he could approve the argument concerning Jesus' moral perfection, on which Unitarianism is based, no more than he could the old argument of orthodox Christianity concerning Christ's divinity. He could not allow that Jesus lived a perfect life, exhibited a perfect character, or passed on a perfect teaching. In this sense, Jesus was not unique, but a "child of his age."[142]

Yet in Montefiore's writings one continually encounters elements that point to Jesus' uniqueness: the inspiration of his teaching, the professed power to forgive sins, the unprecedented claim to authority. Concerning the famous "Johannine passage" in Matthew (11:25ff.), Montefiore writes, "The man who could say these words would necessarily regard himself as wholly different and removed from other men, greater than they in nature as in authority, in kind as in degree."[143] Montefiore, like most Jewish scholars, ascribes this passage and others that do not fit the predetermined pattern to the early church rather than to Jesus. At the same time, however, Montefiore, in his persistent attempt to be fair, says, "He did believe that he stood, or would shortly stand, in some special relation of preeminence or dignity towards the Father. . . . And if he felt like this, it was possible for him to have taken the great, the severing step—severing him, I mean, from the purest Jewish tradition—and to have not only said 'Be-

---

[141]C. G. Montefiore, "The Originality of Jesus," *HJ* 28 (1929–30): 101.

[142]Montefiore, "What a Jew Thinks About Jesus," 516.

[143]Montefiore, "The Significance of Jesus for His Own Age," 777.

lieve in God' but also 'Believe in me.' ''[144] Yet when the Christian scholar A. L. Williams, in his article "My Father," speaks of this unique relationship between Jesus and the Father, concluding that this is a reflection of a relationship that existed before Jesus came into the world, Montefiore says, "I can see no adequate evidence for this opinion."[145] At the same time, Montefiore can say that the person of Jesus was "in many respects unlike that of *any* Old Testament or Rabbinic hero, teacher, or saint," "a new phenomenon among the Jews, which has scarcely been repeated."[146] Montefiore has thus said remarkable things about Jesus, but the line beyond which he will not go is carefully drawn.

Sandmel recognizes a uniqueness in Jesus: "His career must have been exceedingly singular for his followers to say that he has been resurrected."[147] While Jesus is a "great and good" man, however, Sandmel does not feel that he exceeded other such men in excellency of virtue.[148] Stressing the Jewishness of Jesus, Sandmel says that the similarity of his teaching with that of first-century Judaism has been "documented beyond every refutation . . . except for those passages which deal with his supernatural role."[149] Concerning the latter, "Jesus is at variance with both Jews and Judaism."[150] Sandmel adamantly refuses to believe that Jesus has anything to contribute to Judaism. Judaism is self-sufficient and does not need anything that Jesus may have brought. Thus he writes, "I discern no possible religious assessment of Jesus, either by me or by other Jews. I cannot share in the statements of Montefiore which seem to me to fly in the face of

---

[144]Ibid. This kind of statement prompts Friedlander's remark, "Now that the Christian theologians have begun to reject the Jesus of dogma, and to attempt to find the Jesus of history, it has been left to an English Jew to invite his co-religionists to enter into the heritage that is fast slipping away from the Christian grasp." *JSSM*, xxiii.

[145]*RLGT*, 129.

[146]Montefiore, "The Originality of Jesus," 100–101.

[147]*WJJ*, 110.

[148]Ibid., 110.

[149]Ibid., 78.

[150]Ibid., 137.

prudent scholarship, nor in Klausner's distant dream of a re-claimed Jesus.''[151]

Jewish scholars can often speak glowingly of Jesus, but they also make it plain where they must stop short of the Christian view. Flusser writes that ''today we are receptive to Jesus' reap-praisal of all our usual values'' and further, that ''the enormity of his life, too, speaks to us today: the call of his baptism, the severing of ties with his estranged family and his discovery of a new, sublime sonship, the pandemonium of the sick and pos-sessed, and his death on the cross.''[152] For Flusser, Jesus pos-sessed an unusual degree of self-consciousness, yet Flusser finds parallels to this in the Essene writings, especially in ''the men-tality of the charismatic apocalyptist who has access to the mys-teries of God, through which he is able to enlighten the minds of many'' (cf. Matt. 11:25–27).[153] Schoeps forcefully expresses the uniqueness of Jesus in these words:

> There can well be no doubt that one can only speak thus and force men into decision—note well: into decision with regard to his Person—who has a most elevated messianic mission-conscious-ness. It remains beyond understanding how it could ever be doubt-ed in liberal theology.[154]

But Schoeps goes on to separate sharply this messianic-con-sciousness from the later ''church dogma'' of his divine sonship.

Schonfield, of course, has argued that Jesus according to plan only swooned on the cross, then revived for a short time (explaining the first resurrection account) only finally to succumb to his wounds. For Schonfield, nevertheless, ''Jesus had won through to victory. The messianic programme was saved from the grave of all dead hopes to become a guiding light and inspiration to men . . . no other will ever come to be what he was and do what he did.''[155]

> Jesus still counts for so much, and answers so much to human need, that we are anxious to believe that there must have been

---

[151]Ibid., 110–11.

[152]Flusser, *Jesus,* 12.

[153]Ibid., 96.

[154]H. J. Schoeps, ''Jesus,'' in *Gottheit und Menschheit* (Stuttgart, 1950), 73.

[155]*PP,* 174. Cf. *The Authentic New Testament,* xviii.

something special about him, something which eludes our rational grasp and keeps us in our thought of him hovering perilously on the brink of naked superstition. We find in him the symbol both of the martyrdom and the aspirations of man, and therefore we must cling to him as the embodiment of an assurance that our life has a meaning and a purpose. Quite apart from the intrusion into early Christianity of a pagan assessment of his worth in terms of deity, which historically we have to admit, no interpretation of Jesus can content us which does not show that our confidence has not been wholly misplaced. If he was not more than man, he was at the very least a most exceptional man, who placed his own indelible stamp on the story of human experience and achievement.[156]

Vermes too has wonderful things to say about Jesus. "No objective and enlightened student of the Gospels can help but be struck by the incomparable superiority of Jesus," he writes.

Second to none in profundity of insight and grandeur of character, he is in particular an unsurpassed master of the art of laying bare the inmost core of spiritual truth and of bringing every issue back to the essence of religion, the existential relationship of man and man, and man and God.[157]

But this is different from what the Christian church has concluded about Jesus: "Unable or unwilling to establish and admit the historical meaning of words recorded by the evangelists, orthodox Christianity has opted for a doctrinal structure erected on the basis of an arbitrary interpretation of the Gospel sayings, a structure which must by nature be vulnerable to reasoned criticism."[158] Thus Vermes is appreciative of the Jewish Jesus he has reconstructed, but keeps this appreciation sharply delimited from any extraordinary claims of uniqueness such as Christianity affirms.

Writing somewhat defensively about his own positive views of Jesus, and by implication those of other Jewish scholars, Sand-

---

[156]Ibid., 2–3.

[157]*JJ*, 224.

[158]Ibid., 224–25. Vermes adds: "This explains why Christian New Testament scholars of today display an agnostic tendency in regard to the historical authenticity of most of these words. Indeed, they even go so far as to reject the possibility of knowing anything historical about Jesus himself."

mel correctly notes that "Jewish scholarly laudation of Jesus, however generous it may seem to Jews, is niggardly in comparison with Christian laudation of him, for to Jews Jesus is never more than a mortal, fallible man." "Jesus," writes Sandmel, "to my mind, is neither wholly 'ours', nor wholly 'theirs'."[159]

4. It is clear that Jewish scholars regard any claim concerning the deity of Christ in any sense as both difficult and objectionable. The important position that Jesus allocates himself in the plan of God seems astonishing and one-sided to Jewish scholars. For Klausner, the Christian Jesus all but replaces the need for God. The Gospels were written to leave the impression that Jesus

> is already himself God—"God the Son," to whom "God the Father" has entrusted complete control over the creation, and in whose hands he has placed the whole destiny of man, so that he himself, "The Father," has, in truth, nothing more to do in his universe.[160]

Montefiore, for a Jew, is surprisingly tolerant of the doctrine of the Trinity. Not that in any sense he believes that it is correct; it is simply that in his opinion the end result differs little. Thus he writes, "Jews accumulate upon the One (God) what Christians divide up among the Three, but the result is much the same."[161] Nor does Montefiore deny that Christianity is monotheistic. Indeed, he claims that it was Judaism that helped preserve Christianity from tritheism. Moreover, "theism is so big and grand a thing that it may well be content with more than one expression of it, and more than one servant."[162] However, while it must not be denied that the doctrine of the Trinity contains "elements of value and of truth," yet nonetheless "Judaism remains a warning and a beacon. It is like a watchman, silently bidding all those

---

[159]S. Sandmel, "The Jewish Scholar and Early Christianity," in *The Seventy-Fifth Anniversary Volume of the Jewish Quarterly Review,* ed. A. A. Neuman and S. Zeitlin (New York: Ktav, 1967), 480.

[160]J. Klausner, "Christian and Jewish Ethics," *Judaism* 2 (1953): 18.

[161]Montefiore, "Modern Judaism," 648.

[162]C. G. Montefiore, "Has Judaism a Future?" *HJ* 19 (1920–21): 40. A similar conclusion is drawn by Lapide in *Jewish Monotheism and Christian Trinitarian Doctrine: A Dialogue by P. Lapide and J. Moltmann,* trans. L. Swidler (Philadelphia: Fortress, 1981), 59, 72.

without to beware."[163] Sandmel, in contrast to Montefiore
(though in the end, of course, Montefiore would not disagree),
takes a much firmer stand against the Trinity. He says of that
doctrine that "on the one hand it is inherently *incomprehensible*
to Jews, and on the other hand it ascribes to Jesus a divinity
which Jews are unwilling to ascribe to any *man*" (italics his).[164]
Schonfield finds that the message of the deity of Jesus can be
meaningful only to non-Jews: "Where we find Jesus making
statements which no Jewish Messiah could make, and where
Jesus is presented in terms suggestive of deity, we can recognize
these passages as contributions to what could readily be entertained by non-Jews."[165] It is a matter of no surprise that a message directed to Greeks "should have had recourse to the gospel
according to St. Plato."[166]

Any discussion of the uniqueness of Jesus seen from the
viewpoint of Jewish scholarship, as we have seen, inevitably
comes to this: The Jew, as a Jew, denies any uniqueness in Jesus
that cannot be subsumed or contained within a preconceived category of "Jewishness." If this was true, to a degree, of first-
century Judaism, how much more true it is of modern Judaism.
Jewish scholars frankly admit this themselves. Enelow writes:

> It is understood that Jews could not do that [acknowledge the
> divinity of Jesus], and still remain Jews, as the very foundation of
> all Judaism is the unity and the spiritual nature of God, and the
> Jewish religion has never in the least compromised on this funda-
> mental principle.[167]

According to Montefiore, the Jew must select from Jesus' teaching what agrees with and carries forward the best of Judaism, but
he must reject what is contrary to Judaism. "We cannot allow or
approve that another than God should assume the prerogative of
God; so where Jesus speaks of the Son of Man we think only of
God."[168] As much as Liberal Jews may admire Jesus and his

[163]C. G. Montefiore, "Judaism and Europe," *HJ* 21 (1922–23): 732.
[164]*WJJ*, 44.
[165]*FCS*, 21.
[166]Ibid., 94–95.
[167]Enelow, *A Jewish View of Jesus*, 171.
[168]Montefiore, *The Old Testament and After*, 254–55.

teaching, they are "not prepared to call any man master. . . . They still require no mediator between the human child and the Divine Father."[169] For the Master of the modern Jew "is, and can only be, God."[170] Edgar writes concerning the claim of Jesus' divinity that "the Jew has to reject it" in his loyalty to Judaism. "The belief that Jesus was God is an impossibility for Jewish thought."[171] Klausner, knowing the reason to be self-evident, simply states in the conclusion to his book that "Jesus cannot be God or the Son of God."[172] Elsewhere he writes that like every Jew, "Jesus set an unbridgeable gulf between God and even the greatest and holiest of men—the Messiah." Further, Jesus claimed neither to be God, nor the Son of God, but only the Messiah.[173]

Flusser, unlike other Jewish scholars, holds that ancient Judaism did have the concept of a divine Redeemer:

> The one like a man who sits upon the throne of God's glory [Luke 22:69, cf. Ps. 110; Dan. 7:13], the sublime eschatological judge, is the highest conception of the Redeemer ever developed by ancient Judaism. Only one artist has captured it. Van Eyck. He depicted the Son of man, above the altar at Ghent, as a human being who is divine. Could Jesus of Nazareth have understood himself thus? Let us not forget that he felt he was God's chosen one, his servant, the only Son to whom the secrets of the heavenly Father were open. This very sense of sublime dignity could have led him in the end publicly to dare to identify himself with the Son of man; and in Judaism the Son of man was frequently understood as the Messiah.[174]

Flusser's final assessment, however, is to be gleaned from the pathetic final sentence of his book (and the omission of any reference to the resurrection): "And Jesus died."

---

[169]C. G. Montefiore, "Liberal Judaism in England: Its Difficulties and Its Duties, *JQR* 12 (1900): 641.

[170]C. G. Montefiore, "What a Jew Thinks About Jesus," *HJ* 33 (1934–35): 520.

[171]Edgar, *A Jewish View of Jesus*, 4.

[172]*JN*, 413.

[173]Klausner, "Christian and Jewish Ethics," 16.

[174]Flusser, *Jesus*, 103–4. "The Son of man has a superhuman, heavenly sublimity. He is the cosmic judge at the end of time; seated upon the throne of God, he will judge the whole human race with the aid of the heavenly hosts . . . and he will execute the sentence he passes." 102.

Speaking of the claims of Jesus, G. Friedlander excellently sums up the typical Jewish position, in this instance both Orthodox and Liberal (the latter with only slight reservations):

> No Jew could possibly admit these claims, which involve (1) his right to abrogate the Divine law, (2) his power to forgive sins, (3) the efficacy of his vicarious atonement, and (4) his ability to reveal God the Father of man to whomsoever he will. Underlying these stupendous claims is the belief in the divinity of Jesus and his unique divine sonship.[175]

From this survey of Jewish opinion the firm line that is drawn by Jewish scholars with respect to Jesus' uniqueness becomes evident. When confronted by data in the gospels that are not congenial to the Jewish viewpoint, these scholars resort either to *Gemeindetheologie* (the theology of the church) or a complete historical skepticism.

5. The worship of Jesus in the New Testament is therefore exceedingly problematic for Jewish scholars. How did Jesus come to be worshiped by the church? For the Jewish scholar, this worship was certainly not the result of Jesus' direct teaching or intention. It was, rather, the result of the early church looking back on the events reflectively and adapting the sources accordingly. Thus Montefiore writes, "So far as one can judge, his [i.e., Jesus'] estimate of his own power, and of his relation to God, was gradually intensified by the sources and the editors."[176] While Jesus "probably felt himself to be no more divine than his neighbors . . . the sources and the editors went a good deal further. Jesus very soon became, not merely the Son of God as Messiah, but the Son of God in his own nature."[177] Speaking of the lowly service rendered by Jesus, Montefiore suggests the growth of tradition in these words:

> The greater men thought that he was and knew himself to be, the more wonderful this service seemed to them, till, when at last they thought that he was and knew himself to be God, there could be

---

[175]*JSSM*, 265.
[176]*RT*, 161.
[177]Ibid., 162–63.

nothing more passing strange and wonderful in all earth and heaven.[178]

In Montefiore's summary of why Jesus came to be worshiped, one can see from the Jewish perspective how little Jesus himself had to do with it. Montefiore gives four reasons for the worship of Jesus: (1) the manner and occasion of his death, (2) the belief in the resurrection, (3) the life and teaching of Paul, and (4) the religious doctrines and cravings of the Hellenistic world.[179]

Jewish scholars see Paul as the true originator of Christianity. Accordingly Klausner writes:

> Without intending it and without willing it, Jesus nevertheless brought it about that, in the course of time, he was raised to the level of divinity. What was still inchoate and implicit in the words of Jesus was gradually made definite and explicit by Paul.[180]

Thus Paul "clouded and blurred" the pure monotheism of Judaism.

Vermes writes in a similar vein: "Once Paul was acknowledged 'apostle to the Gentiles' and a specifically Gentile mission sanctioned by the church leadership came into being, the original bias of Jesus' ministry suffered a radical transformation."[181] Further, "the example of Jesus' *hasiduth,* his *theo-centric* devoutness, has been overlaid by the ramifications of Paul's *christo-centric* spirituality."[182]

As we have seen, the stress on the Gospels or central elements within them as the creations of the early church can lead ultimately to a full-blown historical skepticism. Montefiore tries to defend the Gospels. In the main they are reliable sources, he argues, and although caution is required, it is "possible and

---

[178]Ibid., 136.

[179]Montefiore, "The Significance of Jesus for His Own Age," 766.

[180]Klausner, "Christian and Jewish Ethics," 16.

[181]*GJJ,* 45.

[182]Ibid., 46. Schonfield, however, regards John and not Paul as the culprit responsible for the idea of the deity of Jesus. Paul, utilizing the concepts of the Jewish mysteries, argued that the Spirit Christ or the Heavenly Man was incarnated in Jesus. Had Paul known of a christology along the lines of the fourth Gospel, "he would have been completely horrified" (*FCS,* 101–2). But Schonfield is alone in this eccentric view.

reasonable to argue back from the results to the living likeness of the actual man.''[183] This is important, for while the non-orthodox Christian can idealize Jesus to his heart's desire, the Jew is necessarily limited to the *actual* life of Jesus.[184] It is, however, extremely difficult to arrive at historically sound conclusions, according to Montefiore, since the Gospels are inconsistent. The result is, he says, that

> press some things, neglect others; urge the historical character of this and that, deny the historical character of one and the other; and you can fairly easily construct a picture of the life and death of Jesus, based upon what you, in all honesty, suppose to be the essential and historical elements in the Gospels themselves.[185]

The present survey of the Jewish understanding of Jesus ironically bears out the truth of these words of Montefiore, though in a way different from what he intended. The modern Jewish picture of Jesus does not do justice to the portrait of him contained in the Gospels. Jesus is of course thoroughly Jewish. But the Jesus of the Gospels transcends the Jewish limits that Jewish scholars attempt to impose on him. The result of Jewish study is a picture of Jesus that is incongruent with the only historical sources about Jesus that we possess, the Gospels. When followed to its logical end, this kind of approach leads to the astonishing conclusion of Enelow, who, having denied Jewish opposition to Jesus during his ministry, writes that "if later on Jesus died for his utterances or enterprises, it was certainly not because of anything he taught in connection with religion or ethics."[186]

Sandmel, though very pessimistic about the historical reliability of the Gospels, is at least fairer to the documents themselves when he writes, "It is my conviction that the Gospels are not telling about the man that scholarship seeks, but about the

---

[183]Montefiore, "The Significance of Jesus for His Own Age," 766–67.

[184]Montefiore, "What a Jew Thinks About Jesus," 519.

[185]*RT*, 123.

[186]Enelow, *A Jewish View of Jesus*, 96–97; thus also Maccoby: "Jesus was never tried by the Jews on a religious issue. . . . Jesus *was* guilty of sedition [against the Romans]," *RJ*, 156.

career of a divine being. . . . New Testament scholarship has not succeeded in isolating the man Jesus, Jesus the Jew.''[187] In the last analysis, the Jewish reconstruction of Jesus is no more faithful to the historical sources than is that of the old liberal lives of Jesus or the newer radical-critical scholarship. In each of these we are left with a picture of Jesus that raises more questions than it answers and one that may be likened to a jig-saw puzzle from which several of the key pieces are missing.

The Hebrew Christian Jacob Jocz, writing of the Jewish understanding of the person of Jesus, has characterized the Jewish conclusion as an example of "wishful thinking." He then asks the disturbing question, "What if the *historic* Jesus did not fulfil modern Jewish hopes?"[188] When confronted with the inescapable uniqueness of Jesus in the Gospels, the Jewish scholar must demur and with an undue confidence insist that Jesus could not have transgressed certain boundaries of "Jewishness." But since it is true that the teaching of Jesus is inseparable from his personal claims, the Jewish scholar finds himself hard pressed to understand and account for much of that teaching on any other grounds. That he was a prophet, or that he claimed to be the Messiah, is not necessarily denied. But these admissions in themselves are not sufficient to explain his teaching. Jesus came announcing the presence of the kingdom of God in his own ministry. Obedience to the kingdom became a matter of personal loyalty to Jesus.[189] It was no accident that Jesus became the object of faith, for through the deeds and the teaching of Jesus the challenge to faith is continually present. The main question in the end, therefore, centers not in the teaching of Jesus, but in his person.

> For, if the Kingdom of God in the Gospels means not some kind of human Utopia to be built on the ethical teaching of Jesus but the saving sovereignty of the transcendent God breaking decisively

187*WJJ*, 108; cf. Sandmel, *A Jewish Understanding of the New Testament*, 201.
188*JPJC*, 36.
189E. F. Scott, "The Originality of Jesus' Ethical Teaching," *JBL* 48 (1929): 115.

into history, and if Jesus, as the Gospels testify, is the Person in whose life, death and resurrection that sovereignty is incarnated in action, a very high Christology is plainly involved.[190]

Not, then, to the early church, but to Jesus himself must we trace these high claims and the origin of Christianity. Jocz correctly concludes that

> Saul of Tarsus with his Jewish background, no matter how influenced he may have been by Greek thought, would have never radically departed from "Jewish" monotheism except for the two facts: (a) that the Master himself made stupendous claims to authority, (b) that these claims were vindicated by the Resurrection.[191]

If Jesus did make unparalleled claims and did assert personal uniqueness, his teaching becomes coherent and meaningful. If, as Jewish scholarship asserts, he claimed no such uniqueness or was mistaken in doing so, his teaching to a large degree remains enigmatic.

---

[190]A. M. Hunter, "Modern Trends in New Testament Theology," in H. Anderson and W. Barclay, eds., *The New Testament in Historical and Contemporary Perspective* (Oxford: Blackwell, 1965), 139.

CHAPTER SEVEN

Conclusion

THE EXTENSIVE DISCUSSION OF Jesus within modern Jewish scholarship must be described as both remarkable and significant. Although there are both positive and negative aspects to this discussion, as we have seen, Christians cannot afford to ignore what Jewish scholars are saying in our day. It is important that Christians become increasingly aware of the Jewishness of Jesus. Yet obviously Christians can only be disturbed over the rejection of extensive and important parts of the Gospels because of the claim that they are incompatible with that Jewishness. The Christian who examines modern Jewish research on Jesus is accordingly filled with appreciation on the one hand and questionings on the other. For the change that has taken place in the Jewish attitude, one can be grateful even though not fully satisfied.

MODERN JUDAISM'S NEW MOOD

The modern period has seen a drastic change in the Jewish appreciation of Jesus. The emergence of a positive attitude toward Jesus and his teaching in light of the preceding centuries of disdain is nothing less than astonishing. And that this positive attitude could be maintained through and beyond the Holocaust is something that in itself speaks of God's grace and something that must bring a spirit of repentance and gratitude to Christians.

It is true, of course, that in some circles Jewish negativism has continued to exist. This negativism continues among the Orthodox Jews and among the Jewish populace generally, much to the chagrin of Liberal Jewish scholars. Enelow once complained that "consideration of Jesus on the part of a Jew is regarded as a sign of weakness, if not disloyalty, as a leaning in the wrong direction, particularly if it shows symptoms of admiration for Jesus."[1] Montefiore in his day lamented that "Judaism does not as yet seem able to take up towards the New Testament and its hero an adequately comprehending attitude."[2] He regards it as a special task of Liberal Judaism to demonstrate that a "less parochial attitude" need not be "less Jewish." And he adds that "if Christendom abandons the folly and the wickedness of anti-Semitism, Jews will be willing to think more accurately and more wisely about the founders and the sacred books of Christianity."[3] Montefiore wrote these words in 1920, long before the atrocities of Hitler in Nazi Germany. Just as for the better part of two millennia Christian oppression of the Jews affected the Jewish attitude toward Jesus, so also the Holocaust resulted in slackening interest. Sandmel notes that "before Hitler, one could document a Jewish interest in Jesus, which, during and after Hitler, understandably receded."[4] There can be no doubt, however, that the situation has improved from that of Montefiore's day. Sandmel, writing in 1956, mentions that he received much encouragement from fellow Jews and concludes that "the task [of writing on Jesus and Christianity] is no longer quite as lonely as it used to be."[5] The following excerpt from a speech by the president of the Union of American Hebrew Congregations (Reform Judaism) reflects well the new Jewish attitude:

> But what about our Jewish attitude towards Christendom, towards Jesus especially? Are we to remain adamant—orthodox—in our refusal to examine our own statements, our own facts, our own interpretations of the significance of the life of Jesus, the Jew? Have we examined our own books, official and otherwise, to reappraise our oft-times jaundiced view of him in whose name

---

[1]H. G. Enelow, *A Jewish View of Jesus* (New York: Macmillan, 1920), 1.

[2]C. G. Montefiore, "Liberal Judaism in England: Its Difficulties and Its Duties," *JQR* 12 (1900): 628.

[3]C. G. Montefiore, "Has Judaism a Future?" *HJ* 19 (1920–21): 35.

[4]*WJJ*, 103.

[5]S. Sandmel, *A Jewish Understanding of the New Testament* (1956; reprint ed., New York: Ktav, 1974), xv.

Christianity was established? How long can we persist in ignoring his lofty and yet so simply stated prophetic and rabbinic teachings, merely on the grounds that he repeated much that was voiced by his prophetic predecessors and rabbinic contemporaries? . . . How long shall we continue pompously to aver that the chief contribution of Jesus was simply a rehash of all that had been said before by his Jewish ancestors? How long before we can admit that his influence was a beneficial one—not only to the pagans but to the Jews of his time as well, and that only those who later took his name in vain profaned his teaching?[6]

Certain changes taking place within Christianity during the modern era have also encouraged Jewish scholars. Lapide notes, for example, that the Jewish view of Jesus can be appropriately described as "neo-ebionite" and that this is not far from the "neo-arian" view of Jesus held by liberal Christianity.[7] Montefiore noted in his day that less stress was placed on doctrines that Judaism finds especially repugnant such as the Atonement and the Trinity, whereas the ethical teaching and character of Jesus were emphasized as constituting essential Christianity.[8] It should be noted, however, that Montefiore wrote in the heyday of Christian liberalism. The present climate in Christian scholarly circles is somewhat different and not nearly so amicable from the Jewish viewpoint. It is Sandmel, the Jewish scholar most conversant with and influenced by Protestant critical scholarship, who has pointed this out from the Jewish side. Sandmel says that whereas during the first two decades of our century it appeared as though Jewish and Christian scholars "were on the threshold of some incipient common understanding of Jesus, today [1965] that common understanding has again become remote." The reason for this is that the focus of attention, according to Sandmel, has shifted from the historical to the theological, from the Jesus

---

[6]Rabbi Maurice N. Eisendrath, "The State of Our Union—47th General Assembly of UAHC," given at the Biennial Conference of the Union of American Hebrew Congregations held in Chicago in November, 1963, subsequently printed as *Jewry and Jesus of Nazareth* by M. Eisendrath and J. Parks (King's Langley, England: Parkes Library, 1964). A longer extract is quoted in P. Lapide, *Israelis, Jews and Jesus,* ET by P. Heinegg (Garden City, N.Y.: Doubleday, 1979), 149–50.

[7]*RN,* 96–97. Cf. Ben-Chorin, *Jesus im Judentum,* 11.

[8]C. G. Montefiore, "Modern Judaism," *HJ* 17 (1918–19): 647–48.

of history to the Christ of faith. Sandmel's important conclusion is that "Jews and Christians are further apart today on the question of Jesus than they have been in the past hundred years."[9] Almost a decade later, Sandmel wrote of "a conservative bent in current scholarship which, instead of confronting the older, 'radical' scholarship and of refuting it, has cavalierly ignored it."[10] This "conservatism"—by which Sandmel appears to mean anything that goes beyond Harnack's definition of the essence of Christianity[11]—has indeed continued to the present, as at least some critical scholars remain sensibly reluctant to impose a historico-critical method recklessly and in inappropriate ways upon the New Testament.

CONTRIBUTIONS OF THE JEWISH QUEST

The new Jewish interest in Jesus and the Gospels made possible initially by the Emancipation and its aftermath has brought forth some important contributions. First and most important, it is largely because of Jewish scholarship that Christians now possess (or at least have accessible to them) a better understanding of both first-century and contemporary Judaism. A vast amount of labor has been devoted by Jewish scholarship to the study and defense of the Pharisaic Judaism of the first century. Motivated by what they regard as a generally unjust portrayal of the Pharisees in the Gospels, Jewish scholars have demonstrated that first-century Pharisaism was a spiritual religion of the highest order, characterized by ethical and religious teaching in no way inferior to, and certainly not opposed to, the teaching of Jesus. This means that there is no longer any place for harshly negative statements about the Pharisees by Christian scholars. Indeed, it is time that Christians speak out positively about the virtues of ideal Pharisaism. This can be done without denying the trustworthiness of the criticisms leveled at Pharisees by Jesus in the Gospel narratives, if only it is recognized that these Pharisees were not representative of Pharisaism at its best and that they

---

[9]*WJJ*, 104.

[10]Sandmel, *A Jewish Understanding of the New Testament*, xxxi.

[11]See A. Harnack, *What Is Christianity?* trans. T. B. Saunders (London, 1912).

would have been criticized with equal severity by the better Pharisees themselves.

This new appreciation of the Pharisees should also have its due effect on the Christian perception of Judaism today, since modern Judaism is the descendant of Pharisaic Judaism. The all-too-common negative stereotypes of Judaism as a religion must come to an end if Christians are to be faithful to the truth. Judaism itself possesses inherent value as a religion and is worthy of our admiration.

Similarly, and again thanks in large measure to Jewish scholarship, the Jewishness of Jesus is today newly appreciated. One can no longer thoughtlessly extol the originality of Jesus over against Judaism. That he was indeed a first-century Jew in the fullest sense of the word and that his teachings in form and content are Jewish has been demonstrated. This remains true even if it must be objected that Jewish scholars have wrongly excluded certain aspects of Jesus' teaching as "un-Jewish" and are therefore unable to do justice to the Jesus portrayed in the Gospels.

Subsidiary to the above contributions, though also of great importance, is the considerable light shed on the Gospel records by the study of the rabbinic literature. To the extent that this literature faithfully reflects religious life of the first century, it serves to illustrate and clarify certain obscurities in the Gospels. By seeing the Jewish context in detail, as made possible by Jewish scholarship, many passages in the Gospels become vividly alive. The unintelligible becomes intelligible and is often granted a startling reality. Furthermore, Jewish scholars have often attested the accuracy of historical details in the Gospels, which under the influence of radical Christian scholarship many have felt obligated to reject. Abrahams calls attention to this remarkable fact when he says that Jewish critics by their study of the Talmud have made "credible details which many Christian expositors have been rather inclined to dispute,"[12] and this in-

---

[12]"Rabbinic Aids to Exegesis," in H. B. Swete, *Cambridge Biblical Essays* (London: Macmillan, 1909), 181. "Most remarkable of all has been the cumulative strength of the arguments adduced by Jewish writers favorable to the authenticity of the discourses in the Fourth Gospel, especially in relation to the circumstances under which they are reported to have been spoken." Ibid.

cludes even the fourth Gospel. Moreover, as Daube's work has shown, many variations in the separate Gospel traditions can now be explained apart from literary criticism, solely on the basis of adjustments according to patterns found in the rabbinic tradition.[13]

It is abundantly clear that the contributions that Jewish scholars have made to the understanding of first-century Judaism, Jesus, and the teaching of Jesus depend to a great extent on the diligent and devoted study of the rabbinic literature. Montefiore wrote the following words more than half a century ago:

> Only in our particular department of scholarship and investigation may Jews as Jews still be of service to knowledge. So far as Biblical science is concerned and the knowledge of Hebrew, the leadership has passed from them. But in Rabbinic learning they still largely hold the field. And Rabbinic learning has still something to say in the interpretation of the New Testament, and more especially, of the first three Gospels.[14]

It is still true that Jews retain mastery over the field of rabbinic studies. Montefiore adds a plea for more Jewish work in this area. Those who are familiar with the excellent contributions already made by Jewish scholars can only join with Montefiore in hoping that the work continues. Montefiore's wish has to some extent been fulfilled, but much room remains for more work on the relation between rabbinic teaching and the New Testament.

SOME REMAINING QUESTIONS

While the contributions of modern Jewish scholarship are to be received with appreciation, the Jewish understanding of Jesus and his teaching can in the end only be regarded by Christians as unsatisfactory. Indeed, the conclusions of Jewish scholarship leave us with several remaining areas of difficulty.

One of these areas concerns the role of the rabbinic literature

---

[13]See D. Daube, *The New Testament and Rabbinic Judaism* (London: Athlone, 1956).

[14]C. G. Montefiore, "Epilogue" in E. R. Bevan and C. Singer, eds., *The Legacy of Israel* (Oxford: Clarendon, 1927), 511.

in elucidating first-century Judaism. As we have seen, some serious questions are being asked by both Jews and Christians about the propriety of using this relatively late literature to establish the nature of first-century Judaism.[15] As G. F. Moore pointed out long ago, when one's interest is the relation of primitive Christianity to its contemporary Judaism, "the critical ordering and evaluation of the Jewish sources" is of the greatest importance.[16] But this is a task that at best necessarily remains speculative and uncertain. Weber, Schürer, Edersheim, Strack-Billerbeck, and Kittel have all received severe criticism for using the rabbinic materials uncritically.[17] Both Jewish (e.g., Sandmel, Neusner) and Christian (e.g., Buchanan, Horbury) scholars now advocate the greatest caution in any use of the rabbinic literature to elucidate the New Testament.[18] Indeed, suggestions have been made that pre-70 Pharisaism was not entirely the same as post-70 rabbinic Judaism. It may be that Christian influence on the rabbinic literature as a whole is negligible (although far from impossible).[19] But at the same time, the possibility of changes in rabbinic Judaism following the catastrophic events of A.D. 70 is not entirely out of the question. Further complicating the matter is the recent acknowledgment that rabbinic Judaism formed only a part of the first-century picture. Thus not only are scholars increasingly hesitant about what can be traced back from the rabbinic literature into the first century, but they also raise the prob-

---

[15]See above, pp. 184–85.

[16]G. F. Moore, "Christian Writers on Judaism," *HTR* 14 (1921): 253.

[17]E.g., see G. Vermes, "Jewish Studies and New Testament Interpretation," *JJS* 31 (1980): 1–17.

[18]See S. Sandmel, *The First Christian Century in Judaism and Christianity* (New York: Oxford, 1969), 61ff.; J. Neusner, *From Politics to Piety: The Emergence of Pharisaic Judaism* (Englewood Cliffs, N.J.: Prentice-Hall, 1973), 1ff., 143; G. W. Buchanan, "The Use of Rabbinic Literature for New Testament Research," *Biblical Theology Bulletin* 7 (1977): 110ff.; W. Horbury, "Rabbinics," *ExpT* 91 (1980): 238.

[19]Cf. I. Abrahams, "Rabbinic Aids to Exegesis," in H. B. Swete, ed., *Cambridge Biblical Essays* (London: Macmillan, 1909), 187. Buchanan writes, "If there is any direct influence between the Jewish literature of the middle ages and the Christian literature of the first and second centuries, it would seem that the later Jewish material would have been influenced by the earlier Christian material and not vice versa." "The Use of Rabbinic Literature," 112. On this problem see G. Friedlander's discussion of the views of E. Bischoff and A. Plummer. *JSSM,* 129ff.

lem that rabbinic Judaism was only a single component of a much
more complicated reality.[20]

An additional factor that complicates the use of the rabbinic
literature for any purpose is its own composite character. Indeed,
it contains such a variety of opinions on most subjects that one
can by careful selection use the rabbinic literature to substantiate
opposite arguments. Montefiore gives this description of the rabbinic literature:

> It is in their theology that they [the rabbis] let their exuberant
> fancy run wild. Thus all is incidental, casual and unsystematic. A
> deliberately playful and fanciful exegesis is pushed to the wildest
> extremes. Earnest and jest go cheek by jowl; wayward exaggera-
> tion and stern simplicity intermingle. Opinions on the one side are
> met by opinions on the other; the widest latitude is freely allowed.
> It is all familiar and among friends; there is no effort or restraint;
> you see the speakers at their worst and best.[21]

The upshot of the matter is that in order to know what is
truly rabbinic in spirit one must have an exhaustive knowledge of
the rabbinic literature or have "a certain instinct—an instinct
which is naturally only possessed by those who are within."[22] It
seems fair enough to conclude that only one who lives and
breathes the rabbinic literature can be in a position to decide what
most characteristically reflects the rabbinic spirit. At the same
time, however, it cannot be guaranteed that such an "instinct" is
altogether uninfluenced by Christianity, even if very indirectly,
or that it will infallibly and without apologetic bias detect the
essence of first-century Judaism, even apart from the problems
mentioned above.

Another question raised by the modern Jewish approach to
Jesus is whether an adequate understanding of Jesus is possible

---

[20]E.g., see M. S. Enslin's prolegomenon to the reprint of I. Abrahams' *Studies in
Pharisaism and the Gospels* (New York: Ktav, 1967), in which Enslin criticizes Abrahams and Moore for neglecting apocalyptic in reconstructing the Judaism of the first
century: "The Pharisees, at least of the rabbinic strain, were but one of several far from
uniform groups." xxi.

[21]C. G. Montefiore, "Rabbinic Judaism and the Epistles of St. Paul," *JQR* 13
(1901): 187; cf. H. Loewe in *RLGT*, 359–60.

[22]C. G. Montefiore, *RT*, 112.

solely on the basis of an analysis of his teachings as contained in the synoptic Gospels. The narratives of the deeds of Jesus are seldom dealt with, and yet the deeds and words of Jesus are often closely linked, as modern scholarship has shown. Furthermore, Jewish scholars prematurely dismiss the fourth Gospel as containing little reliable history and therefore unworthy of consideration.[23] This is a most unfortunate omission given recent scholarly affirmations that John preserves a historical tradition independent of the Synoptics and one worthy of more respect than it has been given in earlier critical scholarship. It would, moreover, be particularly valuable to have additional Jewish attention given to John, and even to Paul, in light of the rabbinic literature.

A related question concerns the adequacy of an atomistic approach that attempts to find rabbinic parallels point by point for the specific sayings of Jesus while neglecting the context and the totality of what Jesus teaches—thus, to use an old metaphor, missing the forest for the trees. Sandmel calls attention to this problem when he cautions about an improper use of the rabbinic literature in illuminating the Gospels: "The methodological error that seems to me to be constantly repeated in the scholarship is the movement from the legitimate generalities into illegitimate specifics, through the failure to recognize that in the specifics, the context, the tone, and the impulses have drastically changed."[24]

THE CENTRAL ISSUE

A further and more important question is whether indeed Jewish research is capable of arriving at a fair and accurate picture of Jesus when it is so characterized by apologetic motives. To be sure, apologetic motives exist on both sides and need not in themselves distort truth. Furthermore, complete objectivity is of course an impossibility for either side. Yet the claim of objectivity is an awkward one when Jewish scholars allow from the

---

[23]Jacobs' conclusion is representative: the fourth Gospel is "practically a work of religious imagination intended to modify opinions in a certain direction." J. Jacobs, "Jesus of Nazareth—In History," *JE*, 7:160.

[24]Sandmel, *The First Christian Century*, 94. Cf. too his caution in "Parallelomania," *JBL* 81 (1962):1–13.

Gospels only that which agrees with their views. Understandably, if regrettably, the Jewish perspective on Jesus is particularly set against the claims of Christianity about Jesus. The consistency of the Jewish conclusion about Jesus' "Jewishness"
itself suggests that the outcome has already been determined
before the study has begun. Despite claims of objectivity, Jewish
scholars begin with an unjustified and overly narrow delimitation
of Jewishness—one that is already in reaction to Christianity—
and proceed to define the historical Jesus accordingly. But the
result is that the portrait of Jesus and the representation of his
teaching that they offer are in truth reflections of the Jewishness
of the interpreters themselves.

As we have noted above, this consistency in the "Jewish"
Jesus reconstructed by Jewish scholars, is possible only by an
inconsistent approach to the synoptic Gospels. Material that supports this reconstruction is accepted; that which does not is rejected. The appeal to *Gemeindetheologie,* the theology of the
postresurrection community, is not made judiciously, but seemingly at the convenience of the interpreter, i.e., at every juncture
where Jesus appears to violate his "Jewishness." Sandmel's virtual agnosticism concerning the historical Jesus is at least not as
arbitrary as this practice of accepting what is congruent with a
particular conclusion and rejecting what is not. But in its irre-
sponsibility toward the historical question, the latter position is as
unrealistic as Sandmel's agnosticism. It is worth asking again
how the evangelists can have been so reliable whenever they
speak about Jesus as a Jew and yet so unreliable at every point
where they describe him as something more.

The synoptic Gospels as they stand assert the uniqueness of
Jesus repeatedly and in a variety of ways. As we have seen, an
examination of the teaching of Jesus shows him again and again
speaking as no rabbi, however exceptional, could have spoken.
He claims an unparalleled authority, providing not only definitive
interpretation of the true meaning of Torah, but acting toward the
Law with an authority that astonishes and offends his contemporaries. He not only overthrows Pharisaic oral law, while acknowledging in principle the authority of the Pharisees, but also
transcends written Torah, while acknowledging its authority and
arguing that his teaching is in full accord with that authority.

These paradoxes are possible only on the assumption of a supreme authority on the part of Jesus. Jesus proclaims the kingdom as present in and through his ministry and proclaims an ethical tradition as a part of the announcement that is so sovereign in its demands that it presupposes movement to a new level of existence. The kingdom that dawns by God's gracious gift brings with it an ethic of response that transcends all ordinary ethics. But the kingdom, and therefore the ethics, is inseparable from the bringer of the kingdom, the person of Jesus. In the same astonishing way, Jesus is himself central to his religious teaching. His death has atoning significance and he possesses a unique relationship with his Father and occupies a unique position of mediation in the relationship between God and humankind. In short, we confront in Jesus one who is without parallel in the authority he assumes, the claims he makes about himself, and the central position he assigns himself in the accomplishment of God's purposes for Israel and the nations.

In addition to such matters as Jesus' authority, his self-consciousness, and his announcement of the presence of the kingdom, the silence of Jesus in certain matters is worth noting, for this too marks him off from his Jewish contemporaries. Thus Jesus is not nationalistic and has nothing to say about a literal realization of Israel's national-political hopes.[25] Indeed, as we have seen, Klausner can fault him for an excessive individualism. Jesus furthermore gives no place in his teaching to the importance of the land.[26] Nor, finally, does the temple or the cult assume a position of any great significance in this teaching; instead, he speaks quite readily of its demise. Neusner has called attention to this important difference between Pharisaism and the Gospels. For the Pharisees the metaphor of the cult is of central significance, whereas for the Gospels it is the historical event of Jesus that is of greatest importance.[27]

If we fully grant the Jewishness of Jesus, as indeed we must,

---

[25]See Jacobs, "Jesus of Nazareth—In History," 165.

[26]See especially W. D. Davies, *The Gospel and the Land* (Berkeley: University of California, 1974).

[27]J. Neusner, "The Use of the Later Rabbinic Evidence for the Study of First-Century Pharisaism," in W. S. Green, ed., *Approaches to Ancient Judaism: Theory and Practice* (Missoula, Mont.: Scholars, 1978), 224–25.

it is also immediately obvious that we cannot force him into a rabbinic mold, *unless* every passage unamenable to the hypothesis is rejected from the beginning as unreliable. But to do this is to be unfair to the evidence of the Gospels. The words of Lindeskog, in the first thorough documentation of the Jewish study of Jesus, remain as appropriate today as when they were first written: "It is not possible to allow the individuality of Jesus to disappear completely and to represent him only as an impersonal mouthpiece of Pharisaic Judaism. The harmonizing method contradicts sound exegetical and historical principles."[28]

RECLAMATION AT AN IMPASSE

As a general trend, the Jewish reclamation of Jesus has become more and more aggressive. A clear shift can be seen from the earlier Jewish scholars who engaged in what may be described as a moderate reclamation of Jesus to the most recent Jewish scholars who attempt a total reclamation of Jesus. Admissions of any uniqueness or originality in Jesus have all but disappeared in recent Jewish writing on the subject. Jesus is seen to belong increasingly and exclusively within the Jewish dimensions set out in advance by these writers. More recent Jewish writers seem to lack the sensitivity and relative objectivity of such earlier masters in this field as Montefiore and Klausner. Sandmel again proves to be the admirable exception. In one of his last expressions on the subject he wrote the following words: "True, Jesus was a Jew. True, there are Jewish presuppositions in virtually every paragraph of the Gospels. Yet it is a Jesus at variance with, or over against, Judaism and Jews that constitutes not all, but a great deal of the warp and woof of the Gospels."[29] Sandmel, of course, is not here talking about the Jesus of history—about whom, as we have seen, he remains quite agnostic. Nevertheless, Sandmel's words can be seen as a fair indictment of the Jewish procedure of treating the Gospels as though they witnessed to a Jesus who was nothing more than a rabbinic Jew.

[28]G. Lindeskog, *Die Jesusfrage im neuzeitlichen Judentum* (Uppsala: Almquist & Wiksells, 1938), 232.

[29]S. Sandmel, *Judaism and Christian Beginnings* (New York: Oxford University Press, 1978), 342.

In fact, the Gospels tell us of a Jew who broke all traditional bounds of propriety, a Jew who proclaimed the kingdom and his own central role in the kingdom. The Gospels tell us of the Jewish Christ who is acknowledged as Lord by the new believing community of Jews. To find anything less than this in the Gospels involves a methodology that is unfair to the sources. And it bears repeating that we have no access to the Jesus of history except through these documents.

Does the Jewish research on Jesus give us better understanding of Jesus than we otherwise would have had? An affirmative answer can be given only concerning the illumination of some details in the Gospels—that is, only in matters of peripheral importance, involving such things as background and context. So far as a better understanding of Jesus himself is concerned, the answer must be only in certain minor respects. Jewish scholars have not truly confronted the Jesus of the Gospels.

Probably the greatest obstacle to a correct understanding of Jesus is the inability of Jews to accept that a new stage in the history of salvation has been reached. The key to understanding the Gospels is in the announcement of the dawning of the kingdom of God. With this key everything forms a coherent pattern; without it all remains strangely enigmatic. The earliest Christians believed both that Jesus was the Messiah and that the kingdom of God had come in advance of the final eschatological events. In no sense were these conclusions felt to be un-Jewish or disloyal to the promises of Scripture. But Jewish scholars begin with the denial that anything new can have occurred without the realization of Israel's national-political expectations and the transformation of the world order. For the Jews nothing new seems to have happened, and therefore the Gospels are approached as though they were timeless, frozen texts analogous to the rabbinic writings and containing no significant forward motion. Neusner, however, senses the important difference. Whereas for the rabbis "regularity, permanence, recurrence, and perpetual activity" are the basis of an "enduring system," what is presupposed in the Gospels is

> an ontology quite distinct from that of the cult, an ontology which centers . . . on a profoundly disruptive historical event, one which has shattered all that has been regular and orderly. So far as

history stands at the center of being, so that the messiah and the conclusion of history form the focus of interest, the ontological conception of Christianity scarcely intersects with that of Pharisaism. So, I think it is clear, the two kinds of piety, the one with its effort to replicate eternity and perpetual order, the other with its interest in the end of an old order and the beginning of a new age of history, scarcely come into contact with one another.[30]

If this is true, then it is a mistake to be content with a simple comparison and paralleling of rabbinic and Gospel texts. It is just here that we again see the paradox: Jesus inevitably stands in continuity with the past, but insofar as he is also the fulfillment of what preceded, he also manifests an astounding newness.

The Jewish approach to Jesus attempts to bypass this newness and thereby falls considerably short of the mark. The Jewish "reclamation" of Jesus is in fact only a reclamation of that which fits with an a priori conclusion and is therefore only a reclamation of Jewish ideas and not of Jesus as he is presented in the synoptic Gospels. Not even the teaching of Jesus can be fully reclaimed, however, since the teaching, as we have argued, cannot be understood apart from the person of Jesus. "The Teacher made himself one with the teaching, and here we must discover the ultimate secret of his originality and power."[31]

The contributions that Jewish scholars have made to the understanding of Jesus' teaching have been possible because of the Jewishness of these scholars. It is an irony that their Jewish perspective also hinders them from a true perception of Jesus and his teaching. What is an invaluable aid in interpreting the Gospels becomes at the same time an unfortunate obstacle. And thus tragically, as in the New Testament era itself, those who in many ways are the closest to Jesus, the Christ, are at the same time the farthest away from him.

THE JEWISHNESS OF THE KERYGMATIC CHRIST

Christians viewing the Jewish study of Jesus are bound to feel both gratitude and frustration. The gratitude stems from the

---

[30]J. Neusner, "The Use of the Later Rabbinic Evidence for the Study of First-Century Pharisaism," in W. S. Green, ed., *Approaches to Judaism: Theory and Practice* (Missoula, Mont.: Scholars, 1978), 225.

[31]E. F. Scott, "The Originality of Jesus' Ethical Teaching," *JBL* 48 (1929): 115.

light shed on the Jesus of history in the exploration of his full Jewishness. The frustration is due to the way in which this presentation of the full and authentic Jewishness of Jesus is sharply polarized against the early church's understanding of him. The clear implication is that the position of the early church is in some sense decidedly un-Jewish. It is, of course, typical of the Jewish perspective to argue that Paul has brought a Hellenistic dimension to the whole matter that transformed the original tradition into a new religion.[32] Without denying that Paul and later writers such as John brought new language and new associations to the primitive tradition, it must be insisted on that they were Jews and *in no way did they regard themselves as departing from their Jewishness or the tradition of their fathers in their exposition of the meaning of Jesus.* Indeed, they regarded the Jesus of the church as continuous with, and the fulfillment of, the hope of the people of Israel as recorded in the Scriptures. But even if Paul is rejected, there is the reality of the pre-Pauline church to consider.[33] In a recent article Flusser has made the remarkable admission that the authority of the Jerusalem church lies behind the development of christology and, in fact, he regards it as probable "that the christology of the church originated from rabbinic Judaism."[34] The earliest Christian church, indeed, was as explicitly Jewish as anything could be in first-century Palestine. It cannot be said, therefore, that to believe in the Christ of the church is to believe in something intrinsically un-Jewish. On the contrary, it is quite Jewish to do so—indeed, from the perspective of the New Testament writers it is the *most* Jewish thing one could choose to do. How were the early Jewish Christians able to come to their beliefs if these were as un-Jewish as we are led to believe by Jewish scholarship?

In this argument of what is and what is not Jewish, the possibility of a reactionary polarization of viewpoints must al-

[32]See D. A. Hagner, "Paul in Modern Jewish Thought," in D. A. Hagner and M. J. Harris, eds., *Pauline Studies: Essays Presented to F. F. Bruce on His 70th Birthday* (Grand Rapids: Eerdmans, 1980), 143–65.

[33]See A. M. Hunter, *Paul and His Predecessors* (London: SCM, new rev. ed., 1961).

[34]D. Flusser, "Das Schisma zwischen Judentum und Christentum," *EvTheol* 40 (1980): 220.

ways be kept in mind. Differences can be exaggerated to the extent that they become totally misleading. This has certainly occurred on both sides of the Jewish-Christian dialogue in the past. The gravity of the problem is in the fact that the sharper such polarization becomes, the more untrue and distorted the picture becomes, not only of the rival faith but *also* of one's own faith. This is true generally between any two religions, but it is true in an especially important way in the relationship between Judaism and Christianity, the mother and the daughter.

ANTI-SEMITISM IN THE NEW TESTAMENT?

Jewish scholars are very sensitive to what they regard as anti-Semitism in the New Testament. It can be argued that the presence of harshly negative statements about, or expressed against, Jews in the New Testament is an indirect confirmation of the un-Jewishness of the Christian gospel and hence the Christian Christ. We cannot, of course, enter into a full discussion of this subject in the closing paragraphs of this book. But some comments, even if general and without sufficient justification, are necessary on this important subject.

In the rapid proliferation of literature on this subject,[35] claims of anti-Semitism have been made, ranging from the presence of anti-Semitic material in the New Testament to the allegation that anti-Semitism is intrinsic to Christian theology, indeed, the "left hand" of christology itself.[36] The discussion is understandably laden with high emotion, especially because of the memory of the Holocaust. Once one has become sensitized to

---

[35]Some of it comes from the Jewish scholars who are the subject of the present study. E.g., D. Flusser, "Die Christenheit nach dem Apostelkonzil," in W. P. Eckert, N. P. Levinson, and M. Stöhr, eds., *Antijudaismus im Neuen Testament?* (Munich: Chr. Kaiser, 1967); cf. also idem, "Ulrich Wilckens und die Juden," *EvTheol* 34 (1974): 236–43, with a response by Wilckens; S. Sandmel, *Anti-Semitism in the New Testament?* (Philadelphia: Fortress, 1978); S. Ben-Chorin, "Antijüdische Elemente im Neuen Testament," *EvTheol* 40 (1980): 203–14.

[36]Rosemary Reuther, *Faith and Fratricide: The Theological Roots of Anti-Semitism* (New York: Seabury, 1974). See the response of T. A. Indinopulos and R. B. Ward, "Is Christology Inherently Anti-Semitic?" *JAAR* 45 (1977): 193–214.

anti-Semitism, it is easy enough to conclude prima facie that a good case has been made against the New Testament.

The first step to clarity in the discussion is to distinguish between anti-Semitism and anti-Judaism. The former is racial hatred, directed toward people—individuals and groups. The latter is fundamental disagreement with the religious teaching of the Jews. Anti-Semitism—racial hatred—is not to be found in the New Testament, despite many claims to the contrary. In the New Testament we encounter what is essentially an in-house dispute, or an intramural debate, carried on between Jews. The objectionable passages sometimes designated as anti-Semitic are spoken by Jews themselves. The Jew, Paul, who makes the sharp statement of 1 Thessalonians 2:14–15, is the same Paul who indicates in no uncertain terms his deep love for his own people in Romans 9–11 (cf. especially 9:3ff., 10:1–2).[37]

Despite the probability that the evangelists reflect to some extent the increasing hostility between the synagogue and church and that this has had some impact on the way in which they have recorded the traditions about Jesus and the Jews, it is a serious mistake to conclude that the Gospels contain anti-Semitic material. Even such passages as Matthew 27:25 and John 8:44 are wrongly understood in this connection, for both passages reflect not racial hatred, but only religious polarization—the former the Jewish rejection of Christ, the latter the polemic against Judaism. Matthew and John, the two most criticized Gospels in this regard, are paradoxically both very Jewish in tone. The evangelists who wrote these Gospels were themselves Jews, and while they had turned against the religion of their contemporaries, it is hardly just to accuse them of anti-Semitism. If all negative statements about Jews and Judaism are to be designated anti-Semitic, then, absurdly, we will also be forced to designate the prophets of Israel as anti-Semitic. When Jews speak in this manner to Jews, the issue is not one of racial hatred, but an argument about truth.

---

[37]W. D. Davies argues that Paul's attitude to the Jews shifts remarkably between these two utterances. "Paul and the People of Israel," *NTS* 24 (1978): 4–39. Although I would not deny that Paul's attitude could and did change on some subjects, it seems to me that these utterances are not mutually exclusive and that Paul could have said both of them at the beginning as well as at the end of his missionary career.

It must be admitted, of course, that we do confront anti-Judaism in the New Testament. This is to be expected, for given the realities of the divergent viewpoints, it could not be otherwise. Sandmel notes correctly that "the exclusivist claims of the two groups are the nub of the controversies of the New Testament age. If one of the two was the only true religion, then the other was necessarily false."[38] Moreover, it is not simply a matter of two religions with counterclaims concerning truth, for in this instance each claims to be the legitimate descendant and representative of the same tradition and collection of Scriptures. There is a certain inappropriateness to the expression "anti-Judaism." One must therefore be careful, for example, in saying that the first Christians turned against the religion of their contemporaries, lest it be implied that what they had come to believe was unrelated, or indeed alien, to the religion of their fathers in which they themselves had been nurtured. Their own description of what they had come to believe was that it was the fulfillment of their earlier faith and in no proper sense a departure from it. Their contemporaries in turn were wrong, not simply because they refused to enter into this fulfillment, but because, as now became apparent, their direction was only leading them into a blind alley.

This "anti-Judaism" is a necessary component in any form of Christianity that seeks to be true to the New Testament. That it can lead and has led to anti-Semitism is not to be denied. But that it is the same as anti-Semitism or *necessarily* leads to anti-Semitism must be denied. It is furthermore completely misleading and unjustifiable to describe the New Testament attitude as anti-Jewish or as necessitating the negation of Jewish existence. Nevertheless, the fact that the New Testament's anti-Judaism can lead so readily to anti-Semitism and anti-Jewish attitudes obligates Christians to be ever diligent in guarding against them. It is to the painful discredit of the church that such un-Christian attitudes have been allowed to exist among its people, let alone to be "justified" from its own Scriptures.

The church should perceive itself as under permanent obligation to distinguish clearly between the anti-Judaism of the New

---

[38]Sandmel, *Anti-Semitism in the New Testament?* 127. See too Jocz, *JPJCA*, 52–62.

Testament and anti-Semitism or anti-Jewish attitudes. It must not allow anti-Semitism to be read back into the New Testament. Even with respect to the New Testament's anti-Judaism, although it cannot be done away with altogether, there is room for correction.[39] As we have seen, this anti-Judaism is obviously, if naturally, biased and reflects the hostility between church and synagogue in the closing decades of the first century. We should not expect the New Testament to go out of its way to point out the positive and admirable aspects of Judaism. If the picture there is excessively negative, we may do our part by pointing out the other side of the picture, providing a more comprehensive and just view of Judaism. There are aspects of the anti-Judaism that can be and should be softened. The tone of hostility is not intrinsic to the truth and need not be perpetuated. The role of the Jews in the death of Jesus need hardly be the focus of attention, since the theology of the epistles relates that death to the sin of all humanity. And certainly, as Ben-Chorin argues, it must be insisted that historical statements expressing bitterness and hostility must be kept from being absolutized and given any present application.[40]

Paul speaks emphatically against any argument that the Jews as a people are under a special curse of God: "As regards election they are beloved for the sake of their forefathers. For the gifts and the call of God are irrevocable. . . . They have now been disobedient in order that by the mercy shown to you they also may receive mercy. For God has consigned all men to disobedience, that he may have mercy upon all" (Rom. 11:28–32). Jesus and the apostles were Jews. "Salvation is from the Jews" (John 4:22). It is unthinkable that Christians should have anything other than a positive attitude to the Jews. If, as we have argued, Christianity necessarily involves anti-Judaism, it by no means necessitates or encourages anti-Semitism or anti-Jewish attitudes. The church owes its existence to the Jews—they are the root that has given life to the branches (Rom. 11:16–24).

---

[39]Cf. Charlotte Klein, *Anti-Judaism in Christian Theology*, trans. E. Quinn (Philadelphia: Fortress, 1978). Klein is helpful even though the argument is overstated and little room is left for any appropriate or necessary anti-Judaism.

[40]Ben-Chorin, "Antijüdische Elemente im Neuen Testament," 203–14.

If the anti-Judaism of the New Testament means that Christians cannot agree with Judaism and that they must sustain their witness to all peoples of the world including the Jews, this in no way excludes the possibility of genuine love and respect for the Jews (regardless of their response to the Christian message). Christians indeed owe love and respect to all people, but especially to the Jews. And Christians must not only guard against any anti-Semitic tendencies in the church but also join together with Jews in resisting anti-Semitism from any front.

JUDAISM AND CHRISTIANITY

Our day is a day of increasing ecumenicity. Liberal Jews and liberal Christians have repeatedly stressed the similarities between modern Judaism and modern Christianity. This trend began in earnest with Montefiore, who argued that the "best" teachings of Christianity are identical to the timeless teachings of Judaism.[41] It is amazing to see the way in which Montefiore anticipated the present ecumenical atmosphere. Christians are expected to see Judaism not as a religion preparatory to Christianity, but an autonomous religion growing and developing along its own legitimate lines.[42] Jews are invited to see the New Testament as expanding and supplementing the best in Judaism. What is good in Jesus and Paul "came from God also."[43] In the end, Christianity is thought of as a Judaism for Gentiles, the vehicle for bringing monotheism and morality to the pagans. Sandmel writes, "Indeed of the many varieties of Judaism which existed in the days of Jesus, two alone have abided with our time, rabbinic Judaism and Christianity."[44] Montefiore expresses in these words what is now widespread Jewish opinion: "The victories of Islam and of Christianity, however strange the statement

---

[41]Montefiore, "Modern Judaism," 646; cf. C. G. Montefiore, "Judaism and Europe," HJ 21 (1922–23): 729.

[42]Montefiore, "Modern Judaism," 650.

[43]C. G. Montefiore, The Old Testament and After (London: Macmillan, 1923), 290–91; RT, 103; idem, "The Religious Teaching of the Gospels in Its Relation to Judaism," HJ 20 (1921–22): 446.

[44]WJJ, 15.

may appear, are steps in the final victory of Judaism."[45] Given the new mood of our times, the enlightened person must be regarded as above any exclusivism. "For surely we," writes Montefiore, "both Jews and Christians, have reached a loftier platform, and breathe a purer air. For us, not only are there many mansions in God's house, but there are many pathways by which to reach it."[46] Ultimately, then, in his view, true Judaism and true Christianity are equivalent religions.[47]

Not all Jews, however, agree with the exponents of Liberal Judaism. Klausner, for example, believes that removing the barrier that separates Judaism from Christianity would be dangerous. He insists that "the difference in beliefs and in religious and ethical views between Judaism and Christianity must not be eliminated or glossed over."[48] Judaism has survived, according to Klausner, because of two main distinctives that mark it off from Christianity: (1) a God without bodily form, and (2) a realistic morality.[49] Loewe too insists that Judaism with its Torah is self-sufficient and needs nothing from the New Testament. Moreover, he argues, the two religions are and must remain distinct: "There can be no merging. The parting of the ways marked the end of unity. The ways may be parallel, indeed they are, but they are definitely separate ways. To combine them, as many attempted in the beginning and as some still do today, is hopeless."[50]

In a day of increasing secularism and the concomitant breakdown of moral values, Judaism and Christianity should not only be on friendly terms but should cooperate against the forces of evil wherever possible. Judaism and Christianity of course have much in common in this regard. But that Christianity and Juda-

---

[45]Montefiore, "Has Judaism a Future?" 28.

[46]C. G. Montefiore, "Rabbinic Judaism and the Epistles of St. Paul," *JQR* 13 (1901); cf. idem, "The Attempted Conversion of the Jews," *HJ* 27 (1928–29): 431, 437; "The Separation of Christianity from Judaism," in A. Kohut, ed., *Jewish Studies in Memory of Israel Abrahams* (New York: Jewish Institute of Religion, 1927), 215.

[47]*RT*, 165.

[48]J. Klausner, "Christian and Jewish Ethics," *Judaism* 2 (1953): 29.

[49]Ibid.

[50]H. M. Loewe, "The Place of the Law in Modern Jewish Teaching," in G. A. Yates, ed., *In Spirit and Truth* (London: Hodder & Stoughton, 1934), 262. Ahad ha' Am also asserts that "there is no room for compromise." "Judaism and the Gospels," in H. Kohn, ed., *Nationalism and the Jewish Ethic* (New York: Schocken, 1962), 317.

ism should amalgamate into one religion by whittling away distinctives until a common substratum is reached seems as impossible as it is undesirable.

Perhaps Jewish scholars can serve the church by helping it to realize anew its own Jewishness and to avoid pagan distortions of its faith. But if the church can be made to see its own Jewishness, it may perhaps learn again to express its faith not in opposition to Jewishness, but in such a way as to strengthen its bonds not only with the religion of the Hebrew Bible but even with the true, inner spirit of Judaism itself. The church should not be regarded as antithetical to the faith of Israel; it is rightly understood when it is seen as the first stage of the culmination of the Jewish expectation, the beginning (but not all there will be) of eschatology. We Christians may thus clearly share pain with the Jews because of the incompleteness of the realization of God's purposes for this world. There is accordingly a sense in which Jews and Christians can pray together, "Thy kingdom come."[51] Although the stumbling block of Christ remains, perhaps the church can nevertheless learn to state its beliefs in such a way—yes, in such a Jewish way—so as to avoid unnecessary obstacles and unnecessary polarizations.

If this is not too much to ask of the church (and it should not be, since it was the way of the earliest Christians), then it may not be too much to ask of our Jewish brethren also to learn not to polarize issues immediately and unnecessarily and above all to avoid a rigid stance, remembering that originally the church was composed of Jews like them with the same fundamental religious commitments and hopes.

This is not to suggest for a moment that Judaism and Christianity can be reconciled or that all the deep-rooted differences between the two can be made to evaporate. Judaism and Christianity can come closer to each other, but they cannot become identical. Christianity remains different—indeed, from the Jewish viewpoint, scandalously different—from Judaism. Although many Jews believed the gospel from the beginning, the majority did not. The supreme obstacle then, as now, was found in the

---

[51]Cf. Ben-Chorin, *Jesus im Judentum*, 67.

teachings and person of Jesus. If Jesus lived and died a Jew, he at the same time lived and died as one conscious of and possessing a personal authority and significance unparalleled in the history of Israel.

It should occasion no surprise that we must declare the Jewish reclamation of Jesus as only partially successful. The significance of the Jesus of the Gospels, as Montefiore admitted, "lies in his character, actions, beliefs and teachings—in a word, it lies in himself."[52] But for Montefiore, Jesus "brought about the difference and universalisation of some fundamental tenets of Judaism" and is thus far more significant to the Gentiles than he is to the Jews. Indeed, to the latter he had comparatively little to say.[53] This, however, does not square with the Gospel accounts. There Jesus comes to Jews, with a Jewish message, and gathers around him Jewish followers who eventually form the nucleus of a Jewish church. Jesus very decidedly came with the Jewish message of fulfillment, a message meant to be "a light for revelation to the Gentiles, [but also] for glory to thy people Israel" (Luke 2:32). Paul writes of his kinsmen: "They are Israelites, and to them belong the sonship, the glory, the covenants, the giving of the law, the worship, and the promises; to them belong the patriarchs, and of their race, according to the flesh is the Christ" (Rom. 9:4–5). For whom was the gospel intended, if not for the Jews? It is precisely because the gospel was for the Jews that Paul struggles with the mystery of Israel's unbelief and, although he himself was called to be the apostle to the Gentiles, never abandoned the important priority expressed in his repeated words "to the Jew first and also to the Greek" (Rom. 1:16; 2:10).

Although there can be no avoidance of the major obstacle of Jesus, and although it is wrong to deny the real differences that separate Jews and Christians, it is also wrong to polarize those differences in such a way as to alienate Christians and Jews unnecessarily. Christians must learn again their Jewishness, the rock out of which they have been hewn, the root into which they

---

[52]C. G. Montefiore, "The Significance of Jesus for His Own Age," *HJ* 10 (1911–12): 767.
[53]Ibid.

have been grafted as unnatural branches. Jews must learn again that the Christ and Christianity they may choose to reject cannot be rejected as being incompatible with true Jewishness.

Christianity rightly understood is not the cancellation of Judaism. It is at the heart of all that Jews hold dear. Jesus the Jew is the Christ of Christianity without being any less a Jew; Jesus the Christ is fully a Jew without being any less the Christ of the church.

Appendix

RECENTLY AN IMPORTANT BOOK from the Roman Catholic scholar John T. Pawlikowski has been published under the title *Christ in the Light of the Christian-Jewish Dialogue* (Ramsey, N.J.: Paulist, 1982). Because Pawlikowski is a leading Christian representative in the Jewish-Christian dialogue and because his book is so pertinent to the subject of the present book, it seems necessary and worthwhile to comment on it by means of this appendix.

The burden of Pawlikowski's book, which grows out of his extensive experience in the Jewish-Christian dialogue, concerns the need for Christians to draw up a new christology that will make possible an affirmation of the continuing validity of Judaism. The traditional christology of the church with its dependence on fulfillment of the Old Testament and the assertion that Christ has introduced the eschatological era is, according to Pawlikowski, unacceptably triumphalist in perspective and allows no possibility of an ongoing significance of the Jewish religion. Although Pawlikowski advocates a thorough rethinking of christology, he says he is against an outright relativizing of Christ such as that advocated, for example, by Rosemary Reuther. His goal is to preserve the uniqueness of Christ, but in such a way as also to preserve the continuing significance and value of modern Judaism (and, indeed, other religious traditions).

In order to meet this large challenge, Pawlikowski proposes an "incarnational" christology that views Christ as a paradigm of the link between God and humanity. What the "incarnation" uniquely revealed was "how profoundly integral humanity was to the self-definition of God. This in turn implied that each human person is somehow divine, that he or she somehow shares in the constitutive nature of God" (pp. 114–15). For Pawlikowski the uniqueness of Jesus lies in his "intimacy with the divine nature," something that was true for him to an extent that it can never be for us. Pawlikowski's "incarnational" christology, unlike the traditional christology of the church, thus seemingly finds the uniqueness of Jesus to be one of degree rather than kind.

Pawlikowski goes on to say that "the revelation of Sinai stands on equal footing with the revelation in Jesus" (p. 122). Probably the primary desideratum that determines his viewpoint is best stated in his own words: "It is necessary to assert that Judaism continues to play a unique and distinctive role in the process of human salvation" (p. 121). Pawlikowski appears indeed to abandon the thought of Christian proselyting not only of Jews but also of the adherents of any religion or ideology (p. 127). It is difficult to know how he believes that his perspective avoids relativizing Christ or the gospel.

Although one cannot help admiring Pawlikowski's desire to affirm Jews and Judaism, it is clear that his proposal is possible, as he admits, only if revelation is not limited to the biblical documents but is an ongoing process. Thus the first of the principles that he says are central to his book is "that revelation remains open and ongoing" (p. 137). Earlier in the book Pawlikowski writes, "To my mind no adequate solution to the Christological problems vis-à-vis Judaism will be attained solely within the framework of the Bible" (p. 6). Those who are limited to a *sola scriptura* perspective, such as Protestants, and especially Evangelicals, will find Pawlikowski's views difficult to accept, as he himself is aware. An inevitable result of Pawlikowski's approach is the relativizing of the New Testament Scriptures.

With his view of revelation as an ongoing process, Pawlikowski does not find it necessary to discuss the biblical data to any extent. He ignores those parts of the New Testament that are not compatible with his reconstructed christology. Pawlikowski writes, it must be said, more as a theologian and social ethicist (his academic field) than as a biblical scholar. In his chapter on the teaching of Jesus, his concern is to show the considerable agreement between Jesus and the Pharisees. With the Pharisees, "a sense of a new intimacy between God and the human person was beginning to dawn" (p. 88), and in Jesus this sense found "an extension, albeit one of quantum proportions" (p. 93). Pawlikowski properly reminds us of the common emphases in Pharisaism and the teaching of Jesus. Throughout his book he correctly insists on the importance of a proper understanding of the Judaism of the second-temple period to any adequate understanding of Jesus and Christian origins.

After discussing the similarities, Pawlikowski turns to the differences between Jesus and the Pharisees. He lists the following seven distinctives found in Jesus (pp. 103–7): (1) "the degree of intimacy involved in Jesus' Abba experience," (2) Jesus' stretching of the idea of the worth of each individual "to its final limits" at the cost of certain social loyalties, (3) Jesus' more favorable attitude to the *am ha 'aretz*, (4) Jesus' view of wealth rather than the "evil inclination" as the primary obstacle to discipleship, (5) Jesus' teaching of love for one's enemy, (6) Jesus' preaching the actual presence of the kingdom of God in his ministry, and (7) Jesus' claiming and delegating of the power to forgive sins.

Having raised these distinctives, however, Pawlikowski for the most part ignores them in the remainder of his book. If even after a reconstruction that appreciates all the glory of Pharisaism Jesus goes far beyond the Pharisees in many of his views, does that not point to a uniqueness that cannot be explained as a mere extension of Pharisaism? To take a specific and startling example (Pawlikowski's sixth distinctive), when Jesus announces that the kingdom of God has come—in the sense of the fulfillment of the Jewish expectation and not merely in a general sense of the presence of God's kingdom, which the Pharisees already accepted—does that not mean that somehow Jesus is the messianic Agent whose work constitutes a turning point in the ages? This point concerning the announcement of the presence of the kingdom is something that Pawlikowski fails to take seriously, primarily because of his abhorrence of any Christian triumphalism over against the Jews. But this proclamation of fulfillment is central to the New Testament, and without it—as the present book has tried to show—the teaching of Jesus defies understanding.

Indeed, it is this denial of the eschatological significance of Christ—the denial that in and through him the key event in salvation history has occurred—that is the main weakness in Pawlikowski's book. By denying this, he sacrifices the normative character of Christ and his saving work in relation to all that preceded and all that follows. It seems obvious that precisely because of his commitment to the Jewish-Christian dialogue Pawlikowski chooses to avoid any such conclusions. He must interpret Christ and the New Testament in such a way as to affirm Judaism in its own right.

Pawlikowski's motives are admirable, but his conclusions can only be unacceptable to those who regard themselves bound by loyalty to the biblical documents. Many of Pawlikowski's concerns, however, can be taken to heart and can be allowed to affect the perspective of conservative Christians without an acceptance of Pawlikowski's implied universalism and relativism. Pawlikowski, indeed, seems unnecessarily pessimistic about some of the implications of orthodox Christian doctrine. An enlightened orthodox perspective of course will hardly solve the problems altogether, but the situation can be expressed much more positively than Pawlikowski has done.

We may, for example, take what is perhaps the central issue: that of fulfillment. As much as the New Testament writers stress fulfillment and the beginning of eschatology, they do not allege that eschatology is fully realized; they are fully aware that the consummation of God's purposes lies in the future. There is therefore no room in Christianity for the kind of arrogant triumphalism that Pawlikowski fears. This does not mean that there is no difference between Christianity and Judaism or that Christianity is not definitive. It does mean, however, that there is a sense in which Christians wait together with Jews for the transformation of the world in accord with God's promises. New Testament Christianity does not claim that all the messianic promises have already been fulfilled in Christ or that the eschaton proper is here. Nor does traditional Christianity argue, as Pawlikowski seems to think, that history has "come to an end as a result of the Christ event" (p. 74).

What about Pawlikowski's overriding concern for the continuing significance of Israel? Many Christian writers have rightly pointed out that the existence of Israel is indeed significant in God's purposes. The apostle Paul, although experiencing anguish at Israel's failure to believe in the gospel, rejoices at the prospect of the "full inclusion" of Israel in the future (Rom. 11:12; cf. 11:15, 23, 26, 31). He regards as a "mystery" the sequence of the present hardening of Israel, the present response of the Gentiles, and the future salvation of Israel (Rom. 11:25–26). Thus Israel continues to have a future in God's plan: "They are beloved for the sake of their forefathers" (Rom. 11:28).

For Paul, however, there is no possibility of salvation outside the work of Christ on the cross. Christians, therefore, cannot recognize in Judaism an alternative route to salvation without being disloyal to the teaching of the New Testament. They can and should, however, appreciate the positive value of Judaism as a religion, particularly because of the high degree of overlap in moral and spiritual commitments but also because of a common faith in the same God. Jews and Christians must stand together against a growing secular materialism.

But does the church have a mission to Israel? Because of the centrality of the incarnation and the cross for any possibility of salvation, the church must continue to evangelize—even the Jews. Although Pawlikowski finds this objectionable, the church cannot be the church and do otherwise. The gospel is not for the Gentiles only; it is meant to be good news to Israel too. Jesus is the Savior not only of non-Jews, but of the whole world, including the Jews. This does not mean that the church has nothing to learn from Judaism. Quite the contrary, Jews, from whom this great salvation has come, may well provide correctives and redirection at important points where the church has allowed itself to be influenced by alien thinking. Moreover, Christians must not proclaim the gospel to Jews as though they were pagans. Nor, as Paul pointed out to the Roman Christians (Rom. 11:18, 20), can there be any pride over against the Jews. Jews are our close relatives, with whom we share very much, who like the disciples of John the Baptist (Acts 19:1–7) have genuinely believed in the beginnings, but not in the fulfillment that Christianity has brought. Although of course illegitimate methods of evangelism must always be avoided, the church remains obligated to proclaim the gospel to both Jew and Gentile.

This is not to say that dialogue is of no value or that it should be regarded as a covert means of evangelism. On the contrary, it is exceptionally important for Christians and Jews to listen to each other and to gain respect for each other. Only through dialogue can misunderstandings and misinterpretations be avoided. The purpose of dialogue is not that Jews and Christians come to agreement, but that they come to a more adequate mutual understanding. Dialogue should thus never require either side to sacrifice any of its central doctrines. Christians should not feel obligated, even for the sake of dialogue, to deny the uniqueness and definitive character of Christ and his work.

Finally, it is true that Christians need to develop much more sensitivity to the Holocaust. Things cannot and should not ever be the same after the Holocaust. This does not mean, however, that the central tenets of the Christian faith must be changed. It means that Christians must exercise more care in how they express the gospel and in particular in how they speak of Judaism. Perhaps even more important, Christians must be on guard against every semblance of anti-Semitism in the church and must stand with Jews in protest against every manifestation of anti-Semitism in the world.

Pawlikowski and others will probably not find these comments very helpful. What is said here is not set forth as a "solution" to the problems raised by the Jewish-Christian dialogue. Rather, these remarks are intended to show that evangelical Christianity need not, because of its very character (as some claim), be oblivious or unresponsive to the kinds of concerns raised by Pawlikowski. More important, these comments, it may be hoped, can help Protestant and evangelical Christians to see that much can be done within a *sola scriptura* viewpoint and that the prospects of such a viewpoint for Jewish-Christian dialogue are not necessarily as grim as Pawlikowski makes them appear.

Pawlikowski has forged a christological position that is meant to facilitate the Jewish-Christian dialogue, but he has done so in what must appear to the evangelical Christian as a most costly way. Others who may share his concerns and sensitivities will work toward a perspective that is more loyal to the teachings of the New Testament. Only through faithfulness to the New Testament will a view of Christ emerge that is worth bringing to Jewish-Christian dialogue, and only then will such dialogue be worth pursuing.

Bibliographical Note on Surveys of the Jewish Study of Jesus

AMONG BOOKS SURVEYING the Jewish study of Jesus, there are several devoted solely or in large part to this task that warrant special attention.

I begin with two volumes that, though quite brief and now somewhat out-dated, still remain useful. The first of these, and the better of the two, is by Canon Herbert Danby, who is best known perhaps for his translation of the Mishna,[1] and who was also the translator of Klausner's well-known *Jesus of Nazareth*. This little volume, *The Jew and Christianity: Some Phases, Ancient and Modern of the Jewish Attitude Towards Christianity* (London: Sheldon, 1927), presents a straightforward chronological survey of Jewish scholarship from the beginning down to the first quarter of our century. Danby shows penetrating insight in his analysis, and, at the same time, his book is conciliatory toward the Jews.

The second little volume is by another Christian who steeped himself in Jewish studies: Thomas Walker, *Jewish Views of Jesus: An Introduction and an Appreciation* (New York: Macmillan, 1931),[2] and now available with a new introduction by Seymour Siegel in a reprint from Arno Press (New York, 1973) as a part of the series called *The Jewish People, History, Religion, Literature*. Walker's book, dedicated to the memory of the Jewish scholars Gerald Friedlander and Israel Abrahams, comprises two main chapters that set in sharp contrast the views of Jesus taken by Orthodox Jews on the one hand (specifically Paul Goodman and Gerald Friedlander) and Liberal Jews on the other (C. G. Montefiore and Israel Abrahams). An additional chapter, called by the author an "addendum," sets forth the views of two additional

---

[1] *The Mishnah* (London: Oxford University Press, 1933).

[2] Cf. by the same author, T. Walker, *The Teaching of Jesus and the Jewish Teaching of His Age* (London: Allen & Unwin, 1923) and *What Jesus Read* (London: Allen & Unwin, 1925).

Jews, Joseph Jacobs and Joseph Klausner. Walker's book is notable for its clarity and usefulness as a brief introduction.

Two much larger volumes, highly significant in the study of the Jewish viewpoint concerning Jesus,[3] have recently been reprinted, each with a brief updating from the author: Gösta Lindeskog, *Die Jesusfrage im neuzeitlichen Judentum* [The Jesus-Question in Modern Judaism] (Uppsala: Almquist and Wiksells, 1938; reprinted with new postscript, Darmstadt: Wissenschaftliche Buchgesellschaft, 1973);[4] and Jacob Jocz, *The Jewish People and Jesus Christ*, 3rd ed. (1949; reprint ed., "substantially unaltered," Grand Rapids: Baker, 1979).

Lindeskog's volume, subtitled *A Contribution to the History of the Leben-Jesu-Forschung,* was originally presented as an inaugural dissertation to the theological faculty of Uppsala University, Sweden. Samuel Sandmel has rightly said that it is with this book that "any serious research on the position of Jesus in Jewish writings must begin."[5] Lindeskog presents us with a comprehensive and masterly survey of Jewish research concerning Jesus. In criticism of what other authors who have written on his theme have failed to do, Lindeskog gives the purpose of his book: (1) to provide "a historical and systematic presentation of the Jewish *Leben-Jesu-Forschung* [Life of Jesus Research] in connection with the origin and development of modern Judaism" but also (2) to place the Jewish representation of Jesus into a *Religionsgeschichte* [history of religions] framework and (3) to examine the Jewish research in its connection with the Christian research.[6] Accordingly, Lindeskog's book has two main divisions: first, an examination of Jewish research up to the rise of modern Judaism, including a description of that new Judaism and its influence, and, second, an examination of modern Jewish research with an attempt to evaluate the results hitherto attained. Lindeskog regards the importance of the Jewish *Jesus-*

---

[3]Both of these volumes fulfill the desire of C. G. Montefiore expressed in 1930 with these words: "A most interesting book could be written which, with adequate learning and detachment, would give a full history of Jewish conceptions of Christianity from the close of the first century to the present day." "Jewish Conceptions of Christianity," *HJ* 28 (1929–30): 249.

[4]Twenty years after his original work, Lindeskog wrote on the same theme in a long essay entitled "Jesus als religionsgeschichtliches und religiöses Problem in der modernen jüdischen Theologie," *Judaica* 6 (1950): 190–229, 241–68. Since the essay is largely based on the aforementioned book, it not only advanced the discussion a step further as Lindeskog indicated, but can at the same time serve as a synopsis of the larger, more detailed volume.

[5]*WJJ*, 156.

[6]Lindeskog, *Die Jesusfrage im neuzeitlichen Judentum*, 7–8.

forschung to be in the contribution made—negatively, in the criticism of Christian research and, positively, in the more correct view of *Spätjudentum,* first-century Judaism, and the correct grasp of the Jewish traits of Jesus and the gospel tradition.[7] Valuable in itself, the study of the Jewish research at the same time leads to a clearer understanding of the essence of Christianity. The author concludes his volume with a summarizing statement entitled "The Significance of Jesus for Modern Judaism."

Lindeskog devotes chapter 11, "The Religious and Ethical View of Jesus,"[8] to the Jewish understanding of Jesus' teaching. His conclusion is worth quoting in full:

> We can—in order to summarize here—distinguish three main types among the Jewish views concerning the teaching of Jesus. The first type, the most frequent, emphasizes the *common* elements. Jesus has taught nothing which does not have its exact parallel in the Jewish writings. The second type, which is characteristic of the Orthodox, represented by Gerald Friedländer, admits that the teaching of Jesus contains *un-Jewish* elements, which from the Jewish standpoint must be rejected. "The good was nothing new, and the new was nothing good." The third type, as we meet with it pre-eminently in Montefiore, stresses the positive, creative *originality* of Jesus. Jesus signifies a new high point in the development of the history of religion. He belongs to the greatest teachers of mankind. All three types emphasize without exception, even when occasionally they frankly concede the revolutionary consequences of the teaching of Jesus for the foundations of Judaism, that Jesus was a true son of his people, that he lived and died as a Jew.[9]

Lindeskog, in addition to providing the reader with a scholarly, detailed survey of Jewish scholarship, including thoughtful analysis and interpretation, has appended to his book exceedingly valuable bibliographies. The first is a nearly exhaustive listing of works by Jewish authors; the second is limited to relevant non-Jewish works.

Recently Lindeskog has published an important book on Jewish views of Jesus available only in Swedish: *Judarnas Jesus* [The Jews' Jesus] (Stockholm: Schalom, 1972). This is largely the representation of an earlier publication that was a Swedish popularization of Lindeskog's major work just mentioned: *Den judiska Jesustolkningen* [The Jewish Interpretation of Jesus] published in 1951. Lindeskog has added

---

[7]Ibid., 1.

[8]Ibid., 215–50.

[9]Ibid., 250; cf. virtually the same paragraph in Lindeskog's article in *Judaica,* 6 (1959): 253.

two new chapters in his most recent book (chapter 7, "A New Epoch: New Ways," including a discussion of Jewish research on Paul, and chapter 8, "The Jewish-Christian Problem").

More recent, of larger scope, and even more detailed than Lindeskog's fine work[10] is Jacob Jocz's impressive volume *The Jewish People and Jesus Christ*. Jocz, himself a Hebrew Christian, writes with sympathetic understanding and yet with incisive logic.[11] He presents the reader with a comprehensive history of the relationship of the Jewish people to Jesus of Nazareth. Among his purposes are to disclose the deepest reasons for the estrangement of the Jews from Jesus, to show the continual presence of a Jewish remnant within the church, to explain the non-Jewish character of Christianity in spite of its Jewish roots, and to provide a history of the Jewish viewpoint concerning Jesus.[12] Jocz conceives the problem of Jesus to be essentially a question of religious faith that transcends the purely historical; he thus describes this work as "in one sense, a continuation of the work done by Lindeskog, in that it brings back the discussion from the purely historical to the religious plane."[13] And like Lindeskog's book, this volume remains an indispensable resource.

After his introductory chapter, Jocz devotes three successive chapters to the Jewish viewpoint of Christianity as exhibited respectively in the period of Jesus' contemporaries and the early church, the period of the ascendancy of the church, and the modern period. Two further chapters trace the history of Hebrew Christianity, and a final chapter focuses on the essential differences between Judaism and Christianity.

Three subsections of Jocz's second chapter ("Jesus Christ and the Synagogue") devoted respectively to "The Law," "The Teaching of Jesus," and "The Claims of Jesus" are directly pertinent to the concerns of this book.[14] Equally relevant is Jocz's description of the contemporary Jewish attitude.[15] Included in his summarizing list of observations are the following:

---

[10]No less than one-fourth of Jocz's book (over one hundred pages of small print) consists of footnotes to the text.

[11]Thus none other than the distinguished Jewish scholar David Daube writes in the preface: "No fair-minded person, Christian or Jewish, will be able to read this book without being deeply moved by the sincerity, humanity and fervour of its author, and without profiting by his profound analysis of, and his balanced judgments about, the problem he has set out to investigate." *JPJC*, ix.

[12]*JPJC*, 1–11.

[13]Ibid., 9.

[14]Ibid., 21–42.

[15]Ibid., 110–45.

A strange unanimity of opinion amongst Jewish scholars concerning some vital historical problems.

The constant emphasis upon the *Jewishness* of Jesus, which invariably leads to an analytical study of his teaching with reference to Rabbinic literature and to minimization of his originality.

The marked change in the general outlook concerning Jesus, expressing itself in sincere appreciation of his teaching.[16]

Jocz's volume also has an excellent bibliography appended to it.

Jocz has now added a sequel to his earlier volume; it is entitled *The Jewish People and Jesus Christ After Auschwitz: A Study in the Controversy Between Church and Synagogue* (Grand Rapids: Baker, 1981). In this new work he traces the impact of the Holocaust on Jewish-Christian relations. A central chapter focuses on the question "Who is Jesus?" Jocz then addresses the questions "What is Judaism?" and "Who is a Jew?"[17] He writes also concerning such things as dialogue, missions, conversion, and Hebrew Christians. Here is a most helpful and enlightening volume, full of down-to-earth wisdom and frankness, a welcome companion to Jocz's earlier volume.

These volumes by Danby, Walker, Lindeskog, and Jocz are invaluable guides to the Jewish viewpoint.[18] Unfortunately, Albert Schweitzer's important book *The Quest of the Historical Jesus* is virtually of no help in understanding the Jewish approach.[19]

Jewish scholars have themselves in recent times turned to the documentation of Jewish research on Jesus. Schalom Ben-Chorin surveys the history of this scholarship in a brief book entitled *Jesus im Judentum* (Wuppertal: Brockhaus, 1970), which appeared as volume 4 in the series entitled "Schriftenreihe für christlich-jüdische Begegnung" (Writings for Christian-Jewish Encounter). The book is excellent and informative despite its brief compass; an English distillation was published under the title "The Image of Jesus in Modern Judaism" in *The*

---

[16]Ibid., 144–45.

[17]Ibid., 425–35.

[18]A recent volume compiled by the Jewish Christian A. W. Kac should also be noted here: *The Messiahship of Jesus: What Jews and Christians Say* (Chicago: Moody, 1980). This volume presents excerpts from Jewish writers, analytical excerpts, and statements by Jewish Christians. Also deserving mention are the following periodical articles: G. F. Moore, "A Jewish Life of Jesus," *HTR* 16 (1923): 93–103; J. S. Connong, "The Changing Attitude of Jews to Jesus," *USR* 48 (1936–37), 323–32; E. S. Tanner, "Recent Jewish Interpretations of Jesus," *JBL* 8 (1940): 80–82.

[19]Cf. Joseph Klausner's criticism in *JN*, 107. Lindeskog rightly says that in Schweitzer's book the very existence of a Jewish *Leben-Jesu-Forschung* is not clear. *Die Jesusfrage*, 2, n. 1.

Journal of Ecumenical Studies 11 (1974): 401–30. Toward the end of the volume Ben-Chorin gives his own views and summarizes his important book *Bruder Jesus*. His summary judgment is that "the faith of Jesus unites us—faith in Jesus separates us." He speaks poignantly of what Jesus means to him. Although he denies that Jesus is the Messiah, the Son of God, the mediator, the fulfiller of the Law, or the sin-bearer, he concludes that Jesus is "a central figure, whom I cannot put out of my Jewish life." Ben-Chorin writes that he has come "closer and closer" to Jesus; that "again and again I have encountered him and we have had conversation"; and that "I am certain he will walk further with me so long as I go on my path."[20] His concluding sentence is "Jesus the Jew—the image of the Jew is so near to me and can be just so near to us, as he cannot be to the common Christian. 'Because he was ours.' "[21]

A second Jewish survey of Jewish research on Jesus is that of Pinchas Lapide, *Ist das nicht Josephs Sohn? Jesus im heutigen Judentum* (Munich: Calwer, Kösel, 1976), now available in an English translation under the title *Israelis, Jews and Jesus,* translated by P. Heinegg, with a foreword by Samuel Sandmel (New York: Doubleday, 1979). Some of the material referred to here appeared earlier in an article in the *Christian Century* entitled "Jesus in Israeli Literature" (87 [1970]: 1248–53). Lapide's book contains a very interesting chapter entitled "Jesus in Israeli Schoolbooks," a chapter called "Jesus in Hebrew Literature," and a long history of Jewish writing on Jesus, "Rabbis Speak of Jesus." The last-named chapter is especially useful in its thorough treatment of premodern Jewish views of Jesus. Lapide begins his book with a note on the importance of dialogue between Jews and Christians, which, given the climate of secularism, is more urgently needed than ever. "Jews and Christians," writes Lapide, "are joined in brotherhood at the deepest level, so deep in fact that we have overlooked it and missed the forest of brotherhood for the trees of theology. We have an intellectual and spiritual kinship which goes deeper than dogmatics, hermeneutics, and exegesis."[22] At the end of his book he concludes that "the old antagonism between the 'Jesus of the Jews' and the 'Christ of the Christians' has been replaced by a theological truce. This is a far cry from the hostility of the Middle Ages, but it is equally far from the ecumenical amity which the Nazarene strove so passionately for."

[20]Ben-Chorin, *Jesus im Judentum,* 72–73.
[21]Ibid., 75.
[22]Lapide, *Israelis, Jews and Jesus.*

A further useful book on the subject before us that deserves mention is W. P. Eckert and H. H. Henrix, eds., *Jesu Jude-Sein als Zugang zum Judentum* [The Jewishness of Jesus as an Approach to Judaism] (Aachen: Einhard, 1976). This volume, which grew out of a symposium held in Aachen in 1974, contains among other essays a survey of Jesus in modern Judaism by Eckert, as well as a fresh Jewish presentation on Jesus from E. L. Ehrlich. Also deserving mention is the article by R. Gradwohl, "Das neue Jesus-Verständnis bei jüdischen Denkern der Gegenwart" [The New Jesus-Understanding in Jewish Thinkers of the Present] in *Freiburger Zeitschrift für Philosophie und Theologie* 20 (1973): 306–23.

Also to be noted is the unpublished doctoral dissertation by Jacobus Adriaan Vorster, "Jewish Views of Jesus. An Assessment of the Jewish Answer to the Gospel of Jesus Christ" (Pretoria, South Africa: University of Pretoria, 1975). Vorster's work, a mine of bibliographical information, surveys the history of Jewish scholarship, describes the Jewish contribution topically, and concludes with a section called "Polemical Influences on Jewish Jesus-Forschung." Vorster is admittedly apologetic in his approach, and this is no doubt in reaction to his perception of Jewish apologetic motivation. His concluding sentence is "As long as the polemical aspects prevail in the study of Jesus, his message and his mission, there can be no thought of a sober scientific research and Jewish writers must accept the verdict that they have failed to understand the meaning of Jesus" (396).

Two further books that are Jewish in origin deserve mention. The first is Trude Weiss-Rosmarin, ed., *Jewish Expressions on Jesus: An Anthology* (New York: Ktav, 1977). This collection focuses on Jesus' Jewishness and on the trial and death of Jesus. In an introductory essay the editor points out the relatively conservative stance of Jewish writers concerning the historicity of the Gospels compared to some radical Christian scholars. The second book is Walter Jacob, *Christianity Through Jewish Eyes: The Quest for Common Ground* (Cincinnati: Hebrew Union College Press, 1974). Jacob surveys and distills the contributions of some twenty important Jewish scholars, from Moses Mendelssohn to Richard L. Rubenstein and Emil Fackenheim. The book is broader in concern than the Jewish understanding of Jesus himself, but nevertheless frequently refers to it. Jacob concludes that "perhaps the best basis for dialogue is the one built by the Jewish scholars who sought to reclaim Jesus, Paul, and early Christian literature for Judaism" (231).

Selected Bibliography

I. Jewish Bibliography

Abrahams, I. "Some Rabbinic Ideas on Prayer." *JQR* 20 (1908): 272–93.
―――. "Rabbinic Aids to Exegesis." In *Cambridge Biblical Essays,* edited by H. B. Swete, 165–213. London: Macmillan, 1909.
―――. *Judaism.* London: Macmillan, 1910.
―――. *Studies in Pharisaism and the Gospels.* First Series, Cambridge: Cambridge University Press, 1917. Second Series, Cambridge: Cambridge University Press, 1924. Reprint. New York: Ktav, 1967.
―――. "'Am Ha-'Areç." In *Synoptic Gospels,* edited by C. G. Montefiore, 2nd ed., 2:647–49. London: Macmillan, 1927.
Ahad ha'Am [Ginsberg, Asher]. "Judaism and the Gospels." In *Nationalism and the Jewish Ethic,* edited by H. Kohn, 289–319. New York: Schocken, 1962.
Baeck, L. "The Gospel as a Document of the History of the Jewish Faith." In *Judaism and Christianity,* ET by W. Kaufmann, 39–136. New York: Leo Baeck Institute, 1958.
Bazes, M. *Jesus the Jew—The Historical Jesus: The True Story of Jesus.* Jerusalem: Alpha, 1976.
Ben-Chorin, S. *Bruder Jesus: Der Nazarener in jüdischer Sicht.* Munich, 1967.
―――. *Jesus im Judentum.* Wuppertal, 1970.
―――. "The Image of Jesus in Modern Judaism." *JES* 11 (1974): 401–30.
―――. "Jesus und Paulus in jüdischer Sicht." *Annual of the Swedish Theological Institute,* vol. 10, edited by B. Knutsson, 17–29. Leiden: Brill, 1976.
Cohen, A. "Jewish History in the First Century." In *Judaism and the Beginnings of Christianity,* 3–47. Lectures at Jews' College, London, 1923.
―――. *The Parting of the Ways.* London: Lincolns-Prager, 1954.
Cohon, S. S. "The Place of Jesus in the Religious Life of His Day." *JBL* 48 (1927): 82–108.
Daube, D. "*Exousia* in Mark 1:22 and 27." *JTS* 29 (1938): 45–59.
―――. "Matthew v.38f." *JTS* 45 (1944): 177–87.
―――. *The New Testament and Rabbinic Judaism.* London: Athlone, 1956.
―――. "The Gospels and the Rabbis." *The Listener* 56 (1956): 342–46.

————. "The Earliest Structure of the Gospels." *NTS* 5 (1958–59): 174–87.

————. "Concessions to Sinfulness in Jewish Law." *JJS* 10 (1959): 1–14.

————. "Responsibilities of Master and Disciples in the Gospels." *NTS* 19 (1972–73): 1–15.

Edgar, L. I. *A Jewish View of Jesus.* London: The Liberal Jewish Synagogue, 1940.

Eisendrath, M., and Parkes, J. *Jewry and Jesus of Nazareth.* Royston: Parkes Library, 1964.

Enelow, H. G. *A Jewish View of Jesus.* New York: Macmillan, 1920.

————. "Review of Montefiore's *Rabbinic Literature and Gospel Teachings.*" *JQR,* New Series 22 (1931–32): 331–38.

Finkel, A. *The Pharisees and the Teacher of Nazareth.* Leiden: Brill, 1964.

Finkelstein, L. "The Pharisees: Their Origin and Their Philosophy." *HTR* 22 (1929): 185–261.

————. *The Pharisees.* 2 vols. 2nd ed. Philadelphia: Jewish Publication Society of America, 1940.

Flusser, D. "A New Sensitivity in Judaism and the Christian Message." *HTR* 61 (1968): 107–27.

————. *Jesus.* ET by R. Walls. New York: Herder & Herder, 1969.

————. "The Son of Man: Jesus in the Context of History." In *The Crucible of Christianity,* edited by A. Toynbee, 215–34. London: Thames & Hudson, 1969.

————. "Jesus." *EJ* 10:10–14.

————. "Das Schisma zwischen Judentum und Christentum." *EvTheol* 40 (1980): 214–39.

Formstecher, S. *Die Religion des Geistes: eine wissenschaftliche Darstellung des Judenthums nach seinem Charakter, Entwicklungsgange und Berufe in der Menschheit.* Frankfurt a.M., 1841.

Friedlander, G. *The Jewish Sources of the Sermon on the Mount.* London: Routledge, 1911. Reprint. New York: Ktav, 1969.

Friedländer, M. "Notes in Reply to My Critic." *JQR* 3 (1892): 430–44.

————. *Zur Entstehungsgeschichte des Christenthums.* Wien, 1894.

————. *Die religiosen Bewegungen innerhalb des Judentums im Zeitalter Jesu.* Berlin, 1905.

————. *Synagogue und Kirche in ihren Anfangen.* Berlin, 1908.

Goldstein, M. *Jesus in the Jewish Tradition.* New York: Macmillan, 1950.

Goodman, P. *The Synagogue and the Church.* London: Routledge, 1908.

Guttmann, A. *Rabbinic Judaism in the Making.* Detroit: Wayne State University, 1970.

Hirsch, S. *Was ist Judenthum und was dessen Verhältnis zu anderen Religionen?* Berlin, 1838.

————. *Das System der religiösen Anschauungen der Juden und sein Verhaltnis zum Heidenthum, Christenthum und zur absoluten Philosophie.* Leipzig, 1842.

Isaac, J. *The Teaching of Contempt: Christian Roots of Anti-Semitism.* ET by Helen Weaver. New York: Holt, Rinehart & Winston, 1964.

———. *Jesus and Israel.* ET by Sally Gran. New York: Holt, Rinehart & Winston, 1971.

Jacob, W. *Christianity Through Jewish Eyes: The Quest for Common Ground.* Cincinnati: Hebrew Union College Press, 1974.

Jacobs, J. "Jesus of Nazareth—In History." *JE* 7:160–66.

———. *Jesus as Others Saw Him.* 1925. Reprint. New York: Arno, 1973.

Klausner, J. *The Messianic Idea in Israel.* ET of 1904 original by W. F. Stinespring. London: Allen & Unwin, 1956.

———. *Jesus of Nazareth: His Life, Times, and Teaching,* ET of 1922 original by H. Danby. New York: Macmillan, 1925. Reprint. New York: Beacon, 1964.

———. *From Jesus to Paul.* ET of 1939 original by W. F. Stinespring. New York: Macmillan, 1943. Reprint. New York: Beacon, 1961.

———. "Christian and Jewish Ethics." *Judaism* 2 (1953): 16–30.

Kohler, K. "Jesus of Nazareth—In Theology." *JE* 7:166–70.

———. "Christianity in Relation to Judaism." *JE* 4:49–59.

———. *Jewish Theology.* New York: Macmillan, 1918.

———. *The Origins of the Synagogue and the Church.* New York: Macmillan, 1929.

Krauss, S. *Das Leben Jesu nach jüdischen Quellen.* Berlin, 1902.

———. "Jesus of Nazareth—In Jewish Legend." *JE* 7:170–73.

Lapide, P. *The Last Three Popes and the Jews.* London, 1967.

———. "Jesus in Israeli Literature." *Christian Century* 87 (1970): 1248–53.

———. *Ökumene aus Christen und Juden.* Neukirchen-Vluyn, 1972.

———. *Der Rabbi von Nazareth: Wandlungen des jüdischen Jesusbildes.* Trier, 1974.

———. *Juden und Christen.* Zurich, 1976.

———. "Two Famous Rabbis." *Annual of the Swedish Theological Institute,* vol. 10, edited by B. Knutsson, 97–109. Leiden: Brill, 1976.

———. *Auferstehung: Ein jüdisches Glaubenserlebnis.* Munich, 1977.

———. (with Hans Küng) "Jesus in Conflict: A Jewish-Christian Dialogue." In H. Küng, *Signposts for the Future,* 64–87. Garden City, N.Y.: Doubleday, 1978.

———. *Israelis, Jews and Jesus,* ET by P. Heinegg. Garden City, N.Y.: Doubleday, 1979.

———. *Er predigte in ihren Synagogen: Jüdische Evangelienauslegung.* Gütersloh, 1981.

———. (with J. Moltmann) *Jewish Monotheism and Christian Trinitarian Doctrine: A Dialogue,* ET by L. Swidler. Philadelphia: Fortress, 1981.

Loewe, H. "On Acting Cleverly." *Rabbinic Literature and Gospel Teachings.* C. G. Montefiore. London: Macmillan, 1918. Appendix II, 380–89.

_____. "The Place of Law in Modern Jewish Teaching." *In Spirit and Truth*, edited by G. Yates, 248–62. London: Hodder & Stoughton, 1934.

_____. "Pharisaism." *The Age of Transition*, Judaism and Christianity I, edited by W. O. E. Oesterley, 105–89. London: Sheldon, 1937.

Maccoby, H. *Revolution in Judaea: Jesus and the Jewish Resistance*. London: Orbach and Chambers, 1973. Reprint. New York: Taplinger, 1981.

Montefiore, C. G. *The Synoptic Gospels*. 2 vols. 2nd ed. London: Macmillan, 1927. Reprint. New York: Ktav, 1968.

_____. *Some Elements of the Religious Teaching of Jesus According to the Synoptic Gospels*. London: Macmillan, 1910. Reprint. New York: Arno, 1973.

_____. *Liberal Judaism and Hellenism*. London: Macmillan, 1918.

_____. *The Old Testament and After*. London: Macmillan, 1923.

_____. *Rabbinic Literature and Gospel Teaching*. London: Macmillan, 1930. Reprint. New York: Ktav, 1970.

_____. "Mr. Smith: A Possibility." *JQR* 6 (1894): 100–110.

_____. "Notes on the Religious Value of the Fourth Gospel." *JQR* 7 (1895): 24–74.

_____. "On Some Misconceptions of Judaism and Christianity by Each Other." *JQR* 8 (1896): 193–216.

_____. "Unitarianism and Judaism in Their Relations to Each Other." *JQR* 9 (1897): 240–53.

_____. "Rabbinic Judaism and the Epistles of St. Paul." *JQR* 13 (1901): 161–217.

_____. "Jewish Scholarship and Christian Silence." *HJ* 1 (1902–03): 335–46.

_____. "Repentance, Rabbinic Conceptions of." *JQR* 16 (1904): 183–226.

_____. "The Synoptic Gospels and the Jewish Consciousness." *HJ* 3 (1904–05): 649–67.

_____. "Liberal Judaism." *JQR* 20 (1908): 363–90.

_____. "The Significance of Jesus for His Own Age." *HJ* 10 (1911–12): 766–79.

_____. "Modern Judaism and the Messianic Hope." *HJ* 11 (1912–13): 366–77.

_____. "The Perfection of Christianity—A Jewish Comment." *HJ* 14 (1915–16): 778–83.

_____. "The Old Testament and Its Ethical Teaching." *HJ* 16 (1917–18): 234–50.

_____. "Modern Judaism." *HJ* 17 (1918–19): 642–50.

_____. "The Spirit of Judaism." In *The Beginnings of Christianity*, edited by F. J. Foakes-Jackson and K. Lake, 1:35–81. London: Macmillan, 1920.

_____. "The Religious Teaching of the Synoptic Gospels in Its Relation to Judaism." *HJ* 20 (1921–22): 435–46.

_____. "The Attempted Conversion of the Jews." *HJ* 27 (1928–29): 424–37.

————. "Jewish Conceptions of Christianity." *HJ* 28 (1929–30): 246–60.

————. "The Originality of Jesus." *HJ* 28 (1929–30): 98–111.

————. "Dr. Robert Eisler on the Beginnings of Christianity." *HJ* 30 (1931–32): 298–318.

————. "Jewish Emancipation and the English Jew." *HJ* 32 (1933–34): 244–52.

————. "What a Jew Thinks About Jesus." *HJ* 33 (1934–35): 511–20.

Montefiore, C. G., and Loewe, H., eds. *A Rabbinic Anthology*. London: Macmillan, 1938.

Neusner, J. *From Politics to Piety: The Emergence of Pharisaic Judaism*. Englewood Cliffs, N.J.: Prentice-Hall, 1973.

————. *Early Rabbinic Judaism*. Leiden: Brill, 1975.

————. "The Use of the Later Rabbinic Evidence for the Study of First-Century Pharisaism." *Approaches to Ancient Judaism: Theory and Practice*. Brown Judaic Studies 1, edited by W. S. Green, 215–28. Missoula, Mont.: Scholars, 1978.

————. "Judaism after Moore: A Programmatic Statement." *JJS* 31 (1980): 141–56.

Rivkin, E. *A Hidden Revolution*. Nashville: Abingdon, 1978.

Sandmel, S. *A Jewish Understanding of the New Testament*. Cincinnati: Hebrew Union College Press, 1956. Reprint. New York: Ktav, Anti-Defamation League, 1974.

————. *We Jews and Jesus*. New York: Oxford University Press, 1965. Reprint. New York: Oxford University Press, 1973.

————. *We Jews and You Christians: An Inquiry into Attitudes*. New York: Lippincott, 1967.

————. "The Jewish Scholar and Early Christianity." *The Seventy-Fifth Anniversary Volume of the Jewish Quarterly Review*, edited by A. A. Neumann and S. Zeitlin. New York: Ktav, 1967.

————. *The First Christian Century in Judaism and Christianity*. New York: Oxford, 1969.

————. *Two Living Traditions: Essays on Religion and the Bible*. Detroit: Wayne State University, 1972.

————. *Judaism and Christian Beginnings*. New York: Oxford University Press, 1978.

————. *Anti-Semitism in the New Testament?* Philadelphia: Fortress, 1978.

————. "Palestinian and Hellenistic Judaism and Christianity: The Question of the Comfortable Theory." *HUCA* 50 (1979): 137–48.

Schechter, S. *Studies in Judaism*. London: Black, 1896.

————. *Some Aspects of Rabbinic Theology*. London: Black, 1909.

————. "The Law and Recent Criticism." *JQR* 3 (1891): 754–66.

————. "Some Rabbinic Parallels to the New Testament." *JQR* 12 (1900): 415–33.

Schoeps, H. J. *The Jewish-Christian Argument*, ET by D. E. Green. 3rd ed. London: Faber & Faber, 1965.

_____. "Jesus." In *Gottheit und Menschheit,* 43–83. Stuttgart, 1950.

_____. "Jesus und das jüdische Gesetz." In *Studien zur unbekannten Religions—und Geistegeschichte,* 41–61. Göttingen, 1963.

Schonfield, H. J. *The Passover Plot: A New Interpretation of the Life and Death of Jesus.* New York: Geis, 1966.

_____. *For Christ's Sake: A Discussion of the Jesus Enigma.* London: Mac-Donald and Jane's, 1975.

_____. *After the Cross.* San Diego: Barnes, 1981.

Trattner, E. R. *As a Jew Sees Jesus.* New York: Scribner, 1931.

Umen, S. *Pharisaism and Jesus.* New York: Philosophical Library, 1963.

Urbach, E. E. *The Sages, Their Concepts and Beliefs,* ET by I. Abrahams. Jerusalem: Magnes, Hebrew University, 1975.

Vermes, G. *Jesus the Jew: A Historian's Reading of the Gospels.* New York: Macmillan, 1973. Reprinted several times.

_____. "Jesus the Jew." The Claude Montefiore Memorial Lecture of 1974. London: The Liberal Jewish Synagogue, 1974.

_____. "Jewish Studies and New Testament Interpretation." *JJS* 31 (1980): 1–17.

_____. *The Gospel of Jesus the Jew.* The Riddell Memorial Lectures, 48th series, 1981. Newcastle upon Tyne: University of Newcastle upon Tyne, 1981.

_____. "The Gospels without Christology." *God Incarnate: Story and Belief,* edited by A. E. Harvey. London: SPCK, 1981.

Weinstock, H. *Jesus the Jew and Other Addresses.* New York/London: Funk & Wagnalls, 1902.

Weiss-Rosmarin, T., ed. *Jewish Expressions on Jesus: An Anthology.* New York: Ktav, 1977.

Wise, I. M. *The Origin of Christianity.* Cincinnati: Hebrew Union College Press, 1868.

_____. *Judaism and Christianity: Their Agreements and Disagreements.* Cincinnati: Hebrew Union College Press, 1883.

Zeitlin, S. "The Pharisees, A Historical Study." *JQR* 52 (1961–62): 97–129.

_____. *The Rise and Fall of the Judean State.* 2 vols. Philadelphia: Jewish Publication Society of America, 1967.

II. Other Relevant Works

Bacon, B. W. "Jesus and the Law." *JBL* 47 (1928): 203–31.

Bammel, E. "Christian Origins in Jewish Tradition." *NTS* 13 (1966–67): 317–35.

Banks, R. *Jesus and the Law in the Synoptic Tradition.* SNTSMS 28. Cambridge: Cambridge University Press, 1975.

Boadt, L.; Croner, H.; and Klenicki, L., eds. *Biblical Studies: Meeting Ground of Jews and Christians.* Ramsey, N.J.: Paulist, 1980.

Bonsirven, J. *Palestinian Judaism in the Time of Jesus Christ,* ET by W. Wolf. New York: Holt, Rinehart & Winston, 1964.

Branscomb, B. H. *Jesus and the Law of Moses.* New York: Smith, 1930.

_____. "Jesus and the Pharisees." *USR* 44 (1932–33): 24–29.

Burkitt, F. C. "Jesus and the 'Pharisees,' " *JTS* 28 (1927): 392–97.

Connong, J. S. "The Changing Attitude of Jews to Jesus." *USR* 48 (1936–37): 323–32.

Dalman, G. *Jesus—Jeshua,* ET by P. P. Levertoff. London: SPCK, 1929.

_____. *Christianity and Judaism,* ET by G. H. Box. London: Williams and Norgate, 1901.

_____. *Jesus Christ in Talmud, Midrash, Zohar and the Liturgy of the Synagogue.* ET by A. W. Streane. Cambridge: Cambridge University Press, 1893. Reprint. New York: Arno, 1973.

Danby, H. *The Jew and Christianity.* London: Sheldon, 1927.

Danby, H., trans. *The Mishnah.* London: Oxford University Press, 1933.

Davies, A. T., ed. *AntiSemitism and the Foundations of Christianity.* Ramsey, N.J./Toronto: Paulist, 1979.

Davies, W. D. *Torah in the Messianic Age and/or the Age to Come. JBLMS* 7. Philadelphia: SBL, 1952.

_____. *Paul and Rabbinic Judaism.* 4th ed. Philadelphia: Fortress, 1980.

_____. *Christian Origins and Judaism.* Philadelphia: Westminster, 1962.

_____. "Contemporary Jewish Religion." *Peake's Commentary on the Bible,* edited by M. Black and H. H. Rowley, 705–11. London: Nelson, 1962.

Eckert, W. P., and Henrix, H. H., eds. *Jesu Jude-Sein als Zugang zum Judentum.* Aachen, 1976.

Foakes-Jackson, F. J., ed. *The Parting of the Roads.* London: Edward Arnold, 1912.

Grant, F. C. *Ancient Judaism and the New Testament.* Edinburgh: Oliver & Boyd, 1960.

_____. "The Teaching of Jesus and First Century Jewish Ethics." *The Study of the Bible Today and Tomorrow.* Edited by H. R. Willoughby. Chicago: University of Chicago Press, 1947, 298–313.

Herford, R. T. *Christianity in Talmud and Midrash.* London: Williams and Norgate, 1903. Reprint. Clifton, N.J.: Reference Book Publishers, 1966.

_____. *The Pharisees.* London: Allen & Unwin, 1924.

_____. *Judaism in the New Testament Period.* London: Lindsey, 1928.

_____. "Christ in Jewish Literature." *DCG* 2:876–82.

_____. "The Fundamentals of Religion, as Interpreted by Christianity and Rabbinic Judaism." *HJ* 21 (1922–23): 314–26.

_____. "The Law and Pharisaism." In *Law and Religion.* Judaism and Christianity III, edited by E. Rosenthal, 91–121. London: Sheldon, 1938.

_____. "The Separation of Christianity from Judaism." *Jewish Studies in Memory of Israel Abrahams,* edited by A. Kohut, 209–20. New York: The Jewish Institute of Religion, 1927.

_____. "Repentance and Forgiveness in the Talmud With Some Reference to the Teaching of the Gospels." *HJ* 40 (1941–42): 55–64.

Jocz, J. *The Jewish People and Jesus Christ.* London: SPCK, 1949.

————. *The Jewish People and Jesus Christ After Auschwitz: A Study in the Controversy Between Church and Synagogue.* Grand Rapids: Baker, 1981.

————. "The Son of God." *Judaica* 13 (1957): 129–42.

————. "The Connection Between the Old and the New Testament." *Judaica* 16 (1960): 129–44.

————. "Das Exegetische Problem und die Judenmission." *Judaica* 12 (1956): 1–24.

Judaism and Christianity. Vol. 1, *The Age of Transition,* edited by W. O. E. Oesterley. London: Sheldon, 1937. Vol. 2, *The Contact of Pharisaism with Other Cultures,* edited by H. Loewe. London: Sheldon, 1937. Vol. 3, *Law and Religion,* edited by E. I. J. Rosenthal. London: Sheldon, 1938.

Kac, A. W., ed. *The Messiahship of Jesus: What Jews and Jewish Christians Say.* Chicago: Moody, 1980.

Klein, C. *Anti-Judaism in Christian Theology,* ET by E. Quinn. Philadelphia: Fortress, 1978.

Lindeskog, G. *Die Jesusfrage im neuzeitlichen Judentum.* Uppsala: Almquist & Wiksells, 1938.

————. "Jesus als religionsgeschichtliches und religiöses Problem in der modernen jüdischen Theologie." *Judaica* 6 (1950): 190–229, 241–68.

————. *Judarnas Jesus.* Stockholm: Schalom, 1972.

Maier, J. *Jesus von Nazareth in der Talmudischen Überlieferung.* Darmstadt, 1978.

Manson, T. W. "Jesus, Paul, and the Law." *Law and Religion.* Judaism and Christianity III, edited by E. Rosenthal, 125–41. London: Sheldon, 1938.

Marcus, R. "The Pharisees in the Light of Modern Scholarship." *JR* 32 (1952): 153–64.

Menzies, A. "A Rejoinder" (to Montefiore's "Jewish Scholarship and Christian Silence"). *HJ* 1 (1902–03): 789–92.

Moore, G. F. "Christian Writers on Judaism." *HTR* 14 (1921): 197–254.

————. "A Jewish Life of Jesus." *HTR* 16 (1923): 93–103.

————. *Judaism.* 3 vols. Cambridge, Mass.: Harvard University Press, 1946.

Moule, C. F. D. "'. . . As we forgive . . .': a Note on the Distinction between Deserts and Capacity in the Understanding of Forgiveness." *Donum Gentilicium.* Studies in honour of David Daube. Edited by E. Bammel, C. K. Barrett, and W. D. Davies, 68–77. Oxford: Clarendon, 1978.

Oesterley, W. O. E. "Judaism in the Days of Christ." *The Parting of the Roads.* Edited by F. J. Foakes-Jackson, 81–131. London: Edward Arnold, 1912.

Parkes, J. *The Conflict of the Church and the Synagogue.* London: Soncino, 1934. Reprint. New York: Atheneum, 1969.

————. *Jesus, Paul and the Jews.* London: SCM, 1936.

————. *Judaism and Christianity.* London: Victor Gollancz, 1948.

————. *The Foundations of Judaism and Christianity*. London: Vallentine, Mitchell, 1960.

Pawlikowski, J. T. *Christ in the Light of the Christian-Jewish Dialogue*. Ramsey, N.J.: Paulist, 1982.

Petuchowski, J. J., and Brocke, M. *The Lord's Prayer and Jewish Liturgy*. New York: Seabury, 1978.

Phipps, W. E. "Jesus, The Prophetic Pharisee." *JES* 14 (1977): 17–31.

Sanders, E. P. *Paul and Palestinian Judaism*. Philadelphia: Fortress, 1977.

Schürer, E. *The History of the Jewish People in the Age of Jesus Christ (175 B.C.–A.D. 135)*. 3 vols. Revised and edited by G. Vermes, F. Millar, and M. Black. Edinburgh: T. & T. Clark, 1979.

Scott, E. F. "The Originality of Jesus' Ethical Teaching." *JBL* 48 (1929): 105–15.

Stendahl, K. "Hate, Non-Retaliation, and Love. 1QS x17–20 and Rom. 12:19–21." *HTR* 55 (1962): 343–55.

Smith, M. "The Jewish Elements in the Gospels." *JBR* 24 (1956): 90–96.

————. "A Comparison of Early Christian and Early Rabbinic Tradition." *JBL* 82 (1963): 169–76.

Strack, H., and Billerbeck, P. *Kommentar zum Neuen Testament aus Talmud und Midrasch*. 5 vols. Munchen: Beck'sche, 1922–28.

Tanenbaum, M. H.; Wilson, M. R.; and Rudin, A. J. *Evangelicals and Jews in Conversation on Scripture, Theology and History*. Grand Rapids: Baker, 1978.

Tanner, E. S. "Recent Jewish Interpretations of Jesus." *JBL* 8 (1940): 80–82.

Walker, T. *The Teaching of Jesus and the Jewish Teaching of His Age*. London: Allen & Unwin, 1923.

————. *What Jesus Read*. London: Allen & Unwin, 1925.

————. *Jewish Views of Jesus*. New York: Macmillan, 1931.

Williams, A. L. *The Doctrines of Modern Judaism Considered*. London: SPCK, 1939.

————. *Talmudic Judaism and Christianity*. London: SPCK, 1933.

————. *The Hebrew-Christian Messiah*. London: SPCK, 1916.

————. "'My Father' in Jewish Thought of the First Century." *JTS* 31 (1930): 42–47.

Index of Persons

Index of Subjects

Index of Scripture References